OCR GCSE (9–1)

BUSINESS

THIRD EDITION

Mike Schofield
Alan Williams

HODDER EDUCATION
AN HACHETTE UK COMPANY

The Publishers would like to thank the following for permission to reproduce copyright material.

Photo credits for this book can be found on page 320.

Acknowledgements

P.88, URL: http://www.managers.org.uk/insights/news/2015/december/six-companies-that-get-employee-engagement-and-what-they-do-right, Copyright © Chartered Management Institute. Used by permission; **p. 160**, Diversity and Inclusion © BP Global. Used by permission.

Every effort has been made to trace all copyright holders, but if any have been inadvertently overlooked, the Publishers will be pleased to make the necessary arrangements at the first opportunity.

Orders: please contact Bookpoint Ltd, 130 Park Drive, Milton Park, Abingdon, Oxon OX14 4SE. Telephone: (44) 01235 827720. Fax: (44) 01235 400454. Email education@bookpoint.co.uk Lines are open from 9 a.m. to 5 p.m., Monday to Saturday, with a 24-hour message answering service. You can also order through our website: www.hoddereducation.co.uk

ISBN: 9781 4718 9936 2

First published in 2001
Second edition published in 2009
This edition published in 2017 by
Hodder Education,
An Hachette UK Company
Carmelite House
50 Victoria Embankment
London EC4Y 0DZ

www.hoddereducation.co.uk

Impression number 10 9 8 7 6 5 4 3 2

Year 2021 2020 2019 2018 2017

Cover photo © blickwinkel/Alamy Stock Photo

Illustrations by Peter Lubach and Integra Software Services
Typeset in Integra Software Services Pvt Ltd, Pondicherry, India
Printed in Italy by Printer Trento

A catalogue record for this title is available from the British Library.

Contents

Business 2: Operations, finance and influences on business

Introduction

The OCR Business GCSE specification is divided into 2 components, each divided into sections. The two components and their sections are:

- Component 1: Business activity, marketing and people
- Component 2: Operations, finance, influences on business and the interdependent nature of business

The specification indicates the content of each section and identifies points to include.

Section 7, The interdependent nature of business, illustrates the links between the different sections of the specification. This section is synoptic, which means that you will need to use content from both components. The specification explains that learners need to make connections between the different elements of the subject. There is a list of bullet points which indicates the knowledge and understanding that learners should have. In the examination the question may guide you as to the sections within the two components that you need to write about.

The examination

There are two examinations. J204/01 covers the content of Component 1 and J204/02 covers that of Component 2. Both components contain **multiple choice** and **data response questions**.

There are fifteen multiple choice questions on each paper. You must select the correct answer from four possible answers.

There are three data response questions on each paper. Each question is divided into a number of parts. The data is based on real or fictional business contexts but there is a greater emphasis on data from real world situations. Business contexts used will be selected so that they are accessible to students who sit GCSE examinations.

Some parts of the final question on J204/02 are designed to be synoptic (requiring you to refer to content from both components of the specification), though this does not mean that you will not be credited if you take a synoptic approach to answering other questions on either paper.

Quantitative skills

The specification expects you to be able to use a range of quantitative skills and mathematical techniques and apply them to business contexts. These are outlined in Appendix C of the OCR GCSE (9¬–1) Business specification. They include being able to perform certain calculations:

- percentages and percentage changes
- averages
- revenue, costs and profit
- gross profit margin and net profit margin ratios
- average rate of return
- cash flow forecasts.

You will also be required to interpret quantitative data to support, inform and justify business decisions, including:

- graphs and charts
- profitability ratios
- financial data
- marketing data
- market data.

A minimum of 10% of the total GCSE marks will be for using quantitative skills.

Assessment Objectives

Assessment objectives here refers to the skills that will be tested in the examinations. The specification identifies 3 assessment objectives (AOs). The weighting of each assessment within the scheme of assessment is given in brackets:

- AO1 (35%) Demonstrate knowledge and understanding of business concepts and issues. Questions in the examination that will test this will use one of the following command words:
  - identify
  - state
  - explain.
- AO2 (35%) Apply knowledge and understanding of business concepts and issues. Questions in the examination that will test the skill of application will use one of the following command words:
  - calculate
  - complete
  - explain.
- AO3 (30%) Analyse and evaluate business information and issues to demonstrate understanding of business activity, make judgements and draw conclusions. Questions in the examination that will test the skills of analysis and/or evaluation will use one of the following command words:
  - analyse
  - discuss
  - evaluate
  - recommend.

Command words are used to signal the highest level of skill required in a question. For example, a question using the command word 'Analyse' will also assess AO1 and AO2.

How to use this book

The textbook has been designed to match the layout of the specification. The final section of the textbook explains and illustrates the interdependent nature of business. It also illustrates the idea of synopticity.

The text of the book, including diagrams and tables, details the knowledge and understanding that learners should have. At the end of each unit there are also lists of 'key ideas' and 'terms to learn' which emphasise the key knowledge.

Each unit contains a number of case studies. The purpose of the case studies is to illustrate the relevance of the content of the business specification to the real world of business. The case studies are very important for illustrating the application of knowledge and understanding.

Case studies also provide an opportunity to demonstrate the skills of evaluation. In addition, each unit in the book contains 'evaluation points' to illustrate the use of this skill in the context of the unit content.

Each unit contains a number of activities. The activities represent opportunities for developing and for reinforcing learning – both knowledge and the skills to be tested.

Each unit contains practice questions. There are multiple choice and data response questions. The data response questions use data from the real world to reflect the type of real world data that may be used in the GCSE examinations. The questions use the command words associated with each assessment objective and indicated in the specification. Advice is given on how to answer the data response questions in order to maximise marks.

Answers to activities

The answers to the activities are published in a companion Answer Guide (9781510409637), which will be available as a digital download in Summer 2017.

A further word about case studies

The case studies in the book were researched at the time of writing. Most were current to that time, some are from earlier years. Inevitably, they will not be current when the books are being used in schools. To an extent, this does not matter as long as they illustrate learning points. However, it can be useful sometimes to follow a story through. Using Google to explore a case study in more detail can enhance your understanding.

A note on the useful words

The specification includes some Business vocabulary that you will need to understand. If a word is used in the specification it can be used in an exam question, so it is very important you understand all of the words in the specification. Words that appear in the specification are highlighted in red in the text and defined in the Useful Words box at the end of each unit. There are other specialist Business terms that it is useful for you to understand, but are not in specification. These can't be asked about directly in an exam paper, but could be useful for you to use in an answer. These terms are also defined in the Useful Words box and are bold and black in the text.

Grades

Candidates will be awarded grades from 9–1. Grade 9 will be awarded to the very highest performing students. Grade 5 represents the new strong pass grade and grade 4 represents to the new standard pass grade.

Acknowledgements

We are grateful to a number of people in helping us to prepare this book. In particular, our wives who have, once again, been very patient and supportive while the researching and writing of the book were carried out. Debbie Malpas (Subject Specialist for Business and Economics) has been an absolute 'brick' answering queries, commenting on drafts and forwarding documentation when requested. We must thank the organisations and individuals who helped out with case studies, particularly busy business owners who gave their time to speak to us and let us take, and use, photographs of them or their businesses. Finally, without the drive, foresight and determination of Beth Cleall from Hodder Education, this publication would not have been possible.

Business 1:

Business activity, marketing and people

UNIT 1.1 The role of business enterprise and entrepreneurship

Learning outcomes

By studying this unit, you will be able to:

- identify why businesses exist
- identify the characteristics of an **entrepreneur**
- understand the role of the entrepreneur in business activity
- evaluate the purpose of business activity and enterprise
- identify the rewards and risks that come with running a business
- evaluate why certain people are more suited to being a successful entrepreneur
- evaluate how risk and reward may lead to business success or failure
- analyse and evaluate whether or not potential entrepreneurs would be successful
- evaluate the merits of risk and reward in deciding whether or not to start a business.

Introductory case study: opening a business – the Torrs Hotel in Ilfracombe

After two years of hard work renovating an old building, entrepreneurs Pamela, Marie and Abu opened the Torrs Hotel in Ilfracombe, Devon, to the public. This was a risk for all concerned, but with room occupancy now at around 90 per cent, the decision to spend time and money preparing the building for guests seems to have paid off.

The hotel is in a quiet part of town, but within easy reach of the town centre, sea front and shopping. This location helped the success of the business, but the determination of the owners is a critical factor, especially in a business where there is a lot of competition.

Introduction

Why do businesses exist?

Businesses exist to satisfy the needs of customers. They provide goods and services at a price that people are willing to pay. In return, the business will be rewarded (hopefully) with profit. If there was no need for a product, then there would be little point in a business producing it. If a product becomes very popular and demand rises, other businesses might also want to make that product, motivated by the fact that there is the prospect of profit.

Developing an idea for business

Once an idea for a business exists, it can be developed. For example, Virgin first started as a mail order business selling records. The business grew and developed to include air travel, which then developed further to include rail travel.

An entrepreneur may also see an existing product and **spot an opportunity** to develop and improve it. For example, Apple did not make the first mobile phone, but saw how it could be developed. On a much smaller scale, an entrepreneur could spot that a particular location lacked quality restaurants. Opening a new, quality restaurant would hopefully satisfy customer needs.

What is enterprise?

In business, enterprise is seeing an opportunity to provide a product or service that people are willing to buy. Enterprise is nothing new. For as long as business activity has taken place, people have shown how enterprising they can be by providing a product or a service that they see others are willing to pay for. This is often seen as 'spotting an opportunity'. For example, when it rains, street sellers will soon appear with umbrellas for sale. In other cases, this has led to small businesses growing into world-wide operations making large profits for the owners. Larry Page and Sergey Brin started their business by meeting in a garage. That small start developed into Google. They spotted the need for a reliable search engine in the fast-growing computer market. Google is now developing interests in drone technology to make sure that the needs of the customer are satisfied because businesses now see that speed of delivery is important for customers. This is also an example of how entrepreneurs develop an idea for business. Google are merely looking ahead and seeing how drone technology will develop, and, along with Amazon, are investing heavily in the technology.

Characteristics of an entrepreneur

Successful entrepreneurs often have a number of **enterprising characteristics** in common. These include:

Creativity

An entrepreneur would normally be creative, possibly designing something that has not been seen before. James Dyson is a good example of this, because his bagless vacuum cleaner had not been seen before. However, being creative does not always mean inventing something new. In the example of the Torrs Hotel above, the owners created a welcoming atmosphere in the hotel that attracted customers and helped them to be successful.

Risk taking

Many people do not like to take risks. An entrepreneur starting a business will certainly have to take risks, possibly using their own money, which may multiply in the future or be lost forever!

Determination

An entrepreneur should have the determination to see things through. Owners of many small businesses find that when they first start, they need to put a lot of time into the business; not everyone will have this level of determination.

Confidence

An enterprising person will be confident that their ideas will succeed, and be able to pass on that feeling of confidence to others who are brought in to develop a business idea. An enterprising person is always very positive. 'Cannot do' is not a phrase they would use.

Programmes like 'Dragons' Den' have highlighted the role of entrepreneurs. Here, people with ideas and the energy to see their businesses prosper try to persuade already wealthy entrepreneurs to put money into the business to help it grow. Not all will succeed; such is the nature of enterprise. There are risks, but there again, there are rewards for those who are successful.

Not all entrepreneurs can persuade others to join them in business.

Activity 1 – Research activity

Use the internet to research the backgrounds of four famous entrepreneurs. You could use entrepreneurs from *Dragons' Den*, or possibly Richard Branson or Walt Disney, or any other local entrepreneur that your teacher may know of.

What made them successful? Do they have anything in common that made them succeed where others have failed? Write a short report on your findings, and present the results to your group, possibly using PowerPoint.

Richard Branson has made a fortune from his Virgin brand.

Activity 2 – Research activity

How enterprising are the students in your business studies group? Use the information in 'Characteristics of an entrepreneur' (page 3) to complete the table started below. Put a tick if you think they have that enterprising feature. A cross means they do not have it!

Compare your results with the rest of the class. Do you have any potential entrepreneurs?

Name	Risk taker	Has determination	Has confidence	Is creative

Table 1.1 Potential entrepreneurs.

Risk and reward in business

When a business starts, the entrepreneur takes a risk. This is all part of the makeup of someone who is enterprising. This risk brings the potential for great rewards, but does come with some possible drawbacks.

Potential rewards for risk taking

- **Financial** – the greater the risk, the greater the reward. This is often said when referring to the amount of money that might be made when taking a risk. Certainly some entrepreneurs have made their personal fortunes from taking a risk and starting their own businesses. Lord Sugar made his initial fortune by selling electrical goods through a business called Amstrad. Sir Richard Branson made millions of pounds from a variety of business activities. The attraction of making a lot of money is an important factor in encouraging people to take a risk and start their own business.
- **Independence** – many people work for others and are quite happy to do the job they are told to do. The risk here is on the owner of the business who employs them. Entrepreneurs often want to be independent, and take the risk of running their own business simply in order to be their own boss. The risk then falls on the entrepreneur, but the feeling of being independent and being their own boss outweighs this.
- **Self-satisfaction** – an entrepreneur may take the risk of starting their own business simply to have the satisfaction of making their idea work. They may not be interested in making a lot of money, but want to retain the satisfaction that they started, and own, their own business. A business may develop out of a hobby that will again bring satisfaction to an entrepreneur if they take the risk in starting such a business.
- **Changing customer habits** – some entrepreneurs are rewarded when customers are persuaded to change their buying habits. Anita Roddick did not

believe that cosmetics should be tested on animals and wanted to persuade customers to buy products that were free from such testing. The success of The Body Shop has changed customer attitudes to choosing cosmetics, with other cosmetic businesses now offering similar products. The risk of starting the original business brought great rewards for its founder. The move to what are known as ethical business practices has made a number of entrepreneurs start businesses in order to see the rewards of changed consumer attitudes.

Potential drawbacks for risk taking

- **Financial** – just as there can be great rewards for risk taking, there are also major potential drawbacks. While fortunes can be made, life savings that are put into a business could also be lost. The possibility of losing money is one of the main reasons why people will not take a risk and start their own business.
- **Health** – if a business idea fails, or more time and effort is needed than originally anticipated, the health of the entrepreneur may be affected. The strain of being in charge of a business that is in difficulty may lead to failing health. Even when a business is successful, the strain of keeping up that success may also affect a person's health.
- **Strained relationships** – taking a risk and starting a business can be very time consuming. It may well take its toll on the health of the entrepreneur and it may also damage personal relationships, with the entrepreneur having to spend so much time developing the business. Holidays may be sacrificed as the business takes time and money to become established. It is often difficult for an entrepreneur to leave the business in the care of someone else, even for a short holiday.

Activity 3 – Explanation activity

Use the information on benefits and drawbacks of risk taking to examine your own attitude to risk taking. If you are a risk taker, what attracts you to taking risks? If you are not a risk taker, what is it that puts you off taking a risk in an enterprise? Write up your thoughts in a suitable chart. Compare your results with others.

Evaluation point

When evaluating the benefits and drawbacks of taking the risk of running a business, remember that there are often no clear correct answers.

Use the information you are given to try and judge whether it is likely that the person involved (the entrepreneur) will make a success of the business or not. Just because an entrepreneur is very confident, determined and is willing to take a risk, it does not mean the business will be a success. There are many other factors to consider.

Key facts

Businesses exist to satisfy the needs of customers.

Entrepreneurs will often spot an opportunity, and develop products and services to meet customer needs.

A successful entrepreneur has many characteristics.

There are a number of risks and rewards in starting and running a business.

Useful words

Entrepreneur is a person who takes the risk of starting and running a business enterprise.

Spotting an opportunity is the ability to see the need for a particular product or service that customers need.

Enterprising characteristics are the features of an entrepreneur, which include being determined, creative and having ability to take risks.

Practice questions

Multiple choice questions

1 Businesses exist to:
   a) provide quality goods only to rich, young people
   b) sell goods to older people
   c) meet the needs of customers
   d) research what customers need.

2 An entrepreneur needs which of the following characteristics?
   a) very well dressed at all times
   b) know a person in business
   c) very good at accounts
   d) confident.

3 Which of the following is **not** a reward for risk taking when starting a business?
   a) being able to invest money
   b) being able to make profits for yourself
   c) being independent
   d) being able to see your own ideas work.

Data response 1

Cathy and Julie are entrepreneurs who set up their own separate hairdressing businesses. They are both successful and have many regular customers. More recently, they have joined forces at Sophisticutz and work together in the business, recognising that being together does have a number of advantages.

1 State two characteristics of an entrepreneur. (2 marks)

2 Explain two possible benefits for Cathy and Julie when joining their two businesses. (4 marks)

3 Evaluate the potential risks of becoming an entrepreneur. (9 marks)

How to answer data response 1

1 You need to 'state' only, so no explanation is required.

2 Make sure that the two benefits you choose are clear to you, so that you can explain them well.

3 This question instructs you to evaluate – this means making a judgement on the drawbacks of being an entrepreneur. Analyse the risks, remembering that it is about becoming an entrepreneur. Is one risk more important than another? Always give reasons for the ideas you put forward.

Sophisticutz.

The staff team at Sophisticutz.

UNIT 1.2 Business planning

Learning outcomes

By studying this unit, you will be able to:

- identify the component parts of a **business plan**
- understand the importance of a business plan
- explain why a business plan is completed for particular businesses
- explain why certain parts of the business plan might be especially important in certain situations
- analyse the advantages and disadvantages of producing a business plan
- evaluate whether or not a given business plan is suitable for use
- evaluate the role, importance and usefulness of a business plan.

Introductory case study: business planning – large and small scale

Almost all businesses, both large and small, will produce a business plan at some time. For many small businesses, the plan will be written before they start, or when they are considering a major change to their operations. Large businesses will have to plan to meet the needs of their owners, who have put money into the business. The decision in 2016 to leave the European Union (EU) will mean that the business plans of companies such as Toyota and BMW, who have assembly operations in Britain, might need to be revised. These businesses are concerned that leaving the EU may add further costs to the cars they sell to other member countries in the EU. In October 2016, Nissan stated that it plans to continue car assembly in Sunderland, despite the Brexit vote.

What is a business plan?

A business plan details how a business aims to achieve its objectives. It is usually written before the business starts, or when there is a major change in what the business plans to do.

The purpose of planning business activity

Reducing risk

Setting up a business can be a risk. There may be a number of competitor businesses and potential customers might not like the products you aim to produce. The point of writing a business plan is to reduce that risk as much as possible. That is *not* to say that by writing a business plan there will be no risk in starting a business, but that there will simply be *less* risk.

Helping a business to succeed

Anyone who is starting a business wants it to be a **success**. Thinking carefully about all aspects of running a business and writing these thoughts down in a business plan allows entrepreneurs to reflect on what they are proposing. The greater the care and thought that is given to this process, the greater the chance of success. Remember though that simply writing a business plan will not guarantee success – there are still a number of things that could affect the business, which no one would have anticipated.

The contents of a business plan

The business idea

This may seem rather obvious, but the starting point for any business plan is a business idea that is practical and stands at least a chance of being successful. Is it a totally new idea, or a development of an existing product or service already being sold?

The people running the business

Details of who is to be involved and their experience in business are included in a business plan. This is important in trying to persuade other people to invest in the business (such as a bank). It is much more likely that others will consider investing in a new idea if that idea comes from someone with a lot of experience in running a business. In fact, a business will stand more chance of success if there are people involved who have relevant experience.

Market research

To back up the original idea and to determine whether consumers are interested in the product or service, some market research should be carried out. The results of this will be included in the plan to show that consumers will use the business. Included in this will be where the business is to be advertised, what price will be charged for the product or service, how it will be sold to the customer (online, through shops etc.) and whether a single product or a range of products is to be produced. By writing a business plan, it makes the person (or people) involved think carefully about these important points that otherwise may be ignored. A business is unlikely to be successful if it does not undertake market research.

Finance

The cost of setting up the business will need to be carefully calculated. A business will include in its plan details of where the **finance** is to come from. A new business may have to find a lot of money to pay for new premises, equipment, advertising and so on. This may come from the owners' own savings or they may borrow the money. Whatever the source of the finance, details of where it is to come from must be in the plan.

Objectives of the business

Just hoping to be successful is not enough. A business should look at a timeline as to when and how certain objectives will be met.

The target market

A business should be clear on who it is selling its products and services to. Is the target market male or female, or both? Is it aimed at a particular age group? Is it aimed simply at wealthy customers?

Competitors

Are there any competitors offering the same or similar products? If so, how will this product be different? A business plan should demonstrate how the new business can stand up against or beat the competition, which may have been established for some time.

There are many parts to a business plan.

The role of a business plan

Identifying markets

A business plan helps a business to think clearly about who it is targeting its products or services at. Remember, this is an important part of business development because it will help determine, for example, the type of marketing the business will need to undertake.

Helping with finance

If a new business requires some finance from a bank, having a business plan will show that careful thought had been given to all aspects of starting and running the business. A bank is more likely to lend a new business money if it is confident in being repaid.

Identifying resources that a business needs to operate

A business plan requires those involved in the business to consider what **resources** they need. This may be equipment, finance (see above), additional people with particular skills or it could be premises where the business will **operate** from. It is vital that a business is clear on the resources it needs, otherwise it will be seen by a potential investor as a business that has not given enough thought to its operations. The potential investor might think the business is too much of a risk and not invest.

Achieving business aims and objectives

Setting out **aims and objectives** within a business plan, with an appropriate timeline, gives a business the best chance of achieving its aims. This is because setting out these aims and objectives requires careful thought, research and consideration of all aspects of running the business.

The importance of a business plan

If a business does not complete a business plan it may not identify the correct **market**, or the resources and staff it needs to succeed. This may be costly for the business.

Usefulness of a business plan

Not writing a plan will, however, put greater risk on the business, because the initial ideas may not have been fully thought through. Would banks offer finance without seeing a business plan? Would a business have well-judged objectives to meet? Does the target market really want the product at the price being offered?

As stated before, writing a plan will only *reduce* the risk to a business, not eliminate it.

The importance of a business plan.

Activity 1 – Research activity

Ask someone you know who owns a business whether they have ever produced a business plan. The business may be very small – perhaps only one person – or much larger, in which case you will need to talk to the person responsible for producing the plan.

Try and find out:

a) when they produced the plan

b) what they put into the plan

c) why the plan was important for the business.

Write your results up in the form of a short report. Present ideas using PowerPoint.

Activity 2 – True or false activity

Is it true or false that the following should be in a business plan? Put a tick in the correct column.

Statement	True	False
Information about the owners of the business		
What marketing is planned		
Information about the hobbies of the owners		
What finance is needed for the business		
A list of favourite school subjects of the business owners		
Analysis of the competitors		
A description of the target market for the product		
Titles of business studies books that the owners have read		

Table 1.2 True or false for a business plan.

Evaluation point

When evaluating the role, importance or usefulness of a business plan, remember that a business plan will usually be completed when a business starts or when a business makes an important change. While a business plan is important for both situations, it is especially important for a new business that needs to use the plan to help judge whether to go ahead or not. When looking at whether a business plan is suitable for a business to use, look at what is missing. Are the parts that are missing of particular importance in the situation you have been given? If so, why?

Activity 3 – Explanation activity

a) Explain why a business plan should be completed by all businesses.

b) Explain why a business plan is especially important for a new business.

Key facts

Planning is a vital part in the successful start-up and development of a business.

A business plan is normally written when a business starts or when an important change to the business takes place.

A number of people, as well as the owners of the business, will be interested in seeing the business plan.

A business plan is useful when someone is simply trying to see if a business idea will really work, before actually starting the business.

Useful words

Business plan is a simple plan which sets out details on the product or service being sold, where the finance is to come from to start the business, how the product or service is to be marketed, and the market research to show there is a need for what is being sold.

Finance is a business word used instead of money. The finance needed to start a business is the money that is needed to do so.

Success for a business can take many forms, including making a profit, surviving and providing a good service to customers.

Markets are where a business sells its goods and services.

Resources are the things a business needs to make it work, including finance (money), staff and materials.

Operate is a term used to explain how a business works.

Aims and objectives are the things that a business is trying to achieve, such as grow larger, or make more profit.

Practice questions

Multiple choice questions

1 A business plan would normally be written:

a) every month
b) a month after a business starts
c) after a business has become established and competitors are known
d) before a business starts.

2 A business plan will:

a) make sure the competitors know you are in business
b) identify the competitors of the business
c) put the competitors out of business
d) allow the competitors to see whether you need finance to start the business.

3 The purpose of identifying resources in a business plan is to:

a) make sure the required resources have been identified and where those resources will come from, so that possible investors will feel safer putting their money into the business
b) make sure that there is a list of some of the resources required for the business
c) make sure that each person involved in the business knows what the word 'resources' means
d) make sure that the resources required cost less than the business first thought.

Data response 2

Ira Rubini is interested in opening an Italian restaurant. She has always loved cooking and feels that she can add a 'homely' touch to her potential business. She has no business experience, but understands that a business plan would help her to make a good start to her new venture.

1 State two items that Ira should include in her business plan. (2 marks)

2 From your answer to question 1, explain why these items should be included in the plan. (4 marks)

3 Analyse two possible problems for Ira and her business if she did **not** complete a business plan. (6 marks)

How to answer data response 2

1 This question simply asks you to 'state'. No explanation is necessary.

2 This question is where you need to explain why your answers to question 1 should be included in the plan. Make sure you give a full answer here.

3 This question asks you to analyse, so you will be looking for the negative effects on the business and Ira. The word 'possible' is used in the question. This is because no one can be sure as to what might happen, but the problems you are analysing must come from Ira **not** completing a business plan.

UNIT 1.3 Business ownership

Learning outcomes

By studying this unit, you will be able to:

- identify the features of different forms of business ownership
- understand and explain the concept of **limited** and **unlimited liability**
- explain the advantages and disadvantages of different forms of business ownership
- apply the knowledge and understanding of business ownership to different situations
- analyse and evaluate the suitability of different types of business ownership in different situations.

Introductory case study: how Marks & Spencer has changed ownership

Marks & Spencer has had four different types of ownership.

Marks & Spencer was started by Michael Marks in 1884 as a **sole trader** when he opened a penny bazaar in Leeds. These shops had only one price for every product – one penny.

In 1894 Michael Marks went into **partnership** with Tom Spencer who provided money to help pay for the expansion of the business. Marks & Spencer was born. Later the business became a **private limited company** (Ltd), before becoming a **public limited company** (plc) in the early twentieth century. These changes all helped to develop and expand the business so that it could sell the wide range of goods and services we see today.

Forms of business ownership

Sole traders

Sole traders are businesses owned by one person. They may have a number of people working at the business, but ownership remains with one person. Sole traders are the most common form of business ownership in the UK.

Plumbers are often sole trader businesses.

Advantages of the sole trader form of business ownership

There would not be so many sole trader businesses in the UK if there were not advantages to this form of business organisation.

The main reasons for this large number of sole traders are shown in the table below.

Easy to set up	A sole trader is the easiest and cheapest form of business ownership to set up. There are few forms to worry about. This is the most popular type of business ownership for businesses just starting.
Finance required	A sole trader can be set up with very little capital, making it a popular choice for those with little savings.
Control	The sole trader is in complete control of the business and can make decisions without consulting anyone.
Profits	Because the business is owned only by the sole trader, all profits will go to the sole trader.
Financial information	All of the financial information about a sole trader is private. Unlike some other types of business ownership, no financial information has to be provided to the public.

Table 1.3 Advantages of sole traders.

Disadvantages of sole trader business ownership

As with most things, there are also some disadvantages. Operating as a sole trader business does have some problems. The main problems that sole traders face are shown in the table below.

Unlimited liability	The sole trader is liable (responsible) for all of the debts (the money a business owes to others) of the business. This may mean that the sole trader might have to sell personal possessions to pay off any of the business's debts. This could be serious, but will only be a problem if the business is in difficulty.
Illness	As the sole trader is the only owner of the business, if he or she is ill then there may be a problem in keeping the business in operation, because there may well be no one else to run it.
Shortage of capital (money)	A sole trader may find it difficult to find enough money to even start the business, because there is only one owner to raise the necessary capital. Should the business need further capital to expand, the same problem may occur.
Hours of work	A sole trader could have to work long hours, especially when the business is starting and the sole trader wants to get the business established. This can cause stress and possibly illness.
Skill shortage	The sole trader may well have skills, but not all of the skills necessary to run the business; this may mean that other workers with specialist skills might have to be employed.
Continuity	If the sole trader dies, then the business will effectively cease to exist.

Table 1.4 Disadvantages of sole traders.

Partnerships

This form of business ownership is very common in certain industries. Solicitors, accountants and dentists are often, but not always, partnerships.

There are very strict rules controlling the creation of partnerships. There must be at least two partners in a partnership, though the partners may not have an equal share in the business. This form of business organisation has many of the advantages, and avoids some of the disadvantages, of the sole trader form of business organisation.

Advantages of the partnership form of business ownership

Capital	As there is more than one owner of the business, it is easier to raise capital to start or expand the business.
Easy to set up	As with sole traders, a partnership is easy to set up, although a deed of partnership should be completed – see page 14.

More skills in the business	With more than one owner, there are often a number of different skills within a partnership. With solicitors, for example, different partners will specialise in different areas of the law.
Workload is shared	Unlike a sole trader, the partners can share out work if necessary, reducing possible stress. If a partner is ill, there are others to cover the necessary work.
Financial information is private	This is the same as for a sole trader – financial information does not have to be shared with anyone.

Table 1.5 Advantages of partnerships.

Disadvantages of partnership business ownership

As with sole traders, partnerships do have their disadvantages. These are shown in the table below.

Profit is shared	Any profit that the business makes is shared between the partners. This could cause problems if one partner feels they are the only person doing any work.
Unlimited liability	This is the same as for sole traders. Each partner is liable for the debts of the business, so personal possessions may have to be sold to pay debts if the business is in difficulty.
Shortage of capital	There may be a shortage of capital in the business if there are only a few partners in the business.
Slower decision-making	With more partners involved in the running of the business, there may be disagreements, which could result in decision-making being slower than for a sole trader.
Continuity	If one or more of the partners dies then the business could cease to exist.

Table 1.6 Disadvantages of partnerships.

Deed of partnership

Because a partnership is a more complicated form of business ownership than a sole proprietor, most partnerships draw up a **deed of partnership**. If there is no deed of partnership, the law states that each partner is equal regardless of the amount of **capital** that they have put into the business.

What is in a deed of partnership?

- Information on the way in which the business operates.
- The role of each partner within the business.
- How profits and losses will be shared among the partners.
- Details of how much capital each partner has contributed to the business. This is important because partners do not need to provide an equal amount of capital.

Sleeping partners

Sleeping partners provide capital for the business but take no part in the running of the business. Their liability for any losses within the business is limited to the amount of capital that they have contributed.

Limited liability partnerships

You may have seen the letters 'LLP' after the name of some businesses. This is because a recent change in the law now allows partnerships to operate as **limited liability partnerships**. This means that their liability (responsibility) for the debts of the business is limited to the amount of money they put into the business. Many solicitors are choosing to operate this type of business organisation.

Evaluation point

You will need to be able to recommend whether a business should be a sole trader or partnership. To do this, you need to compare the advantages and disadvantages of each, in order to give reasons for any recommendation you make.

Activity 1 – Research activity

Draw up a deed of partnership between you and another member of your class. Try to make the agreement a good one for you to sign and a poor agreement for your 'partner'. For example, think about the capital you both put into the business. See if your partner thinks it is a good agreement for them to sign. If someone asks you to sign an agreement, check it carefully!

Activity 2 – True or false activity

Tick a box in the table below to indicate if each statement is true or false.

Statement	True	False
A partnership has at least four partners.		
A sole trader has one owner.		
A deed of partnership will state how much capital partners should contribute to a business.		
A sleeping partner is always asleep.		
Ordinary partners in a partnership and sole traders have unlimited liability.		
Sole traders often have difficulty raising money for their business.		
Partners will often use their own savings to start their business.		
A partnership has shareholders.		
Anyone can see the financial details of a sole trader.		
A sole trader can employ as many people as they wish.		

Table 1.7 True or false.

Activity 3 – Presentation activity

Prepare a PowerPoint presentation comparing the key features of sole traders and partnerships. In your presentation, try to show how each has advantages over the other.

Activity 4 – Missing words activity

Use the words below to help you fill in the gaps in the following paragraph.

- duties
- capital
- traders
- unlimited
- decisions
- debts
- deed
- one
- personal

Sole ___ have one owner, are very easy to set up and can make ___ quickly because there is ___ owner. Like partnerships, sole traders have ___ liability, which means that they are responsible for all of the ___ of the business. This means that they may have to sell ___ possessions. A partnership would normally have a ___ of partnership, which sets out the ___ of the partners and the amount of ___ they put into the business.

Private limited companies

There are many private limited companies in the UK. You may well have seen 'Ltd' after a business name – this will show that it is a private limited company. The owners of a limited company are called **shareholders**, because each has invested money in the business and so has a share of that business.

Limited liability

Limited liability means that the liability (responsibility) for the debts of the business is limited to the amount that the shareholder has put into the business. Compare this to sole traders and partnerships where the liability is unlimited and personal possessions may have to be sold to pay debts. In a limited company, this will not happen and for this reason, it is for some people a very attractive advantage of setting up a limited company.

Advantages of private limited companies

Limited liability	As stated above, liability (responsibility) for debts is limited to the amount of money a shareholder invests in the business. This often encourages others to invest in the business because they are clear on just how much money they are putting at risk.
Continuity	Unlike sole traders and partnerships, if an owner (shareholder) of a limited company dies, the business can continue to operate.
Can raise money more easily	Banks are often more prepared to lend money to limited companies, which they see as less of a risk than sole traders and partnerships. However, in some cases the owners may still be required to guarantee the loans they receive from a bank.
Control over share sale	As shares can only be sold with agreement from the existing shareholders, there is no chance of the business being taken over by another business without shareholder agreement. This is why a number of private limited companies are 'family' businesses, with shares being owned only by family members, who remain in full control.

Table 1.8 Advantages of private limited companies.

Disadvantages of private limited companies

Financial information available to the public	Unlike sole traders and partnerships, the financial information of a limited company can be seen by the public and competitors of the business.
Administration	Private limited companies are more complex and can be expensive to set up and operate. There are many forms to complete, particularly financial information, which must be sent to the Registrar of Companies. Failure to submit the necessary forms on time will result in a fine.
Sale of shares is restricted	A private limited company is unable to sell shares to the general public, which will restrict the amount of capital that can be raised.
Dividends	**Dividends** are amounts of money paid to shareholders from the profits of the business. A shareholder who has put money into a business may expect a dividend each year, when the directors who run the business may want to use profit to expand. This can cause conflict.

Table 1.9 Disadvantages of private limited companies.

Some thought needs to be put into setting up a private limited company.

Public limited companies

There are a large number of public limited companies (plc) registered in the UK. A look at the share pages of most newspapers will give the names of just a few of the public limited companies that trade their shares on the London Stock Exchange.

So what does the 'public' mean in a public limited company? If you see a business with 'plc' after its name, it will show that it is a public limited company. This means that it can sell its shares to the general public – in Britain that means selling the shares through the Stock Exchange in London.

Advantages of public limited companies

Ability to raise large amounts of capital	As shares can be sold to the general public, much more capital can be raised. Share buyers may also be other organisations, such as those who provide pensions. This ability to raise large sums of money is a key advantage to being a plc.
Easier to borrow money	Should a plc need to borrow money, they may find it easier, because banks will often see them as low risk and so lend money as needed.
Limited liability for shareholders	As with a private limited company, shareholders in a plc are only liable for the amount they invested in the business (the value of their shares) should the business get into difficulties.

Table 1.10 Advantages of public limited companies.

Disadvantages of public limited companies

Possibility of takeover	As shares are sold to the general public through the stock exchange, a plc has no control over who buys its shares. If any person or group buys 51% of the shares, the overall ownership of the business will change. This cannot happen with a private limited company without full agreement of existing shareholders.
Cost of setting up and operating	It is more complex and expensive to set up a plc compared to a private limited company. A plc must have £50,000 of shares as a minimum.
Problems of size	A plc is a large business often with complex management structures necessary to control all of the operations of the business. This may be inefficient compared to a smaller business.
Financial information available to the public	A public limited company has to publish its accounts each year and make them available, on request, to anyone who would like to see them. This is especially important to a plc because competitors can see how it is performing. This may lead to other businesses buying its shares with a view to taking over.

Table 1.11 Disadvantages of public limited companies.

As accounts in a plc must be published, competitors have vital information on whether to try to take over the business.

Activity 5 – Research activity

Using a newspaper that publishes share prices (or the internet), choose a plc that you would like to invest £500 in. It may be a business you know, or one you have never heard of. Look at the share price and consider how many shares you will get. You could pick a company with a share price of £1, in which case you will have 500 shares. A company with a £10 share price will give you 50 shares.

Track the share price over the next month. At the end of the month calculate how much the shares you bought for £500 are now worth. See who in your group has made the most, and lost the most money. Can you identify any reasons for changes in your company's share price?

Evaluation point

You will need to be able to use your knowledge and understanding of forms of limited companies to recommend whether or not a business should change from a private limited company to a public limited company. You should always be able to give reasons for any recommendations you make, taking into account the circumstances of the business in question.

You will need to consider and explain why so many large companies choose to become plcs.

Some businesses that have become plcs decided that this is the wrong form of business organisation and have returned to being private limited companies. You will need to consider why this may have happened.

Activity 6 – Zone activity

The following list shows some features of private limited companies and plcs. Some features are common to both forms of business organisation. Place a tick in the column(s) to which the feature applies.

Feature	Private limited company	Public limited company	Both private limited company and plc
Financial information is available to the public.			
Shareholders have limited liability.			
Shares are sold on the stock market.			
Dividends are paid to shareholders.			
Shares are usually sold to family and friends.			
Can be taken over without the consent of original shareholders.			
Can have any number of shareholders.			
Share capital must be at least £50,000.			
Has Ltd after its name.			
Can only be taken over with consent of existing shareholders.			
Often a family owned company.			

Table 1.12 Private limited company or plc?

Suitability of differing types of business ownership in different business contexts

Start-ups

When a business is just starting, it will begin as a sole trader, partnership or private limited company. Public limited companies are not used for start-ups (businesses just starting).

One consideration for start-ups is the amount of money required. If the amount is small, then someone could easily find the finance and open as a sole trader. If a larger amount of money is required, then a partnership or private limited company may be appropriate because there will be more than one person providing capital.

Limited liability can be useful for start-ups. If a person has large personal wealth, they may not want to put that at risk if a new business fails with large debts. Here, a private limited company would be appropriate because liability (responsibility for debts) is limited to the amount invested in the business. In this way, a person who puts money into a private limited company will know clearly just what their level of risk is, and personal possessions are protected.

A single person starting a business on their own may feel that they do not have the skills to run a business. They may benefit from a partner who can bring in other skills to help the business run smoothly and take some pressure off a single owner.

Private limited companies are more complex to set up and operate, so this may not be attractive to someone setting up a simple one-person business. Sole trading would be a better choice.

Established businesses

Once a business becomes established, it may change its ownership, especially if it aims to grow. Do remember that many sole traders are well-established businesses who will see no need to change their ownership, preferring to stay as they are.

Growth in a business often requires extra capital. If the business is a private limited company, it could change to a public limited company. This will be a big step and will itself require money to complete the change. The benefits are that the business will be able to raise the capital it requires much more easily as a plc. The amount of capital for expansion is important in the decision. It is only when very large amounts of money (into the millions) are required that a plc is a realistic option. A private limited company would normally not be able to raise such an amount. There are exceptions to this: Clarks shoes is a private limited company that makes millions of pounds' profits. This is perhaps an unusual case.

Partnerships in professions such as dentists and solicitors are often well-established businesses and will see that as a suitable form of ownership. If expansion takes place, it may only require another desk in a solicitor's office, or slightly larger premises elsewhere. The money involved will be small and would not require a change of ownership to raise the necessary finance.

The biggest businesses are almost always plcs, examples include Sky, Burberry and Next. They require very large amounts of capital to operate and this only comes from being able to sell shares through the Stock Exchange.

Always remember that a change from a private to a public limited company will mean that shareholders lose the control they have on the sale of shares. This means that competitors or any interested group could buy up the shares and take over the business. This loss of control would be a real disadvantage to many private limited company shareholders who wish to keep their control and influence.

Activity 7 – Explanation activity

For each of the following situations, recommend a suitable form of business ownership. Give reasons for your recommendation.

a) Three newly qualified vets want to set up a veterinary surgery.

b) John Jones wants to start a painting and decorating business.

c) Friends Stuart and Tracy, both very wealthy, want to open a new high-class jewellery shop.

d) An established family bakery business, already a private limited company, wants to move to a new, larger bakery.

e) An established, large petroleum exploration business wants to expand its area of exploration.

f) Melissa is concerned that she is under stress as a sole trader trying to do everything in her dressmaking business.

Activity 8 – Research activity

In your local area, interview a business owner. It could be a corner shop, a hairdresser or a larger business where you have some contact with the owner.

Find out:

a) their type of ownership – is it a sole trader, partnership etc.?

b) why they have that type of business ownership

c) are there any plans to change the type of ownership? Whatever the answer, find out why they might or might not change.

Write your findings up as a report. Compare your results with other members of your class. Do all businesses give the same reasons for choosing their type of business ownership?

Key facts

There are four types of business ownership that you must be familiar with – sole trader, partnership, private limited company and public limited company.

Each type of business ownership has its own unique advantages and disadvantages.

Changing circumstances may mean that a different type of ownership could be appropriate.

Many successful small businesses do not change their type of ownership.

Private limited companies are more expensive to set up and operate than a sole trader or partnership. A public limited company is much more expensive than a private limited company to set up and operate.

A new business would not start as a public limited company.

Private and public limited companies are owned by their shareholders.

The main reason for a business becoming a public limited company is the ability to raise large amounts of capital.

Useful words

Limited liability is where the responsibility for the debts of a business is limited to the amount invested by a shareholder. A feature of private and public limited companies.

Unlimited liability is where the responsibility for all the debts of a business rests with the owners of the business. A feature of sole traders and partnerships.

Sole trader is a business owned by one person.

Partnership is a business owned by between two and 20 partners.

Private limited company is often (but not always) a smaller business. Owned by at least two shareholders. Shares cannot be sold to the general public. Has Ltd after its name.

Public limited company is a large business, where shares can be sold to the general public enabling vast sums of money to be raised to develop the company. Has plc after its name.

Deed of partnership is a document setting out the operations of the partnership, including amount of capital to be invested and how profits will be shared.

Capital is money raised to start or develop a business.

Sleeping partner is a partner who invests in a partnership but has no part in the running of the business.

Limited liability partnerships are part partnership part limited company. Owners are members, not partners. They have limited liability and have to make their finances available to the public.

Shareholders are the owners of a private or public limited company.

Dividend is the money paid to a shareholder from the profits of a limited company. This is the reward for the shareholder taking a risk by investing money in the company.

Practice questions

Multiple choice questions

1 A sole trader can:
  a) only employ one person
  b) employ as many people as the owner wishes
  c) only employ workers where other workers agree
  d) not employ any workers because it is a sole trader working on their own.

2 A partnership has:
  a) a maximum of 20 partners
  b) a maximum of 2 partners
  c) a minimum of 2 partners
  d) a minimum of 20 partners.

3 A private limited company:
  a) is easier to set up than a plc
  b) is just as difficult to set up as a plc
  c) always has one main shareholder
  d) can sell shares to anyone with the agreement of the main shareholder.

4 A public limited company:
  a) must have a minimum of £500,000 share capital
  b) must have a minimum of £50,000 share capital
  c) must have a maximum of £50,000 share capital
  d) has no minimum share capital.

Data response 3

Clarks shoes.

Clarks began making slippers in Somerset in 1825, using scrap pieces of material from sheepskin rugs. For many years, all of Clarks' shoes were made in Britain, However, with many more people wanting to buy their shoes, Clarks decided to move production overseas, where large factories – often built specially for Clarks – were able to meet the growing need for their shoes.

Despite this huge growth, Clarks has remained a family owned private limited company. It is one of the largest private limited companies in Britain, and made a profit of over £45 million in 2016. 25 per cent of the business is owned by Lance Clark.

1 State two advantages of Clarks being a private limited company. (2 marks)
2 State two disadvantages of Clarks being a private limited company. (2 marks)
3 Evaluate whether or not Clarks should become a plc or stay as a private limited company. Give reasons for your answer. (9 marks)

How to answer data response 3

1 This question simply asks you to 'state', so there is no need for any explanation.
2 This question simply asks you to 'state', so there is no need for any explanation.
3 This question tells you to evaluate, so here you must make a judgement, giving reasons for the judgement you make. In this type of question there is no clear right or wrong decision. What you must do is look at Clarks as a business from the information you are given, and use your knowledge and understanding of the benefits of being a private limited company compared to the benefits of becoming a plc.

UNIT 1.4 Business aims and objectives

Learning outcomes

By studying this unit, you will be able to:

- identify and explain the different aims and objectives of businesses
- understand that not all businesses have the same aims and objectives
- evaluate why aims and objectives change as businesses evolve
- explain why certain aims and objectives are suitable for a particular business in different situations
- analyse the benefits to a business of having aims and objectives
- analyse and evaluate different possible aims and objectives of a business, and recommend which are more appropriate in different situations.

Introductory case study: how EE aims to achieve its vision

EE shop and logo.

The EE website states:

'Our vision is to provide the best network and best service so our customers trust us with their digital lives. Here's how we will achieve it:

Best network: building a new digital backbone for Britain.

Best service: delivering outstanding service to our customers through our stores, in our centres and online.

Customer trust and relevance: providing a personalised experience for our customers – from the products and services we offer, to the way we sell them.

We believe in giving the UK the best network and best service so our customers trust us with their digital lives.'

Marc Allera CEO of EE.

Taken from www.ee.co.uk

Business aims and objectives

All businesses have one or more objective. The objectives themselves will vary according to the size and situation of the business. A large well-established public limited company will have very different objectives to a sole trader just starting in business. The aims of EE, for example, are to build the best network, deliver the best service and achieve the trust of its customers.

Profit

Most businesses will make achieving profit one of their objectives. For many businesses, it will be the *main* objective. Some businesses may want to 'maximise profits', which means they will try to make as much profit as possible. This may, however, mean that consumers feel they are not being treated well, if a business is seen to make too much profit. Sales may fall as a result.

Other businesses may aim to make just enough profit to pay for their general needs. This is called **satisficing**. Sole traders are often in this situation, being content to earn just enough profit to give them a decent living.

Growth

Growth is important to a business, as it is seen as a way to raise profits. This is especially important to larger businesses such as public limited companies, which need the growth to pay increased dividends to their shareholders. However, do not assume that all businesses are interested in growth. Smaller businesses may be quite content to stay as they are and see the idea of growth as simply too much bother.

Growth itself can take different forms, including sales growth. A business may want to see sales grow, which may not necessarily mean an increase in profit, as prices may have to be lowered in order to attract more customers. Sales growth is often achieved by a business opening more outlets – for example, opening shops in different towns. Growth might also take the form of increased **market share**.

Market share

A business may wish to see its market share grow. This means that the business has a greater percentage share of a market. For example, if 1,000 tables were sold in a country, and a business sold 100 of those tables, it would have 10 per cent share of the market. If the total number of tables sold rose from 1,000 to 2,000, the business would have to sell more than 200 tables (10 per cent of 2,000) if it were to increase its market share. Supermarkets will compare how much of the total market they have for the goods they sell. A business might take over a competitor to help achieve higher market share.

Survival

A rather more basic **business objective** is **survival**. This objective is particularly important to a new business for the first few months. Just to keep going after first opening a business may be something of an achievement! Other more established businesses may see survival as an important objective when they are faced with problems such as falling sales, reduced market share and so on. In most cases, survival should normally be seen as a temporary but also vital objective.

Providing a service

Providing a service may be closely linked to making a **profit** – the better the service, the more customers it will attract and therefore profits will grow. For some businesses, however, providing a service may be the main objective, even if it means making less profit. This may be important in businesses that see customer satisfaction as being a high priority. See earlier in this unit how EE has made excellent customer service a main part of their vision for the future. With good service, the business gets a good reputation, possibly winning awards, which may well be enough to satisfy the owners of the business. Such a business may not even think of **growth**, being content to continue in its present form, providing a service to customers. This is often found in smaller businesses, which serve the local community.

How and why business objectives might change as businesses evolve

Businesses will always start with the best intentions.

When a business starts

When a small business starts, its main objective may well be to simply survive the first few months. This could be because:

- It will probably face competition from other established businesses who may not like to see a new competitor. Competitors may lower their prices to make sure the new business does not survive.
- It needs to establish its name. Other businesses may have established a good reputation, and a new business may have to 'steal' some of their customers or find new customers to buy their product or service.

Note here that to achieve the above main objective, a business may put excellent customer service as an aim, because this may tempt potential customers to try the new products and services on offer.

Other businesses may set their sights higher than simply surviving and aim for profit in the first year. For example, partners may be coming into business with some experience, possibly with some contacts, and feel confident that they can make profit from the start.

As a business evolves

As the business evolves, aims and objectives may change; though remember that some businesses are quite happy to not change at all, and simply make enough profit to provide a decent standard of living. Their aims and objectives will stay very much the same. Businesses might change their objectives as they grow because:

- For some entrepreneurs (see Unit 1.1) simply making enough profit to live on is just not enough. Ambitions may drive the business on to aim for greater profit.
- This profit could then be used to pay for the growth of the business. New premises could be built, a competitor may be taken over and the market share could be increased. This change in aims and objectives is usually down to the owner and their desire to make more profit.
- A sole trader or partnership may wish to become a limited company with the growth of a business. With profits being made and an increase in wealth of the owner(s), the attraction of limited liability (see Unit 1.3) will mean that personal possessions (and all of the profit) is not put at risk.
- A business may grow to a point where it simply does not wish to grow any more. For example, there could be enough shops for a business to control effectively, and further growth would mean that control, and possibly customer service, would not be as good. The aim then becomes one of keeping the profits at a particular level, or making more profit by improving the existing shops or through better customer service.
- If a business grows too quickly it may lose sight of how it is treating its customers. This may mean that there needs to be a switch to providing a good service to avoid losing customers.

When a business is in difficulty

Sometimes it is necessary to change business objectives.

When businesses evolve, it could mean that they grow, as shown above. It could also mean that they are in some difficulty and have to change their aims and objectives. This is because:

- profits may be reduced or the business might be running at a loss. This means that for a short time, there is no realistic point in making profit an objective. The objective may be to keep losses at a certain level, or in extreme cases, to survive
- expansion plans would be scrapped or postponed if a business was in difficulty. Businesses that have tried to expand too much have had to set new aims and objectives that can include closing down some of their operations.

Why different businesses have different objectives

Small businesses such as sole traders are owned by one person. If the owner simply wants a quiet life running a small business, they can decide for themselves what aim or objective they set.

As businesses become bigger, this can change. In the case of large businesses such as public limited companies, the shareholders will normally want more in dividends from the business. As this comes from profit, the business has to make enough money to keep the shareholders happy. A plc may wish to increase sales as an aim. This may be done by reducing prices, but if sales only increase by a little, then less profit may be made, and shareholders will not be happy!

Some business owners may be in business because they want to serve the community as well as possible. This may be done by keeping prices low so that everyone can afford their product or service, therefore the aim for greater profit does not exist. Here, the provision of a good service is of greater importance than profit.

A business facing a lot of competition may have different objectives to a business with no competition. In a competitive market, there may be less emphasis on growth, simply because there are so many other businesses providing the same product or service. Always consider in this situation that small differences can have a real impact on a business. There are many supermarkets in the UK, but his has not stopped Aldi and Lidl from growing their businesses, because they offer something different from supermarkets such as Tesco and Asda.

Evaluation point

You will need to be able to explain in detail why a particular business has certain aims and objectives. You will need to consider the size of the business and the likely attitude of the owner(s). Whether the business is doing well or is in difficulty will also affect your answer.

You will need to be able to evaluate how and why objectives change as the business evolves. Some changes may be outside the control of a business, for example, new competitors. Some changes might be because the business has changed from a family run private limited company to a public limited company, with shareholders demanding high profits to pay them dividends.

Not all businesses will have the same objectives.

Activity 1 – Explanation activity

Look back to the start of this unit and the future vision of EE.

Explain why EE might have chosen the aims and objectives in its vision statement.

Activity 2 – Zone activity

Complete the table below by selecting one of the following business objectives for each of the following business situations:

- profit
- growth
- market share
- survival
- providing a service

Give a reason for your choice of objective.

Business situation	Possible objective	Reason for choice of objective
A public limited company making car parts		
A family run high-class fashion business		
A school leaver wanting to start a motor cycle repair business		
A computer manufacturer who is seeing a fall in sales		
A well-established international airline facing competition from low-cost airlines		

Table 1.13 Business objectives.

Activity 3 – Explanation activity

Imagine you were to go into business. Complete the table below by making a list of your business objectives in order of importance to you. Explain why your objectives are in that particular order.

Type of business:

Objective	Explanation for choice of objective

Table 1.14 Business objectives.

In pairs or small groups, compare and discuss your individual lists of business objectives. Are the objectives in the same order for everyone? Why might different businesses within your class have different objectives?

Key facts

Businesses in different situations will often have different objectives.

Although some objectives might differ, there are often common objectives in businesses.

Aims and objectives may remain the same, especially in small businesses. In other situations, aims and objectives change as businesses evolve.

The aims and objectives of a business are often influenced by the attitude of the business owner(s).

The objectives of a business are often linked. For example, providing a good service should lead to more customers, which in turn will help increase sales, which will then help the profitability of a business.

Useful words

Satisficing is making just enough profit to provide the business owner with a decent living. More common in smaller businesses.

Market share is the share of the total market for a product or service and is shown as a percentage.

Business objectives are what the business aims to achieve, and include survival, profit, growth and providing a service.

Profit is the difference between revenue and costs.

Survival is when a business just manages to keep going.

Growth is where a business becomes larger, for example by making more products or opening more places where goods and services are sold.

Providing a service is where a business makes sure that the needs of the customer are being met.

Practice questions

Multiple choice questions

1 Survival in a business situation means:
 a) making products cheaper than competitors
 b) making sure the business continues to operate
 c) making less profit than last year
 d) providing good service rather than making profit.

2 A business might want to grow because:
 a) it sees the opportunity of making more profit
 b) growth will mean more people working in the business
 c) it is the best objective to have
 d) it will guarantee more profit.

3 A business might change its aims and objectives because:
 a) all businesses change their objectives after a year
 b) a new competitor has become very successful
 c) it feels that a change will always bring more profits
 d) it is essential to change objectives as a business grows.

Data response 4

Pen and Sword books and staff: Amy Jordan, Heather Williams and Jodie Butterwood

Pen and Sword are book publishers based in Barnsley, South Yorkshire. It is a family owned private limited company, and specialises in military history and transport books. The business has seen growth since it started with only 50 books published per year. It now employs 42 people and published 450 books in 2016.

The business is ambitious and is aiming to expand into publishing books related to science, space and the environment as well as more general social history.

The business has also seen growth in digital publishing, which it is aiming to develop further.

1 State one aim of Pen and Sword books. (1 mark)

2 Explain how providing a good service might help Pen and Sword to achieve its aims. (4 marks)

3 Analyse why the aims and objectives of Pen and Sword might evolve as the business grows. (7 marks)

How to answer data response 4

1 This question tells you to 'state', so no explanation is necessary.

2 This question needs an understanding of good service as a business aim, applied to the details you know of Pen and Sword books.

3 In this question you are asked to 'analyse', so look for possible effects on the business. You have to consider reasons why Pen and Sword might change their objectives due to growth – this *could* mean a change in the type of ownership.

UNIT 1.5 Stakeholders in business

Learning outcomes

By studying this unit, you will be able to:

- identify the different **stakeholders** in businesses
- understand that stakeholders have an effect on business, and business has an effect on stakeholders
- understand the roles and objectives of internal and external stakeholders
- evaluate the roles and objectives of different **stakeholder groups**
- explain how the interests of stakeholders might be different in particular business situations
- analyse and evaluate the effect that stakeholders have on businesses (and businesses have on stakeholders) in particular situations.

Introductory case study: stakeholders in Barratt Developments plc

Barratt Developments.

Barratt Developments plc is a leading house builder in the UK. It has many groups of people – stakeholders – who have an interest in the business.

The owners (shareholders) of the business want to see Barratt do well so that they can share higher profits through the payment of dividends. Barratt's employees are interested in the business succeeding so that they can have a reliable job which pays well. Local communities are interested in Barratt because they may want to see new housing in their area. Some communities may of course have an interest in *not* seeing any new development! The government wants taxes from Barratt and its employees. Businesses who supply Barratt with building materials will also have an interest in seeing the business succeeding.

Barratt Developments is typical of large businesses that have a variety of people who are interested in their success.

What are stakeholders?

A stakeholder can be an individual or group(s) of people who have an interest in a business. There are many different stakeholders in a business, and they often go beyond the business itself.

The main stakeholders in business are:

- owners
- employees
- customers
- suppliers
- government
- local community.

There will probably be many other stakeholders who will have an interest in the business. Much will depend on the type of business and where it is located. Stakeholders can be classed as internal or external. **Internal stakeholders** are the owners and people who work in the business. **External stakeholders** are 'outside' the business and include customers, suppliers, government and local community.

Internal stakeholders

Owners

The owners of a business are not the same for all businesses. For a sole trader, there is one owner who would normally work in the business. The same would apply to partners working in a partnership – the owners are also employees working in the business. In the case of limited companies, shareholders are the owners of the business.

Employees

Employees have a clear interest in the business where they work. They rely on work for their pay, which they will use to live on. Employees will also look upon work to provide them with some security for the future, and possibly a place to meet and work with other people. An employee, whether a manager or a worker, has every interest in keeping the business going.

External stakeholders

Customers

Customers want to see a business continue in operation. They may, for example, rely on a local corner shop for their daily needs. Other customers might have a different view and just look for low prices and good service. Some may be pleased if a large superstore opens in the area because it will give them a choice of shops and possibly lower prices.

Suppliers

A business that supplies goods and services to another business will clearly want that business to continue and to grow. If a business fails for any reason, other businesses are often affected in some way. If a business finds that another business that it supplies materials to is in difficulty, it may stop supplying those materials in order to reduce the risk of losses.

Government

The government has an interest in all businesses succeeding because this means that more people are in work and paying taxes, as well as the business paying taxes, which in turn gives the government more money to spend on areas such as health and education. With more people in work, the government also has to pay less unemployment pay – once again saving money.

Local community

The local community has an interest in business development. This may not mean that every business is welcome in an area. A business dealing in toxic waste processing may well provide jobs for some people, but the local community may be against such a development. Successful business will also bring general prosperity to a local community, which could help to reduce crime and contribute to local projects by donations and other support.

Evaluation point

You will need to be able to explain the reasons why a stakeholder may have an interest in the business, and to analyse and evaluate the importance of different **stakeholder groups**.

Activity 1 – Research and explanation activity

Research who the stakeholders are in your school or college. Explain their interest in your school. Do some stakeholders have more effect on the running of the school than others? Give reasons for your answer.

A school has many stakeholders, but which has the greatest effect on its operation?

Activity 2 – True or false activity

Tick **one** box to indicate if the statement is true or false.

Statement	True	False
All stakeholders are owners of a business.		
All businesses have stakeholders.		
All stakeholders have the same interests.		
Stakeholders can influence the activity of a business.		
Stakeholders are only interested in the profits of the business.		
Stakeholders generally want a business to succeed.		
All of the employees of a business are stakeholders.		

Table 1.15 Stakeholders.

The effect that business activity has on stakeholders

Business activity will affect stakeholders in a number of ways.

As a business grows, it may need more employees. These may come from the local community who will appreciate the fact that more people are employed, because spending in the local shops may increase. Suppliers will benefit from having increased orders from the expanding business, and the government will be happy to see more people employed who can pay taxes. Customers will possibly have a greater range of products and services from an expanding business and will be able to buy those goods and services in more places. Last but not least, the owners will have higher profits, which they will see as a reward for starting the business or in the case of shareholders, a reward for investing money in the business.

If a business is having difficulties and has to decrease in size, the reverse of the above will occur. Employees might lose jobs, suppliers may be put out of business because they have no one to supply goods to, and the government may see a rise in unemployment that will result in fewer taxes being paid and more unemployment benefit being paid out. The local community suffers with more people out of work, and the business owners have less profit for themselves. Customers may have less choice of goods and services with fewer places to buy them.

A business may be unwelcome in an area, such as the fracking that is currently proposed in various parts of the UK. This involves high pressure water, sand and chemicals being injected into rocks at great depths from the surface. This fractures the rocks below, releasing gas that can be used in homes or to generate electricity. This will have mixed effects on stakeholders. The government sees this as a way of making sure the country has sufficient energy for the future. Some members of the local community might see it as a job opportunity. Others are very much opposed to the project because they claim it will spoil the environment and potentially cause earthquakes and flooding. The disposal of any waste chemicals and water may also have a negative impact locally. Other projects that may have similar impacts are the High Speed 2 (HS2) high speed rail link and wind farms.

The effect stakeholders have on business

Stakeholders, as we have seen, have different interests in businesses. In order to see that their interests are met, stakeholders have different effects on business activity.

Owners

Owners will usually, but not always, see profit as their main interest in running a business. To achieve higher levels of profit they would want to see the business run as effectively as possible. This may mean making workers redundant in order to save costs. Profit could also be increased by growth in the business.

Employees

Employees can influence business activity by objecting to changes in their work. Workers could go on strike in order to try and persuade the owners not to take a particular course of action. A common issue is often wages, where employees want to see higher wages. This would make employees happy, but would possibly add costs to the business, making products more expensive and therefore potentially less are sold.

Employees are, however, the foundations of the business. Good, reliable, hard-working employees will go a long way to making a business successful. There must always be a balance between what a business (in the form of the owners) can afford to pay, and what the employees see as a reasonable wage or salary. Pay is not the only issue that can cause problems within a workplace. Levels of staffing, pensions and work patterns are just three other potential areas where there can be conflict between employees and business owners, which in turn may affect business activity.

Customers

A business cannot survive without customers. By simply not buying the goods or services a business has to sell, this will send a message to the business owners that something has to change. Customers may be unhappy with the price, the level of service being provided or the quality of the goods and so on. Whatever the reason, the business will have to first find out what the problem is, and then take steps to change how it operates or potentially face closure. Conversely, if customers really like a product or service, this will possibly encourage a business to grow and provide an increased range of goods.

Suppliers

Suppliers can affect business activity through the quality of goods they supply. If a car maker relies on another business to supply parts for their cars and these parts develop a fault, then the car maker's reputation will be harmed and sales might fall.

The reliability of supply is also important (see Unit 4.6). If a shop sells milk and the supplier fails to deliver, then the shop will be seen as unreliable. Shoppers will simply go elsewhere. Suppliers must be both reliable and provide consistent quality to have a positive effect on a business.

Government

As we have seen, the government has a great interest in business as a stakeholder. It also can affect business activity in a number of ways:

- **Changing taxation levels** – if taxes such as income tax are increased, people will have less money to spend on products and services. If tax levels are cut then people will have more money to spend and businesses benefit with possibly higher profits due to increased sales. The government also taxes the profits of businesses. If this tax is reduced, the business will have more money to invest in expansion or reward its owners.
- **Giving grants to businesses and organisations** – this will help businesses to establish themselves when they might not have succeeded. This is seen as a benefit to the community and a boost to jobs.
- **Changing laws, such as the national living wage** – a business has to pay the necessary amount required by law. This may cause businesses some difficulty. For others, they may be paying more than the necessary level already.
- **Spending** – the government is a huge spender. Simply by spending money on projects such as defence, railways and roads, the government increases business activity.

Local community

As explained above with the proposed fracking in parts of the UK, local communities are affected by businesses and they, in turn, can affect business. If protests about potential harm to the environment are successful, then business activity will be stopped. The planned route for HS2 through Yorkshire has been changed due to protests from groups in Sheffield. Other groups along the line of the proposed railway are now protesting about potential harm to *their* local environment. It remains to be seen whether or not the railway will be built.

Different stakeholder groups do not always agree.

Activity 3 – Research activity

a) Research any proposed business activity where there are arguments for and against the proposals. This may be in your local area or something that is happening elsewhere in the country.

b) Identify the stakeholders involved.

c) Explain why the stakeholders have an interest in the proposal.

d) Analyse the effect that each stakeholder is having on the proposal. Is anything being changed from the original idea?

e) Present your findings in a PowerPoint report.

Key facts

There are a number of stakeholder groups who have an interest in business activity.

Stakeholder groups can influence business activity, and business activity can influence stakeholders.

Stakeholders may not always agree on the way a business should develop.

The government, as a stakeholder, can affect business activity in a number of different ways.

Useful words

Stakeholders are groups or individuals who have an interest in a business.

Internal stakeholders are the business owners and people who work in the business.

External stakeholders are the local community, suppliers, customers and government.

Stakeholder group are owners, employees, customers, suppliers, government, local community.

Practice questions

Multiple choice questions

1 A stakeholder is:

a) someone who objects to a business development they do not like

b) a person or group of people who have an interest in business activity

c) a person or group who always support business activity

d) someone who will organise others in developing business activity.

2 Employees as stakeholders are interested in the business activity because:

a) they rely on the business for their income

b) they want the business to be taxed more

c) they feel that the business should do just as they say

d) they want the government to help them get a higher living wage.

3 Which of the following is not a method by which government as a stakeholder can affect business activity?

- **a)** increasing the taxation on business profits
- **b)** giving grants to businesses to help new developments
- **c)** increasing the number of MPs in parliament
- **d)** spending money on new road projects.

Data response 5

Steve Loy owns Lineside Repairs, a small garage in Elsecar, South Yorkshire. It is a family business that opened in 1968, and deals in car sales, servicing and repairs. Steve started working in the business with his brother in the early 1980s, and has been servicing and repairing all types of cars since then without ever having to advertise the business.

Josh and Steve at Lineside Repairs.

Steve employs Josh to help him in the business because he has too much work from the local community to complete himself and needs someone to operate the business for him when he is on holiday.

1 Other than government, identify two stakeholders in Lineside Repairs. (2 marks)

2 Analyse one effect that the government might have as a stakeholder in Lineside Repairs. (3 marks)

3 Evaluate the effect that different stakeholders have on the successful running of Lineside Repairs. (9 marks)

How to answer data response 5

1 This question asks you to identify stakeholders, so no explanation of their interest in a business is necessary.

2 In this question you must look at the effect that the government as a stakeholder has on Lineside Repairs. Look at the information provided for help but also use your understanding of how government as a stakeholder affects businesses. How much of this is applicable to Lineside Repairs?

3 In this question 'evaluate' means that you should make a judgement on the effect that different stakeholders have on the business. Use your knowledge of different stakeholders – which will have the *most* effect on the *successful running* of Lineside Repairs?

UNIT 1.6 Business growth

Learning outcomes

By studying this unit, you will be able to:

- identify the methods by which a business might grow
- explain how different businesses might grow in different ways
- analyse and evaluate the different methods of growth and recommend a particular method suitable to a given situation.

Introductory case study: the growth of Pets at Home

Pets at Home store.

Pets at Home opened its first store in Chester in 1991. In 1999, it bought Petsmart, which took the number of stores to 140. In the same year, it introduced Companion Care – instore vet practices. In 2007, the 200th store was opened in Barnstaple. In 2013, the veterinary service was expanded with the takeover of Vets4Pets and by 2015, the number of veterinary practices had reached 300. The number of stores is now over 360 making Pets at Home the biggest pet store chain in the UK.

Adapted from www.petsathome.com

How businesses grow

There are two main methods of business growth:

1 organic

2 external.

Organic growth

Organic growth is concerned with increasing sales of products and services. It is *internal*, as in it grows by increasing its own size rather than taking over another business. This can be done in a number of ways:

Increasing output

If a business makes a product, it can expand by increasing the amount that it produces. This could be by introducing more efficient technology, building more factory space or taking on more workers. Growth in this way can be quick if there is spare capacity at the factory and simply by employing more workers, production can be increased. If a new factory has to be built, this growth will be much slower.

Gaining new customers

A business might gain more customers in a number of ways:

- **Reducing the prices of its products or services** – for customers who cannot afford a particular product, a reduction in price will possibly persuade them to buy.
- **Opening shops in new places** – Aldi and Lidl have opened many new shops to help their growth in the UK.
- **Better marketing** (see Unit 2.1) – a business may advertise itself more effectively and so reach new customers, therefore helping the business to grow. This could be costly, depending on the business involved and how much competitors are putting into marketing.

Developing new products

A business might develop new products and services that appeal to a wider range of customers. As shown in the case of Pets at Home, veterinary services were added to the products that the business already sold, enabling further growth to take place. Apple have grown from first producing computers to introducing the iPod, iPhone, iPad and the Apple watch. In technology-based businesses in particular, the introduction of new and updated products is essential if the business is to grow and not lose out to its competitors.

Increasing market share

A business might grow by increasing its market share – increasing its share of the overall market for a product (see Unit 1.4 Business aims and objectives). It is a means of measuring whether or not a business has grown in relation to the total market. If, for example, the number of cars sold in the UK increases by 20 per cent, a business must increase its sales by 20 per cent simply to have the same share of the market. If it increases sales by 10 per cent, it will have lost out to competitors, even though it has sold more products.

If a business does increase its market share, it could be that sales have actually fallen. If the total market for cars falls by 20 per cent over 12 months and a business sells 10 per cent fewer cars over 12 months, it will have increased its market share, even though fewer cars are sold. Care must be taken with using market share as a means of establishing whether a business has grown or not.

Note: All of the methods of organic growth will often work together. A business will hope to increase its number of customers by increasing the number of products and services it sells. Output might be increased because a greater variety of products are being sold.

Activity 1 – Explanation activity

Using the information about Pets at Home, explain how the business has grown organically.

Activity 2 – True or false activity

Put a tick in the correct column to indicate whether the statements are true or false.

Statement	True	False
Organic growth in a business is about growing vegetables organically.		
More effective marketing will help a business to grow.		
Market share is the share that a worker has in the business.		
It is important for technology-based businesses to constantly bring out new products if they are to grow.		
Reducing prices will help attract new customers to a business.		
With a 30% increase in the total market, a business that increases its sales by 20% will have increased its market share.		

Table 1.16 Organic growth.

External growth

There are two ways that a business could grow externally:

1 merger
2 takeover.

It is not always the case that a big business takes over a smaller business.

Merger

A **merger** is a form of **external growth** where two businesses agree to join together to form one larger business, and it is a quick way for a business to grow.

Takeover

A **takeover** occurs when one business buys control of another. In the case of a limited company, it would mean buying more than 50 per cent of its shares. As with mergers, this can lead to a business growing very quickly.

Types of merger and takeover

Both mergers and takeovers can themselves be divided into different types, depending on the *type* of businesses involved.

Horizontal

Here the two businesses that join together are in the same type of business, such as two businesses making furniture. The businesses concerned need not be identical, for example, a business making chairs merging with a business making tables would be **horizontal growth**. This means that the bigger business will control more of the market, and will possibly be able to get discounts from suppliers as the enlarged business will be ordering more goods. A potential problem, as with any sudden growth of a business, is whether the enlarged business can be controlled effectively. Sometimes it is easier to control two smaller businesses than one larger one!

Vertical

Here, the business will merge with (or take over) a business that supplies it with goods (**backwards vertical growth**), or with a business that it supplies (**forwards vertical growth**). In the case of a furniture maker, a backwards vertical merger might be with a wood supplier. A forwards vertical merger or takeover might be with a shop selling furniture. This type of growth would enable the furniture maker to make sure that it had supplies of wood (backwards vertical) and could make sure it had somewhere to sell the furniture it made (forwards vertical).

Diversification

With **diversification**, the business merges with, or takes over, a business with which it has no real connection. This might mean a furniture maker takes over a pizza delivery business. The benefit of this is to spread risk as well as achieving growth. Running any business is risky, but if the risk is spread (if people stop buying furniture, the hope is that they may still want their pizzas delivered) then the business will not only survive, but be able to grow. Any business that relies on a single product or service is at risk if customers stop buying that one product. The problem with this attempt at growth is that the furniture maker may know very little about pizza delivery, and that this poor knowledge might affect the operation of the enlarged business.

Activity 3 – Matching terms activity

Match each of the following with the statement in the table below.

a) A maker of pottery takes over a pottery shop.

b) A business buys control of another business.

c) A business making radios merges with a business making televisions.

d) A business assembling computers merges with a microchip supplier.

e) Two businesses agree to join together.

An example of a horizontal merger or takeover.	
An example of a backwards vertical merger.	
A definition of a merger.	
An example of a forwards vertical merger.	
A definition of a takeover.	

Table 1.17 External growth.

Activity 4 – Research activity

Using newspapers or the internet, research a merger or takeover that is being planned between two businesses. Look into:

a) why they want to join together

b) what type of merger or takeover it is

c) whether there are any possible problems with the merger/takeover.

Write a short report on your findings.

Evaluation point

When evaluating the advantages or disadvantages of mergers, always look carefully at the situation you are given in a question. Is it a case that a business has to merge or go out of business? Does one business really have to take over another or can it manage as it is without the risks that any takeover brings?

Key facts

Businesses can grow organically (internally) and/or externally.

Mergers and takeovers are not the same.

There are a number of types of merger/takeover.

Useful words

Organic growth is growth of a business internally by increasing sales. Sales can be increased in a number of different ways.

Merger is where two or more businesses agree to join together.

External growth is growth of a business by takeover or merger.

Takeover is where a business takes a controlling interest in another business.

Horizontal growth is a merger or takeover where two businesses are involved in a similar operation e.g. two electrical producers or two shops selling fashion clothing.

Backwards vertical growth is when a business merges with, or takes over a business that supplies it with goods or services.

Forwards vertical growth is when a business merges with or takes over a business that it supplies goods or services to.

Diversification is when a business merges with or takes over another business with which there is no connection.

Practice questions

Multiple choice questions

1 A forwards vertical merger is when:

- a) a business merges with another similar business
- b) a business merges with a supplier
- c) a business merges with a business it supplies goods to
- d) a business merges with a totally different business.

2 A takeover is when:

- a) a business agrees to join with another business
- b) a business buys more than 50 per cent of another business
- c) a business buys any share of another business
- d) a business takes over paying the workers at another business.

3 Which of the following is not an example of organic growth?

- a) increasing output
- b) merging with a supplier
- c) developing new products
- d) gaining new customers.

Data response 6

Vice Media is a successful digital media and broadcasting company targeting the youth market. Its co-founder, Shane Smith, said he has refused offers of a buyout from Time Warner (international television and film company) and Viacom (another mass media company). Disney already has an 18 per cent share of Vice Media. Shane fears that there is not enough business for so many similar companies, especially in the social media market, and that some will simply have to close.

Vice Media is now diversifying into the more traditional pay-TV market with Viceland – a new channel on Sky.

Adapted from Daily Telegraph *business section, 25 August 2016*

1 State two examples of how a business might grow. (2 marks)

2 Explain two reasons why Time Warner, Disney and Viacom might be interested in taking over Vice Media. (4 marks)

3 Evaluate the possible benefits to Vice Media in diversifying into pay-TV. (9 marks)

How to answer data response 6

1 Here you need to simply 'state' examples, so no explanation is necessary.

2 In this question, you should think first of why any business might benefit from taking over another. Then look at the reasons why *these* businesses might be interested in Vice Media. Look carefully at the information you have been given.

3 As with question 2, first look at the general reasons for diversification and then go onto Vice Media and diversification. 'Evaluate' means making a judgement – is it really a benefit? Is the benefit really significant? Again, look at the information you are given.

UNIT 2.1 The role of marketing

Learning outcomes

By studying this unit, you will be able to:

- identify and explain the roles of **marketing** in business activity
- explain how different businesses might have a different approach to marketing
- analyse and evaluate the purpose and importance of marketing in business activity.

Introductory case study: Fairy Liquid

From cars to washing-up liquid, businesses must market their products in order to make them successful. Fairy Liquid was introduced in 1950. Prior to that, people used powders to wash their dishes. Since then it has become a well-known name in the UK and abroad, now being sold with different scents and as a dishwasher product.

All of this has been achieved through marketing. The demand for a product was identified. There was a clear target market in the 1950s – housewives, with the slogan 'now hands that do dishes can feel as soft as your face with mild green Fairy Liquid'. Advertising on the newly created ITV channel was used to inform potential customers. The use of television, newspaper and other advertising media has continued to be used to keep sales high, with Fairy Liquid maintaining its position as one of the best-known product names in the country.

The role of marketing within business

Marketing is concerned with finding the needs of customers and demonstrating how a business fulfils those needs. It is vital to the success of any business. Some large businesses will spend millions of pounds on marketing; other more local businesses may spend a few pounds on a local newspaper advertisement. Both of these examples have the same objective: they want to increase sales. This is done by:

1 identifying and understanding customers – a business must be clear on who it is trying to sell its products or services to. Is it trying to sell to all ages, both male and female, or just females between 20 and 40 years old? This will influence how the business is marketed. A business needs to understand its customers. Their views will be collected using **market research** (see Unit 2.2), and then analysed to make sure that the business really is providing what the customer wants. There have been many examples in the past where a business *thinks* it understands the needs of the customer. Without checking with the customer, mistakes can be made and these mistakes can prove very costly for businesses.

2 informing customers – customers need to be informed by the business of the products and services they are selling. There is no real point in researching what customers want, making

that product, and then not informing customers through advertising that it is available. Informing customers would normally be achieved through advertising (see Unit 2.4). There are a number of different ways a business might advertise a product or service, including television, radio and social media. There are costs to be considered here. Procter and Gamble, who own Fairy, are a very large company and have huge resources they can put into informing customers of additions to the Fairy range, or a new offer on price. A small corner shop that is starting to sell newspapers might simply put leaflets through doors in the local area informing them of the new service. Each business has a different *market* to inform. For the corner shop, it is a very local market with local customers. Fairy's market is throughout the country.

3 increasing sales – as stated above, marketing aims to increase sales. This could be achieved by:

a) advertising the product or service more in order to raise awareness of what is on offer
b) introducing a new model that will appeal to more customers, for example, higher definition televisions
c) increasing the range of products or services available. Fairy Liquid is now in different scents. Cars, such as the Ford Fiesta, come in many different models
d) reducing the price – sales may increase, but will profits go up? Selling a new car at £1,000 may well increase sales but no profit will be made. A business must make sure that the price it charges for a product or service will be low enough to attract customers but high enough for the business to make a profit.
e) selling the product in different places – as stated above, Fairy Liquid was initially only available in the UK. It is now sold successfully in many countries, increasing overall sales
f) selling by different methods – selling online, or offering digital distribution (see Unit 2.4) will help increase the sales of products such as books and music.

Evaluation point

You will need to be able to evaluate whether or not a business should undertake marketing activities, using the role of marketing as a basis for your answer. Remember that not all businesses will spend money, time and effort on marketing themselves. It will often depend on the size and circumstances of the business. Money spent on marketing does not always bring about the required increase in sales.

Activity 1 – True or false activity

Put a tick in the correct column to show whether the statements are true or false.

Statement – the role of marketing is to:	True	False
increase the production of products		
give workers a better place to work		
inform customers of new products		
make higher quality products		
increase the sales of products and services		
undertake market research in order to understand the needs of customers.		

Table 2.1 The role of marketing.

Activity 2 – Research and explanation activity

Identify a product that you own. It may be an item of clothing, technology or any other item. Then research and answer the following questions:

a) How well is the product aimed at your needs? How do you think the business that made the product identified just what you wanted? If it does not quite meet your needs, could the business do more to meet them?

b) How were you informed about the product – was it an advertisement or another way? Do you think the business used the best way to keep you informed? Are there other methods the business could use?

c) Overall do you think that the product you have chosen is a good product for the business, in that sales are high and profit will be made? How would you explain the success of the product?

d) Make a PowerPoint report of your findings.

There are a number of roles within marketing.

Key facts

Marketing has a number of roles within a business.

Marketing plays a key part in business success.

Small businesses may not market themselves in any way.

Large businesses may spend millions of pounds each year on marketing.

Useful words

Marketing is finding the needs of consumers and demonstrating how a business fulfils those needs in a way that increases sales.

Market research is the collection of data on consumer habits to help decision-making in marketing. (See Unit 2.2.)

Practice questions

Multiple choice questions

1 The principal role of marketing is to:

- **a)** increase sales
- **b)** increase profit
- **c)** increase the number of products made
- **d)** increase the skills of the workers.

2 The way a business informs customers about a new product or service:

- **a)** is the same operation for all businesses
- **b)** can vary depending on the size of the business
- **c)** is only done at a local level
- **d)** is only done at a national level.

3 A business can understand the needs of its customers by:

- **a)** conducting market research
- **b)** making the best possible product
- **c)** setting a lower price than competitors
- **d)** having special offers such as buy one get one free.

Data response 7

Everything Voice is a Yorkshire-based business specialising in improving communications in businesses – whether this is between its workers or with customers. This allows people to communicate more effectively using phone, video and instant messaging, whatever device they are on and wherever they are.

The business markets itself using a combination of elements, including social media, emailing and attending events. They take care to target their messages, so that the messages are relevant to the business concerned. They employ a marketing and social media executive to make sure that the marketing section of the business operates effectively.

1. Identify two methods by which Everything Voice could inform its present and potential customers of new developments in technology. (2 marks)
2. Explain three ways in which a business such as Everything Voice might increase sales. (6 marks)
3. Evaluate the importance for a business to clearly identify and understand its customers (9 marks)

How to answer data response 7

1. This question is simply an 'identify' question, so no explanation is necessary.
2. Here you need to apply your understanding to a business such as Everything Voice. This question is not about *any* business that wants to increase sales. Consider the type of business you are dealing with from the information provided. Remember too that this is an 'explain' question – make sure there is an explanation in your answer.
3. This question requires you to make a judgement, because there is an instruction to evaluate. What will be the effect on a business if it did not understand its customers? Just how important is this element of marketing?

UNIT 2.2 Market research

Learning outcomes

By studying this unit, you will be able to:

- define the different methods of **market research** undertaken by businesses
- explain how and why primary and secondary market research are used in different business situations
- explain the advantages and disadvantages of methods of market research
- analyse the different types of market research and make justified recommendations as to which method is suitable in a particular situation
- evaluate the purpose of market research
- interpret quantitative and qualitative research.

Introductory case study: the importance of market research

Sarah's Gourmet Dishes.

Sarah Jones thought she had a good idea for a business in selling organic gourmet food online. She thought that high-class food would appeal to many people who wanted to have something special, perhaps at the weekend or for parties.

Sarah had sufficient money to start the business, and despite reservations from her family, she ordered her first stock of food from selected producers.

Sarah did not undertake any market research. She did not really know what competition she had in the gourmet online food market. She only had a general idea about the price she should be charging. There was no clear view on exactly who her customers were likely to be. Deliveries were disorganised.

After a disastrous first six months Sarah had lost much of her savings in the business. Her orders picked up after she began to understand more about the business she was involved in and the customers she was hoping to serve.

Sarah would have benefited from undertaking market research before she started her business.

Market research

Introduction

Before a business starts, it is important that the owners check exactly who their customers are likely to be. Are they old or young, male or female, rich or poor? There is little point in starting a business and then wondering why you are not selling anything! This analysis of the market will normally be part of the business plan (see Unit 1.2) and it is an important part in setting up a successful business. Who a business aims its product or service at is called the **target market**. Understanding your target market is important because it can help a business segment its market; which means aiming different products at different groups of people. Think of watches – there are many different types and styles made by the same maker, all targeting different groups of people.

Activity 1 – Explanation activity

Catherine Fraguela wants to start her own business making cakes. She has no business experience, but has been working part time in a small bakery business for 12 months. She realises that she must look carefully at the way she sets up the business, in particular what she should make and who she should aim her products at. She has come to you for advice and has the following questions. What advice would you give to Catherine? Give reasons for any recommendations you make.

a) Should Catherine research whether or not people will buy her product before she starts making cakes? Research will take time and cost money.

b) Should she make any type of cake, or just certain styles?

c) If Catherine wanted to find out who might buy her products, what should she do?

d) Should she make cakes aimed at everyone, or just concentrate on something specific, like wedding cakes?

What is market research?

Market research is how businesses collect information on whether or not their products or services will be bought.

Why is market research important?

Market research will help a business be clear on whether there is demand for their product or service. Put quite simply: will customers buy the product or not? There is clearly no use making a product or providing a service if no one wants it!

Market research avoids unnecessary investment. If a business is considering investing lots of money into a project, it is in its own interests to make sure that there is demand; otherwise that investment will be wasted.

Methods of market research

Primary research

Market research can be split into two main parts: **primary research** and **secondary research**. Primary research is sometimes called 'field' research and involves collecting information that is new. Secondary research is sometimes referred to as 'desk' research and involves looking at research information that has been collected by another organisation.

Businesses will use one or more of the following methods when they perform primary research:

- **questionnaires**
- **interviews**
- **trials**
- **focus groups.**

Questionnaires

This is a common way of collecting primary information. Questionnaires may be sent to consumers in the post or put in with guarantee forms for products. Online questionnaires are also used to try and get information from consumers. Whenever a business considers using a questionnaire, it is important that the information is returned to the business. In some cases, an entry into a free prize draw is offered to make sure the questionnaire is completed.

Advantages of using questionnaires

- They are cheaper than interviews to collect data.
- They can easily target particular consumers, for example, a questionnaire sent with a guarantee for a product.

Disadvantages of using questionnaires

- It is difficult to predict how many completed questionnaires will be available
- The people filling in the forms may not understand the questions being asked.

Interviews

In an interview, customers are asked questions and the person asking the questions (the interviewer) fills in the answers. Group interviews are sometimes used where a group of customers are asked the same questions at the same time. Interviews can also take place over the telephone.

Advantages of using interviews

- The interviewer can explain questions if there is a misunderstanding.
- Customers can be targeted easily, for example, picking out certain age groups in a street to interview.

Disadvantages of using interviews

- They can be expensive because an interviewer has to be paid.
- Customers may feel uncomfortable being interviewed, whether it is being stopped in the street or on the phone.

Activity 2 – Explanation activity

a) Design a questionnaire on a new type of energy bar Zonetime, an exciting combination of exotic fruits and nuts with a new energy formula. You should aim to have between eight and ten questions.

b) Briefly explain why you included each of your questions.

Trials

For some businesses, the use of trials is important in identifying whether or not there is demand for a product or service.

In a trial, the product or service is sold for a short time as a test to see whether or not consumers like the product. For a large business, which might normally sell products across the UK, a trial may be set up in a much smaller area. A smaller business might simply add a new product to sell for a short period of time without buying in large quantities.

Advantages of trials

- As trials are conducted in a small area, a business may save money by having a trial for a product or service, just in case it finds out that customers don't want what the business has for sale.

Disadvantages of trials

- Trials are still costly to set up. The area chosen must fully reflect the target market of the business. If not then money will be wasted. The business may conduct a trial and only find out what they first thought.

Focus groups

Focus groups are small groups of people (around ten) who are carefully selected to represent the target market for a product or service. They are given information and then asked questions. The answers they give can then be analysed to provide valuable data. For example, an advertising agency might show a focus group different posters that they are considering using to advertise a new product. The feedback from the focus group will then help to choose the most effective poster to use.

Advantages of focus groups

- Because focus groups are chosen to represent the target market for a business, the data from them is usually very accurate and can be relied upon to make important decisions.

Disadvantages of focus groups

- Focus groups, though carefully chosen, are still small groups which makes the collection of data from them more expensive per person than interviews and questionnaires. The selection of people to take part in a focus group is time-consuming and so costly.

Focus groups are a useful way of collecting opinions from a target market.

Activity 3 – Zone activity

Complete the following table by matching the correct starting phrase with one of the phrases below.

Primary research

Primary research is also known as
Trials are used to
Smaller businesses often do not use primary research
Focus groups are usually

Table 2.2 Primary research.

Phrases to add:

- made up of people who represent the target market
- because it can be expensive
- field research
- establish whether there is demand without committing fully to the idea.

Activity 4 – Evaluation activity

When choosing an appropriate method of research to use, there are many factors to be considered. One important decision is whether a business wants precise, up-to-date information about particular consumers. If this is the case, then it is more likely that specially designed primary research will be used because there may not be any suitable secondary research available. If more general data is required, cheaper secondary research may well be suitable.

Recommend which primary method of research is most suited for the following:

a) a new chocolate bar

b) a new computer game

c) collecting information on consumer views on double glazing.

In your answer, you should include details on the following:

- the method of primary research you would use
- why it is suitable for the product
- who should be asked.

Evaluation point

When answering a question on market research, it is vital that you look carefully at the business in the question. Is it likely to need research? Does it have the money to complete expensive research? Remember that some businesses will not complete any market research, with owners relying on their own judgement.

Secondary research

Secondary research, sometimes called desk research, is research that another organisation has already completed.

Sources of secondary research

Census data

For the **census**, every person living in Britain is questioned on how they live, what their income is and so on. The information is extremely useful for businesses, and is collected every ten years. For example, a business planning a nightclub aimed at 18 to 40 year olds could look at how many people at that age are living in a particular area. The census can help schools plan ahead for classroom numbers. The last census was in April 2011. The next one will be in 2021. Data collected by the census can be seen at www.statistics.gov.uk.

Websites

There is a huge amount of information available on the internet. Many companies now put information about themselves and their products on the internet, all of which can be used by other competitor businesses as secondary research.

Internal data

Many businesses have their own secondary data. This is in the form of past sales figures, profits from departments as well as comments from customers. This is usually kept on computers and can be used by a business when it is making decisions for the future.

Newspapers and magazines

Newspapers and magazines are full of information that is useful to businesses. This information might be on other businesses, it might be on trends in fashion and interests that could be used to develop new products and services. As much of this information is now online, searching for it is easier for businesses.

Advantages and disadvantages of secondary research

Advantages

As the research has already been completed by another organisation, secondary research is usually much cheaper to collect than primary research.

A wide range of data is readily available, especially with the growth of the internet.

Disadvantages

The research information might not be exactly what a business wants. Remember that someone else has completed the research, unless it is **internal data**.

The data may not be up to date. There are possible problems for a business that makes decisions based on outdated market research.

The data might not be in a form that the business can analyse easily. Only by designing its own research (primary) can a business be sure that it is in the form it requires.

Activity 5 – Explanation activity

What type of secondary research could be useful in the following situations? Give reasons for your answer and try to be as precise as possible with your choices.

A business wanting to know:

a) how many banks are in the local area

b) how many competitor businesses sell a particular range of products

c) the number of people over 65 years of age living in a particular area

d) the prices charged by competitor businesses.

Activity 6 – Zone activity

Complete the following table, which shows a comparison of primary and secondary research. Use the statements below to help you.

	Primary research	Secondary research
Advantage 1		
Advantage 2		
Disadvantage 1		
Disadvantage 2		

Table 2.3 Comparing primary and secondary research.

Statements:

- It is designed exactly how the business wants.
- A risk that it could be out of date – the census, for example, is only every ten years.
- Research collected may not be exactly in the form the business requires.
- It could be expensive to complete.
- Generally, it is the cheaper option.
- Interview questions can be explained to avoid confusion and incorrect data.
- A wide range of data is readily available.
- It may be difficult getting consumers to co-operate and provide answers to questions.

Activity 7 – Explanation activity

Using the details you have completed in Table 2.3 on primary and secondary research, which advantage and disadvantage is most important to:

a) a new business

b) a well-established business

c) a small business

d) a large business operating in many countries?

Give reasons for your choice.

Qualitative data and quantitative data

Qualitative data

Qualitative data is collected when the opinion of consumers is needed. Because of this it is usually collected using primary research methods, often with interviews or the use of a focus group, though secondary research could be used as well. This data can then be interpreted and used to help make decisions within the business, although it is sometimes difficult to interpret opinions. For example, someone could say they dislike a product, but they may still be willing to buy it for someone else.

Quantitative data

Quantitative data is related to facts and numbers. It may be the number of products sold, or how many people eat cereals for breakfast. Quantitative data could be collected using primary or secondary data. For example, people could be asked how often they eat chocolate (not their opinion on chocolate, as that would be qualitative), or businesses could use research collected by other organisations (secondary). This data is often easier to interpret than qualitative, because it is simply dealing with facts and numbers.

Activity 8 – Explanation activity

Design two short questionnaires of five questions each to collect data on a new cinema that is to open in the local area. One questionnaire should be designed to collect quantitative data; the other one should be for qualitative data.

a) Explain why you asked the questions.

b) Explain any problems you might have in analysing the data you have collected.

c) From your analysis, what changes might be made to improve your original questionnaires?

Key facts

Market research is important to the success of most businesses.

There are many reasons why market research should be undertaken. The most important is to determine whether consumers will buy a product and whether they will buy it at the price the business requires.

The two main types of research are primary (or field) and secondary (or desk).

Internal data, from past sales figures for example, is important for many businesses in helping decision-making.

Primary research is often more useful to a business, because it can be designed for its exact needs and be up to date.

Surveys, in the form of questionnaires and interviews, are the most common form of market research.

Market research, especially primary, can be expensive.

The census is an important source of secondary data.

The internet is of growing importance for the availability of data.

Market research should always be aimed at the target market for the product.

Not all businesses use all types of market research. Smaller businesses may use very little, if any!

Useful words

Market research is the collection of data on customer habits to help decision-making in marketing.

Target market is the group of customers to whom a business aims to sell its products. The target market may be other businesses as well as consumers.

Primary research is data collected first-hand, often in the form of surveys. Sometimes referred to as field research.

Secondary research is the collection of data using research or information provided by others, such as magazines, journals and the internet. Often called desk research.

Questionnaire is a question sheet filled in by the consumer.

Interview is a question sheet filled in by the person conducting the interview.

Trials are used to test whether customers will buy a product.

Focus groups are selected small groups of customers who give their opinion on products.

Census data is data collected by the government every ten years, questioning the entire population on their income, occupation etc.

Internal data is data already within a business based on past performance.

Qualitative data is data based on opinions of those being asked.

Quantitative data is data collected that is based on facts or numbers, usually easier to analyse than qualitative data.

Practice questions

Multiple choice questions

1 Which of the following is an example of primary research?
  - **a)** collecting data from the internet
  - **b)** collecting data by asking consumers questions in the local shopping centre
  - **c)** collecting data published in the local newspapers
  - **d)** collecting data from the last census for a particular age group.

2 Market research is important to a business because:
  - **a)** it helps develop a good working atmosphere in a business
  - **b)** it provides information to help develop products
  - **c)** it shows managers how to motivate their staff
  - **d)** it keeps staff busy.

3 Quantitative research is:
  - **a)** research undertaken asking a wide variety of people
  - **b)** research that concentrates on one part of the population
  - **c)** research that deals only with facts and numbers
  - **d)** research that has been completed by a competitor business.

Data response 8

There is a lot of work to be put into market research.

Jon and Jo are experienced teachers and want to open a child nursery in their local village. They want to make sure that there is sufficient demand for the service and require advice on how to approach the research that they need to carry out.

Their target market is parents who have children from 12 months to 4 years old. They have made a start on their market research, with the following questions:

- How important is good quality childcare?
- How old are your children?
- If you need childcare, how many days of childcare per week are you interested in?

1 Identify which of the above questions will produce qualitative data. (1 mark)

2 Explain two reasons why Jon and Jo should complete market research before they consider opening a childcare business. (4 marks)

3 Jon and Jo need to collect suitable data for their business. The following options are available:
  - **a)** a focus group made up of local parents with young children
  - **b)** a study of the last census from the local area
  - **c)** interviewing grandparents who look after young children.

  Evaluate which one of the options Jon and Jo should use. (9 marks)

How to answer data response 8

1 Remember qualitative data is about opinions; quantitative data is concerned with facts and figures.

2 Think about what might happen if no data was collected and the business was opened on the basis of an idea rather than facts. What might that mean for Jon and Jo?

3 This question requires you to evaluate each method of gathering data. Consider each option – would it provide useful data for Jon and Jo? If so why? What exactly could they learn from a census for example? Remember to explain why you rejected certain options.

UNIT 2.3 Market segmentation

Learning outcomes

By studying this unit, you will be able to:

- explain the meaning of segmentation
- explain how **market segmentation** helps a business target customers
- explain how and why different methods of segmentation are used in different business situations
- analyse and evaluate the methods of segmentation and recommend, with reasons, why a method of segmentation is suitable in a particular situation.

Introductory case study: Adidas

Adidas started in Germany in 1924, when Adi Dassler decided he wanted to make the best possible sportswear for athletes.

By 1949, Adi had 47 employees and launched the famous three striped shoe that would come to define Adidas. Their design of a lightweight football boot, which was used by the German team who won the 1954 World Cup, made Adidas a household name.

When the world-famous German footballer Franz Beckenbauer modelled the first Adidas tracksuit in 1967, there was a sudden expansion in the business, which until that time was only famous for shoes and boots.

Adidas has since further expanded by taking over Reebok sportswear and Taylormade (golfing equipment).

Adidas is a very large business and has a carefully segmented market:

- different sports, e.g. football, athletics and golf
- different needs of consumers, e.g. footwear, clothing
- male and female market
- budget and professional products.

Adapted from adidas-group.com

Adidas has products aimed at many market segments.

Market segments

Segmentation is the splitting of the market for a product or service into different parts, or segments.

Clothing might be split into the male segment, the female segment, the children's segment, teenage fashion and so on. Splitting the market for a product (or service) into different segments helps the business to identify its **target market** more effectively. This is done by targeting the market and involves looking at the different types of customers that might buy the product. For example, Adidas will have trainers that are made for serious runners, and trainers made for simple everyday wear. The trainers for serious runners would be advertised in running magazines whereas the more general trainers would not be advertised in such places. Businesses need to be aware of which segment they are targeting with their products. With good segmentation, the advertising for a product can be much more accurate.

Although each product will have its own market segments, common ways in which customers can be divided are shown below.

Methods by which a market can be segmented

Age

Different age groups will buy different products. This is at times difficult to plan with total accuracy. While the latest technology may be aimed at younger people, it is not to say that some older people will not buy such products. Recent changes in the population structure of the UK have meant there is a growing number of older people who have the wealth, health and time to enjoy themselves. This has resulted in holiday businesses targeting more (and often more expensive) holidays at this age group.

Gender

Men and women will often (but not always) buy different products. As with age, it can be difficult to segment all products clearly. Clothing is more easily segmented along gender lines. But what about cars – are there some cars that are targeted at females and some at males? Many businesses make products for both men and women, for example, Adidas.

Income

People with higher levels of income will want particular products, often simply to show that they have wealth. This could include selected watches, yachts, certain cars, particular designer clothes and so on. Businesses will target these customers because there could be a lot of profit to be made.

Location

Consumers living in different parts of the country will have different tastes and needs. If customers live in an expensive area, their tastes in products may well be at the more luxury level compared to someone living in a poorer part of the country. Another aspect of this is practicality. Those living in a city may want a smaller car that they can park easily; those living in the country may want a car that will cope with off-road driving. However, there are a number of people who may want a larger car even when they live in a city. This again makes it difficult at times to clearly segment a market. The stock in a shop may be chosen to match the expected local population. A clothes shop in the country will stock different styles than those in the centre of the city.

Lifestyle

Different people have different hobbies and interests. This will mean that a range of products is needed to satisfy all tastes. This may also be connected to income and location, because those wanting to sail a yacht may be living in a coastal location and have plenty of money.

Lifestyle can go beyond having a hobby or interest. Many people follow celebrities and wherever possible copy their lifestyle, opting for similar hairstyles and clothing. This creates demand for particular products and services that gives businesses an opportunity for profit.

It is easier to identify a clear market segment for some products than for others.

Example of market segmentation: watches

Watches can be segmented in a number of ways:

- Age – watches can be bright, big and colourful for younger people, but perhaps less so for older people.
- Gender – watches are aimed at both men and women.
- Income – watches can cost thousands of pounds or less than £10.
- Lifestyle – there are special watches for diving, running and other outdoor pursuits. Many watches do much more than tell the time! Some watches are made especially for certain jobs, such as nursing.

Evaluation point

Segmentation can be used in any business situation. All businesses target their market in some way. When evaluating, look for the ways in which the market for a business can be split and how this splitting, or segmentation, will benefit the business. Remember that if a business is clear on its market (due to segmentation) it can target advertising much better.

Activity 1 – Explanation and research activity

a) Divide the following products into as many different segments as you can. Use the information just given on market segments to help you, though not all of the methods of segmenting a market may apply.

- cars
- books
- clothing.

b) Demonstrate your research in a PowerPoint presentation.

Activity 2 – Explanation activity

Explain, using examples, why businesses should use segmentation. In your answer, use a variety of different products to illustrate the fact that for most products there is some segmentation. Some products and services (can you think of any?) are aimed at everyone, no matter what age, gender or the lifestyle or income they have, or where they live.

Key facts

Segmentation is an important part of marketing for many, but not all businesses.

Markets can be split into a number of different segments, or parts.

Understanding segmentation will help a business to market its products much more accurately.

Useful words

Market segmentation is splitting the market for a product into different parts, or segments.

Target market is the group of customers at which a product or service is aimed, or targeted.

Practice questions

Multiple choice questions

1 Segmentation is:

a) splitting the number of products you sell each year

b) splitting the market for a product into different parts

c) splitting the staff in a business so they produce goods quicker

d) splitting the holidays that staff take so that not all staff are away at the same time.

2 Which of the following is not a method of segmentation?

a) age

b) gender

c) income

d) target.

3 Segmentation of a market is done to help with:

a) targeting advertising more accurately

b) increasing the amount of products being made

c) improving the quality of goods being sold

d) making sure that workers are happy at work.

Data response 9

Amala and her family own a business that makes a wide range of garden furniture, from outdoor suites (made to customers' own requirements) that cost thousands of pounds, to chairs that cost £20. Sales have been falling at the business and Amala is concerned that the business does not really understand the market segments that would be interested in their products. She feels that a meeting with the family is needed to resolve the problem.

1 Explain what is meant by 'market segment'. (2 marks)

2 Explain how Amala could segment the outdoor furniture market. (4 marks)

3 Analyse the benefits to Amala and her family business in understanding market segmentation. (6 marks)

How to answer data response 9

1 Here you need to 'explain'. The question is worth two marks, so no great detail is required.

2 In this question, you should apply your knowledge of how a market could be segmented. There are some clues in the information on Amala's business. Remember in this question there is no instruction to explain *why*.

3 The analysis here is about explaining the benefits of segmentation *to the business*. You should link the benefits wherever possible. For example, one benefit might lead directly to something else that will also help the business.

UNIT 2.4 The marketing mix

Learning outcomes

By studying this unit, you will be able to:

- identify the different parts of the marketing mix
- explain how the different parts of the marketing mix work together to help inform business decisions
- explain how different businesses might use the marketing mix to market their products and services
- explain how parts of the marketing mix might not be used by all businesses
- evaluate the importance of the 4 Ps of the marketing mix
- evaluate how the 4 Ps of the marketing mix work together
- identify examples of market data and how to use this data to make recommendations in a marketing context
- evaluate the use of the marketing mix to inform and implement business decisions
- understand how the marketing mix links to the interdependent nature of business.

What is the marketing mix?

The marketing mix is made up of different parts, often referred to as the **4 Ps**. These are:

- price
- product
- place
- promotion

You will need to understand each one of these Ps and how they can work together to help a business successfully sell its products and services.

Introductory case study: the 'big four' supermarkets

The big four supermarkets are always looking at the way they market their products and services.

The big four supermarkets, Asda, Tesco, Sainsbury's and Morrisons, are in fierce competition with each other and also have to watch the activities of Aldi and Lidl, which are growing fast.

Asda has concentrated on 'everyday low prices', Tesco introduced a price match guarantee to make sure that customers pay no more than at other supermarkets on certain products. Sainsbury's has stopped offering 'buy one get one free' in favour of offering lower prices. Morrisons aims to 'provide a range of prices that are simpler, more competitive'.

Price

A business must take great care when deciding what price to charge for a product or service. The business may have many competitors selling similar products, which will influence the pricing. A business may be new to consumers, so price reductions may be offered to entice customers.

The different situations businesses find themselves in will have an important impact on how the price of a product or service is set. For this reason, the method of deciding the price will change over time.

The importance of price in marketing

Most consumers take notice of the price of a product when they buy it. Only a few very rich people can afford to buy products and services without bothering about the price. Because consumers are so concerned about price, businesses must make sure that the price they charge is at a level that consumers are prepared to pay. If a business sets a price too high, it will soon see its mistake when sales fall. A business cannot set a price that is too low because it will not make the profits needed both for investment and to reward those who have invested money in the business in the first place.

Factors that affect the price of products and services

There are many factors that affect the price a business could charge.

- A business may look at the price charged by competitors.
- A new business may have to take into account the fact that consumers are not familiar with their name and may be reluctant to buy products unless the price is really low.
- All businesses must consider their costs when setting a price for a product, as well as the profits they are hoping to make.

Businesses try to solve these problems by using different pricing strategies in different situations.

Activity 1 – Explanation activity

Heather Williams has a market stall at a busy town market, where there are a number of other stallholders selling the same or very similar products. She has not had her stall as long as some of the other market traders and so she cannot rely on old customers coming back each week to buy from her. Heather knows that she must get the price of her products right if she is to have a successful business. She would appreciate your views on the following, and your reasons for any advice given:

a) How important is it to consider the prices charged by other stallholders?

b) What can Heather do with price to try and attract customers who have always gone to other stalls? Setting her prices too low will result in her making a loss.

c) Are customers really bothered whether the price is £1.99 a kilo rather than £2 a kilo?

d) Explain how Heather's approach to setting prices may be different from, and similar to, a much larger business such as Tesco.

Methods of pricing used by businesses

Businesses in different situations will use different pricing methods. The most commonly used methods are:

- **competitor pricing**
- **cost-plus pricing**
- **penetration pricing**
- **skimming**
- **promotional pricing**.

Competitor pricing

This method simply looks at the price being charged by competitors, to give a business an indication of the price it should charge. If someone was hoping to set up a new café, it would be sensible to see what prices any competitors were charging before the business opened. The new business may well charge slightly less than others, but the price will be based on the competition. If there are few, or no competitors in the area, this pricing method will not be as important. If a business is an online operation, then competitors are any other similar online business.

Cost-plus pricing

It is vitally important for a business to look carefully at its costs before deciding on a price to charge. If the costs of a business were greater than the price it charged, it would eventually close. Businesses will look at their cost to make the product and add the profit they wish to make (the 'plus' part). Calculating price in this way makes sure a business makes a profit, providing that it can sell the amount it needs to.

Penetration pricing

When a business is unknown to the public it may have a problem persuading consumers to buy its products. Consumers are often reluctant to try new names, preferring to stay with trusted brand names. To 'penetrate' or break into this new market, a business may reduce its price in order to tempt consumers away from the established companies. Once it has established a name, the 'new' business can put its prices up to the level of the competition. Penetration should therefore only last for a short period of time, if it has been successful. As the price is lower than the business may want, it would be impossible for the price to remain low for long. Penetration pricing will not usually be used by a business that is well-known.

Skimming

When a business introduces a new product that is clearly superior to that of its competitor, especially if it is a technical product, the new product can often be sold at a higher price. This is because many consumers are prepared to pay more to have the latest products. The setting of price in this way is called skimming. The mobile phone market is a good example of skimming. When Apple or Samsung, for example, bring out a new model, it is priced at a higher level because consumers want to be seen with the most up-to-date technology. After a while the product is no longer seen as up to date and the price will fall. Like penetration pricing, skimming would normally be used for a short period of time only.

Promotional pricing

Promotional pricing is a reduction in price used either to attract customers to an existing product or to sell off old products (as in a sale). Sales of a product may be falling and in need of a boost, or stock may need to be sold to make room for the next range of products. In both cases, promotional pricing can help the business. As with skimming and penetration pricing, it is only used for a short period of time, though sales in certain stores often seem to go on for most of the year!

Activity 2 – Zone activity

Complete the following summary table of pricing strategies used by businesses, by using the phrases below.

Pricing method	Definition
Skimming	
Cost-plus	
Competitor	
Penetration	
Promotional	

Table 2.4 Pricing strategies.

- A method of pricing used when there are a lot of other businesses selling the same or similar products.
- Prices are reduced for a short period of time, often to sell off old stock.
- A method of pricing where the business looks at the price it paid for a product and then adds on profit to arrive at the price to be charged.
- Where a business lowers the price of products or services to gain customers from other businesses.
- A method of pricing where the business has a higher price than competitors because it has a better product, for which customers are willing to pay a higher price.

Promotional pricing is an almost constant feature in shopping.

Evaluation point

When you are evaluating different pricing methods to make a recommendation, never lose sight of the product that is being sold. The product may have competitors, which will affect price. The product may only be aimed at a few select wealthy customers, which will again affect the pricing strategy. The product may be new and unknown. This will again have implications on the choice of pricing method.

Key facts

The setting of a suitable price is vital in the marketing of a product.

There are many factors that affect the price of a product or service.

There are many pricing methods that businesses might use.

Different circumstances mean that a business might use several pricing methods.

Activity 3 – Explanation activity

What pricing method would you recommend for the following situations?

Give reasons for your recommendations, which may include a range of different methods:

a) an existing breakfast cereal from a well-known maker

b) Apple introducing its latest iPhone

c) a new brand of hair shampoo; the maker is unknown in the UK

d) a luxury hotel just opening

e) a computer repair business that is well established but with new competitors opening nearby

f) a coach operator introducing a new long-distance service from Birmingham to London.

Activity 4 – Missing words activity

Insert the correct word into the spaces in the paragraph below.

- profit
- penetration
- high
- skimming
- promotional
- better
- lower
- competitors

When a business first introduces a new product, it may use ___ pricing if it wants to gain market share from ___. If the product or service is thought to be much ___ than the competition, a business might use ___ in order to make as much ___ as they can.

After time, when the product becomes older, a business might have to ___ the price in order to keep sales ___ as consumers see the product as being dated. To finally get rid of old stock when the product or model is no longer made, then ___ pricing may be used.

Useful words

4 Ps of the marketing mix are price, product, place and promotion.

Competitor pricing is when a price is set based on prices charged by competitor businesses for a similar product.

Cost-plus pricing is a pricing method that adds a percentage of profit to the total costs of making a product. This gives the selling price.

Penetration pricing is when a price is set lower than the competitor businesses. Often used by new businesses to break into a market. This should only be seen as a short-term strategy.

Skimming is where a new product is more advanced than that of competitors; a price is set high as some customers are willing to pay higher prices to own the newest technology. Sometimes called 'creaming'.

Promotional pricing is where prices are reduced to give products a boost or to sell off old stock. Most commonly seen as sales in shops.

Practice questions

Multiple choice questions

1 Skimming is:

a) charging a lower price when a product becomes old

b) keeping the price of a product the same as competitors

c) making sure your price is always more than competitors

d) setting a higher price when a product has an advantage over its competitors.

2 Penetration pricing would normally be used when:

a) a business has been in operation some time and has few competitors

b) a product is being introduced that is thought to be at the cutting edge of technology

c) a business is new and needs to establish its place in the market

d) there is high demand for a product.

3 If a business wishes to dispose of old stock to make way for new products it would normally consider:

a) competitor pricing

b) promotional pricing

c) cost-plus pricing

d) skimming.

Data response 10

Dixons Carphone started as two separate stores. Dixons opened in 1937, selling electrical goods, and Carphone Warehouse started in 1989, selling mobile phones. Dixons merged with Currys and PC World, and then merged with Carphone Warehouse in 2014 to form Dixons Carphone.

In all this time, there was great competition on price with competitors. The growth of online sales at competitor businesses has put further pressure on price, with customers often looking at goods in store and then buying online.

What Dixons Carphone must do to survive is to make sure that their pricing strategy attracts the numbers of customers that the business requires.

1 Explain why a business such as Dixons Carphone should be so concerned about the price of the products it sells. (4 marks)

2 Recommend a pricing method for Dixons Carphone to use to make sure it maintains its sales. Give reasons for your recommendations. (9 marks)

3 Discuss other steps that Dixons Carphone could take to make sure that sales are kept at a high level without reducing profitability. (9 marks)

How to answer data response 10

1 Here you must consider whether or not Dixons Carphone has any competitors – without competitors there is much less need to worry about price. Is everyone selling the same goods? If so there is more to worry about on price. If a business sells a unique product, price is less of a concern.

2 This question asks you to recommend a method, which can be a number of different pricing methods used at different times. Remember what is being sold, the level of competition, the size of the business (smaller businesses are often less flexible on what they might do with price). Also remember to give reasons for your answer.

3 This question broadens the scope of marketing a little beyond pricing – the parts of the marketing mix are closely linked. Here you should consider the difference between selling in shops and the internet – can the business make more of the service it gives? Can it make on-the-spot decisions to make sure a customer buys? What offers could be put in place?

Product

Introductory case study: Dyson vacuum cleaners

In 1978, James Dyson was unhappy about vacuum cleaner performance. Cleaners in 1978 used bags to collect dust. The bags clogged causing vacuum cleaners to not work as well as they should have done. James had an idea to design a new bagless vacuum cleaner that used cyclone technology. It was not easy. It took James five years and 5,127 attempts before he successfully developed his first bagless cleaner.

Dyson vacuum cleaners are now sold in 65 countries, and over 1,000 engineers are working to design the next products, as the business knows that it cannot stand still. Continuous improvement in design and **innovation** is vital if its products are to remain at the cutting edge of cleaner technology.

Introduction

Product is another vital part of the marketing mix. Businesses that make products to sell must make sure that they are making products that customers actually want to buy. Businesses that sell products (rather than making them) have to think carefully about the number of different products they sell. A large business such as Tesco will sell thousands of different products; a corner shop will sell far fewer. Whatever the number, the same question is asked: will customers buy the product or service? If they will, then fine, if not, then stop selling!

The style of a product may need updating. Some products are changed once a year or more. Others will last much longer with little change to their style or design. This – the life of a product – is another consideration for a business. Just how long can a business continue to try and sell a product or service before it has to be replaced?

The importance of product in marketing

Businesses will always try to supply products that customers will want to buy, at a price at which the business can make the profit it requires. This will often come as a result of analysing market research, where customer needs are identified (see Unit 2.2). A business can then make the product with more confidence that it will be a success.

Even with this 'preparation', there are still some considerations that a business will have to make when marketing the product.

Activity 5 – Explanation activity

Matt Williams owns a small business that sells fashion clothing aimed at 14–18 year olds. He is becoming concerned that the products he sells do not have a long life before they either go out of fashion or the weather changes and he has the wrong stock. Matt is keen to avoid having old stock that he cannot sell, but also wants to sell other products and services that will help increase the profit he makes. Another consideration for Matt is whether he should sell products with a well-known brand name. At present, he sells products from makers who are not so well-known, as these are cheaper.

Write a report to Matt on how he should develop the products in his business, giving reasons for any recommendations you make. You should consider the following in your work:

a) how the life of the products he has may be extended

b) other products and services that Matt may offer

c) whether or not Matt should only sell products from well-known makers.

Image and design

How a customer feels about owning a product may be used in marketing. It is more common in relation to exclusive products such as expensive sports cars and perfume, where customers like to be seen to own certain goods. At times, it is difficult to say whether a product has been sold because it is a great **design** or whether it has a particular image that the customer wants to be associated with.

If an image is damaged in any way, it may take some time to restore customer belief in the product. In 2015, Volkswagen (VW) diesel cars were found to have a device that illegally gave lower pollution readings when put under tests. Prior to this, VW cars had a very strong positive image among the car buying public. This had helped VW to become the second largest car maker in the world. However, its negative image now could affect sales for some time to come.

Invention, design and innovation

Where an entirely new product is invented, in theory, that product has an advantage over its competitors. In reality, there are few totally new products invented. Most are improvements or developments of existing ideas. It is here that innovation takes place, with businesses trying to develop an advantage over their competitors in order to increase the demand for their products and services.

Technology has a large part to play in this process, either in the making of a product or in how that product is used. Internet banking is now seen as being quite normal. A few years ago, it was unknown and when first introduced it was thought of as an innovation. Banking was not new but the way people conducted their banking was very different. Now the challenge for banks is to think of new innovative ways to make internet banking easier and safer for those who use it. Banks that can develop in this way will have an advantage over others. The internet itself was the **invention**; it is now being used in an increasing number of innovative ways to sell products and services that will only increase in the future.

Many businesses spend large sums of money on researching and developing their products. Part of the research is investigating the needs of customers, though **research and development (R&D)** can also include testing whether an idea will work or not. In developing his bagless cleaner, James Dyson built many different versions of his vacuum cleaner before those we know today were ready to be sold. In the medical industry, new drugs are developed and tested over many years before they are allowed to be used on the general public. For a business to stay ahead of the competition, or even just to keep up with it, there may be large financial investment in research and development which in turn can lead to innovation.

Design also plays a large part in the success of a product. It may be clothing that follows particular fashions, or design in mobile phones. In the case of mobile phones, when they were first developed the race was to make them as small as possible (the very first ones were the size of a brick!). Now the designers are coming up with bigger screens to cope with the need to display web pages more clearly.

Phone design is always changing.

Branding

Branding is closely linked to design and image. Many companies do not need to put their name on a product – we know the make simply by a symbol, sometimes referred to as the **trade mark**. We understand from that symbol that this 'brand' has a certain quality. It may be high quality or it could be lower quality 'budget' standard, but we know where we stand with it. This even works well with fast food. We know the brand name (KFC, McDonald's etc.) and so have a clear idea of the standard of product we are buying. If it was an unknown make with a brand name we did not recognise, we might not buy the product.

Activity 6 – Artwork activity

a) Using books, magazines, newspapers and the internet, make a collection of brand names and trade mark logos that different businesses use. In your collection, try to include a number of different types of businesses, such as clothing, electrical, toiletries, food and so on.

b) Make a collage of your collection. What proportion of the logos does not include the name of the business?

c) Make up a quiz to try on other members of your business studies group to see if they can identify a business just from its trade mark logo.

Activity 7 – Explanation activity

When marketing the products A to D listed below, which of the following considerations is most important to you and to other people in your group?

a) price

b) design

c) image

d) brand

Products:

A toiletries

B a mobile phone

C a waste-paper bin

D a laptop computer

Give reasons for the choices you make. For some products, you may want to recommend more than one consideration.

Activity 8 – Explanation activity

Explain how much the following products are marketed as inventions, just good design, or an innovation on what has gone before:

a) the latest Samsung television

b) the latest electrical battery car

c) the latest L'Oréal foundation make-up.

Invention, design and innovation are important to product development.

Activity 9 – Research activity

Research any product that you feel is:

a) a new invention

b) a really good innovation on what has been developed before

c) simply a great new design.

Explain how the features of the product will help in its marketing.

The product life cycle

Most products have a time span over which consumers will want them. This is called the **product life cycle**. Customers' tastes change and products have to change to reflect that. Sometimes products come back into fashion after a time when they would not sell; clothes are a good example where different styles come and go. The life cycle of a mobile phone is short – technology and design change quickly and a 'new and improved' product is ready to sell. Other products have a longer life cycle; many food products such as Kellogg's Corn Flakes have changed little over the years.

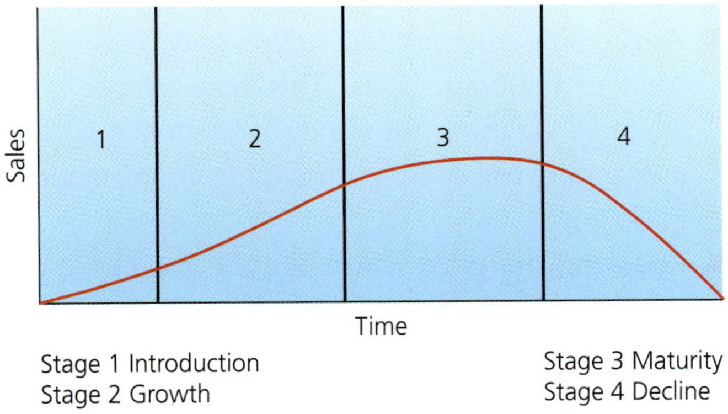

Figure 2.1 The life cycle of a product.

How the product life cycle is used in marketing

As you can see, the graph (Figure 2.1) is split into four sections which are used to demonstrate stages, and different marketing techniques need to be applied to each stage of the product in order to make it successful.

Introduction is when the product is launched or first put on sale. Before this, a business may well have conducted some market research and invested money in developing the product. When the product is launched, a business may advertise it in a number of ways, in order to make sure that it gets off to a successful start. Remember, at this stage the product is unknown and customers need to be told about it. Sales should rise steadily.

Growth is the second stage, where the sales show their most rapid growth. Advertising and other promotion support change slightly as the product will be generally known to customers. There is no need for special offers because the product is new and in high demand.

Maturity is the next stage, where sales are towards their highest, but most importantly the rate of growth is slowing down. It may be necessary to support a product with further advertising and offers at this time, to maintain sales against the competition.

Decline is the final stage in the life cycle. Here, sales are falling and though the product may be given some support in the form of further special promotional offers, customers see the product as old and switch to those of competitors or a newer replacement. It is at this stage that a successful business will have already developed a new product to replace the one that is in decline.

Activity 10 – Explanation activity

At what stage of the product life cycle are the following?

a) desktop computers

b) denim jeans

c) Kellogg's Corn Flakes

d) iPhone 7

Give reasons for your answers.

Activity 11 – Explanation activity

Draw a product life cycle to show the life of the following products. Note that some may have a very short life cycle, some a very long one. This should be shown clearly by how you label the axis on your graphs. You must consider how long they last before they are replaced and no longer sold. Give reasons for drawing your graphs in this way, and label the graphs fully.

Products:

a) a Dairy Milk chocolate bar

b) a chart single

c) a particular model of television

d) a home shirt for a Premier League football club.

Activity 12 – Missing words activity

Use the words given below to complete the paragraph about the product life cycle.

- decline
- four
- time
- introduction
- replacement
- high
- maturity
- growth
- life
- slowing

The product life cycle is divided into ___ parts and shows the ___ of a product measured against ___ The first stage is called ___ and is where the product is new. Advertising is often ___ at this stage to make sure that customers are aware of the product. The next stage is ___ where the product is becoming well-known. When the product reaches ___ sales are at their highest, though sales growth is ___ The final stage is ___ where the sales are falling and a business might be thinking of introducing a ___ product.

Extending the product life cycle

As can be seen from the graph of the product life cycle (Figure 2.1), the highest level of sales is at the end of growth and into the maturity section. Businesses try to keep the sales of a product at this high level for as long as they can, as it will increase sales and profit.

A number of methods are used to try to extend the life cycle and keep the sales as high as possible for as long as possible. These include the following:

- Advertising the product more widely is often used to maintain sales. This may simply be a business claiming the product or service is new and improved, or by putting it in more modern packaging.
- Reducing the price will make the product more attractive to consumers, and so help to maintain sales.
- Other markets may be developed. For example, if a business was at maturity level in Britain with a product, it might export to countries where the product was only at the introduction stage, with plenty of future sales opportunities. In other cases, a business might simply try to sell its product to a different target market than the one first used.

Evaluation point

It is very difficult for a business to judge the right time to replace a product. For some businesses, such as car manufacturing, the cost of designing and making a new model is very high, so will only be done every five or six years. In this case, there is a strong argument for trying to extend the life of an existing model. Where there are rapid changes in technology, such as computers and phones, new models must be brought out in order to keep up with competitors, so the life cycle of any model is much shorter. In these businesses, there is much less effort put into extending the life of the older version. Other businesses, for example, food businesses, can see the life cycle run for many years. Here it is simply a case of maintaining customer interest in the product, (often through advertising) especially where there is a lot of competition.

Activity 13 – Research activity

a) Research the history of Rice Krispies. Include in your work:

- when it was first introduced
- the stage of the product life cycle you think Rice Krispies is now in
- changes that have been made over the years to the product (if any) and the way it is packaged
- how the product has developed – what related products are now available and what 'new' uses can be made of the original product.

b) Explain how important Kellogg's, as a brand name, has been to the development and success of Rice Krispies.

Activity 14 – Presentation activity

Choose one of the following products, or a product of your own choice, and consider how the product life cycle for the product can be extended. Remember that the time a product's life can be extended does vary, before it is replaced by the next model or different product. Give a short presentation to the rest of the group.

a) a mobile phone

b) a bike

c) a spray-on deodorant.

Key facts

Many businesses invest large sums of money in research and development in order to keep their products ahead of the competition.

Having a varied product mix is helpful to a business when the sales of one or more products start to fall.

Design is very important in a number of products.

For technology products in particular, innovation is vital if a business is to keep ahead of competitors.

Branding is becoming increasingly important in the marketing of a product.

The different stages of the product life cycle require different marketing techniques.

The length of the product life cycle is not the same for every product.

Extending the product life cycle is important if a business is faced with large investment needed to develop a new product.

Product is one part of the marketing mix. A business cannot simply concentrate on developing a product and ignore the other parts of the mix.

Useful words

Innovation is the improvement on an original idea, which will often involve using new processes. It is closely linked to design, where new ideas can be used in a product due to changes in the design.

Design is an important element in a number of different products, especially where style and technology work together.

Invention is the introduction of a totally new product or feature.

Research and development (R&D) is used to help introduce both new and existing products. The research may be testing products in a laboratory or conducting market research by interviewing customers.

Product life cycle is the life of a product, usually shown as a graph divided up into four stages: introduction, growth, maturity and decline.

Introduction is when a product or service is first on sale.

Growth is when sales are growing strongly as the new product or service becomes known.

Maturity is when sales are at their highest level.

Decline is when sales are falling as the product or service is seen by customers as being old and they switch to newer products and services.

Practice questions

Multiple choice questions

1 The second stage in the product life cycle is:
  - **a)** maturity
  - **b)** introduction
  - **c)** decline
  - **d)** growth.

2 Product innovation is concerned with:
  - **a)** changing the colour of a product
  - **b)** developing new features in a product that have not been seen before
  - **c)** selling the product at a lower price than competitors
  - **d)** making sure a competitor does not copy your product.

3 Which of the following would not be used to extend the product life cycle of a product?
  - **a)** bring out a new product
  - **b)** increase the advertising
  - **c)** decrease the price
  - **d)** offer additional features free of charge.

Data response 11

British Telecom (BT) is a business that provides phone services through landlines. In August 2013, it widened its range of products by launching BT Sport, in direct competition with Sky. BT Sport now has English Premier League matches, as well as football from the French and German Leagues, and the Champions League. It also covers premiership rugby union matches in England.

Early in 2016, BT bought EE, the mobile phone service provider. BT has now moved to football 'on the go' by offering EE customers streamed live matches. After an initial free six-month period, there would be a monthly fee payable. Football 'on the go' as a product is seen as a money-making proposition for BT, especially with the growth of the 4G network and more reliable streaming of live action.

Sky is not to be left out of this development. It is looking at launching a mobile phone service using O2.

1 Explain why BT might have chosen to introduce BT Sport. (3 marks)

2 Analyse why BT might have wanted to buy EE to develop its products. (4 marks)

3 Evaluate whether or not the idea of football on a mobile phone could be a good product development for BT. (9 marks)

How to answer data response 11

1 Here you need to think about why it might be good for a business to have a range of products. Think about only having one product – what if the public no longer want that product?

2 This question asks you to 'analyse', so you need to look at the benefits it can give the business. Think about reaching a large number of new customers.

3 This is an evaluation question, so you must reach a judgement on whether the idea is good or not. Always give reasons for your answer in an evaluation question. This is all about the cost of setting up the business (or is it set up already?). Is it a product that customers want? Will competitors such as Sky take business from BT?

Place

Introductory case study: Morrisons and online food delivery

Morrisons.

After starting with a market stall in Bradford in 1899, Morrisons grew to be one of the 'big four' supermarkets in the UK.

It was, however, rather late into online food ordering and only started this aspect of its business in January 2014. Its rival Tesco had started in 2000. In an increasingly competitive market, Morrisons may have lost a number of customers with such a late start to online ordering. Businesses can no longer rely simply on the distribution systems that they have been using for many years. They must adapt quickly to changes that are made possible by new technology, and make sure that they meet the changing needs of their customers.

Morrisons has now teamed up with Amazon to develop online ordering.

Introductory case study: Sony and the changing nature of distribution

Sony is a world-wide organisation which sells the music of many artists from all types of musical backgrounds.

One of Sony's artists is Elvis Presley. When Elvis was recording his music from the 1950s to the 1970s the way his fans bought music was very different from today. Back then, the product, a record, was a physical thing you could touch. You bought it in a record shop. Later CDs came in to replace records (records are now coming back into fashion) but it was still a physical product, bought from a shop.

In 2017, it is all very different. The music of Elvis can still be bought, but will more likely be downloaded. This digital method of distributing music has replaced much of the music bought throughout the world, though some older people may still prefer to go into a shop and buy a CD!

Introduction

Place is concerned with the distribution of goods and services, that is, how those goods and services reach the customer. There are two main methods – the more traditional **physical distribution** and the growing **digital distribution**. Consider a book. Not that many years ago, it was sold in a physical form in a bookshop. Now most books are available digitally. The same is true with music – CDs are no longer needed by many as music can be downloaded. The way a business distributes its products or services is called the distribution channel.

Activity 15 – Research activity

Complete a survey in your business group to find out who has products delivered digitally and who has products delivered physically. Products to investigate could include music, books and computer and console games.

Make a chart of your findings.

Which distribution channel to use: physical or digital?

The importance of place in marketing

There is an old saying in business that to be successful you must have 'the right product in the right place at the right time'. The place in this saying has two parts in business activity:

1. The place where a product is sold.
2. How the business gets the product to the consumer. This is called the distribution channel.

Where products and services are sold

The place where businesses sell products is changing. It used to be the case that businesses selling to the public (remember that businesses also sell to other businesses) would sell through a shop, which would be located in the high street in towns and cities or on street corners. Much of this has now changed to out-of-town shopping, with high streets seeing shop closures now that many customers prefer to visit shopping malls with free parking. It is important that businesses respond to the needs of customers as they must offer their products and services for sale where customers want to buy.

The distribution channel

The method of distribution used by businesses has changed significantly in recent years, especially with the growth of technology that enables digital distribution. Businesses must adapt if they want to keep up with these changes in technology. If customers prefer to download books and music, then businesses selling books and music must offer that service.

In physical distribution it is important that businesses choose the right method (see below) for their goods. Should they use their own distribution network, or rely on others? It is important to get this aspect of marketing right. If customers find that there are no goods for sale in a shop (wherever it might be) then the business will lose those customers.

Yes, the business must get the right product, in the right *place* at the right time.

Physical and digital distribution

Physical distribution

This is the most common type of distribution, although its importance has declined somewhat as digital distribution grows.

Physical distribution is the movement of goods that we can see. It includes:

- household products that are made in a factory, sent to a retailer (shop) and are then bought by a customer
- food that is grown by a farmer, again sent to a shop to be sold to customers
- products that may be mined from the ground and then sent to be made into steel, for example.

In these cases, movement of goods will usually be by road. Air transport is sometimes used for goods of high value or goods that might perish easily and have to be transported long distances quickly.

Physical distribution channels

Physical distribution method 1

Producer

↕

Customer

In this example, the producer is distributing a product directly to the customer. As the business will have to deal with each person who buys from it, this method is only possible with a small business. Imagine Cadbury trying to supply all of the different shops that sold its chocolate! The type of business where this method will be found is, for example, a small craft centre, which will sell its products direct to its customers. Small bakeries will often do the same.

A business selling its products to another business will often use this method of distribution. This is because the number of customers will once again be small and can be managed easily. As soon as the number of different customers becomes too large, a business must consider another method of distribution.

Physical distribution method 2

Producer
↕
Retailer
↕
Customer

In this method of distribution, the producer sells to a retailer (a shop), who then sells to the customer. This method is common in electrical goods, with producers such as Sony and Panasonic selling to shops such as Currys, and customers then buying from these shops. Once again, it would be difficult for Sony to sell its products directly to each person who wanted a television. It is easier for Sony to sell a number of products to a retailer who then sells the products to the customer.

Physical distribution method 3

Producer
↕
Wholesaler/Regional distribution centre
↕
Retailer
↕
Customer

In this method of distribution, the producer sells to a **wholesaler** or sends goods to a **regional distribution centre (RDC)**.

A wholesaler is a large storage centre able to take in deliveries direct from producers.

The role of a wholesaler is to 'break the bulk' of goods sent by the producer. This means buying in large quantities from a manufacturer and then selling smaller amounts to a retailer. This is especially important in the distribution of food, where small shops are often not able to store large quantities and so need to buy their stock in amounts they can cope with. Take the example of soup. Large producers such as Heinz will be unable to deal directly with every shop that sells its products. It will distribute cans of soup in large quantities to the wholesaler, who will have a large warehouse to store the goods. Small retailers will then go to the wholesaler to buy, say, a tray of 24 tins of soup to sell in their shops.

Although the main role of the wholesaler is to break the bulk of goods between the producer and retailer, it does provide these other services:

- Credit can be given to the retailer, which enables the retailer to have the goods before paying for them. This 'trade credit' means that a retailer can sell the goods, which provides the money to pay the wholesaler.
- The wholesaler may be able to deliver products to the retailer. This may be very helpful when the products are bulky and heavy, or if the products are frozen and require special transport.

It should be remembered that the wholesaler provides a useful service to the producer, who would otherwise be unable to supply goods direct to the many customers it might have.

The role of the regional distribution centre is slightly different. The RDC is owned by the retailer and is used to store the products it will later sell in its shops. Marks & Spencer and Next are just two examples of large businesses who use this system, where producers send goods to the RDC, which then sends the products to the shops as they are needed.

A number of large businesses have their own regional distribution centres.

Digital distribution

With the increased importance of the internet, many goods and services are now distributed digitally. This process involves no physical product being moved. The goods or services are downloaded digitally, though they may not need to be purchased digitally. This is separate from e-commerce (see Unit 4.3) where there may still be some physical movement of goods when they are delivered.

Examples of businesses that provide digital distribution:

- music
- books
- insurance
- banking
- newspapers.

Advantages of digital distribution

- Customers can access products and services 24 hours a day.
- Goods are downloaded, so are available quickly.
- Cost saving to a business, as there is no physical product to deliver.
- Some products, such as console games, can be purchased as a code in a shop and downloaded digitally at home, meaning that the customer does not need to share their credit card details online.

Disadvantages of digital distribution

- Not all goods are suitable for digital distribution.
- Businesses may be forced into digital distribution simply to match the service offered by a competitor.
- Not all customers have access to the internet.
- Digital distribution has made it easier to illegally copy content and distribute it for free. This means that businesses lose sales and have less income to invest in other areas of the business or in creating new products.

The future of distribution

It is likely that digital distribution will increase at the expense of physical distribution, as the population as a whole becomes used to downloading goods and services.

The growing importance of the mobile phone in particular cannot be ignored by businesses. Banks, for example, are now seeing that more people use their online services from a phone than from a desktop or laptop computer. Businesses must make sure that their app technology keeps up with developments or they will lose customers to competitors.

Evaluation point

When recommending a method of distribution, remember that if there are a lot of buyers for a physical product, a business that makes the product is unlikely to be able to supply directly to those customers. A retailer or a wholesaler is much more likely to be used.

In choosing a distribution channel, you must keep up to date with recent developments to see how businesses are reacting to changes in technology.

Activity 16 – Missing words activity

Use the words given below to complete the paragraph about physical distribution:

- regional
- product
- small
- consumer
- retailer
- wholesaler
- the bulk
- direct.

Physical distribution is all about getting the ___ to the ___ Some businesses sell ___ to the consumer. These businesses are usually ___ Other businesses may sell to a ___ such as Currys who then sells to the customer. Larger businesses may sell to a ___ whose job it is to break ___ and sell smaller amounts to a retailer. Businesses such as Tesco and Marks & Spencer have their own ___ distribution centres where much of their stock is stored.

Activity 17 – Explanation activity

Which method of distribution, physical or digital, would you use for the following businesses? Give reasons for your choice.

a) a business making watches
b) a small bakery
c) a farmer selling strawberries
d) a business selling travel insurance.

Activity 18 – Research activity

a) For any 20 different products you have at home (for example, books, electrical/phones, food, clothing etc.) find out how they were bought. Was it:

- from a shop
- direct from the maker
- from a catalogue
- downloaded from the internet?

b) Display your results in a graph with suitable illustrations. Explain why products are bought from different places.

Activity 19 – Zone activity

Put the following advantages and disadvantages of a business using digital distribution into the correct column in the table below.

Advantages of digital distribution	Disadvantages of digital distribution

Table 2.5 The advantages and disadvantages of using digital distribution.

- A business can sell throughout the world and so has more potential customers.
- A business may be able to improve its image with skilful use of websites.
- All businesses can sell throughout the world so there is more competition.
- A business can promote products much easier to more potential customers using digital distribution. This will help increase sales.
- There may be a need to recruit or retrain workers with the introduction of digital distribution, which can add to business costs.
- Less staff may be required, which will cut costs.
- A business is able to sell to new markets. This will help increase profits.
- Digital content can easily be copied and illegally shared for free online.
- There are costs with the building and maintenance of the website.
- A business can be open at all hours throughout the year.

Useful words

Physical distribution is the distribution of goods using a physical presence such as a shop or office.

Digital distribution is the distribution of goods and services digitally by downloading from a website.

Key facts

Place includes both where a product is sold and the method of distribution used to get the product to the customer.

Distribution can be divided into physical and digital.

Some products are not suited to both physical and digital distribution.

More recently digital distribution is becoming much more important for certain products.

Smaller businesses usually have a simpler method of distribution; larger businesses tend to have a more complex system.

Although the main role of the wholesaler is to break bulk, they do offer other services.

There are advantages for both businesses and customers when using digital distribution.

Digital distribution is changing the way in which many businesses operate. This is linked to work on location, training and recruitment.

Because digital distribution is changing so rapidly, businesses must keep up to date with new developments.

Practice questions

Multiple choice questions

1 Digital distribution is suited to:

a) selling goods and services from a shop

b) selling goods and services through a large warehouse

c) selling and delivering goods in a digital format

d) selling goods and services at airports.

2 A distribution channel is:

a) A method of improving the quality of goods and services

b) A method of getting goods and services to customers

c) A method of seeing how products can be advertised on television

d) A method of testing whether customers will buy a product.

3 Which of the following products would be suited to both physical and digital distribution?

a) Potatoes

b) Newspapers

c) Watches

d) Clothes.

Data response 12

Netflix is the world's leading internet television network with over 83 million members in over 190 countries enjoying more than 125 million hours of TV shows and movies per day, including original series, documentaries and feature films. Members can watch as much as they want, anytime, anywhere, on nearly any internet-connected screen. Members can play, pause and resume watching, all without commercials or commitments.

From www.netflix.com

1 Using the information above, explain how Netflix can be described as a user of digital distribution. (2 marks)

2 Explain two benefits to a business such as Netflix of using digital distribution for its products and services. (4 marks)

3 Evaluate how the growth of digital distribution has affected business activity. (9 marks)

How to answer data response 12

1 Here you need to make sure you use information from the paragraph you are given on Netflix.

2 Remember, for this type of question, to make sure you refer to businesses such as Netflix. You can use any businesses (including Netflix) but they must be operating in a similar way with similar products and services.

3 In this question, you should look at the advantages and disadvantages of digital distribution and then analyse how this will affect businesses. The evaluation element requires you to make a judgement – has there been a significant effect on all businesses? Note that Netflix is not in this question so you must look at a range of businesses, though Netflix could be included.

Promotion

Introductory case study: the mobile phone promotion war

Choosing a mobile phone service provider is never easy. Once the phone has been chosen, there is a vast choice of options that the service providers offer their prospective customers. This is big business. Should a customer go for contract, pay as you go or sim only? Then there are the offers on texts, data and minutes to consider. Is there an upfront cost to the phone, is there 4G coverage?

The combinations are endless. There could then be 'special' offers added into the mix to further complicate the choice, including vouchers to spend in shops and online, reductions in upfront costs and discounts on other items such as tablets.

Promotions on all of the above are changing all the time, with each company trying to make sure that it is in the lead in attracting, and keeping customers. A customer persuaded to pay £30 a month over a two-year contract will pay at least £720 to the service provider. Promotions are a vital part of the marketing mix.

Introduction

When a business has a good product, or is offering a good price for a service, or perhaps is moving to a new place, it needs to inform its customers. This part of promotion – advertising – is therefore very much connected with the other 'Ps' in the marketing mix. Promotion in marketing also includes all the various offers such as 'buy one get one free' that we have become used to seeing.

Businesses spend a lot of money on promotion each year. Care must be taken to make sure that the money is used to good effect.

Activity 20 – Explanation activity

a) Research and read information about mobile phone companies.

b) Why do the mobile phone companies put so much into promotion?

c) Which of the mobile phone companies has the most effective promotions at present (you may have to complete some research on this)?

The importance of promotion in marketing

Promotion is concerned with how a business informs its customers about a product or service and then persuades them to buy. A business must inform customers that it has a product to sell, and make customers feel that they need to buy the product. To do this, businesses will use a variety of methods, which need to be chosen carefully to have the greatest effect on customers. Without promotion, a business may have an excellent product that fails because customers were not persuaded to buy it.

Note that it must be remembered that many businesses do not promote themselves very much at all. Small, well-established, locally-based businesses might simply rely on word of mouth and their local reputation to keep their customers. There is little justification for these businesses to spend money on promotion. (See Introductory case study in Unit 1.5.)

Aims of promotion

Promotion has the following aims:

- to inform customers about a product or service (especially when new or changed)
- to keep a business ahead of its competitors
- to create or change the image of a business, its products and services
- to maintain or increase sales.

These aims will vary from business to business, though they all try to keep sales at a level that is satisfactory for the business concerned. As a business develops, the emphasis of promotion will change. When a business starts, effort is put into promoting the business as well as the products it may be selling. As the name of the business becomes established, there is less need to promote the name, and promotion is concentrated more on the product or service.

It must be remembered that even the best-known companies and their products still need promotion. Well-known products such as Cadbury Dairy Milk still requires promotion to keep it in the minds of potential buyers.

Methods of promotion

Promotion is divided into two main areas:

- **point of sale promotion**
- advertising.

Point of sale promotion

There are a number of parts to sales promotion. Remember that not all businesses will use all of the parts below. Some businesses will not use any!

Price reductions

These are often seen in shops in January and July in order to sell off all the old stock that a shop no longer wants to keep. This will boost sales at a time when the products (such as Christmas cards) would not normally sell. Price reductions may also be used to sell off the stock of an old model, in order to make space for the newer model. In this example, customers who know that an old model is about to be replaced will not want to own the old model unless, of course, there is a large price reduction!

Loss leaders

Loss leaders are another form of price reduction, often used by supermarkets. Here a business will lower the price of one or two items to such a point that there is little or no profit. The idea is that a customer will be attracted to the supermarket by the price reductions, but while they are there they will also buy a number of other items (at normal prices) so the supermarket makes the profit it needs.

Competitions

Competitions can be used to boost sales, where customers are entered into a monthly prize draw, offering a variety of prizes. With higher-priced products – for example, cars – the value of the prize is often very high, such as a continental holiday, or even the money you paid for the car being returned.

Free samples

These are often used in cosmetics and other businesses to let the customer try the product. Customers may be reluctant to buy the full size of a product they do not know, as they may not like it. By providing a small sample, which may be posted through a letter box, or included in a magazine, customers can try the sample and then potentially buy the full size.

> **Activity 21** – Explanation activity
>
> For each of the following situations, explain what sales promotion method(s) you would use. Give reasons for your choice(s).
>
> **a)** A well-known watch maker is introducing a new fashion model. It also has a lot of old model watches still unsold.
>
> **b)** Sniff Cosmetics wants to promote its deodorant range, which has not sold as many as expected.
>
> **c)** A soft drinks maker wants to increase the amount of cola it sells.
>
> **d)** McWilliams Cars feels that its new model is not selling as well as expected and it needs ideas on sales promotion.
>
> **e)** A famous cereal manufacturer has seen sales fall slightly. It feels that a new promotion is needed to push sales back up.

Obviously, this can only be used for certain products. A business such as Apple is unlikely to give away a free sample of one of its phones.

Free samples might also be given away at the point of sale. Supermarkets are again a good example here, where small samples of food are offered to the consumer in the hope that they will buy the product. This is especially important when a new product is being launched.

Activity 22 – True or false activity

Are the following statements on promotion true or false? Put a tick in the correct column.

Statement	True	False
A loss leader is meant to make a loss to keep the business in the lead.		
Competitions are only used by supermarkets to promote the food they sell.		
Price reductions are often seen in shops in January.		
Free samples are often seen in products such as cosmetics.		
Supermarkets use loss leaders to encourage shoppers to visit their stores.		
Promotion is mainly concerned with making sure that old stock is sold at the best possible price.		
Not all businesses use promotion to help them sell products and services.		

Table 2.6 True or false for promotions.

Advertising

Advertising is one of the most important parts of promotion. We all see and hear advertisements for a huge range of products. On television, they often seem to be more entertaining than the programmes!

The type of advertising to be used needs to be carefully chosen, as do the advertising media – that is, where the product is to be advertised. You would not normally expect to see the latest designer kitchens and cheap denim jeans being advertised in the same place.

For some products, an **advertising campaign** is launched, which involves a series of advertisements in different forms over a period of time. In this way, a producer can build up customer knowledge of a product that will increase sales or get a new product off to a successful start.

Advertising media

A business must carefully choose where it advertises its products and services. The different places a business can advertise are known as **advertising media**.

In making that choice, businesses will consider the following:

- the cost of advertising: a small business may not have much money to spend. Some small businesses may simply not advertise at all
- the target market for the product: a business selling teenage fashions will advertise where teenagers will see those adverts
- whether the advertisement is part of a campaign, or a single advert.

Advertising media used by a business

A business has a choice of the following advertising media:

- social media
- websites
- printed media
- television
- radio.

Social media

Social media have seen a huge growth in importance over the last ten years for business advertising. They are cheap to operate and because of this, they are popular with businesses. Larger businesses will encourage customers to sign up and follow its activities and promotions on Facebook or Twitter among others. This has the advantage of targeting customers more easily, because those following a business have an interest in it and will be more likely to take notice of advertisements for new products. The vast numbers of people who regularly use social media make them an ideal way of reaching a wide audience with any advertising and messages.

Not all people, however, use social media. If a product is targeted at the elderly, then social media may not be a good choice as they are less likely to use Facebook or Twitter compared to a younger generation.

Social media sites such as Facebook have become more important to business advertising.

Websites

Most businesses will have their own website, which is sometimes a vital part of advertising their products and services. It can include the use of full video, with links to sites such as YouTube to further impress the potential buyer. With the use of search engines such as Google, the website of a business is the main point of contact for many consumers.

While setting up and maintaining a complex website can be expensive, smaller, more simple versions are available to suit local businesses.

Once again, consideration must be given to the target market. Will potential customers make use of the internet? If the answer is no, then other advertising media should be considered.

Printed media

These include:

- newspapers
- magazines
- leaflets.

Newspapers (both national and local) are still an important way for businesses to advertise. Local newspapers are ideal for low-cost advertising that only reaches the target market in the local area. It is of little use to a corner shop to advertise in a national newspaper because most of the readers will not know the business and it would cost too much. National newspapers such as the *Daily Mail* and *Daily Mirror* are more suited to big business advertising that is of interest to people throughout the country. It will cost much more than local newspaper advertising, but is worth it for a large business if it results in increased sales.

Magazines are an ideal way for a business to target its market. There are many different magazines in the UK that are aimed at particular interest groups. A business wanting to advertise caravan accessories can make sure it reaches caravan enthusiasts by advertising in one of the specialist caravan magazines.

Magazines are usually published on a monthly basis. This may not be enough for some advertisers who want to constantly put their products in front of the buyer.

Leaflets are used in a number of ways to advertise a business. Local fast-food outlets may simply post leaflets through the doors of potential customers in their area to promote a new menu or delivery service. Holiday attractions often publish leaflets to advertise themselves, making the leaflets available at tourist information centres where their target market is likely to see them.

Leaflets are cheap to produce and can be cost effective in that they can be targeted at the correct market.

Television

Television advertising is important for large businesses that need their advertisements to reach a wide audience throughout the country. Groups of customers can be targeted by choosing the correct programme in which to advertise. If there was a history series on Rome for example, then that could be an ideal place to advertise a holiday tour that takes in places of historical interest.

Costs will be very high (sometimes reaching into thousands of pounds) for television advertising, so only large businesses consider this as an option. It does, however, reach millions of people.

Radio

Radio is much cheaper than television for advertising. It is usually local and is therefore suitable for smaller businesses who sell their products and services to a smaller area. Radio is much more portable and so advertising can get through to customers anywhere, anytime.

One problem is that the product cannot be seen, which may be important if a business wants to show off a stylish new model.

Activity 23 – Explanation activity

Which advertising media would you recommend in the following situations? Give reasons for any choices you make, bearing in mind that more than one media may be appropriate.

a) a new flavour of yoghurt from a well-known maker

b) a famous perfume brand launching a new fragrance

c) a special offer from a well-known washing-machine maker

d) a new high specification satellite-navigation system

e) a local café just opening.

Activity 24 – Poster activity

Using magazines, newspapers, the internet or any other source of information, collect at least ten advertisements that are advertising different types of products. Make a collage poster of your results, labelling underneath each advertisement where it came from.

Evaluation point

When evaluating different methods of promotion and advertising, it is vital to consider the product, the size of the business and the market at which the product is targeted.

Where products or services have a lot of competitors, then there is likely to be more advertising and promotion.

When looking at the target market, think about what type of media the target market will see before recommending where to place an advertisement.

The size of the business has a large impact on promotion. How much advertising and promotion does your local shop do compared to, say, Sainsbury's? For many smaller businesses, advertising may be restricted to small adverts in a local newspaper, or they may decide not to advertise at all simply because of the cost.

Key facts

Promotion is a vital part of the marketing mix.

Methods of promotion are varied and must be chosen carefully to fit a given business in a given situation.

There are a range of places and methods for a business to advertise its products and services.

Businesses must be inventive in trying to think of different ways to promote their products.

Advertising can be expensive and must lead to increased sales that pay for the advertising that has been used.

The internet is a fast-growing method of advertising, but is not suitable for all products. Social media is a vital part of internet-based advertising and promotion.

The size of the market and money available are important considerations when choosing a method of promotion.

Many smaller businesses may choose not to advertise at all because of the expense involved.

Useful words

Point of sale promotions include price reductions, loss leaders, competitions and free samples.

Advertising campaign is a series of advertisements, often using different advertising media.

Advertising media are the methods by which a business can advertise a product. Includes newspapers, TV and radio.

Practice questions

Multiple choice questions

1 Loss leaders are:
   a) leaders who always lose their way
   b) losses that a business makes when it sells leading products
   c) the losses a business makes every time it has a sale
   d) items that are sold at a low price to attract customers into a store.

2 Social media include:
   a) all advertising media
   b) Twitter and Facebook
   c) point-of-sale promotions
   d) all special offers a business might make.

3 A local chip shop wanting to advertise its new menu would most likely use:
   a) a leaflet drop through letter boxes
   b) nationwide television advertising
   c) radio advertising at peak times
   d) magazine advertising.

Data response 13

Go Compare and Compare the Market are two internet-based companies offering links to insurance and finance products that consumers can then buy. The use of these 'comparison sites' has increased dramatically in recent years. Both businesses have expanded since starting in 2006 and now offer a range of products such as insurance for bikes, homes and travel of which consumers can compare prices and service. The businesses are also linked to credit card and mortgage providers as well as mobile phone, broadband and other services.

Both businesses promote themselves widely on television. Compare the Market introduced 'the Meerkat' toy to further promote the business in 2011, offering a range of collectable toys to customers buying products linked to their comparison website. Go Compare featured a fictional Italian singer in their advertising, with celebrities also being used in their television advertising campaign.

1 Explain two reasons why television advertising is a suitable medium for businesses such as Go Compare and Compare the Market to promote their services (4 marks)

2 Analyse the advantages to internet-based comparison sites of offering to compare a wide range of services. (6 marks)

3 Explain one reason why businesses might offer goods such as toys to promote their business. (2 marks)

4 Discuss how a new price comparison website might promote itself in order to complete with Go Compare and Compare the Market. (7 marks)

How to answer data response 13

1 This question asks you to give two reasons why businesses such as Go Compare should use television advertising. Think here about the size of the business, what it can afford, and the numbers of possible customers that it is likely to reach.

2 This question asks you to analyse the advantages of offering a wide range of service comparisons. Think about the cost to the business of setting up a website – once this is done it is less work to add different products. There is no separate website for each type of insurance. Think too about the customer – while they are comparing, say house insurance, perhaps they have a holiday coming up and want to take out travel insurance?

3 Advertising alone is often not enough to sell a service. The Meerkat was a very popular way of making people remember the company name – vital in marketing. If children want a toy, perhaps they might persuade parents to look at the website.

4 In this question, you must make recommendations and give reasons for those recommendations. Consider the comparison site market; there are lots of well-established names. How can you make sure that a new name becomes well-known and trusted (important in insurance and financial products)? It may require a wide range of ideas from promotion and advertising. Remember to give reasons for each idea you put forward.

How the 4 Ps of the marketing mix work together

The **4 Ps of the marketing mix** need to work together.

Obviously, a business must have a product (or service) that customers want to buy and it must be distributed or sold in a place and in a way that customers are happy with. In addition to this, the price of the product must be acceptable to the customer. If customers are to be attracted to the product, for example, through advertising, the business must undertake some promotion.

If a business wanted to increase sales, the marketing mix might work together in the following way:

- **Price** – the price must be at a level to attract an increased number of customers.
- **Product** – does the product justify the price? If it is an older model, then the price might be lowered in order to increase sales. If a new model, the price could even be higher and still see sales increase, for example, new computer games consoles.
- **Place** – sales could be increased by selling through different channels of distribution. Is the product suitable for digital distribution? If so, could the price be lower because there is no physical product to make or deliver?
- **Promotion** – all of the above may be fine, but the customer needs to know about the product or service, otherwise there will be no increase in sales. If there is a lot of competition, a business may need to be inventive with promotions to further attract enough customers to increase sales. Should there be an introductory price reduction? Should there be free delivery if physical distribution is being used?

The marketing mix and new businesses

It is clear from the above that all parts of the marketing mix work together. While all parts of the mix are important, in certain circumstances, one part may be more important than the others. For example, when a product is first introduced, more advertising is required so that potential customers are aware that the product is available. When a mobile phone is more than a year old, it is important that a new product is ready for release; but a lower price on the old model will help keep sales high. If a business such as a new café is being opened in an area with lots of competition, then the prices to be charged will be important, otherwise customers will go elsewhere. The café could, however, offer a superior product to attract customers, or offer delivery to local businesses to help sales.

For a new business, there is a greater need for advertising and promotion – customers need to be educated as to where and how they can buy the product, which itself is unknown. The price will need to be carefully set; otherwise possible customers will not use the new business.

The marketing mix and established businesses

It is important to recognise that established businesses will often take a different view of the marketing mix. When a business is well established, customers will be familiar with the product, accept the price being charged, understand how and where they will buy the product or service, and have less need for advertising because customers are well aware of the product on offer. This does not mean that they will not use the marketing mix. When there is a lot of competition, it is still important for the biggest, most established business to keep their customers informed of new products, lower prices and so on.

The marketing mix and market research

The marketing mix is closely linked to market research. From good market research, a business will have a clear idea of whether the product is something a customer wants to buy. Research will also identify the price that customers are willing to pay, the places where they buy similar products and the types of promotion that interest them.

How the marketing mix is used to inform and implement business decisions

The marketing mix can help business decision-making.

The marketing mix can help business in its decision-making. It is linked closely to market research because data from research will help to make decisions as to how the marketing mix should be used.

- **Price** – what price consumers will pay for a product or service is vital for a business as it sets its prices. If the product is different or more advanced than competitors, pricing could be set higher (skimming). If there is competition then competitor or penetration pricing may be considered. Businesses must be alert to changing circumstances and adjust prices if necessary. How supermarkets compete on price is a good example of how price considerations affect decision-making.
- **Place** – as the method of distribution for many goods changes, then businesses must be prepared to change the way they get their products and services to consumers. The late decision by Morrisons to enter the online delivery market is an example of how the successful actions of others (Tesco and Asda in particular) forced Morrisons to make a decision to provide online services. Businesses must take into consideration the growth of digital distribution and e-commerce (see Unit 4.3) – is it suitable?
- **Product** – a product or service that consumers want to buy is another key element of a successful business. Businesses such as car manufacturers must make decisions as to when to introduce a new model. Looking at the product life cycle would help the decision-making process because it must be timed carefully to come out as sales of the old model decline. Products must be developed to take account of changing tastes and technology. There are few products that have remained the same for many years. Competitor action will often drive that change – successful businesses cannot afford to be left behind.
- **Promotion** – most customers are influenced in some way by promotion; whether it is that special offer that cannot be refused or an advertisement that simply makes you buy a product. Decision-making will be based around the potential for a promotional activity to work by increasing the demand for a product or service. **Market data** will help here in the decision-making process. Have past promotions worked? Does a price promotion really increase sales enough to compensate for the lower price a customer is to be charged?

Remember that all parts of the marketing mix, and other considerations such as market research, work together to influence the decision-making process within a business. As discussed earlier, there is no point in making a decision to introduce a new product if there is no promotion to tell people about it. A car maker may spend many thousands of pounds on informing customers with television advertisements. A local pizza takeaway may have a few hundred leaflets delivered to inform local people of a change in menu. Both will hope that the money spent on advertising will be justified.

Playball centres need to consider all parts of the marketing mix.

Activity 25 – Explanation activity

Beth plans to open a playball centre targeting children from 2 to 12 years old. She would like advice on how she might use the marketing mix to make sure her business is a success.

She is interested in your advice in the following areas:

a) Where should she advertise the business? Or should they simply not advertise at all and rely on local word of mouth?

b) What range of activities and facilities does she need to provide for children and the waiting parents?

c) What offers could she make to tempt parents to bring their children?

d) How should she decide on the price to charge for each session?

e) Would they be able to sell their services in any other way, such as parties?

Write a short report for Beth on how you think the business should be marketed, making sure you cover all the points above. Always give reasons for any recommendations you make. Complete the work on a computer if possible to help with presentation.

Activity 26 – Research activity

a) Ask your parents if they can remember any products that were a failure, or perhaps did not last very long at all.

What was the reason for the failure? Was the price wrong? Was it because no one wanted the product? Use the marketing mix to help your answer.

Can you think of any such failures yourself?

Write up your report on a computer if possible. Title it 'Business failures and the marketing mix'.

b) Now title a new piece of work 'Business successes'. Think of a range of different products that always seem to have been with us (some food products will make a good start). What has made these products last so long? Explain how the marketing mix helps show us why these products have been with us for such a long time.

Evaluation point

When evaluating the most important part of the marketing mix, there are many considerations. An important one is simply producing a product at that time that customers actually want to buy. Some products come and go; others are still going strong after many years. KitKat, first sold in 1937, is something that has always been popular with customers with no real change to the product, apart from the addition of different flavours.

What is market data?

Market data is information that will help a business make marketing decisions.

What data might be included?

- **Changes in demand** – here a business will look at any data that shows how a product is selling. If there is an increase in demand then there is no real problem for marketing (it may cause issues in production!). If there is a fall in sales, is it because the price is too high compared with competitors? Is the product simply old and customers have switched to competitors? Does the product need a boost with some special offers that will increase sales? Or have customers switched to buying the product in a different way, perhaps online? Whatever the reason, a business must react if demand for a product or service begins to fall.
- **Target market** – this is who the business is selling its products and services to. However, the target market can change. Older people are now using smartphones much more than in the past – an example of how technology in general is being used by more elderly people. A new business must be clear on its target market otherwise it will have difficulties with sales.
- **Market share** – this is a business' share of the total market for a product or service. For example, if the total market for washing machines in the UK is 100,000 sales per year, and a business sells 20,000, the business has a 20 per cent share of the market. The problem here is that a business can actually sell more of its products (good news) but have a falling share of the market (bad news).
- **Product change** – when a business introduces a new product (or service) the data on how that product is performing (or not) is vital for a business. Should the product be changed in any way? If the product is selling well, does a business need to change, or should it start planning a change?
- **Effect of promotion** – if a business is spending large amounts of money on promotions and advertising, it is important that the business has data on whether the promotion is having some effect. If there is no increase in sales after thousands of pounds have been spent on promotion, then there needs to be a rethink on just what is causing the promotion to be ineffective.

Activity 26 – Calculation activity

Look at the table below for the sales of fridges by LXFridges and the total fridge market.

	Sales of fridges by LXFridges	Total fridge market
2014	120,000	500,000
2015	132,000	600,000
2016	145,200	720,000

Table 2.7 Fridge market.

a) Explain whether or not the owners of LXFridges will be happy with the sales figures in the table above. Give reasons for your answer.

b) Explain the possible causes of any change in LXFridges' market share.

c) What action should LXFridges take for the years after 2016?

Activity 27 – Calculation activity

Study the following data collected by a maker of chocolate, where 5,000 people were asked what type of chocolate bar they preferred over a three-year period.

	Fruit and nut	Hazelnut	Plain milk chocolate
2014	1,500	1,500	2,000
2015	1,600	1,300	2,100
2016	1,650	1,300	2,050

Table 2.8 Chocolate types.

Explain how the above data might influence the future production of chocolate bars.

Evaluation point

When looking at any data where you are asked to make a decision, remember that there is always an option to do nothing; that is, do not recommend any change. In this case, as in any others, you must give full reasons why you take that particular view. Market data can influence business decisions beyond marketing. If demand falls for a product, it may be the case that the business might have to close factories or make workers redundant.

Key facts

Although the marketing mix is usually based on the 4 Ps, other considerations, such as packaging, could also be influential.

The different parts of the marketing mix should not be seen in isolation. They work together to form a marketing plan or strategy.

There is a close link between the data from the marketing mix and other market data when decisions are being made in a business.

While all parts of the marketing mix are important, in certain situations, one part may be more important than the others.

Useful words

4 Ps of the marketing mix are price, product, place and promotion.

Market data is information that can help marketing decisions. It includes data on such things as market share, changes in demand and the effect of promotions.

Target market is the group of customers who the business tries to sell its product to. It can be based on such areas as gender, age and lifestyle and will influence methods of advertising and promotions.

Market share is the percentage of total sales of a product that a business has made. If a business sells 20,000 products and the total market for that product is 50,000, then the business has a market share of 40 per cent.

Practice questions

Multiple choice questions

1 Market data includes:
- **a)** changes in school curriculum
- **b)** changes in demand
- **c)** changes in number of workers
- **d)** changes in workers' pay.

2 Which of the following will not normally be helped by the use of market data?
- **a)** decisions on whether to increase production
- **b)** decisions on what questions to ask a candidate at interview
- **c)** decisions on whether to build a new factory
- **d)** decisions on whether to start television advertising.

3 Market share is:

a) the product share of the marketing mix

b) the amount of goods a business sells in a 12-month period

c) the amount of goods a business sells as a percentage of the total market for a product

d) the goods that a business sells as a percentage of the previous year's sales.

Data response 14

Halfords cycle/car parts store and Halfords Autocentre.

Halfords is a well-known business selling a range of cycles, car parts and leisure goods, as well as offering car servicing through its autocentres.

Poor weather can reduce cycle sales, though it is hoped the use of celebrity endorsement in advertisements will improve sales. A number of cyclists who have won Olympic gold medals have been used to help develop new bikes for sale in the shops.

Popular products in the shops are changing. Satellite-navigation sales are down because many cars have them fitted when built, but dashboard cameras are becoming popular.

Halfords has a number of shops and autocentres to sell its products and services, but online sales are rising. Price competition is fierce from other car service centres and online cycle stores.

1 Explain how the use of celebrities might help increase the sale of cycles at Halfords. (4 marks)

2 Explain why products sold by a business such as Halfords are continually changing. (4 marks)

3 Recommend a suitable marketing mix for Halfords that is designed to increase sales. Give reasons for your recommendations. (9 marks)

How to answer data response 14

1 Think of the effect of celebrities and how they can influence consumers. If a well-known personality is seen with a product, others will often buy that same product. What will the effect of someone from the very top (Olympic gold medallist) have on the sales at Halfords?

2 Consider here how technology changes. Halfords sells a lot of technology-related products.

3 In this question, cover all parts of the marketing mix. Make sure that your ideas are applicable to Halfords, not any business. Better answers will look at how the different parts of the marketing mix will work together. Remember that online sales are rising and that Halfords still has many stores selling direct to the public. How will this development affect the marketing mix you recommend?

3 People

UNIT 3.1 The role of human resources

Learning outcomes

By studying this unit, you will be able to:

- explain the meaning of the term **human resources**
- evaluate the **purpose of human resources** in business
- explain how a business **identifies its human resource needs**
- perform calculations of the type that are used in the analysis of the human resource needs of a business
- evaluate the benefits and costs to businesses of completing an analysis of their human resource needs.

The purpose of human resources

Read the following two case studies. They show two businesses that have thought about their human resources.

Introductory case study: Virgin listening

Virgin.

'This multi-industry organisation has a habit of listening to its employees, to show that they are valued, to listen to their opinions and take care of their ideas, to have healthy debates and continuously innovate. It's a win-win: the organisation keeps learning and employees feel important and engage with the organisation. Listening is at the heart of engagement. In our experience, everyone wants to be seen and heard – it's a minimum requirement of leadership, yet often overlooked for the immense value it can bring. On top of it simply being the right thing to do. Employee engagement is the fuel of the organisation. And even if an organisation is good at it, we can all get better at it – and maximise that fuel.'

From managers.org.uk

Introductory case study: human resource needs at Noah's Arf dog and cat kennel

Noah's Arf is based in Portland, Oregon, USA. The extract from its business plan starts with an outline of the company.

'Noah's Arf is a full-service animal care facility dedicated to consistently providing high customer satisfaction by rendering excellent service, quality pet care, and furnishing a fun, clean, enjoyable atmosphere at an acceptable price. We will maintain a friendly creative work environment that respects diversity, ideas and hard work.'

The website from which the plan was taken gives the plan in full. A key extract for this unit is the **human resource plan**. It details the human resource needs for Noah's Arf in its first three years.

Human resource plan

The human resource plan will be as follows:

- One manager to oversee and fill in for all areas.
- Two front desk receptionists to greet customers, receive payments for services/products, set appointments, answer phones, check-in pets and maintain files of clients with data entry.
- Four playground supervisors will feed and water pets, keep area clean, walk and exercise, collect pets at check-out time. Two will be on staff full-time and two will work part-time.

Contract employees:

- One pet groomer.
- One behavioural trainer.

In the first year, assumptions are that there will be only one receptionist, four playground supervisors, and the manager will serve as part-time receptionist and night staff until the business can build. The groomer and trainer will work on contract. In the second year, a second receptionist, two playground supervisors and a groomer will be added to the payroll.

From bplans.co.uk

Human resource plan			
	Year 1	**Year 2**	**Year 3**
Production staff			
Playground supervisor	£14,720	£15,840	£16,320
Playground supervisor	£11,200	£11,880	£12,240
Playground supervisor part-time	£5,520	£5,952	£6,144
Playground supervisor part-time	£2,760	£2,976	£3,072
Playground supervisor	£0	£15,840	£16,320
Playground supervisor	£0	£11,880	£12,240
Groomer	£0	£23,040	£24,000
Pet taxi/in-home care/dog walker	£0	£15,360	£15,840
Subtotal	£34,200	£102,768	£106,176
Sales and marketing staff			
Other	£0	£0	£0
Other	£0	£0	£0
Subtotal	£0	£0	£0
General and administrative staff			
Manager	£36,000	£36,000	£36,000
Reception 1	£16,560	£17,760	£18,240
Reception 2	£0	£6,912	£7,104
Subtotal	£52,560	£60,672	£61,344
Other staff			
Other	£0	£0	£0
Other	£0	£0	£0
Subtotal	£0	£0	£0
Total people	6	11	11
Total payroll	£86,760	£163,440	£167,520

Table 3.1 Human resource plan from bplans.co.uk. (Note: This is an American firm. Figures have been converted from US dollars to pounds for the UK version of the website.)

Human resources are the people who do the work for a business. They include the owner(s) of the business if they work in the business, people who are employed by the business and contractors who carry out jobs for it.

The two case studies on pages 88–89 give examples of what is involved in the management of human resources. The Virgin case study shows the importance of engagement for motivating workers and for getting ideas from them so that the business will continue to improve. The Noah's Arf case study illustrates how businesses think about the purpose of human resources and what staff to employ.

The purpose of human resources is to carry out the **functions** of a businesses. Production workers make the product or provide the service. Finance workers send out bills and collect in payments. Marketing workers encourage buyers for goods or services that the business provides. This involves making the decisions about what to sell, where to sell it, how to promote it and what price to charge. Human resources workers are essential to the success of any business, even those that are very high-tech.

There is more about the motivation of workers in Unit 3.5. Other considerations about human resources covered in later units are organisation charts (Unit 3.2), communications (Unit 3.3), recruitment and selection (Unit 3.4), retention (Unit 3.5) role training (Unit 3.6) and employment laws (Unit 3.7). This unit deals with the purpose of human resources and how businesses may identify their needs.

Identifying and meeting the human resource needs

Businesses plan their human resources. They work out the purposes that can be met by human resources and what workers they will need to make sure that this work is done. Noah's Arf planned its human resources for the first three years. Well-run businesses will think about their human resource needs regularly so that they can try and predict any changes that might affect the business. If good predictions are made, the business will be better able to recruit the workers it needs so that it is efficient and competitive. It is likely that Noah's Arf would have reviewed its need for workers before the three years was up.

Some of the changes that a business may need to consider when looking at their human resource needs include:

- Workers may have to be replaced, for example, because they might retire, leave for jobs in other businesses or because they may be promoted in their current business.
- The business may grow or shrink, which means it may need more or fewer workers. This may be caused by changes in the level of economic growth that affects demand, or by changes in the competitor landscape and so on.
- The business may change its method of production, for example, from job to batch or by introducing new technology. It may need more or fewer skilled workers. It may need workers with different skills to those of the current workers.
- The business may decide to relocate. It may have to recruit workers who live near the new location but also may decide it wants to take some of its current workforce to the new location.
- The budget available for paying for workers may change. The budget may be reduced if other costs of production increase or it may increase if the business can raise product prices.
- Changes in the law may affect employment – how much workers need to be paid and the **regulations** controlling the employment of workers.

You should note that some of the changes referred to above are examples of 'the interdependent nature of business.' Decision-making in business involves thinking about the links between different areas of business activities. For more on the interdependent nature of business, read Unit 7.

The list below shows some of the things that businesses will have to think about when planning their human resource needs:

- the number of workers it needs
- the number of workers who will work full-time or part-time
- the number who should be employed on **zero-hours contracts**

- the number of workers to hire as contractors as and when needed
- when the workers will be needed – the times of the day, the days of the week
- where the workers will work
- the skills that the workers will need to have
- the need to manage and supervise some of the workers
- the age, gender or ethnicity of the workers it will need (bearing in mind the laws that affect the employment of workers)
- how many staff members the business can afford to employ.

Evaluation point

Businesses must spend time and therefore money identifying their human resource needs. This is a worthwhile activity because if they have identified their needs accurately, it will help them to recruit the workers that will do the work that should be done. With appropriate workers in place, and at the time that they are needed, the business will be able to operate efficiently. It is more likely to be competitive and so be able to survive and make good profits. It is time and money well spent.

Activity 1 – Missing words activity

Complete the paragraph below using the words provided.

- many
- skilled
- full
- regularly
- start
- changing
- growing

Businesses must identify their human needs when they ___ up. The purpose of identifying human resource needs is to decide ___ . They need what kind of staff and how ___ workers to employ. Other decisions will be whether to employ ___ workers or unskilled, whether the workers will be ___ time or part time. Well-run businesses plan ahead. They will look at their staffing needs ___ to see if they are changing, for example, because the business is ___ or ___ the way it produces its goods or services.

Activity 2 – Matching activity

Match the change given in the table below with its effect on business.

Change		Effect on the business
1 A kitchen fitting business increases its sales as a result of the growth of incomes and employment in the economy.		(a) Some workers may lose their jobs but the business may want some workers to work in the new factory.
2 A car manufacturer introduces high-tech robotic equipment.		(b) It will have to ask the workers to work different hours.
3 Next plc has to pay its shop assistants more as the government raises the national living wage.		(c) More of the same kind of workers will be needed.
4 A bicycle manufacturer decides to switch production to a factory abroad.		(d) The business may look to reduce the number of workers it employs.
5 A family activity centre decides to close on a Wednesday and open at the weekends instead.		(e) Skilled workers will be needed to program the equipment.

Table 3.2 Changes in a business and its effect on its human resource needs.

Activity 3 – Identifying the human resource needs of a business

Read the information below and then come up with a plan of the workers that you will employ.

You have decided to start up a take-away pizza shop. You are thinking about the following:

- Customers can collect pizzas from the shop or have them delivered to their homes or places of work.
- Your shop will open from 11 a.m. until 3 p.m. and then again from 5 p.m. to 11 p.m., from Monday to Saturday and close all day Sunday.
- You think you will sell 250 pizzas per day on average in the first three months.
- From research, you have discovered that pizza chefs who work only on cooking pizzas will cook 25 pizzas per hour working with ingredients that have already been prepared.
- The ingredients used in a day can be prepared in four hours.
- Completed pizzas will need to be put in boxes to take away and to be ready to be delivered.
- The same person may be able to take calls and serve customers, taking payment from them. It is expected that this person will be able to box 25 pizza meals per hour in addition to their other responsibilities.
- Someone will also be needed to take orders over the telephone, order stock, manage the other workers and keep the accounts of the business.
- You have estimated that delivery drivers will be able to make five deliveries per hour in the evenings when your customers will mainly want the pizzas brought to their homes.
- You are hoping to sell to ten customers every hour in the evening.
- At lunchtime, you expect to make ten deliveries per hour also, because the deliveries will be mainly to offices and shops nearby.
- You will not make lunchtime deliveries on Saturdays. You expect that you will do 50 per cent more deliveries on a Saturday night than on other nights in the week.

a) Come up with some ideas about:
- What different types of workers will the business need?
- How many of each type of worker will it need to employ?
- What hours will each worker have to work?

b) Once you have completed the activity, write down how useful you think it would be for a business to identify its human resource needs before starting up.

Key facts

Businesses must think about the human resources they will need.

The human resource needs of a business will depend on the purposes that those resources must fulfil.

It is good practice for businesses to think about their human resource needs regularly.

Identifying human resource needs will help the business to have the correct workers in place as and when they are needed.

Useful words

Human resources are the workers employed by a business.

The purpose of human resources is the work that must be done by human resources. It is usually broken down into a number of different jobs.

Identifying human resource needs is the activity of thinking about the purposes of human resources, and how many and what types of workers will be needed.

Human resources plan is a plan detailing workers a business needs – how many, whether they will be full- or part-time, the skills they should have and when they will work.

Useful words

Functions are different types of work that need to be done in business including production, finance and marketing.

Regulations are rules imposed on businesses by the government.

Zero-hours contracts are contracts given to employees which do not guarantee any work. The business will call workers if and when they are needed to ask them to come in to work.

Practice questions

Multiple choice questions

1 Which of these statements is false?

a) An analysis of human resource needs will help a business to decide how many workers it requires.

b) An analysis of human resource needs will help a business to decide if it needs to recruit workers with different skills.

c) An analysis of human resource needs will help a business to decide if it is producing the right product for its customers.

d) An analysis of human resource needs should be done when the business starts up and regularly after that.

2 A business has an order to make 7,200 T-shirts. It has three weeks to get the order ready. The business operates five days each week and for eight hours each day. A worker can sew 20 T-shirts in an hour on average. The number of workers the business needs to employ to make the T-shirts to meet this order is:

a) 3 b) 4 c) 300 d) 8.

3 Which of the following statements are false?

a) Human resources are the people who work for a business.

b) Human resources are the people the business sells its goods to.

c) Human resources can help to make a business succeed.

d) Human resource needs may change as technology changes.

Data response 15

E.Leclerc is a supermarket chain in France. It has introduced electronic price tags. These are small, electronic screens that are fixed to the shelves in the shops below the goods on display. The prices of the goods are displayed on the screen. Decisions about what prices to charge are taken at the supermarket chain's head office. If a decision is made to change a price, a worker at head office can send a communication to each of the electronic price tags in every E.Leclerc shop in France. Previously, prices were displayed on paper tags that were inserted into small, plastic wallets fixed to the shelf near the item on the shelf.

1 Businesses like E.Leclerc must think about identifying their human resource needs. Explain what this means. (2 marks)

2 Analyse how the human resource needs of the E.Leclerc supermarket chain might change as a result of the introduction of electronic price tags in its shops. (4 marks)

3 Evaluate the benefits and costs to businesses like the E.Leclerc supermarket chain of doing an analysis of human resource needs on a regular basis. (7 marks)

How to answer data response 15

1 This questions needs a straightforward explanation of what an analysis of human resource needs is.

2 Think how the work of displaying prices changes, whether E.Leclerc will need more or less workers and if there will be any change in the types of worker it needs to employ.

3 The benefits will include having the right staff in order for the business to function properly and to save costs by not employing staff who are not needed. The cost is in terms of paying for staff to spend time reviewing the business' human resource needs. Overall, the cost is worthwhile as it should make the business competitive and help it to be profitable.

UNIT 3.2 Organisational structures and different ways of working

Learning outcomes

By studying this unit, you will be able to:

- explain an **organisation structure** and use the terminology related to it
- explain the benefits of organisation structure for businesses
- explain the different organisational structures, for example, tall and flat organisations
- evaluate why businesses have different organisational structures
- evaluate the suitability of tall and flat organisation structure for different kinds of businesses
- explain the different ways of working and the changes that have taken place to these in the UK
- evaluate the impact of changes in the ways in which people work on businesses and on workers.

Organisation structure

An organisation structure is how people and departments are organised within a business. An **organisation chart** is a way of displaying the organisation structure. They show how responsibilities in an organisation are divided up among different departments and people. An example of an organisation chart is shown in Figure 3.1.

Understanding the Griffin Engineering Ltd organisation chart

Griffin Engineering Ltd makes components for cars. The departments in the business are organised by function, which means that each department has a specific job to do. For example, the purchasing

Introductory case study: Griffin Engineering Ltd

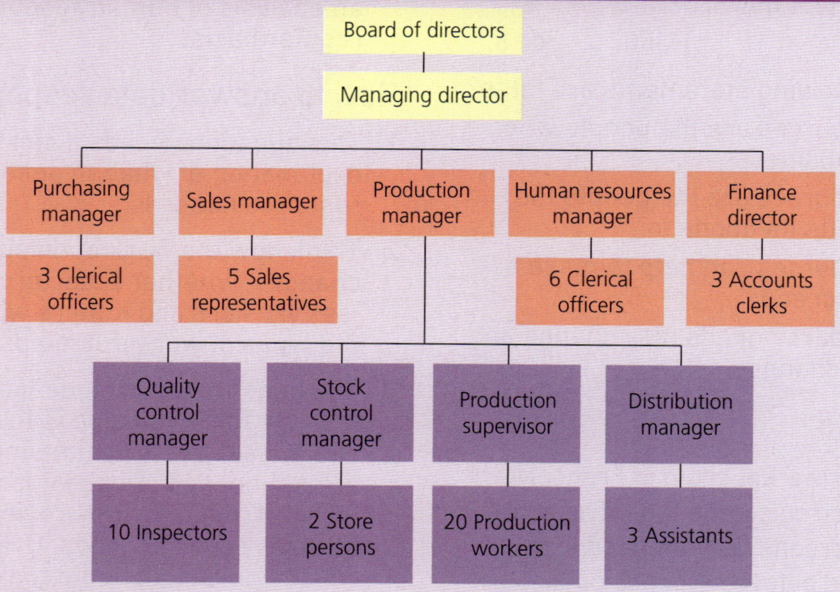

Figure 3.1 Griffin Engineering Ltd – organisation chart.

department will be responsible for buying in the materials that are needed to make the components, the sales department will be responsible for finding customers to buy the components and human resources will carry out the jobs connected with recruitment, training and relations with the workforce. The information technology and research departments have responsibility for helping all the other departments when they need it. For example, the IT manager will give advice to departments about the kind of hardware and software they should use.

The organisation of Griffin Engineering Ltd is a hierarchy with several **layers**. Employees on the higher layers have more responsibility and **authority** than those on the layers below. Authority is the power to make decisions and the right to tell other workers what they have to do.

There is a **chain of command** with those at the top of the hierarchy being able to send instructions to those lower down. The managing director of Griffin Engineering Ltd has more authority than the production manager, who is on a lower layer of the organisation. The managing director could send an order to the quality control manager through the production manager. This would represent the line of communication through which the order was made.

The person a worker is responsible to is their line manager. The workers who someone is responsible for are known as their **subordinates**. The **span of control** refers to the number of subordinates a manager is responsible for. The sales manager has a span of control of five subordinates – they are the line manager for the five sales representatives who are their subordinates in that department. **Delegation** is the act of giving another person a specific responsibility for doing something. The line manager will have been delegated responsibility by their line manager. This means that they will have been given authority to make certain decisions and to carry out specific responsibilities. For example, the production manager may have delegated responsibility to the quality control manager for how the quality of production will be monitored.

Activity 1 – Identifying activity

Answer the following questions based on the organisation chart of Griffin Engineering Ltd.

a) Who is at the top of the hierarchy?

b) Who is the line manager for the sales representatives?

c) Who are the subordinates of the finance director?

d) What is the span of control of the production manager?

e) How many layers are there in the organisation?

f) To whom would the production manager delegate responsibility for the stocks of raw materials?

g) Who would be involved in the line of communication between the managing director and the stock control manager?

h) Who would be accountable if the sales of the business did not reach the target set by the managing director?

i) The human resource manager delegates responsibility for advertising jobs and dealing with application forms to a subordinate. Which of the following statements are benefits that would result from delegating in this way?

- The subordinate may work harder because they feel that they have been given a specific area of responsibility.
- The subordinate may feel that the human resource manager is taking advantage of them.
- The human resource manager may feel that they are losing responsibility and may not be paid as much by the firm.
- The human resource manager may have more time to oversee the work of all the members of the department rather than getting tied down by detailed work.
- The subordinate may improve their management skills and this could lead to future promotion.
- The work will be done by a specialist and so the quality of the work should improve.

Benefits of organisation charts

Organisation charts help businesses by showing:

- who is responsible for which functions and tasks
- what a person is **accountable** for
- which work is delegated to others in the business
- who a worker is managed by and from whom they must take orders
- lines of communication within the organisation
- how different departments are linked together.

Different organisation structures – tall and flat organisations

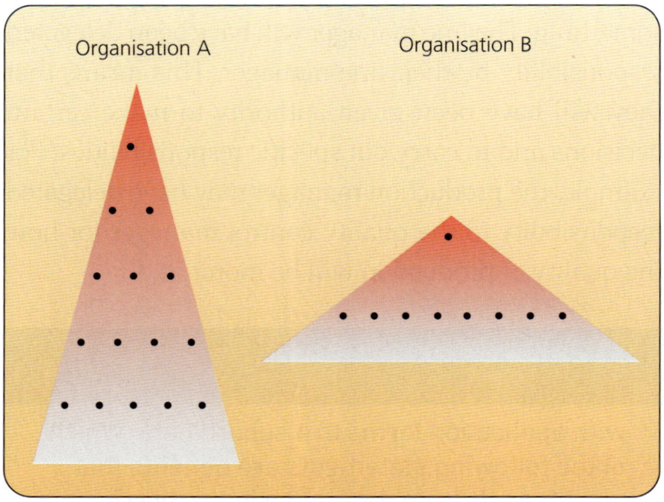

Figure 3.2 Tall and flat organisations.

The height of an organisation chart depends on how many layers there are in it.

Organisation A has a tall structure. Organisation B has a flat structure. Table 3.3 below shows the advantages of tall and flat structures.

Activity 2 – Zone activity

Put each of the statements under the correct heading in the table below to give the advantages of tall and flat organisations:

a) Workers will feel trusted because the managers will need to delegate responsibility as their span of control will be very wide.

b) It is easier to share ideas because people are more likely to know the bosses and the idea does not pass through so many people.

c) There are only a few layers so communications will be faster.

d) Managers may find it easier to supervise their subordinates because they will have fewer workers working directly for them.

e) The message is less likely to get changed – it only passes through a small number of layers.

f) Workers will be clear who they are responsible to.

g) Workers may be motivated to get promotion and move up the hierarchy.

Advantages of tall organisations	Advantages of flat organisations

Table 3.4 Advantages of tall and flat organisations.

Advantages of tall structures	Advantages of flat structures
■ The span of control of managers is likely to be narrower than in flat structures, meaning that he or she does not have too many people to look after. ■ There will be plenty of opportunities for workers to gain promotion that will motivate them.	■ The lines of communication and the responsibilities of the workers are clear. Communication from top to bottom might be quicker than in tall structures because there are not as many layers. ■ It is likely that fewer mistakes in communication will occur because messages do not have to be passed through so many layers. ■ People at the bottom may be encouraged to share ideas with those at the top because they will know who they are and what they are like. ■ The wider spans of control of managers will mean that they must delegate work and share authority. This will make the workers feel trusted and may encourage then to work harder.

Table 3.3 Advantages of tall and flat structures.

Evaluation point

Why do businesses have different organisational structures?

The type of organisation structure that a business adopts will depend on:

- the scale of business – large businesses usually require a hierarchical structure so that there are clear lines of communication and control from the top to the bottom. This is less important in small businesses. Effective communication is very important for making businesses successful
- the roles and responsibilities of each worker – these roles and responsibilities will be detailed in the job descriptions for the workers
- the nature of the business – flat organisational structures suit creative businesses. This type of organisation encourages two-way communication between workers at different levels and it is this that can lead to the development of new ideas
- the type of leadership – some leaders are autocratic by nature, they like to have control over all decisions. A tall, hierarchical structure will give these leaders the control they want.

Ways of working

The way in which people work has changed significantly in recent years. Many older adults will remember when working hours were typically nine to five, Monday to Friday in a regular place of work. Now people can be working on seven days a week and they may not have regular hours each day. They are just as likely to be working from home, on the train or in a café as they are to be working from their office or factory or shop. The changes that have taken place have created what is known as the 'flexible labour market.'

The two case studies illustrate ways in which working in the UK is changing. This section explains some of the changes that are taking place. These changes are dealt with individually but in reality, changing work practices may involve more than one type of work. For example, a firm might introduce both part-time and flexible working.

Case study: zero-hours contracts and flexible working at Sports Direct

In the mid-2010s, Mike Ashley, owner of Sports Direct (and also Newcastle United Football Club) was regularly in the news. One reason was that 75 per cent of Sports Directs 19,000 employees were employed on **zero-hours contracts**. Most of these were either shop assistants working in the retail outlets or warehouse workers. The business was criticised because some people thought zero-hours contracts were unfair on workers as they were not guaranteed any hours of work and this made their financial position unstable. For Sports Direct, these contracts helped to keep costs down because staff were not paid when not needed. Also, some workers liked being on zero-hours contracts as it gave them flexibility.

Case study: working at Wokingham Council

Flexible working at Wokingham Council.

Wokingham Council has introduced **flexible working** arrangements for many of its workers. The Council realised that society had changed and that workers' (the amount of work done by a worker) and customers' needs were changing. Workers can work at home when they are not needed in the office and can be flexible about the hours they work. People working outside of the office have had to learn to use technology so that they can communicate effectively, for example, telephone calls made to an office number may be transferred to a mobile number. They also need to be able to use computers at home to work on. When workers go into the office, they regularly 'hot desk' – they no longer have their own desk in the office but use whatever desk is available when they come in. These desks can often be booked in advance to ensure there is one available for the worker coming in. Workers indicate on a calendar when and where they are working and give their contact details so that colleagues know how and where to find them. There are some restrictions, for example, if a member of staff is needed for a meeting with other staff or with customers or a supplier, they will need to be in the office during working hours.

The Council has been able to save money by introducing flexible working arrangements because less office space is needed. The productivity of workers has improved because many find that they work better from home and the flexible arrangements can suit some workers with family commitments. The Council has also found that absenteeism has fallen, perhaps because people are happier and healthier with this way of working or they can look after sick children without taking time off.

Adapted from flexibility.co.uk

Full-time and part-time work

There is no official definition of **full-** and **part-time working** in the UK. It is generally thought that full-time work is when a person works 35 hours per week or more and part-time working is any job that involves fewer than 35 hours per week. The hours of a part-time worker may be made up in a number of ways. For example, they could work one or two full days per week, a number of half days or flexible hours.

There has been a big growth in part-time working in the UK, partly through the use of zero-hours contracts. (Zero-hours contracts are used here as an illustration of part-time working, but it should be noted that many part-time workers receive contracts for a specified number of hours.) When a person is given a zero-hours contract by an employer, the person is said to be employed but there is no guarantee of any work. The employer will contact the employee when they are needed, sometimes at very short notice. The worker may work fewer than 35 hours and so be considered a part-time worker but many will also work 35 or more hours per week. If this is the case, the workers are not part-time. Increasingly, companies are using zero-hours contracts as a way of employing workers or a part-time basis, including Wetherspoon, Cineworld, local councils and Buckingham Palace. In 2014, 1.8 million people had zero-hours contracts. Of these, nearly 700,000 were considered to be the person's main job. More women than men had zero-hours contracts.

The table below (Table 3.5) shows the advantages and disadvantages of part-time work for the worker and for the business.

Activity 3 – Explanation activity

a) Explain one advantage and one disadvantage to someone of working part-time.

b) Explain one advantage and one disadvantage to a business of employing a part-time worker.

	For the worker	For the business
Advantages	■ It suits people who need to look after their family, who need to pick children up from school or look after elderly relatives. ■ The success of UK businesses using part-time workers has helped to create more jobs. ■ It suits semi-retired workers who do not want to work a full week. ■ It suits students who want to earn some money while studying.	■ Experienced workers such as retired people or those who do not wish to work full-time still contribute to the business. ■ The business may have more choice when recruiting as not everyone wants full-time work. ■ The business can respond to demand – employing more staff in peak hours or fewer workers in off-peak hours so saving money. ■ It can reduce overtime costs by employing part-time workers. ■ Many UK businesses have been successful, perhaps because they have been able to keep costs low by employing workers only when they are needed.
Disadvantages	■ Part-time work may mean a lower income for a worker who really wants full-time work. ■ Workers may not be certain of earning income if they do not have fixed hours. ■ The hours may be inconvenient for the worker, e.g. three hours in early morning and two in late afternoon.	■ Recruitment and training costs may be higher if more people are needed than if full-time workers were used. ■ It may be time-consuming for managers to have to look after larger numbers of workers.

Table 3.5 Advantages and disadvantages of part-time working for the worker and the business.

Flexible working

There are many ways of flexible working:

- zero-hours contracts are an example of flexible working as well as possibly involving part-time working. The worker is called in when the business needs them.
- working from home for part of the week
- working flexi-time, where the worker can work their weekly hours in as few or as many days as they wish. If they complete their working hours in four days, they would then have a day when they did not need to work. It should be noted that the business may put some restrictions on when work can be done and how much time can be taken off
- shift working, which is when work times change. For example, a worker may work 8am–4pm one week, then 4pm–12pm the next week and 12pm–8am in another week.

All workers are now entitled to ask their employers to work in a flexible way. However, businesses do not have to let workers work in a flexible way. Businesses will make decisions that depend on whether flexible working suits them.

Activity 4 – Zone activity

The statements below are advantages or disadvantages of flexible working. Decide if they apply to the worker or the business. Put them in the correct place in the table below. You may find it useful to reread the case study on Wokingham Council.

- Flexible working suits some people with family commitments.
- Communications between workers may not be as good because workers may not meet each other regularly.
- Job sharing may mean that the business is able to retain experienced workers.
- Workers enjoy having some freedom to work where and when they want (within limits).
- The business may save costs by needing less office space and less storage space.
- Some workers may miss the social side of working with other people.
- Workers may need more supervision to make sure they are working well.
- Workers may save time and money by not having to travel to work.
- The business may benefit from the increased productivity of workers who find it better to work from home.

	For the worker	For the business
Advantages		
Disadvantages		

Table 3.6 Advantages and disadvantages of flexible working.

Temporary working

Temporary work is also known as casual labour. Workers only work for a business for a short period of time. They may be given a fixed-term contract, for example, for three months. Alternatively, they may not have a contract at all and just work when they are called up by the business. **Temporary working** is common in seasonal industries such as agriculture (when the harvest needs bringing in) and tourism (in peak tourist periods in summer or around Christmas). During these periods, temporary workers may work long hours.

Like part-time working, temporary workers suit businesses because they only need to be employed when there is a demand and this saves having to pay workers during less busy periods. A possible problem is that when they need workers there may be a shortage, particularly if they need workers with skills. The business may not have the time to train workers and, for this reason, temporary employment may be limited to unskilled workers. This can make life insecure for some people as they do not have work all year round. However, some prefer periods with a heavy workload in which they can earn a lot of money and then enjoy the rest of their time pursuing leisure interests.

Many businesses get their workers through employment agencies such as POWERpeople (which is also a recruitment agency – see Unit 3.4). You will not be asked questions directly about employment and recruitment agencies. However, they are very relevant to the way that businesses now operate and are included to help you know about the real world of business. You may be able to use your understanding of them as part of an answer to another question. These

Case study: POWERpeople employment agency

'What we do

We provide a full engineering personnel support to our clients in the energy industry. We specialise in the supply of high calibre blue or white collar engineers, either in the form of full project teams, main trade labourers on major projects or as individual specialist engineers for specific roles.'

From PowerPeople.biz

agencies recruit workers and keep their names on their books. When other businesses contact them seeking workers, the employment agency will offer the work to the people on their books. Often the work may be for a limited time. Many agencies are quite formal, like POWERpeople. Others are informal such as those run by 'gang masters' who will have contact with a group of workers and who will contact them when work is needed, sometimes picking them up in a minibus to take them to work. This is common in agriculture.

Working from home

Many workers are now able to work from home. They may have an office in their home containing a computer, telephone and so on. They contact their employer or clients by telephone or email. Reports can be written on the computer and sent by email to the client or to the employer. Meetings at the offices of the employer may not take place very often – perhaps only when problems arise that require face to face discussions to produce solutions. Some businesses use video-conferencing so that workers do not even have to come to work for meetings. (All this is very good environmentally since it reduces the amount of travel that workers need to do – see Unit 6.1.)

More people work at home.

The table below gives the advantages and disadvantages of home working.

To the business		To the worker	
Advantages	**Disadvantages**	**Advantages**	**Disadvantages**
■ Workers can work longer – they save on travel time.	■ The worker may not be able to exchange ideas with fellow workers if they do not see them very often.	■ The worker may have freedom about how much they do and when they work.	■ The worker may miss the social side of working with other people.
■ Workers may be more motivated because of the freedom about how much they work and when.	■ The worker may produce less. Some workers need the discipline of clocking on and off.	■ The worker may save money by not having to travel to work.	
■ Workers may work better if there are fewer distractions at home.	■ The worker may need to be trained in how to use the technology needed to be able to work at home.	■ The workers may be less stressed by not having to travel to work.	
	■ The worker may be less efficient if there are distractions at home.		
	■ The business may have to buy the technology, for example computers, for the worker to use at home.		

Table 3.7 Advantages and disadvantages of working from home.

Activity 5 – Zone activity

The following statements are either advantages or disadvantages to businesses of allowing workers to work at home. Put them under the correct heading in the table below.

- Workers feel trusted that they will do their work.
- It is not as easy for workers to talk to each other to discuss ideas about a job.
- The worker can concentrate better without the distractions of others at work.
- Workers will need to be trained to use the technology, which costs time and money.
- The technology the worker needs may be expensive to buy.
- The worker is less stressed because there is no need to travel to work.
- Some workers like the social side of work and may not be as happy working on their own.
- Some workers may find that there are distractions at home from family and friends.
- Time may be wasted if unsupervised workers do not focus or do not understand properly what they need to do.
- The worker feels good because they save the cost of travelling to work.
- The worker can work whatever hours they wish as long as they get the job done, and this can take some stress away.
- Some workers need the discipline of having to start work at certain times and having to be supervised.

Working at home	
Advantages	**Disadvantages**

Table 3.7 Advantages and disadvantages of working from home.

Working while mobile

Working while mobile! Of course, he could be watching a film and not working!

Working while mobile refers to people who work when they are not at a place of work, such as an office or their home. It has become more important partly due to improvements in technology that have made communication easier. People can work while they are, for example, on a train journey or in a café or even while away on holiday, sending in reports, making and receiving calls and holding video-conference meetings.

Businesses like it because it improves the productivity of their employees – they are able to do more work in the time that they are employed. Workers like it because it gives them the flexibility over where and when they work. They can continue to work while travelling and so make full use of their time. All of this can help to reduce business costs and improve the competitiveness of business.

Activity 6 – Research activity

Write a short account of a worker who works in a mobile way. Use the internet or speak to someone you know who is a mobile worker. Mention in your account any advantages or disadvantages to them or to their business of the way they work.

Self-employment

Case study: Philip Aaron, electrician

Philip Aaron.

Philip Aaron is a trained electrician. Like many other tradespeople, he used to be employed by a firm on a permanent, full-time contract that guaranteed him work, holidays, sick pay and other employment rights. (See Unit 3.7 Employment law.) He became self-employed, setting up a private limited company with another electrician. Philip will put in a quote for the electrical work on a job such as re-wiring a student hall of residence that is being refurbished. If the main contractor is happy with the quote, Philip will do the job. He likes this. He is guaranteed the payment however long it takes to complete the job. He can complete the contract as quickly as possible by working hard and often for long days and then move on to a new job to earn more money. There are risks – he may not be successful tendering for work and, usually, there are payment penalties if the work is not completed on time.

Self-employment in the UK is now at the highest level it has been since records began. There are over 4.5 million people who are self-employed. Common jobs are in construction (plumbing, electrics, bricklaying and so on) and taxi driving. 15 per cent of the work force were self-employed in 2014–2016 compared with 8.7 per cent in 1975 and 13 per cent in 2008 according to figures from the Office for National Statistics (ONS). Once people have become self-employed, they are more likely to stay self-employed now than ever before.

Many people like to be their own boss as they can work hard and earn good money, but there are problems. Being self-employed means they lose their employment rights such as holiday pay, sick pay and pension contributions from their employers. They also often work longer hours than employed people. Many self-employed people have also seen their incomes fall as increased competition has reduced the amount that contracting companies are willing to pay them.

Many businesses like using self-employed workers as it reduces their costs. They pay them only for the work they do. They do not have the costs of pension contributions and national insurance. Workers, like Philip Aaron, will supply their own tools. Self-employed people tend to be highly motivated and so will work hard to do the job well and quickly, and so be able to move on to another job or to keep their contractor happy so they get more work in the future. They are much less likely to take days off for illness, childminding and holidays.

Activity 7 – Poster activity

Draw a poster that shows the main advantages and disadvantages of being self-employed to the self-employed person and to the business that pays them for work done.

Evaluation point

This section describes some of the changes that have taken place with regards to work. The changes have brought benefits to businesses. For example, flexible working practices and the increase in part-time employment means businesses are able to employ people when they need them and do not need to pay them if there is no work for them to do. In addition, the changes help some workers to be more productive or more efficient, for example, by working while mobile. This helps businesses to minimise their costs and so keep the prices they charge low whilst still being able to make a profit. In short, this helps businesses to be more competitive which is important as globalisation develops and firms must compete with more businesses in more countries. Some of the changes have also benefited workers, by giving them more flexibility over when and where they work, for example However, for many workers how much work they do and how much they are paid has become increasingly uncertain and insecure. For many workers, incomes have fallen.

Key facts

Organisation charts show the organisation structure of a business. They are useful for showing who does what in an organisation and who is responsible to whom.

Organisation charts help communications in a business by showing the lines that communication can take.

Different types of organisation suit different kinds of businesses.

The way we work has changed significantly in recent years.

More people are working part-time, working from home, working while mobile and are self-employed.

Useful words

Organisation chart is a diagram that shows how the workers are organised in a business and who is in charge of whom.

Layers are the number of levels of authority that there are in a chain of command.

Authority is the power that one person has to make decisions and to control what other workers do.

Accountability is the responsibility that a person has for a job meaning that they will take the blame for what goes wrong as well as the credit for what goes well.

Chain of command is the links in the levels of authority from those at the top with the most authority to those at the bottom with the least.

Subordinates are the workers that a line manager is responsible for.

Span of control is the number of subordinates who report directly to the line manager.

Delegation is the process of giving a manager authority to a subordinate to make decisions for which that manager is responsible.

Job description states the main duties or tasks or responsibilities of the worker.

Zero-hours contract is when a person has a contract to work for an employer but is not guaranteed any work. The employer will inform them if and when they are needed.

Flexible working is the practice of people working partly at their place of work and partly elsewhere, perhaps at home or while they are mobile.

Full-time working is when a person works 35 hours or more per week.

Part-time working is when a person works fewer than 35 hours per week.

Temporary working is when a person only works for a short period of time for an employer, sometimes on a short-term contract or sometimes just on a day-to-day basis as needed.

Working while mobile is when people work when they are on the move, travelling or on holiday.

Self-employment is when people work as their own business, selling their work to buyers who may be consumers or other businesses.

Practice questions

Multiple choice questions

The diagram below shows the organisation chart for Leigh Hire Ltd. Leigh Hire Ltd hires out equipment such as cherry pickers and forklift trucks.

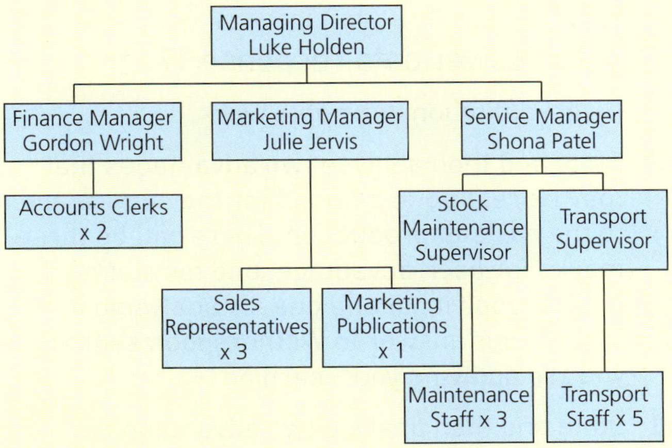

Figure 3.3 Organisation chart for Leigh Hire Ltd.

Using the information in the organisation chart for Leigh Hire Ltd, answer the following questions:

1 How many layers are there in the organisation?

a) 2 **b)** 3 **c)** 4 **d)** 5.

2 Which of the following is a subordinate of the marketing manager, Julie Jervis?

a) an accounts clerk

b) a sales representative

c) a maintenance supervisor

d) the managing director.

3 What is the span of control of the managing director, Luke Holden?

a) 2 **b)** 3 **c)** 4 **d)** 5.

Data response 16

Organisation charts

Using the organisation chart for Leigh Hire Ltd, answer the following questions.

1 Analyse one benefit to Leigh Hire Ltd of its organisational structure. (3 marks)

2 Analyse one benefit that Leigh Hire Ltd would gain if it changed its structure to a flat organisation. (3 marks)

3 Recommend whether Leigh Hire Ltd should change its structure to a flat organisation. Give reasons for your answer. (3 marks)

How to answer data response 16

1 State and explain one advantage of organisation charts and analyse it. Relate it to the diagram for Leigh Hire Ltd so that your answer is applied.

2 State one advantage of a flat organisation and analyse it. Relate it to the diagram for Leigh Hire Ltd so that your answer is applied.

3 Decide whether a tall or a flat organisation chart is suitable and then justify your decision. Consider the type of product or service that is provided in giving your justification.

Practice questions

Multiple choice questions

1 Which of the following statements is true?
  a) Part-time working in the UK has fallen.
  b) Part-time workers are not given contracts
  c) Part-time working is said to be when a person works fewer than 35 hours a week.
  d) Part-time working suits businesses, like travel companies, that have a steady, all-year-round demand for their services.

2 Which of the following is not typical of a flexible labour market?
  a) Workers can work at home if they wish.
  b) Workers are often self-employed.
  c) Workers' employment rights are increasing.
  d) Workers are employed on a casual basis or temporary contract.

3 Which of the following statements about self-employed people is not true?
  a) People like to be self-employed because they can be their own boss.
  b) There are more self-employed people in the UK now than there were 25 years ago.
  c) Businesses like to use self-employed people because it saves on costs.
  d) People like to be self-employed because it makes life easier as they do not need to work hard.

Data response 17

Wetherspoon is a public house business. It runs a chain of over 750 pubs throughout the UK. It offers meals and drinks throughout the day and is particularly busy at lunchtimes and in the evenings. Many of its workers are on flexible work contracts. Wetherspoon claims that not only do these contracts help it to keep its prices low but also that many of its employees like them.

1 Explain the meaning of the term 'flexible work'. (2 marks)

2 Analyse two advantages to Wetherspoon of having workers on flexible work. (6 marks)

3 Analyse two advantages to employees of Wetherspoon of having flexible work. (6 marks)

4 Analyse two disadvantages to employees of Wetherspoon of having flexible work. (4 marks)

How to answer data response 17

1 Give a definition of flexible work.

2 State and then analyse two advantages that may be related to demand for the service and to the costs of production. There will be three marks for each advantage, one for stating it, one for applying it and one for analysing it. Relate your answer to Wetherspoon so that you are applying your learning.

3 State and then analyse two advantages to the employees that may be related to being flexible when they work or the creation of jobs that might not exist otherwise. There will be three marks for each advantage, one for stating it, one for applying it and one for analysing it. Relate your answer to the workers of Wetherspoon so that you are applying your learning.

4 Analyse two disadvantages to the employees that may be related to uncertainty about work and income. Relate your answer to workers of Wetherspoon so that you are applying your learning.

UNIT 3.3 Communication in business

Learning outcomes

By studying this unit, you will be able to:

- explain the **importance of communications** to businesses
- evaluate the importance of business communications
- explain the different types and ways of **communicating**, and give examples of each
- discuss when the different ways of communicating are appropriate for businesses to use
- analyse ways in which **digital communications** have influenced businesses and evaluate these changes.

The importance of business communications

'Good communication is the lifeblood of business.'

While ICT has revolutionised the way we communicate, personal contact and **written communications** are still important in business. This unit looks at communications in business in detail.

Read the four case studies below. They illustrate how communication is important for all areas of business.

Introductory case study: communications and marketing – Coca-Cola

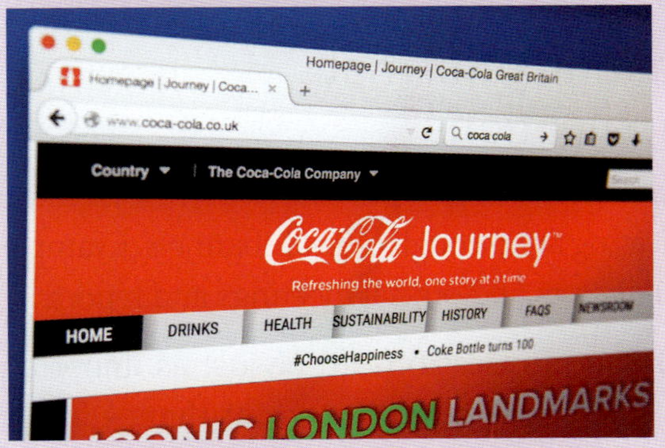

Coca-Cola marketing communications.

The use of Twitter for marketing campaigns has increased significantly. One of the most successful campaigns on Twitter has been the 'choose happiness' campaign by Coca-Cola.

Introductory case study: communications and finance – FreeAgent.com

Trusted by over 40,000 businesses already!

FreeAgent's online accounting software brings everything together, from invoice and expense management to VAT, payroll and self-assessment tax return filing.

Invoices that send and chase themselves.

FreeAgent lets you set up recurring invoices that can send themselves automatically, and nudge those pesky late-paying clients with automated reminders. It's hands-free invoicing!

From freeagent.com

Introductory case study: communications and recruitment – selecting a mathematics teacher at Maricourt Catholic High School

A shortlist of candidates had been drawn up using the CVs and letters of application for the post of mathematics teacher. Short-listed candidates were invited to the school. A 'selection team' was formed for the day consisting of the head teacher, the chair of governors of the school and the head of mathematics. On the day, the candidates taught a short lesson that was observed by a member of the senior leadership team and an experienced teacher of mathematics. The observers gave feedback to the selection team about what they liked about each of the lessons. The selection team interviewed each of the candidates. Using the information from the lesson observations, the interviews and the references sent on behalf of the applicants, the selection team chose the candidate to be appointed.

Introductory case study: communications and the production process – Tait Radio

Tait is an Australian company that produces radios. Production is kept lean, meaning that the company only produces radios that have been ordered. It quality tests products during the production process so that faults can be identified quickly and resolved. Communication is essential to the whole process. Information needs to be sent from the marketing department about the number and type of radios ordered. Issues regarding quality need to be brought to the attention of quality controllers who can then discuss solutions and implement them.

(You can see a video of production at Tait – blog.taitradio.com.)

What is communication?

Communication is the transmission of a message from a sender to a receiver.

One-way communication is when the message is sent but there is no reply. If an announcement is made over the tannoy at a pop concert you are attending, this is one-way communication because you cannot reply to the message. Another example would be an advertising leaflet pushed through your door. One-way communication is good for giving information.

Two-way communication takes place when the person receiving the message can reply to the sender. Having a conversation is an example of two-way communication. Two-way communication is important because:

- **feedback** from the receiver makes it clear that the message has been received and understood
- it is good for generating ideas and coming up with solutions to problems.

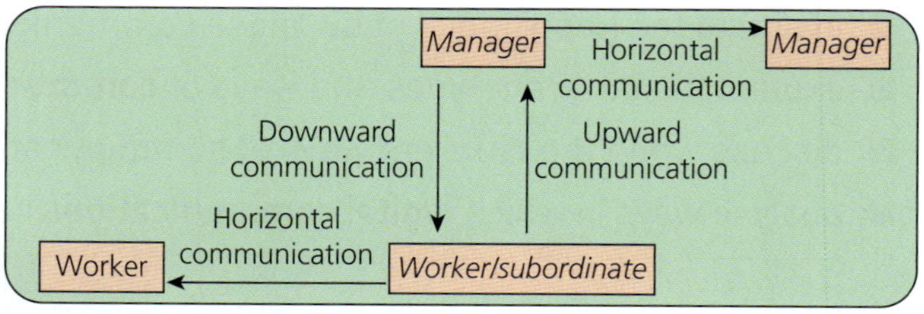

Figure 3.4 Horizontal and vertical communications.

Internal communication takes place between people who work in the same organisation. It may be vertical or horizontal.

Vertical communication is between people on different layers of the organisation's hierarchy. It can be upward or downward. If a manager talks to workers (subordinates) it is an example of downward vertical communication. If a worker sends an email to their boss, this is upward vertical communication.

Horizontal communication takes place when two people at the same level within the organisation structure communicate with each other.

External communication takes place between one person in an organisation and someone outside that organisation.

Formal and informal communications

Formal communication takes place when the means of communicating are through official channels. Examples of these are letters and official meetings and reports.

Informal communication can be just as important as – and sometimes more important than – formal communication. An example of an informal communication is a conversation during a break or at a social event.

Activity 1 – Types of communication classification activity

Table 3.8 below shows some of the communications connected with Bolton Wanderers Football Club.

Tick the boxes next to each item to say whether:

a) the communication is an example of internal or external communication

b) the communication is an example of formal or informal communication

c) the communication is likely to be one-way or two-way.

Example of communication	Internal	External	Formal	Informal	One-way	Two-way
The team manager must talk with the directors about buying a new player.						
The ticket office must let the fans know that tickets for the cup final will be on sale from next Monday.						
Club officials talk to the police to agree security arrangements at games.						
The manager needs to discuss tactics with his coaching staff.						
The players complain about the manager's tactics as they get changed after the game.						
The personnel officer needs to write for references about applicants for a job.						
The stadium announcer must tell away supporters that their coaches will meet them in Car Park A after the match.						
The chief groundsman must tell one of his staff to mark the lines more clearly on the pitch.						
The marketing manager discusses an idea with the personnel manager over lunch.						
The marketing department must negotiate prices of replica shirts with a supplier.						
The marketing department must tell customers about the special Christmas gifts on sale in the club shop.						
The ticket office manager must agree a rota with the office workers to make sure there is someone there during all opening hours.						

Table 3.8 Examples of communication.

The importance of communications in business

Table 3.9 indicates some of the benefits of communication.

Area of business activity	Examples of communication
Marketing	External communication is needed for effective market research and advertising that informs and/or persuades the customer to buy the product. Internal communication is needed to plan promotion campaigns.
Finance	External communication may be needed to explain a business plan to a bank manager to persuade them to provide a loan. Internal communication about income and expenditure is needed so that accurate accounts are kept (though this may be external communication if the accounting is outsourced).
Human resources	Both external and internal communication may be needed to encourage applications and to get information about applicants for a job. Internal and external communication may be needed so that a person is trained properly to do a good job. Internal communication may be needed to resolve a problem between workers to avoid disruption or to motivate workers to improve their performance.
Operations	Internal communication is needed to discuss quality so that wastage of materials is avoided. Internal communication is involved when the marketing department informs the production facility about the number of goods ordered. External communication is needed to enquire about a delivery of raw materials.
Government and trade	External communication is needed so that businesses understand government regulations that control business. External communication is needed so that businesses can make applications for grants from government.

Table 3.9 Communication and different kinds of business activity.

Activity 2 – Matching terms activity

Match the kind of business activity given in the first column with the example of communication in the second column.

Kind of business activity	Example of communication
Marketing	A computer-controlled robot is programmed to paint cars on the assembly line.
Finance	A sales representative visits a possible customer.
Human resources	Information about new health and safety regulations is posted on a website.
Government and trade	A business sends out a bill to a customer for money that is owed.
Operations	An employee is given a telling off for repeatedly being late for work.

Table 3.10 Examples of how communication is important in business.

Ways of communicating in a business context

ICT has revolutionised the way we communicate and the way we work. However, personal contact and written information on paper are still used by many businesses for particular uses.

'What is that new-fangled thing you are using, Jess?'

Verbal communication

Phone

For many mobile phone users, texting is the main method of communicating but, of course, actually speaking to someone is still common and is an example of **verbal communication**.

Meetings

Meetings often take place when people come together in a room but, increasingly, businesses are using video- and phone-conferencing facilities to enable meetings to take place between people who are not in the same place. Meetings can be formal when there will be a chairperson who conducts the meeting, following an agenda (a list of the items to be discussed during the meeting). Meetings can also be informal when people communicate without any agenda or chairperson. These can be arranged in advance or be 'impromptu' because people meet up, for example, in the office or the work's canteen.

Presentations

Presentations are very common in business. They may or may not be supported with slide projections such as PowerPoint. A presentation is a way for a speaker to explain their thinking and then to respond to questions. A salesperson may present a product to a potential customer, in a shop or during a visit to their place of work, to show and describe the product.

The general advantages and disadvantages of verbal communication are shown in the table below.

Written communication

Letters

Letters can be handwritten or typed, sent through the post or electronically as an attachment to an email. In

Verbal communication. e.g. phone calls, meeting, presentations	
Advantages	**Disadvantages**
■ The person can check that the message has been understood by asking for feedback. ■ The person giving a message can emphasise points through their tone of voice and/or their body language. ■ The speaker can use diagrams, pictures and slides to help to explain something even when the communicators are not in the same place, if the communication is supported by digital technology.	■ If there are a lot of people listening to a message it may not be clear that all have heard or understood it. ■ If the receiver of the message does not like what they hear, they may disrupt the message. ■ There is no permanent record of the message (unless minutes are taken, or a recording made). This may be important if a worker is being disciplined, for example, or if major business decisions are being made that need to be communicated to others later. ■ Some forms of verbal communication can be expensive, for example, if workers from different parts of the world need to travel to meet together.

Table 3.11 Advantages and disadvantages of using verbal communication.

business, letters are usually quite a formal method of communication and are often used when the sender wants to keep a formal record and to ensure that the person receiving the communication has actually received it. Letters sent through the post can be sent by 'recorded delivery' so that delivery can be tracked because the receiver has to sign for it.

Important documents are often sent by in the post so that there can be an official record of the sending and receiving of it. For example, a contract may be sent in the post.

Emails and texts

Emails and texts are now widely used in business. Emails (electronic messages) and texts (written messages sent from one phone to another) can be used to send a specific message to a colleague, supplier or customer. They may also be used to communicate general messages such as advertising to potential customers. A disadvantage of these 'bulk' emails is that people often delete them before reading them.

The general advantages and disadvantages of written communication are shown in the table below.

Written communication, e.g. letters, emails and texts	
Advantages	**Disadvantages**
■ There is a record of the message. ■ The receiver can read and reread the message to make sure they understand it. ■ The message can be sent to more than one person at a time – for example, circular letters or advertising flyers. ■ A written message can avoid confrontation. ■ Some written communication can be transmitted very swiftly, particularly text and email if the sender and receiver keep their mobile phones and/or computers or tablets switched on and with them.	■ It is not always possible to check immediately that the receiver has understood the message properly. ■ The success of the message depends on how clearly it has been written. ■ There is a risk of the computer becoming infected with a virus from an email unless there is adequate protection. ■ Emails may get lost in spam. ■ Some people can get overwhelmed by the number of emails they receive.

Table 3.12 Advantages and disadvantages of using written communication.

Activity 3 – Explanation activity

1 Write a short description of each of the methods of communication listed below. Note the advantages and disadvantages of each to business:

- telephone
- business letter
- email
- social media
- text
- website
- meeting.

2 For each of the cases i) – vii) below:

a) You should say whether you would use verbal or written communications or use images. You may recommend more than one kind of communication.

b) You should also should state what form the communication should take; for example, if you recommend written communication, state whether a letter, text or email or other form of written communication should be used.

Give reasons for your recommendations and include in your answer reference to the advantages and disadvantages of the different methods of communication.

i) A school with 1,500 pupils wishes to let pupils know that the school will not be open today because of problems with the central heating boiler. It is 7.30 in the morning when the school finds out there is a problem. School starts at 8.45. Pupils, parents and teachers need to be informed.

ii) A salesperson wishes to demonstrate the features of a new computer to a potential customer.

iii) A holiday firm wishes to advertise its new brochure for next summer's holidays.
iv) A project manager for a construction firm wishes to remind colleagues who work in several different departments located on different sites that there will be a meeting for all concerned later in the week.
v) The social committee wants to advertise its summer barbecue to all workers.
vi) A manager wishes to find out from workers in her department about an accusation made by a worker that he was racially abused by a colleague.
vii) A firm wishes to advertise special offers for all its shareholders.

Social media

The use of **social media** is now very widespread. It involves online platforms that allow people to create and share communication and participate in social networking. Facebook has 1.5 billion users worldwide, Instagram 400 million, and other media such as Twitter and Pinterest are also hugely popular. Social media often combine photographs and text, and they are all particularly good mediums for advertising. They also have other uses, for example, businesses can get feedback from customers about the quality of service provided, through feedback on Twitter or Facebook. Some social networks also suit particular types of users. Over half of Pinterest's users are under 25 so this is good for advertising to young people. More women than men use Pinterest and it is popular for communications about DIY, fashion, exercise, beauty, photography and food. Instagram, which is also visual like Pinterest, requires good quality pictures, otherwise poor images of products may be presented. Instagram is commonly used for presenting information about food, art, travel and fashion.

Social media can also be used for internal communications. Groups of workers can be linked through the media to message each other, for example, they can arrange meetings, send information, share ideas and receive instructions. The advantage of this is that they can receive these communications wherever they are in the world and at any time of day.

The general advantages and disadvantages of social media are shown in the table below.

Websites

A **website** is an online location that links pages of information. Internet users can connect with the website using its address. Having an online presence through a website is now a must for many businesses. Websites can be used to advertise, to receive orders and to get feedback from customers.

The general advantages and disadvantages of websites are shown in Table 3.14.

Social media	
Advantages	**Disadvantages**
■ There are a huge number of users. ■ Information can be updated regularly. ■ Visual images may be used to enhance communications. ■ It can be cheaper to advertise than using traditional media such as TV, radio, newspapers and magazines. ■ You can involve customers by allowing feedback. ■ Customers can help to promote your message by passing on information to other users. ■ Social media are a good way for staff to communicate.	■ There is a cost because the information on the social media needs to be managed – updating and feeding back regularly. ■ It can be difficult to measure the effectiveness of the businesses' use of the social media or of using one channel or another.

Table 3.13 Advantages and disadvantages of social media.

Websites	
Advantages	**Disadvantages**
■ Sales can be made online. ■ Products and services can be promoted to millions of potential customers around the world. ■ Websites operate 24/7. ■ Detailed information about products can be given including specifications and prices. ■ Images can be used. ■ Links can be used to offer 'chat' services so the potential buyer can ask questions about specific needs. ■ Customers often use search engines to find sellers and to locate their premises or shops. ■ Internet shopping continues to increase and so offers a way of setting up a new business or of expanding. ■ Website design and purchasing a domain name are both fairly cheap making a website a lower cost way of advertising and selling than traditional methods. ■ Customers can post feedback which, if positive, can encourage other customers.	■ There is the risk of the website crashing resulting in a (temporary) halt to business activity. ■ A business can receive a lot of spam emails unless it protects against this. ■ Not everyone likes using websites, for example, they may prefer to speak to sales staff in a shop or on the telephone. ■ Websites need to be maintained and updated regularly.

Table 3.14 Advantages and disadvantages of websites.

Activity 4 – Making a presentation or writing a report activity

Saskia Dimiancuk is a retired art teacher. Her hobby has been designing and making jewellery and she now wants to set up a business selling her products, but she is not familiar with social media. Saskia wants to know what benefits there will be in using social media, any problems she might have and which, if any, of the social media she should use.

Create a presentation or report to give her advice about what to do. You might want to research examples of other similar businesses and include information about these or links to them.

Activity 5 – Poster activity

Imagine you are a website designer. You are going to attend an exhibition for small businesses in your region where ICT specialists can display the services they offer. You want to tell the representatives of the small businesses about the benefits and the problems of having a website. Design a poster that you could display at the exhibition, which would show the benefits and the problems to small businesses of having a website.

Evaluation point

Which methods to use?

When deciding how to communicate, businesses must consider who they are communicating with, what the purpose of the communication is and what methods of communicating are available and affordable. For example, if a business wishes to advertise to its potential customers, it can use a number of different media. If there are not many customers and they need technical information, it might be appropriate to send a representative for an individual meeting. If there are a lot of customers for a mass consumer product such as an antiperspirant deodorant, it might be appropriate to use social media that can be used to send a persuasive message to a lot of people. If the communication is internal, different methods will be appropriate. If there is a need to inform all workers about something, perhaps email will work best but if there is a need to talk about problems at work, people may need to meet to have a discussion.

Why can't you just speak to someone anymore to get an answer?

How digital communication influences business activity

Digital communication is the electronic exchange of information such as voice, text, diagrams, pictures and video. Developments in digital communication have had an enormous impact on business activity. To understand this, we need to think about what has already been discussed. Examples of the impact of digital communication on various parts of businesses are outlined below.

Marketing

The digital communication revolution has led to the use of websites and social media. Businesses can promote their goods and services through these, which means that larger numbers of potential customers can be targeted both in the home country and abroad. There is the greater possibility for businesses to grow.

Businesses can now sell their products online. This has reduced the need for retailers to have shops, instead having huge warehouses where goods are stored until they are sent out to customers. This has encouraged the growth of large businesses such as Amazon and eBay. Their selling costs have been significantly reduced, leading to price reductions and/or increases in profits. Many small retailers have been driven out of business as a result.

Competition has increased. Customers are better able to compare the products and the prices of different businesses. They can buy from the high street or online, from sellers in their own country and from sellers abroad. Businesses have had to improve their competitiveness to survive and to grow focusing even more on quality and price and the service they provide.

New services and products are on offer. Gone are the days when there were only five TV channels. The digital streaming of media content now means there are more TV channels available and we can use Netflix, BT and Amazon to watch TV on demand. Ebooks that depend on digital streaming are also now very common.

Human resources

The ways of working have been changed dramatically by digital communication. Working while mobile and working from home are two of the key changes brought about by the development of digital communication.

The recruitment and selection of staff now involve digital communications for many businesses. Jobs are advertised on websites, applications received and invitations sent out for selection procedures using email. People can be interviewed using video-conferencing such as Skype.

Jobs have been lost as productivity has increased. Workers have had to be retrained to learn the skills needed in the digital age.

Operations

Production is now often highly automated as computers communicate digitally with robots to control the production process. Banks have been able to provide banking services using digital communications and as a result, employ less staff.

Quality control has improved as machines can inspect and relay information digitally to people overseeing the production process. Problems can be spotted earlier and dealt with sooner, reducing waste.

Production is leaner. What is being produced can be changed more quickly in response to changes in demand. The marketing department can inform the production department of changes in demand that can then reprogram production.

Digital communication has allowed an increase in the outsourcing of production. Businesses can communicate more easily with other producers, at home or abroad.

Staff can be monitored more easily. Delivery drives can be tracked using GPS. Engineers visiting homes to carry out services can be tracked so that their managers know where they are, what jobs they are doing and how long they are taking.

It is easier for the producer to find materials and stock and to compare prices by using internet searches.

Finance

The second case study on Chatsworth House below illustrates how the finance function of business has been affected by digital communications.

Case study: tracking at Mindshare

As part of an experiment, the University of London asked employees at London media agency Mindshare to wear one of three different activity trackers as they worked: an accelerometer wristband, a portable brainwave monitor or a posture coach. After a month, productivity had risen by 8.5 per cent and job satisfaction by 3.5 per cent overall. Most improvement was seen in employees who wore non-invasive devices that collected data quietly rather than interrupting with ongoing feedback. "People recognise that effectively they're on the clock, that they're being tracked, and as a result they raise their game," said a representative of the University of London.

Adapted from newscientist.com, October, 2014

Case study: accounting at the Chatsworth Estate

Chatsworth House, Derbyshire.

Michael Isherwood used to be the accountant for the Duke of Devonshire who owned various business interests including Chatsworth House in Derbyshire and an industrial estate in Sheffield. Michael started as the only accountant employed. During the years that he worked for the Duke, the revenues of his business grew by twenty times but when he retired, there was only one other accountant. Digital technology meant that Michael and his colleague could handle a lot more information than when he had started and records were kept manually.

Accounting information such as invoices and records of payments can be communicated more quickly and easily, and stored and then processed to prepare documentation such as cash flow forecasts, break-even analyses, profit and loss accounts and balance sheets.

Payments can be made digitally.

Improved employee performance, productivity and costs

Digital communication has improved employee performance, increasing the productivity of workers (output per worker) which in turn has reduced the costs of production. This is true for workers in all the different functional areas as shown in the sections above.

More clearly presented financial information can improve decision-making, reduce costs, give better predictions of cash flow and therefore support business activities like loan applications.

Competition

The digital communication revolution has led to an increase in competition and has helped with the process of globalisation.

New business opportunities

The development of digital communications has led to many new business opportunities. Businesses are needed to make the hardware (computers, phones, tablets and so on) needed, computer analysts and programmers are required to create digital information systems, technical experts are required to install and maintain the hardware and software used in the systems and ICT trainers are required to train staff in businesses how to use digital communication systems.

This unit covers an area that illustrates the 'interdependent nature of business.' For more on this see Unit 7.

Activity 6 – Missing words activity

Complete the following paragraph using the words below.

- jobs
- leaner
- costs
- home
- electronically
- global
- social media
- productivity
- retraining
- competition
- accounting
- mobile

Digital communication is about sending and receiving information ___ It has transformed business activity. There is now greater ___ and trade has become more ___ The ___ of workers has been increased and production ___ have fallen as a result. All the functional departments of businesses have been affected. Finance departments can store and process ___ information more quickly. Marketing departments use websites and ___ to reach potentially huge markets. Production is now ___ as what is being produced can be changed much more quickly. Human resource departments have seen more staff working while ___ or working from ___ Many workers have benefited from the changes to business activity but some have lost their ___ or had to undergo ___

Evaluation point

The influence of digital communication

The digital communications revolution has had a major impact on all of the different functions in businesses and brought many benefits. Competition has increased between UK firms and with businesses from all over the world. So too have opportunities for businesses. Whether or not UK businesses have survived or thrived because of the changes in digital communication has depended, in part, on how well they adapted to the changes to help to give them a competitive edge. The big supermarkets have had to adapt by offering online ordering and delivery services. Not all UK businesses have been successful. Some have closed because they were slow to respond and others have closed because digital communications changed the nature of their business, a point well-illustrated by changes to retailing with the introduction of online trading and a fall in the importance of physical shops. Workers have been affected, sometimes being able to work in better ways but for others their skills and jobs are no longer needed.

Activity 7 – Research activity

Choose one business function that you are interested in – marketing, human resources, production or finance. Use a search engine such as Google to find out information about a business. Write a report summarising the main ways in which the business function within the business has benefited from the use of digital communications. For example, you might want to find out more about the 'Choose happiness' Twitter campaign run by Coca-Cola. Come up with some facts and figures, such as sales, market share, costs and profits, if you can that measure the impact on the business.

Key facts

Communication is about sending and receiving messages.

Good communication is essential to business.

There are many different ways of communicating.

Different ways of communicating are appropriate for different kinds of businesses and for what needs to be communicated.

Developments in digital technology have improved the speed and effectiveness of communications in business.

Developments in digital communications have helped to reduce business costs and increase competition. They are a major reason for the increase in globalisation.

Developments in digital technology have affected every functional area of business – marketing, human resources, production and finance.

Developments in digital technology have changed how businesses operate and how workers work.

Useful words

Communication is the transmission of a message from a sender to a receiver through a means of communication.

Digital communication is the exchange of information electronically using ICT.

Written communication is communication by written words and diagrams – text, email, letters.

Feedback is the response made by a person who receives a communication that indicates that they have, or have not, understood the communication.

Internal communication is communication between people employed in the same organisation.

Vertical communication is communication up or down the hierarchy within an organisation.

Horizontal communication is communication between people on the same level of the hierarchy in an organisation.

External communication is communication between people in an organisation and others outside that organisation.

Formal communication is communication that uses the official channels of communication within an organisation.

Informal communication is communication that is outside the official channels of communication within an organisation.

Verbal communication is communication by speaking – in meetings, by telephone, the use of video-conferencing.

Social media are online applications that allow people to create and share content to participate in social networking.

Website is an online location with several pages that can be contacted by internet users through its address.

Practice questions

Multiple choice questions

1 Which of these statements is false?

a) Digital communication involves the electronic transfer of information.

b) Mobile phones, computers and tablets are ways in which information can be transferred electronically.

c) Digital communication is always better than non-digital communication such as people coming together in meetings.

d) Digital communication has been a major force behind the globalisation of business activity.

2 Which of the following is always an advantage of meetings?

a) There is always a record of what has been said.

b) The sender of the message can always be seen as well as heard by the receiver.

c) The sender can check immediately with the receiver that they have understood the message.

d) It is a way of avoiding confrontation when the message is given.

3 Which of the following is **not** true about developments in digital communication?

a) It has helped to increase the globalisation of business activity.

b) The development of digital communication has benefited all workers.

c) The development of digital communication has increased competition between businesses often leading to lower prices for customers.

d) The development of digital communication has made it possible for some workers to work at home and while travelling.

Data response 18

Ryan and White Ltd is a small business that makes and sells upmarket, expensive wedding dresses. Ryan and White Ltd has shop premises in Formby, a town where the average income of people is well above the national average. It currently advertises by using a website and advertisements in local newspapers.

1 Explain two ways in which Ryan and White Ltd may use digital communications. (4 marks)

2 Evaluate the importance to Ryan and White Ltd of having a shop where sales staff can meet with customers. (3 marks)

How to answer data response 18

1 You need to choose two methods that are appropriate for this kind of business – consider who the customers are and what they want. You must suggest methods that are relevant to a wedding dress business, so think about who the customers are likely to be. Remember also that it is small-sized and that it sells expensive dresses, as these factors will affect what it can afford to do.

2 Again you need to focus on the nature of the business. Personal contact and being able to see and try on the product will be essential for most people buying a wedding dress.

Data response 19

Amazon is one the best examples of a business that benefited from the revolution in digital communication. It started as a bookseller in the 1990s and by introducing a website listing the books and then selling online, it did not need shops on the high street and so stored books in warehouses. Books were sold at cut prices. It sold to customers all over the USA and then expanded to other countries, including the UK. Amazon has always stressed good customer service and has efficiently run warehouses where, once ordered, books are located quickly and sent off to the customer by rapid delivery. It has also encouraged innovation. The invention of the Kindle e-reader is an example of how digital technology has introduced new products. Books no longer need posting and can be downloaded directly to the

Kindle. Nowadays, Amazon is a multinational giant selling a wide range of products.

1 Explain how product innovation has helped Amazon to grow. (2 marks)

2 Explain why Amazon was able to offer books 'at cut prices.' (2 marks)

3 Analyse how the digital technology helped Amazon to increase the size of its potential market compared to traditional, high street bookshops. (3 marks)

How to answer data response 19

1 Define 'product innovation'. Explain what a Kindle is and how people can download electronic books to them. Explain the advantages of this in terms of speed and cost, which are services that customers like.

2 Use the data in the case study. Explain how having a warehouse, perhaps on cheap land, would save money compared to having shops on the high street where rents may be high. Explain possible savings in wages as sales assistants are not needed, only workers in the warehouse to store and pack the books, and people controlling the website. Show that the costs of these workers could be spread across huge numbers of sales, which makes the cost per item sold low.

3 The key is to link your answer to the data and add your own knowledge about digital communications. Amazon was able to reach a larger market by advertising online. It created a website. This could be accessed by people from all over the USA. By offering delivery, Amazon could sell all over the USA and eventually all over the world. In comparison, there was no point in high street book sellers advertising much more widely than the local town because customers would not travel very far for books usually. This limited their market size.

UNIT 3.4 Recruitment and selection

Learning outcomes

By studying this unit, you will be able to:

- explain and evaluate why businesses recruit
- explain the different stages in the process of recruitment and **selection**
- explain what is included in **job descriptions** and **person specifications** and evaluate their use
- explain the difference between **internal** and **external recruitment**
- analyse the advantages and disadvantages of internal and external recruitment and evaluate the use of each
- analyse the advantages and disadvantages of the different recruitment methods and evaluate the use of each
- identify and explain the different methods of selecting from applicants for jobs
- analyse the advantages and disadvantages of the different methods of selection and evaluate the use of each.

The importance of recruitment for businesses

Read the following two case studies and then answer the questions in Activity 1.

Introductory case study: it costs over £30,000 to replace a staff member

Research carried out by Oxford Economics reveals that replacing members of staff incurs significant costs for employers: £30,614 per employee (but more for some such as Mario Balotelli). There are two main factors that make up this cost.

First is the cost of lost output during the time that a new worker gets up to speed with their job compared to the previous, experienced employee. On average the research says that it takes 28 weeks for a worker to get up to speed, so that is 28 weeks in which the worker is not as efficient as they could be. The report says that this will cost a business, on average, £25,181.

Second is the cost during the process of recruiting the employee. The costs include:

- hiring temporary workers before the replacement starts: £3,618
- management time spent interviewing candidates: £767
- recruitment agency fees: £454
- advertising the new role: £398
- time spent by human resources staff processing the replacement: £196
- total recruitment cost: £5,433.

Introductory case study: problems with Mario

Mario Balotelli.

Mario Balotelli is a wonderfully-gifted Italian football player. He was signed by Liverpool Football Club in September 2014 for a fee of £16 million. However, the football press reported a number of problems – which may or may not be true. José Mourinho, one of the most successful football managers and who had managed Mario, described him as 'unmanageable'. The press claims he has a history of falling out with managers and doing silly and dangerous things, such as setting off fireworks in his bathroom, and, as a result, setting his house on fire. More seriously, from a football point of view, allegedly, he has had fights with other players in the team and has not always tried his best on the pitch.

When he signed for Liverpool, Mario's contract required him to stick to a strict code of conduct or he would be disciplined and fined. It did not work out at Liverpool. He was judged to have rarely played to the level he was capable of. He scored only four goals in 28 games – a key measure of productivity for a striker – for Liverpool and only one of these was in a Premier League game. It was said that there was some resentment from other players in the team towards him. At the end of the season, Mario was loaned to AC Milan and when this loan finished he was sold. The general consensus was that Mario was an expensive mistake for Liverpool FC, a poor employee with a negative effect on the business. Mario, himself, might give a different story, of course.

The Oxford Economics report on page 121 recognises that costs will vary depending on the type of business, the location of the business and the type of worker required.

What do the two case studies tell you about the importance of recruitment for businesses?

Evaluation point

The message from the case studies is clear: successful recruitment is very important. Businesses need to appoint the right workers for the job because recruiting new staff costs a lot of money. The costs of recruitment will usually be higher for skilled workers than for unskilled workers so businesses should take care when appointing this kind of worker.

Activity 1 – Missing words activity

Use the words given below to complete the paragraph about the importance of recruitment and selection.

- expensive
- costs
- wasted
- interviews
- selection
- workers
- success
- methods.

Recruitment and ___ are very important to businesses. The ___ in a business make it successful or not. Recruiting new staff is ___ If good staff are not recruited by firms, money spent on the recruitment process is ___ Also the productivity of workers may fall, which may raise the ___ of the firm. For this reason, using correct recruitment and selection ___ is important. ___ are one way of finding out about people but they can give the wrong impression. Many firms now plan their recruitment and selection very carefully – employing good workers can be the difference between ___ and failure for a business.

Why businesses recruit

There are three main reasons why businesses recruit new workers.

First, because the firm is starting up or growing. A new business must recruit workers from scratch. A business that is getting increased orders or making more sales may decide to increase its production and so it needs to employ more workers.

Second, to replace staff who leave. Staff leave a job for all kinds of reasons – for promotion, retirement, to do something different or because they have been sacked.

Third, the business may have a skill shortage. Recruiting skilled workers can be very difficult, particularly if the economy is doing well and there are lots of businesses all looking to fill a **skills gap**. It is not unusual for businesses to have to look abroad when recruiting skilled workers. Larger, well-known companies usually find it easier to attract new workers but small and medium businesses, particularly those outside the main population centres, can struggle to recruit. Recruiting engineers is a real problem in the UK as there are simply not enough people graduating with engineering degrees who then want to work in industry. Businesses like Jaguar Land Rover and Dyson have invested heavily in staff development to fill their skills gaps but still cannot recruit sufficient workers from the UK.

Activity 2 – Evaluation activity

With reference to the case studies about Mario Balotelli (page 122) and the costs of replacing staff (page 121) and any other business you are familiar with, evaluate the importance to businesses of recruiting staff effectively.

The use of different recruitment and selection methods to meet different needs

In larger organisations, recruitment and selection is usually one of the jobs of the **personnel** or **human resources (HR) department**. In smaller businesses, the owner, or one of the partners, may have to do it.

The different parts of the recruitment and selection process followed by a business are as follows.

Recruitment

- **Analysis of human resource needs** – the business needs to decide the number and type of workers and when it needs to employ them. (See Unit 3.1.)
- Advertising a vacant job – the business needs to decide where to advertise the vacancy. This will depend on where the business is located, what type of worker it is looking for and how much it has to spend on advertising.

Selection

- Shortlisting – people interested in the job will show their interest by making an **application**. Businesses often ask for written information such as a **letter of application** and a **CV**. The business will use this information to choose which applicants it wants to find out more about. These applicants form the shortlist for the job.
- Selecting from the shortlisted candidates – the business will need to choose somehow between the candidates who apply for any post. Typically, this will involve **interviews**, **tests** or **group activities**, or a combination of these.

You will find more detail about selecting from applicants later in this unit.

Job description and person specification

There are two documents that are very useful to a business when recruiting new workers.

A job description lists the tasks and the responsibilities the worker must perform. Writing this helps the business to be clear about what work it wants the employee to do. It is also important for possible applicants because it helps them to decide if they are able to do the job and if they want to apply for it. Figure 3.5 below shows the job description for an administrator employed by Marston Children's Services Department.

A person specification states the knowledge, qualifications, experience, personal qualities and skills the worker will need in order to do the job. As with the job description, writing the person specification helps the business to be clear about what kind of person it should appoint and which selection methods to use. The possible applicants can decide if they have the skills and qualities needed and, if they decide to apply, it can help them to write their application. The image below shows the person specification for the administrator.

Activity 3 – Explanation activity

Draw up a job description and a person specification for one of the following:

a) a teacher of business

b) a job that you have done – the work experience or part-time employment that you have had

c) a job that a relative or friend does.

Compare your job description and person specification with those drawn up by a fellow pupil. Evaluate each other's work – what is good about it, how could it be improved and explain your suggestions?

Marston Children's Services Department Job Description

Post: Administrator, Functional Skills Project

Grade: 4

Responsible to: 14 – 19 Development Officer

Job purpose: To manage the accounts of the project and to provide administrative assistance support.

Main duties

1 To ensure that the accounts are up to date and readily available

2 To assist the 14 – 19 Development Officer in the preparation and presentation of reports.

3 To establish good working relationships with the partners in the project.

4 To carry out other duties that it would be reasonable to ask for.

Figure 3.5 Sample job description.

Marston Children's Services Department
Administrator, Functional Skills Project – Person Specification

Personal attributes required	*Essential/desirable*	*Method of assessment*
Qualifications		
Educated to Level 3 of the National Framework of Qualifications – A levels or Diploma	E	AF
Experience		
Managing accounts	E	AF/I
Taking minutes at meetings	D	AF/I
General adiministrative work	E	AF/I
Knowledge/skills/abilities		
Good interpersonal and communications skills,both spoken and written	E	AF/R/I
Ability to work as part of a team	E	R/I
Knowledge of managing budgets	E	AF/R/T
Computer literacy – setting up and using spreadsheets,databases,word-processing and presentation packages	E	AF/R/T
Special requirements		
Current driving licence	E	AF
Able to work unsociable hours	D	I
Flexible and adaptable	E	R/I
Methods of assessment: AF (Application form), R (Reference), I (Interview), T (Test)		

Figure 3.6 Sample person specification.

Internal or external recruitment

Businesses may choose whether to recruit internally or externally. This decision will influence where a business advertises the job (and the methods of selection it decides to use).

Internal recruitment is when a job is filled by someone who already works in the organisation. Methods used for advertising a job internally include:

- a noticeboard
- word of mouth, such as making announcements in staff meetings
- a company (in-house) magazine for the workers
- the firm's website
- social media used by workers
- emails to workers who might be interested in the job.

The advantages of internal recruitment methods are:

- It is often cheaper to advertise internally rather than externally.
- It may be quicker to recruit someone who is already employed within the organisation.
- The person appointed will already know about the organisation, its aims and objectives and its ways of doing things and **induction training** may not be needed, which will save money.
- The organisation can be confident, because the person appointed will be known well, that the person appointed will be suitable.
- It can be good for the morale of the workforce to give opportunities for promotion.

The disadvantages of internal recruitment methods include:

- Existing staff may not add new ideas to help the business to improve.
- There may not be many people who are able and willing to apply for the job so the choice is restricted.
- If an employee is promoted within the company some other workers may be jealous and it can cause resentment.
- The job of the person who is appointed to the post will probably need to be filled so then further recruitment is needed.

External recruitment is when the organisation fills a post with someone from outside the organisation. Media used for advertising a job externally are discussed on pages 128–9. There are many advantages of external employment, for example in the following situations:

- when the business is starting up
- when there is no one in the organisation who would be able to do the job i.e. there is a skills gap
- when someone with new ideas is required
- when it would cause unpleasantness between workers if the one of them was promoted
- when more workers are needed than the business currently employs.

The disadvantages of external recruitment methods are:

- It usually takes longer than recruiting internally.
- It usually costs more than recruiting internally because of, for example, the need for advertising and paying expenses for people attending the interview.
- The managers will not know external candidates as well as they know internal applicants and this increases the risk of appointing someone who is not suitable for the job.

Activity 4 – Explanation activity

For each case below, state whether you would recommend the use of internal or external recruitment and the method you would use. Give reasons for your choice. What problems, if any, may the firm have to deal with as a result of your recommendation?

a) The local council needs to appoint someone to cover for the office manager while she is on maternity leave. She is expected to be on leave for six months.

b) Computec Ltd assembles computers. Its production of computers has increased by 20 per cent in the past year and is expected to rise by a further 15 per cent in the coming year. It needs to employ one more technician.

Advertising vacant jobs

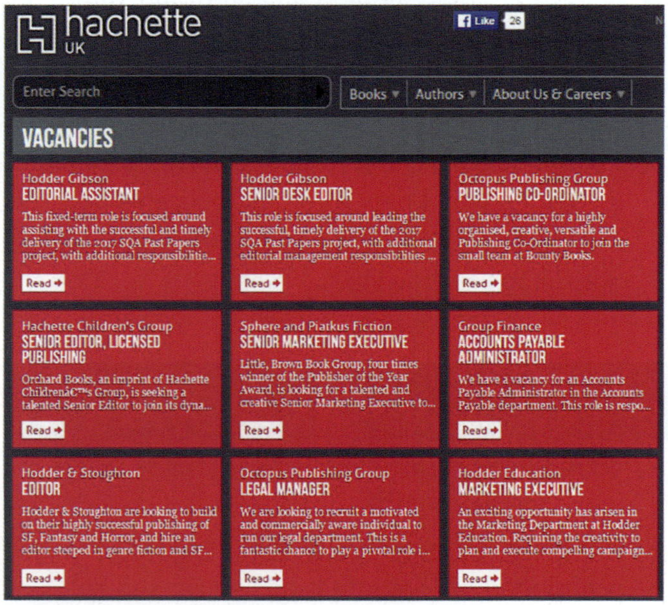

Advertising vacant jobs.

Designing the advertisement

Activity 5 – Explanation activity

Look at the following advertisement. Explain why it is not very good.

> Ingham's Catering Ltd
>
> Clerical Assistant required
>
> *Start as soon as possible*
>
> ***Contact:* John Meeks**

The advertisement for the job advertised in Activity 5 does not give potential applicants enough information. If people apply who do not have the necessary qualifications, skills and experience it will waste their time – as well as that of workers at Ingham's, who will have to read the applications and write back to these applicants to tell them that they have not got the job. It is important that a job advertisement contains information that will encourage people with appropriate skills and experience to apply and it must tell potential applicants how to apply. The design of the advertisement is important as it has to catch the attention of the potential applicant.

The following information may be included in a job advertisement:

- duties or tasks
- qualifications needed
- experience needed
- salary details
- description of work
- hours of work
- place of work
- training opportunities
- future prospects
- contact address
- details of how to apply for the job.

Activity 6 – Explanation activity

Embassy Caravans makes folding trailer tents. The business was set up in 1953. It now needs to recruit a production worker to work in the factory making the tents. All production workers need to be able to do some woodwork, welding and sewing of materials. The basic pay will be between £20,000 and £25,000 per year, depending on experience. Overtime is available when the factory is busy. The address is Unit 10, Industrial Estate, Ormkskirk L31 5XY. The telephone number is 01695 558899. Applicants will be expected to telephone for a discussion about the job and to ask for an application form.

a) Draw up an advertisement for this post. You should use some of the information provided but you do not have to use it all. The advertisement will go in the local newspaper, which charges according to the number of words – so keep the number of words to a minimum.

b) Explain why the firm would ask people to telephone for a discussion about the job before sending out an application form.

c) Write a short explanation as to why you have included each piece of information in the advertisement.

d) If possible, use a computer to create the advertisement.

Deciding where to advertise

Case study: Indeed.co.uk and Reed.co.uk advertising online

Indeed and Reed.

Indeed.co.uk is widely used for advertising jobs. 'Indeed' offers 'organic' and 'sponsored jobs.' Sponsored jobs are the first jobs that people will see when they do a job search online and those that are not sponsored are organic jobs. There is no fixed fee for sponsored advertising but instead a charge is made for every time someone clicks on the job that a business has advertised. The cost of each click is between 12 pence and 70 pence. A higher cost per click guarantees a greater prominence of the advertisement on the website. People interested in jobs can post their CVs on the Indeed website and businesses can search the CVs of people on the website. There is no charge for this. A business can also get 'alerts' when people post new CVs that are relevant to their search criteria. Indeed charges £1 to permit a business to contact relevant candidates.

Another website for advertising jobs is Reed.co.uk. Reed charges £159 for advertising a job for a six-week period. The company will also email the advertisement to the best 100 people whose CVs match the requirements for the job. Reed will send on applications to the business free of charge.

(Charges quoted were current at the time of writing, you can find up-to-date charges by searching reed.co.uk and indeed.co.uk.)

Case study: the increasing use of social media in recruiting and selecting staff

A report by Jobvite shows that 40 per cent of businesses recruiting staff use social media – a percentage that is expected to grow. Facebook is the most widely used social medium for recruitment. LinkedIn is also widely used. At first, social media were used for checking what people were like:

- to find out if they had a positive social media profile
- to find out whether they could use grammar and spell correctly
- to check they were not communicating about things that might be considered inappropriate such as consuming (a lot of) alcohol or using drugs.

However, businesses are now using social media for advertising posts and inviting applicants for interview.

Adapted from The Independent, *30 September 2015*

When a business advertises a job, it needs to think about a number of things:

- whether it will recruit internally or externally
- the type of worker required
- the number of workers needed
- the location of the work
- the amount of money the organisation has available to spend on advertising for workers.

The table below lists the media that can be used to advertise a job externally (note that the first two of these methods could be used for interval recruitment also, along with word of mouth and the company noticeboard). It also gives examples of when each of the media might be used.

Medium	Description	Job examples
Websites (other than social media)	Firms recruiting workers can use their own websites or advertise on specialist sites specifically set up to advertise jobs including, for example, indeed.co.uk and monster.co.uk. Applicants can get 'alerts' from these sites about jobs they might be interested in. Applicants can search for jobs by type, salary and location.	These websites are now very commonly used and for all kinds of jobs, both local and national. Information about the jobs is accessible nationally.
Social media	These are websites and applications that can be used to provide information about jobs and to find out about candidates.	Increasingly used for many kinds of jobs because of the wide use of social media and the information that can be discovered about applicants.
Local newspapers	These usually contain a jobs section that local people would know to look in. It is not usually expensive to advertise in these. There may also be newspaper websites that are used to advertise jobs.	Local newspapers can be useful when the business knows that there are people in the local community who will be able and willing to do the job. Jobs for hairdressers, carers, restaurant and local council workers are often advertised in local papers.

Medium	Description	Job examples
National newspapers	These may contain sections and supplements for advertising jobs. It is usually more expensive to advertise in national rather than local newspapers. Like local newspapers, the national paper may have its own website on which jobs can be advertised. Advertising in both local and national newspapers has declined as the use of the internet and social media has increased.	National advertising is often used when a business wants to recruit skilled workers and there may be a shortage in the local community.
Specialist magazines (for example, the *Times Educational Supplement* (jobs in education) and *The Lancet* (for doctors))	These magazines, often now also available online, will contain articles of interest to specific types of workers who will also be aware that jobs will be advertised in them. Often the magazine will have a website where jobs are advertised.	Specialist magazines (and their websites) are often used to recruit highly skilled workers such as consultants, doctors, engineers, scientists and personnel staff.
Job centres	These centres are run by the government. They let people use computers to search for jobs.	They are very useful for people who might not be able to access the internet in any other way. They are also useful for people who need advice about searching and applying for jobs.
Word of mouth	The business lets existing employees know that there is a job available and hopes that some of them will tell people they know about the job.	This is useful when the business is looking for people who will live locally. If successful, it saves the cost of advertising.

Table 3.15 Media used to advertise jobs.

Methods of selection

When an organisation needs to find out information about the people who apply for jobs, they will often use more than one method to do so. The methods of selection process may be divided into two stages. First, the organisation may want to draw up a shortlist of applicants, and to do this it may use letters of application, application forms and CVs. Those shortlisted are the applicants who will be invited to the next stage of the selection process. At this stage, sometimes called the 'final stage of selection', it might be enough just to interview the candidate. However, other methods such as tests, presentations and group activities are often used for jobs that require a lot of skill. Of course, the information that had been used for shortlisting may be used again at this stage.

References may be called for from an applicant's employer or someone of authority who knows them well enough and can provide useful information about them.

Activity 7 – Explanation activity

Recommend suitable media to use to advertise the jobs given below. In each case give reasons for your recommendations. Note that there may be no single correct answer; you may want to recommend more than one medium.

a) Bowton Hospital wishes to appoint a doctor who is a cancer specialist.

b) A large, multinational sports clothing firm needs to employ an experienced sales manager to head its European section.

c) The supermarket in Marston needs to appoint three part-time check-out staff.

Method	Description	Advantages
Letter of application	A letter written by the applicant explaining why they believe they are suitable for the post.	Letters are good for showing a person's communication skills, including their use of punctuation and grammar, as well as giving them an opportunity to write about their experience and their qualities.
Application form	Applicants provide information in answer to questions on a form. The form has spaces for specific information to be written.	The business can make sure that all applicants supply the type of information it requires so it can make easy comparisons.
CV (curriculum vitae)	The applicant writes down personal details such as their address, qualifications, employment history and names of referees. The CV may include a section about their ambitions and why the applicant feels they are suitable for the post.	A CV shows the ability of the applicant to organise information. It is, or should be, easy for the business to see essential details about the applicant at a glance.
Interviews	The applicant meets people from the firm for a discussion. Often the interviewers will ask all the candidates the same series of questions and then compare the answers that they give. Sometimes the candidates may be interviewed as a group.	The employer sees the candidates and can judge how well they present themselves and communicate and how well they are likely to get on with other workers. Group interviews are very useful for seeing how people might get on in a team.
Tests and presentations	The applicant may be given a pencil and paper test or a practical test. The candidate may have to present ideas they have for the job.	These tests give very specific information, such as how good the applicant is at mathematics, typing or using equipment. A presentation can show how well a candidate can communicate and what ideas they have.
Group activities	A group of people who have applied for a job may be asked to work together on some kind of task. It may be a practical task (they have to make or do something) or it might be, for example, that they have to discuss a problem together to produce a solution to it.	Group activities can reveal a lot about a person. For example, they are good for seeing how well people work with others (their inter-personal skills) and for seeing who has good practical skills and ideas.
References	Someone who knows the applicant well provides information about their personal qualities, what work they did and how well they did it. They may provide or comment on their attendance and punctuality records and any other information that may be relevant to the post. It may be written by the applicant's current employer or by someone in a responsible position in society.	References can be very honest assessments that can recommend whether someone should be appointed or not. Sometimes, though, firms give employees good references because they want them to leave!

Table 3.16 Sources of information about applicants and the advantages of these.

Sixty words per minute? More like sixty mistakes per minute!

Evaluation point

Selecting who to employ from a number of applicants can be really tricky. One of the main problems is assessing how good the information is that has been gathered about each applicant. Sometimes applicants tell lies about what they have done, perhaps on their CV, or in a letter of application, or during an interview; referees give incorrect information in a reference in support of an applicant. For this reason, organisations often use more than one source of information and try to build up a true picture of what the person is capable of by piecing the information together. Even so, it often comes down to the gut instinct of the recruiters.

Activity 8 – Role play activity

a) Plan an interview for a job. Choose either the job of Administrator for the Functional Skills Project advertised by Marston's Childrens' Service Department using the information from page 124, or the job that you wrote about in Activity 3. Using the information in the job description and the person specification, write down some questions that you would ask.

b) Carry out the interview. One of the people in the class will need to volunteer to be the applicant. The applicant may need some time to prepare their answers.

c) Discuss what was good about the interview and what could have been better. For example, what information did you get that you needed? What further information do you need to make a decision about whether the person would be suitable or not? How would you change the interview? What other sources of information would you use?

Activity 9 – Explanation activity

For each of the situations described below, recommend how the organisation should get information about applicants for the job. You may recommend more than one source. Give reasons for your recommendations. Each of the organisations expects to receive a large number of applicants for the jobs.

a) Homesafe Insurance plc requires experienced clerks able to use spreadsheets to keep financial data, word-processing for writing letters and electronic presentation software for creating presentations.

b) Bowton Borough Council requires five road sweepers for the summer period when the town is busy.

c) Abbey Homes Ltd builds and sells houses in most regions in the UK. Sales have been poor for the past two years compared with other house builders. The firm needs a marketing director with responsibility for sales throughout the country.

Activity 10 – Zone activity

Complete the flow chart below by putting the terms about recruitment and selection next to the appropriate stage in the process. The first one, interviews, has been done for you.

- interview
- letter of application
- job centre
- national newspaper
- number of employees
- CV
- specialist magazine
- application form
- type of employee
- references
- job description
- tests
- website
- when the worker will work
- word of mouth
- local newspaper
- person specification

Stage	Terms
Analysis of human resource needs	
Advertising the post	
Shortlisting	
Final stage of selection	interview

Table 3.17 Recruitment and selection flow chart.

Recruitment agencies

The use of **recruitment agencies** for external recruitment has increased dramatically in the UK in recent years. (See the POWERpeople case study in Unit 3.2.). These agencies will do a lot of the work involved in recruiting and selecting staff. For example, if a firm wants to appoint a new sales manager, it may discuss its needs with a **recruitment agency**. The agency will draw up a job description and a person specification in consultation with the firm, and it will then advertise for applications from interested people. From these applications, it may recommend a small number of people it thinks are most suitable for the job. The firm may then interview the people recommended before finally deciding which one to appoint.

Using a recruitment agency saves time and money if it reduces the number of people employed in the firm's human resources department. The recruitment agency is a specialist organisation and will know how and where to advertise the post, as well as what kind of information will be needed about the applicants in order to decide which of them to employ.

Employment agencies

These agencies keep lists of people who are willing to do certain kinds of work – for example, lists of receptionists or office typists. A firm may ask the agency to provide a worker for a short period of time. The firm pays the wage of the worker and the **employment agency** also receives a payment. Sometimes, if the worker is good, the firm will offer the temporary worker a full-time post. This is a good way of recruiting staff because it gives the firm a chance to get to know how good the person is. However, the agency may then ask for an extra fee for introducing the worker to the firm as it had recruited the person in the first place! This fee can be quite a lot of money.

Key facts

Workers are very important to businesses. They are often the most important resource in a business.

Although expensive, it is often worth taking time and trouble over recruitment.

An analysis of the human resources needs of the business helps the firm to be absolutely sure about what kind of person they need to recruit and what that person will do.

It is important to advertise the job correctly so that the firm gets applications from people who can and are willing to do the job.

A lot of jobs are now advertised on websites or using social media.

When selecting who to employ from a number of applicants, firms often use more than one source of information about them.

Sometimes firms can save time and money by employing recruitment agencies to recruit and select staff on their behalf.

Sometimes firms prefer to employ temporary staff from employment agencies rather than take on full-time workers.

Useful words

Selection is the process of choosing between applicants for a job.

Job description lists the main duties, tasks and responsibilities of a worker.

Person specification lists the qualities, qualifications and knowledge that a person should have to do a particular job.

Internal recruitment is when a job vacancy is filled by employing someone who is already an employee of the business.

External recruitment is when a job vacancy is filled by employing someone from outside the business.

Personnel or **human resources department** is the department in a business that deals with the recruitment and selection of workers, with pay and other employment matters.

Analysing HR needs is when the organisation decides how many and what type of workers it should employ.

Induction training is training to introduce a new worker to the business, place of work and their fellow workers as well as their job.

Recruitment agency is a specialist agency that carries out all the tasks involved in recruitment and selection of workers on behalf of an organisation.

Employment agency is an agency that has workers readily available for business hire, usually for a short period of time.

Skills gap is when the business recruits skilled workers because it is short of them.

Internal methods of recruitment include notice boards, word of mouth, company website and emails to staff.

External methods of recruitment include websites, newspapers, social media and specialist magazines.

CV is a document on which the applicant outlines their personal details, experience and skills.

Application form is a form which asks applicants for personal details, experience and skills.

Letter of application is a letter written by the applicant usually explaining why they think they are suitable for the job.

Interviews are sessions in which the people making the appointment ask questions of the applicants.

Tests are activities completed by applicants which check their skills.

Group activities are usually designed to test how well an applicant works with others.

References are statements from a previous or current employer or other responsible person about the suitability of the applicant for the job.

Practice questions

Multiple choice questions

Danielle Smith runs BWHF Ltd. The franchise sells bottled water to organisations in the Bowton area. She needs to recruit a worker to help with the delivery of the water and to act as a salesperson.

1 Which of the following items should Danielle include in a job description?
   - a) The person must deliver water to the customers.
   - b) The person must have a clean driving licence.
   - c) The person has to have good communication skills.
   - d) The person must have good inter-personal skills.

2 Which of the following items should Danielle write in the person specification for the job?
   - a) The person should collect empty bottles from customers.
   - b) The person is responsible for finding new customers.
   - c) The person will be punctual and reliable.
   - d) The person will keep records of customers visited.

3 Danielle has decided to advertise a job on the website indeed.co.uk. Indeed will charge 60 pence per click and £1 for each time BWHF Ltd contacts an applicant. 350 people clicked on the advertisement and BWHF Ltd contacted 16 people who had posted CVs. How much did it cost BWHF Ltd to advertise the job?
   a) £226 b) £262 c) £622 d) £662.

Data response 20

The Met Office, which provides weather forecasts, wants to appoint an executive personal assistant. The person appointed would provide administrative support such as arranging meetings and booking accommodation and transport for two directors of the Met Office. The Met Office wants to appoint someone with experience of working as a PA. The premises of the Met Office are in Exeter in Devon. The job is permanent and full-time, and will pay £20,400 per year. The person appointed will need to be polite and tactful, have excellent organisational and time-management skills, good typing skills and be familiar with Microsoft Word, Excel and Outlook software.

1 Explain two advantages of using external recruitment methods for this job. (4 marks)

2a) Explain one possible advantage of advertising this job on a recruitment website. (3 marks)

2b) Explain one possible advantage of advertising this job in a national newspaper. (3 marks)

2c) Recommend whether the Met Office should use a recruitment website or a national newspaper to advertise the job. Give reasons for your recommendation. (3 marks)

3 Recommend two methods of selection that the Met Office should use to select from short-listed candidates for the job. Give reasons for your recommendation. (7 marks)

How to answer data response 20

1 Choose two possible advantages of external recruitment and write at least one point about each to explain why it would be an advantage when recruiting for this job.

2a) Choose one possible advantage of using a website and write at least two points to explain why it would be an advantage to use a website to advertise this job.

2b) Choose one possible advantage of using a national newspaper and write at least two points to explain why it would be an advantage to use a national newspaper to advertise this job.

2c) Make a recommendation and justify it. You must say why one medium is better than the other. You can mention the advantages that apply to one of the media compared to the advantages or disadvantages of the other.

3 Choose the two methods of selection and justify them by saying how the Met Office recruiters would be able to find out from them about the skills and qualities that are needed for the job (as indicated in the case study).

UNIT 3.5 Motivation and retention

Learning outcomes

By studying this unit, you will be able to:

- define the terms **motivation** and 'retention'
- explain each of the financial and non-financial methods of motivation
- explain the importance of motivation and retention to businesses
- explain how businesses may use financial and non-financial methods of motivation
- perform calculations connected with financial methods of motivation
- analyse and evaluate the benefits and costs of motivation and retention
- evaluate methods of motivation.

Introductory case study: the benefits of motivation at Aldi

Aldi.

Aldi Says:

'We believe in creating a culture where employees feel valued and have pride in their work. Engaged employees are more productive ... Unhappy employees tend to leave quickly, so turnover is another important measure of employee satisfaction ... our UK turnover of Store Managers in 2017 is only 9 per cent.

Our Employment Satisfaction Survey results are market-leading, putting us at the very top of the industry.'

From aldi.co.uk/corporate responsibility/people

Motivation

Motivation is the encouragement given to workers to work well. A motivated worker will feel responsible, fulfilled and happy in their work.

The importance of employee motivation and retention

Motivation is all about improving the performance of workers. Well-motivated workers bring several key benefits to firms and these are discussed below.

- **High employee performance** – workers are efficient in what they do because they gain rewards for good quality work.
- **High retention and low turnover of workers** – workers are happy to continue working for the employer because they are rewarded and feel valued.
- **Ease of recruitment of new workers** – if a firm needs to recruit new staff, good motivation will make this easier. The firm will gain a good reputation for the way it treats its staff and this will attract applications from workers who want

to work there. The firm is more likely to have a range of applicants to choose from which should help it to recruit good-quality staff.

- **Less need for the supervision of workers** – motivated staff need less supervision. They will be focused on their work, therefore improving their performance. This will save on the costs of paying people to supervise other workers.
- **Low absenteeism** – motivated staff will be absent less often. They will want to be at work to earn their rewards or because they enjoy being at work. Absenteeism costs money if firms have to pay sick pay and no products are being made by the workers.
- **Reduced waste of raw materials** – motivated staff will want to produce good quality work. This will reduce waste because fewer goods will not be up to standard.
- **Better delivery of services** – staff who deliver services will want to do this better, leading to fewer complaints and more satisfied customers who are more likely to buy again in the future.
- **Increased custom** – due to the improved quality of goods and services, custom is increased, making the business more successful.

Retention

Retention refers to workers staying with a firm for a long period of time. Firms have a high **turnover of labour** when workers leave after only a short period of time and new workers need to be recruited. Poor retention and high turnover can cause problems.

First, there is the cost of recruiting and selecting staff, which can be very expensive. Second, retained workers are familiar with the business and its customers. This helps production to be more efficient and also it helps to provide better service to customers because of the knowledge the worker has. If a new worker has to be recruited, they may need training to know the job and that can be very expensive. Research suggests that for some workers it can cost as much as 50 per cent to 60 per cent of their annual salary to replace them. A firm that pays a worker £40,000 a year could save £20,000 to £24,000 by motivating them to stay.

Third, if there is a stable staff team in a business, it is often good for morale. It means that people are happy in their place of work and get on well with other workers. In turn, this can help performance as happy workers tend to be motivated and willing to work with colleagues to produce good work. Finally, low turnover is often an indication to potential recruits that the business is a good place to work and this will make it easier, and probably cheaper, for the business to recruit new workers when they are needed.

Evaluation point

Are the costs of motivation worth paying?

There may be costs for motivation. For financial methods of motivation, the firm must use money to reward its workers rather than adding this to profits for the benefit of the owners. Some managers will need paying to manage the motivation system, deciding which workers should be given rewards, how much each one should be given and then arranging for this to be given. The managers who decide on rewards will need to do this fairly as workers may be de-motivated if they do not receive rewards while others do, unless it is clear and seen to be fair why the rewards were given.

Whether or not a motivation system is worthwhile will depend on how effective it is in improving the performance of workers, increasing retention, reducing supervision, absenteeism, waste and increasing sales compared to how much it costs. It is possible that the benefits in terms of higher productivity and reduced production costs may pay for the costs of the methods of motivation used. Good motivation should improve the competitiveness and profitability of the business.

Activity 1 – True or false activity

Place a tick next to each of the statements to indicate whether they are true or false.

Statement	True	False
If a worker improves productivity, they will produce more than they used to in the same amount of time.		
If workers in a car factory improve their productivity, the cost of producing each car will fall.		
Motivated workers will always want to leave the business to work elsewhere.		
Training costs will usually fall if staff turnover is high.		
Increased motivation reduces costs because workers are less likely to be absent.		
Motivated workers need a lot of supervision to make sure they work hard.		
Increased motivation saves on training costs because workers are likely to remain working for the firm for longer and fewer new recruits are needed.		
Motivated workers may help to reduce business costs because they will take pride in working accurately, so reducing waste.		
Motivation systems can be expensive as managers need to be paid to run them.		
Financial methods of motivation increase total business costs.		
Motivating workers always reduces the average costs of producing goods and services.		

Table 3.18 True or false motivation.

Methods of motivation

All workers need enough money so that they can buy the basic necessities – food, clothing and shelter – for themselves and for their families. However, many other factors will also encourage workers. Workers will be more motivated if they are safe at work, if they feel they are part of a team, if they get status that raises their self-esteem or if they feel that their talents are being challenged and used fully.

The following quotes are from people who have worked at the sports retailer, Sports Direct. They are interesting because they are from two people working for the same organisation but who have different views about the business. The first is from a cleaner, the second from a salesperson working in one of the Sports Direct shops.

'I was happy to be a part of a small team of cleaners making sure the shop was fit for custom before the doors opened every morning. The management were down to earth and regularly discussed ways to improve in certain areas as opposed to ordering me about.'

'Worst place to work. First week was okay but after that it just did not make you want to go. They put so much pressure on the staff and expect you to do more than what you are supposed to. Even the pay I had problems with as someone did not put my bank information right and the manager could not care less to get that fixed. Not the greatest experience.'

From: www.indeed.co.uk

Evaluation point

The quotes above show that people who work in the same business can have very different experiences. Different workers need motivating in different ways. The appropriate method of motivation will depend on what kind of work they do. Whether the method of motivation is effective or not may depend on how well it is implemented by the managers and on the personalities of the workers.

Methods of motivation can be divided into two categories:

- financial methods of motivation
- non-financial methods of motivation.

Financial methods of motivation

Figure 3.8 shows four methods of motivating workers that involve paying money to them.

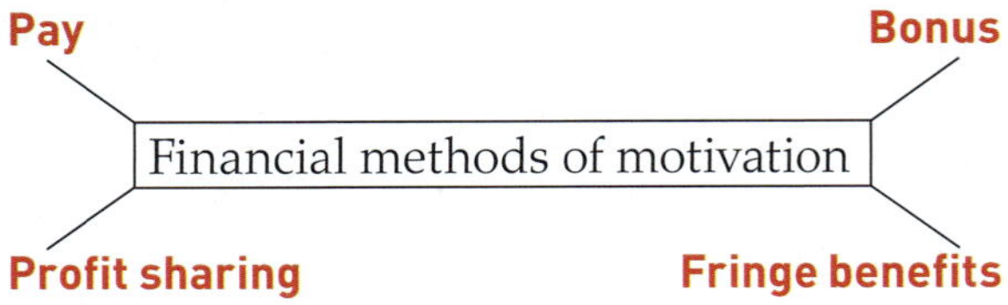

Figure 3.8 Financial methods of motivation.

The following four case studies are examples of the financial methods of motivating workers.

Case study: Ikea raises pay

In 2016, Ikea decided to raise the rates of pay for 7,300 employees. Some employees got a pay rise because Ikea introduced the Living Wage Foundation recommended rate of £8.25 per hour outside London (well above the National Living Wage, which was £7.20 at the time). Other employees received a pay rise so that their pay remained proportionately higher than those who received the Living Wage Foundation rate.

The HR manager at Ikea said that motivating workers was good for the business as it helped to retain workers and to attract new ones who would be needed as the business expanded. He also said that Ikea would be able to provide a better experience for customers as a result.

Case study: profit-sharing at American Airlines

American Airlines.

Five per cent of the profit that American Airlines makes before tax is put into a pool of money. This is then shared among employees. The workers receive this share of profit on top of the hourly rates of pay. American Airlines believes the profit-sharing scheme helps the business because workers will work hard to make the company profitable knowing that they will benefit. In the end, this benefits the shareholders when receiving dividends, as well as the workers.

Case study: motivation at McDonald's

McDonald's employees.

Every month, McDonald's gives a bonus to employees who work in the top ten per cent of its restaurants. McDonald's has 400 restaurants the UK. The top ten per cent are decided on the basis of reports from mystery shoppers who visit the shops pretending to be ordinary customers but who are checking that staff are working as they should. Store managers also get a bonus that is linked to mystery shopper scores, sales growth and profitability.

Case study: Travis Perkins' fringe benefits

Travis Perkins.

Travis Perkins is a timber and building merchant. The company offers a wide range of fringe benefits to its workers.

A generous contribution to the employee's pension is made, with the amount depending on the seniority and length of service. Workers can also receive private medical insurance and discounted gym membership. Share 'buy-as-you earn' schemes are open to all employees. There is also a company car scheme and a subsidised bike-buying scheme. Travis Perkins offers childcare vouchers and an enhanced maternity scheme.

The table below summarises the main methods of financial motivation.

Pay	How it might work	Pay motivates workers because it enables them to buy the goods and services that improve their standard of living. Pay is also important in retaining workers. If competitor firms offer better pay for the same work, workers will leave. Competitive pay rates also help to attract new employees. Workers will feel valued if they are paid well and will be motivated to do their job well and give a good level of service – just like the workers at Ikea.
	Salary	Two basic methods of pay are salary and wages. Salary is when a worker receives a set amount for a year's work, usually paid out in 12 equal monthly payments. Salaried workers are often motivated by the possibility of promotion and the higher salaries attached to more senior jobs.
	Wage	A wage is usually a weekly system of pay. One way of deciding how much a worker's wage will be is a time-rate system of pay. This is when workers receive a certain amount for each hour worked. The longer the person works, the more they will receive. To calculate the weekly pay of a shop assistant who works a 40-hour week and is paid on an hourly rate of £9 the following sum would be used:
	Example calculation	Number of hours worked times hourly rate = total pay for the week. This would be: 40 x £9 = £360

	Problems	Pay is a business cost. High costs may reduce profits. A disadvantage of time-rate pay is that it does not depend on how much or the quality of work done in the time. Without some kind of additional reward, wages and salaries may not motivate workers very well.
Profit-sharing	How it might work	The American Airlines scheme is typical of how profit-sharing schemes work. In a profit-sharing scheme, a business usually sets aside a proportion of profits which is then shared out in some way among its workers. The bigger the profit that the company makes, the greater will be the sum to be shared out. This will encourage their workers to work harder.
	Example calculation	An example calculation for a profit-share scheme and how it might be shared out is shown below: Total profit of the business: £5 million Percentage to be shared out: 10% Amount to be shared out: £5 million ÷ 100 x 10 = £500,000 Number of workers: 160 Amount of profit for each: £500,000 ÷ 160 = £3,125 per worker.
	Problems	Shareholders may feel that money is being taken away from the dividends they might earn on their shares but if the profit-sharing scheme works, the overall profits may increase so much that dividends rise even once a share of the profits has been given to the workers. (See Unit 1.3 Business ownership.) Pay is a cost. High costs may reduce profits.
Bonus	How it might work	Bonuses are payments that workers receive on top of their pay. They are a kind of performance-related pay. A bonus payment will be triggered by some measurable level of performance. This might be a salesperson or team reaching a target level of sales, production line workers reaching or exceeding a target level of output or the business achieving a target level of profits. As for some of the employees at McDonald's, awarding a bonus might depend on the quality of service provided.
	Example calculation	An example calculation for a bonus is: Total bonus available: £100,000 for a team of 40 workers who reach a target level of output Bonus per worker: £100,000 ÷ 40 = £2,500
	Problem	Targets need to be realistic or workers will not be motivated to achieve them.
Fringe benefits	How they might work	These are benefits other than money that a worker may receive on top of their pay. A major benefit is when the firm contributes money into a pension scheme for its workers. From April 2016, it became compulsory for all firms to offer a contributory pension scheme. Other benefits include: a car allowance, childcare vouchers, private medical insurance, share-buying schemes and subsidised canteen meals.
	Problem	Fringe benefits are a cost to the business that may reduce profits.

Table 3.19 The main methods of financial motivation.

Evaluation point

Using financial methods to motivate workers will cost the business money. However, this cost could be covered by lower average costs of production and increased revenues. The type of financial method to be used would depend on the type of worker to be motivated.

Activity 2 – Calculation activity

For each of the following:

a) state the method or methods of pay being used to reward each of the following workers

b) state the amount of pay that each worker would receive in the given time period.

- Angus Deade receives £6 per hour and works a 35-hour week. In May, he worked four weeks. He also worked 12 hours of overtime at time and a half.
- Fabrice N'gono is paid a basic salary of £800 per month to pack spices. The team he works with are entitled to share a bonus of £960 each month if they achieve the target number of packets. There are eight workers in the team including Fabrice.
- Alastair Munro is the managing director of a firm. He receives £80,000 per year. He is also paid two per cent of any profit that the company makes. In the last year, the company made £2 million in profit. He has a company car and is given free health insurance.
- Wasim Ikram earns a basic salary of £30,000 per year. In October, he received a bonus of 15 per cent of his salary when the output of the production department that he manages was 25 per cent greater than the target level.

Activity 3 – Explanation activity

For each of the following financial methods of motivation:

a) explain briefly how it works to motivate workers

b) explain one problem or disadvantage to a business of using that method.

Methods of motivation:

- pay
- profit-sharing
- bonus
- fringe benefits.

Non-financial methods of motivation.

These methods of motivation do not involve any payments of money or fringe benefits. Figure 3.9 shows three non-financial methods of motivation.

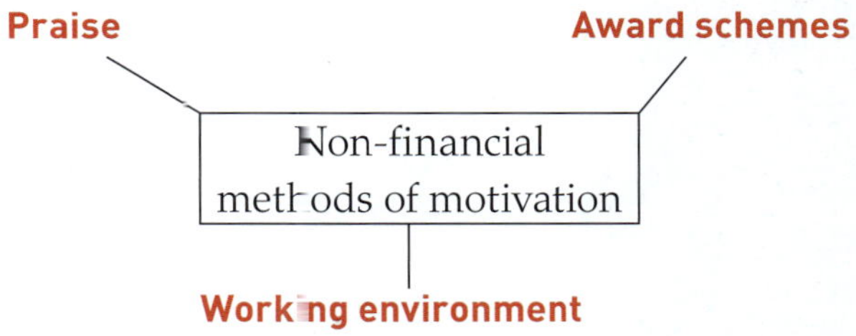

Figure 3.9 Non-financial methods of motivation.

Case study: praise and the Cartwright Group

Praise can be given in many ways.

Followers of football will notice how often, when a player comes off the pitch after having been substituted or at the end of a match, the manager will shake hands, hug or give the player a pat on the back. This demonstrates that praise is important, even for these often very highly-paid workers. It makes them feel valued and appreciated.

The Cartwright Group makes vehicle bodies and trailers. The company states its commitment to recognising apprentices who have received praise from their peers. Praise is generally given to apprentices for 'making a valuable contribution to the Cartwright manufacturing operation.'

Adapted from cartwright-group.co.uk

Case study: awards at Asda and McDonald's

When workers at Asda reach a monthly sales target, the worker is given a lapel badge. Workers at McDonald's restaurants are given stars when they do well, in order to recognise their competence. Workers are often proud to display the number of stars they have received.

Case study: the working environment at Alphabet

Alphabet provides maintenance services for fleets of vehicles owned by transport companies. One way in which Alphabet motivates its workers is by involving them in a range of activities. One of these is the company choir. The choir was a way of bringing together workers. Another is its APE (alphabet proactive experts) initiative. Workers can write suggestions on a blackboard about how to make the company a better place to work. Alphabet managers always respond to these suggestions, even when they are not adopted.

The table below summarises the main methods of non-financial motivation.

Praise	How it might work	The importance of managers giving praise to workers, formally as in the Cartwright Group or informally, should not be underestimated. A 'quiet word' of praise can make workers feel good because they know that their effort has been noticed and appreciated. Publicly praising a worker can raise the self-esteem of that worker as well as presenting an example to others of what the firm expects.
Award schemes	How they might work	These may be closely linked to praise. An award is a tangible way of recognising someone's effort. It might take the form of a 'worker of the month' notice in the staff newspaper or noticeboard or the presentation of a certificate at an award ceremony. Awards can take many forms. It could be a voucher for goods from the shop, a choice of Red Letter Days, a free holiday, a car or a wide range of other things. Even awards as simple as the lapel badges given at Asda and the stars at McDonald's can have a very positive effect on worker morale and productivity.
Working environment	How it might work	The safer a place of work is, and the more comfortable and pleasant the surroundings are, the more staff will be motivated. The working environment is also about the atmosphere created in the place of work. Do workers get on well with each other? Are their views respected and are they made to feel responsible for their work? Is there a 'can do' confidence about the workplace? Much of this will depend on how managers treat the workers, how they speak to them, whether they trust them or not and are willing to be flexible with them. All of this is about the culture of the business or the climate in the workplace. Sometimes businesses will do specific things to create a positive environment. For example, a firm may arrange an activity, such as a day of outdoor pursuits, to bond a group of workers as a team. Sometimes it is just about the way in which people are treated on a day-to-day basis. Alphabet has achieved a positive climate partly through the specific activity of a company choir, but also through the respect that workers are shown on a day-to-day basis.

Table 3.20 Non-financial methods of motivation.

Evaluation point

Non-financial methods of motivation may cost a business money, for example, to pay for awards and bonding activities and possibly in lost production if the worker is taken away from the job. However, they do not need to cost anything. They focus on relationships between workers – recognising and valuing workers who do good work and creating a positive attitude towards achievement.

Activity 4 – Explanation activity

For each of the following non-financial methods of motivation:

a) explain briefly, with the aid of an example, how it motivates workers

b) explain one problem or disadvantage to a business of using that method.

Methods of motivation:

- praise
- awards
- the working environment.

Activity 5 – Zone activity

Match the non-financial method of motivation listed below to the example given in the table. You need to use them more than once.

a) Praise for good workers.

b) Awards for good workers.

c) A positive working environment.

Examples of non-financial methods of motivation	Non-financial method of motivation
Some firms have an annual event when these are given out to workers to recognise their good work.	
This might involve consulting with workers to make them feel valued.	
This might just be a word of thanks over a coffee break, but it acknowledges good work by the worker.	
These might include certificates or gifts.	
This might be created by team-bonding sessions such as a firm's day out at the races.	
This might result from painting an office and putting new furniture in it to make the workers feel that they are being treated well.	

Table 3.21 Examples of non-financial methods of motivation.

Key facts

The motivation of workers can help to reduce the costs of a business and make it more competitive.

Pay is an important reward for workers.

Basic pay can be determined by the amount of time a worker works.

Bonuses, profit-shares and fringe benefits can be added to basic pay.

Workers can be motivated by things other than pay, for example, by feeling valued and having their efforts recognised.

Praise, awards and a good working environment all help to motivate workers.

Useful words

Motivation is how workers are encouraged to work hard.

Retention of workers is when workers choose to stay in a firm rather than move elsewhere.

Turnover of labour is a measure of the number or proportion of a staff who leave a firm each year and need replacing.

Productivity is a measure of output per worker. It is one way of measuring the performance of workers.

Pay is the money earned by workers as a reward for the work they do.

Profit sharing is when workers receive some of the profits made by a business.

Bonus is an additional payment to workers for achieving a target.

Fringe benefits are additional benefits that workers receive on top of their pay. They include pensions, childcare vouchers, subsidised canteen meals.

Praise is a method of motivating a worker by complimenting their work and so making their work recognised and valued.

Award scheme is a presentation of some kind to recognise somebody's effort.

Working environment is the quality of the physical workplace and its climate.

Practice questions

Multiple choice questions

1 A worker is paid £8 per hour for working a 35-hour week. On top of this, the worker is paid a bonus of 10 per cent of their wage for the week. Calculate how much the worker earned in the week.

- **a)** £280
- **b)** £282.80
- **c)** £308
- **d)** £420.

2 Which of these is a financial method of motivating workers?

- **a)** award
- **b)** praise
- **c)** a good working environment
- **d)** profit-sharing.

3 Which of these is a disadvantage of a method of motivating workers?

- **a)** an increase in some of the costs of the business
- **b)** increased retention of workers
- **c)** increased productivity of staff
- **d)** a reduction in absenteeism.

Data response 21

United Utilities supplies water and sewage removal services to households and businesses in the north-west of England. Some staff, such as the managers of the different departments and clerical and cleaning staff, work in its offices in the headquarters in Warrington. Other staff work in different parts of the north-west, for example, manual workers who dig up and repair water supply pipes underneath our roads. These manual workers work to tight deadlines to get their jobs done and to minimise disruption to traffic when they need to dig up roads. United Utilities offers the following to its workers:

- competitive salaries
- participation in a pension scheme
- free transport to work for some local workers
- bonuses for staff who exceed their targets.

United Utilities has a good reputation as an employer in the north-west of England.

1 State one financial method of motivation that United Utilities uses. (1 mark)

2 State one non-financial method of motivation that United Utilities uses. (1 mark)

3a) Analyse one possible advantage to United Utilities of paying a bonus to its workers. (3 marks)

3b) Analyse one possible disadvantage to United Utilities of paying a bonus to its workers. (3 marks)

3c) Recommend whether or not United Utilities should use bonuses when paying all staff. Give reasons for your answer. (3 marks)

How to answer data response 21

1 This question simply needs a statement of one financial method of motivation listed in the data.

2 This question simply needs a statement of one non-financial method of motivation listed in the data.

3a) This question needs a statement of the advantage and then a clear analysis of how this results from rewarding workers with a bonus.

3b) This question needs a statement of the disadvantage and then a clear analysis of how this results from rewarding workers with a bonus.

3c) This question needs a justification of whether the method of motivation is appropriate for United Utilities. You should consider other methods of motivation which might be suitable for some or all of the workers that United Utilities employs.

UNIT 3.6 Training and development

Learning outcomes

By studying this unit, you will be able to:

- define **training** and staff **development**
- identify and explain why businesses train their workers
- explain the different methods of training of workers – **on-the-job**, **off-the-job** and **induction training**
- analyse the advantages and disadvantages of different training methods to workers and to businesses
- evaluate why businesses train their workers and the use of different training methods
- explain different methods of development – apprenticeships and professional development, including vocational and academic development
- analyse and evaluate the benefits of staff development to businesses and to employees.

Introduction

Introductory case study: training as a barista at Starbucks

Starbucks.

Customers at Starbucks want their crema – that thin layer of foam on top of an espresso coffee – to be 'just right'. In fact, they want all of their coffees to be good whether it is a flat white, a cappuccino or an Americano. The baristas in coffee shops are the people with the responsibility for making and serving the coffees. Clearly, the success of Starbucks depends on the quality of its baristas. There are around 550 Starbucks shops in the UK. New baristas receive on-the-job training. An experienced barista will work with a new member of staff on a one-to-one basis, showing them how to make the different kinds of coffees that Starbucks sells.

Introductory case study: team development at Beaverbrooks jewellers

Beaverbrooks is a family owned jewellers established in 1919 with 71 stores across the UK. Their website makes this statement:

'We are very proud of our commitment to promoting from within at Beaverbrooks, and feel that it is vital to our mission to enrich people's lives. The management development programme is available to everyone and, through a programme of home study, accelerated learning and individual coaching, you will be enabled to achieve promotion to assistant branch manager, and onwards to branch manager.'

From beaverbrooks.co.uk

The difference between training and development

The difference between training and development is a quite fine distinction.

Training is more job specific and short term. It is about teaching the knowledge and skills needed to do a particular job. It is about preparing the employee to do a job or to improve their performance in the job that they do.

Development is about the overall growth of the worker, and is longer term. It is about teaching knowledge and skills that will be useful to the business and the employee at some time in the future. While the learning activities may seek to develop practical skills, there will also be a stress on the theoretical knowledge and understanding that the worker may need in future roles. Development is about improving the potential of an employee.

Both training and development can involve on- and off-the-job activities.

Activity 1 – Explanation activity

a) Read the case studies about Starbucks and Beaverbrooks.

Using the information from the case studies:

i) explain the difference between training and development

ii) write down the benefits that the workers may gain from training or development

iii) write down the benefits that the businesses may gain from training and developing workers.

b) Training and development costs money. Explain why it might have helped these firms to increase their profits.

Why businesses train their workers

Training is about developing the knowledge, skills and abilities of workers. Different kinds of workers need training for different reasons. Some of these are suggested below:

- **Technical skills** – workers may need to learn the skills to use machinery or to upgrade their skills to deal with new machinery.
- **Personal skills** – workers may need to develop personal skills such as communication skills.
- **Health and safety training** – this is provided to workers to reduce their risk of being injured at work. It can protect the business from expensive claims for compensation if it can show the worker was given the proper training.
- **Diversity in the workplace** – workers may need to be trained to deal with issues that can be very sensitive in the workplace. These will include, for example, racial, gender and disability discrimination.
- **Management skills** – workers may have been given a promotion or may be seeking promotion. They will have to learn the skills needed to manage other people, control budgets, solve problems and so on.
- **New workers** – they will need induction training to introduce them to the organisation.
- **Group working** – workers may need training about how to work together well and how to get the best out of each other.
- **Knowledge of new products** – workers may need to be trained on new products that they have to sell.
- **Flexibility** – a firm may want to provide workers with a range of different skills so that they can do different jobs.
- **Retraining** – a person may change jobs within a company, perhaps because a machine now does the job and they will need to develop new skills. Unit 3.3 explores developments in technology further.
- **Personal development** – this is about developing the person in ways that may not be connected directly to work. This can raise the worker's self-esteem, their ambitions and their motivation.

The table below summarises some of the ways in which businesses benefit from training workers to improve their knowledge, skills and abilities.

Benefit of training	Explanation
Development of the business	The business may be able to develop new products or services to keep it ahead of competitors or so that it can grow.
Improving **productivity**	Productivity is a measure of how much each worker produces. Improving productivity increases output per worker and will lead to lower costs. Lowering costs means the business can lower prices so it can increase sales and/or profits. (See Unit 3.3 Communication in business for examples of how digital communications can improve productivity.)
Solving skill shortages	Sometimes businesses need to recruit skilled workers – to replace workers who have left or because the business wishes to expand. The skilled labour required may not be available. Training its existing or new staff can help the business to deal with such skill shortages.
Improving **customer service**	Customer care is critical in competitive markets. It can increase sales because customers are made to feel welcome or because they get the information that they need about the goods or services they want to buy from properly trained staff.
Improving motivation and retention	Workers who receive training may feel valued by their employer and may see opportunities for progressing in the business. This may motivate them, which means they perform better, therefore increasing their productivity. It may also encourage workers to stay with their employers, so reducing the costs to the business of recruitment and training. (See Unit 3.5 Motivation and retention.)

Table 3.22 Benefits of training to businesses.

Activity 2 – Matching terms activity

The left-hand column of the table below gives business situations where people need training. Match the situation to the different training needs given in the right-hand column. You will need to explain your answers.

Situation	Training need
Business development	Annabel's, a hairdressing salon, has taken on a young trainee, Colin Wynne. Colin starts work next week. He needs to be told about the business, how he is paid, what he can do at lunchtime and other basic, practical matters.
New products	The owner of Annabel's hairdressing salon wants to extend the range of services it offers. She has taken a lease on the shop next door and will offer a range of beauty and therapy treatments. One of her assistant hairdressers – Jamelia – has shown a lot of initiative, and she has booked her on to a series of courses so that she knows how to provide the services when the shop opens.
Induction training	Hattersley Engineering Ltd is finding it difficult to recruit engineers for its plant in Shrewsbury. It has offered training opportunities to two technicians it employs, to make them fully-qualified engineers.
Motivation and/or retention	Ian Daly has been a machine operator at Lathom's Paints for 15 years. New machinery has been developed to do the work he did. The firm does not want to make him redundant. It has sent him on a training course to learn how to work in the warehouse.
Improving productivity	TechWorld Ltd provides training each week for sales assistants on the new computers and games consoles that it sells.
Solving skill shortages	Hudson Solicitors has bought new accounting software and has sent its two accounts staff on a one-day training course to find out how to use this. The software should mean that the accounts staff can do their work more quickly and, as the business takes on more work, it will not need to employ an additional accounts person.

Table 3.23 Situations and training needed.

Different training methods

This section looks at three types of training: on-the-job-training, off-the-job training and induction training.

On-the-job training

This training or development is done while the employee is working, as happens at Starbucks. The table below shows the advantages and disadvantages of on-the-job training.

Advantages	Disadvantages
■ The trainee is given individual training so it improves their performance.	■ The trainer may need to leave their work to help the trainee, so production may fall.
■ It is cheaper than off-the-job training because there are no travel or accommodation costs.	■ The quality of the work may not be very good if a trainee does it This could lead to wasted resources and/or a poor reputation for quality.
■ The trainee produces goods and services while training and so the firm earns money from their work.	■ The quality of the training depends on the skills of the trainer both as a worker and as a trainer. If the trainer has poor communication skills or is not very skilled at the job, the quality of the training may be poor.
■ The trainee is trained to do the job in the way that the firm wants it done.	■ The skills may be specific to that firm and this may make it difficult for the trained worker to find work in another firm. This may restrict the opportunities for the worker if they lose their job or want to gain promotion by moving.
■ The skills may be specific to that firm and this may make it difficult for the trained worker to find work in another firm. This can improve the retention of workers and ensure that the firm gets a return on the time and effort it spends on training.	■ The trainee does not usually gain any specific qualification from on-the-job training.
	■ Not suitable for groups of trainees, it is more effective in one-on-one situations.

Table 3.24 The advantages and disadvantages of on-the-job training.

Activity 3 – Zone activity

Read the statements below and decide which concerns the worker and which the employer. Write each one in the correct place in the table below. Some statements may apply to both the worker and the employer and can be used twice.

- The quality of the training depends on the skills of the trainer both as a worker and as a trainer. If the trainer has poor communication skills, the quality of the training may be poor.
- The trainee is given individual training to meet their needs to improve their performance.
- The worker produces goods and services while training, and so the firm earns money.
- The trainer may need to leave their work to help the trainee and so production may fall.
- The quality of the work may not be very good if a trainee does it. This could lead to wasted resources and/or a poor reputation for quality.
- It is cheaper than off-the-job training because there are no travel or accommodation costs.
- The skills may be specific to that firm and this may make it difficult for the worker to find work in another firm. This can improve the retention of workers and ensure the firm gets a return on the time and effort it spends on training.
- The worker does not usually gain any specific qualification from on-the-job training. The worker is trained to do the job in the way that the firm wants it done.

Advantages to the worker	Disadvantages to the worker

Advantages to the business	Disadvantages to the business

Off-the-job training

Off-the-job training is when employees are trained or developed away from their work. It might take place on the premises where the worker is employed but they will not be doing their normal job while they are receiving training. The following case study shows some of the kinds of off-the-job training available.

Case study: staff training in your own school

Teachers often go out of school for training and development – this is off-the-job training. For example, your teacher might go on a course organised by the examination board to find out about a new examination or go to a training organisation to find out about teaching strategies that can be used in business lessons. They may study for a professional qualification such as a master's degree or a leadership qualification at the National College for Teaching and Leadership. Your teacher will be able to give more ideas about the training teachers in your school receive.

Activities used in off-the-job training are:

Lectures

These are good for telling people about things, for giving information. They are not good for improving skills.

Demonstrations

The trainee watches someone show them how to do a job. These are good because you learn from an expert. It is often necessary to practise the work after the demonstration in order to develop the skills.

Role play or simulation

The worker experiences a situation as if it were a real work situation. The trainee practises the skills or practises how they would deal with the situation.

Team-building

A group performs tasks together in order to develop. It helps them to learn how to work well in teams and to appreciate the different qualities that other people have. The tasks might be connected to the work that the people do, but often they are not. Non-work connected activities can include outdoor pursuits such as climbing and raft-building, or they may be problem-solving activities.

Reading and reflecting on online materials

The worker may have access to training materials that are online. Usually there are tasks or exercises that the worker must do to develop their understanding of the materials.

Table 3.25 on page 151 shows the advantages and disadvantages of off-the-job training.

Activity 4 – Explanation activity

a) Explain the benefits of off-the-job training for workers.

b) Explain the benefits of off-the-job training for a business.

c) Explain the problems of off-the-job training for a business.

Advantages	Disadvantages
■ Experts may provide the training, making it high-quality. ■ The worker can use specially designed training equipment. ■ Workers often enjoy the change of environment. ■ Workers feel valued when the firm pays for them and gives them time to attend training courses. ■ The training is essential when the safety of workers and customers is a risk of the job.	■ Usually it is more expensive because of fees, travel and accommodation costs. ■ The absence from work means that the worker is not producing goods or services for the business when training. ■ There is a risk that the employee may want to leave the firm once they gain new skills and qualifications.

Table 3.25 Advantages and disadvantages of off-the-job training.

Induction training

Induction training is for new workers. It can be delivered on- or off-the-job. The purpose of induction may be to introduce a worker to their job, but it is usually about introducing them to their workplace to help them to settle in. Sometimes, as part of induction, businesses offer further training to help the worker develop their job-specific skills.

The specific advantages of induction to the new worker are:

- They get to know colleagues.
- They are made to feel welcome.
- They get to know the place of work e.g. rest facilities etc.
- They learn what is expected of them.
- They learn about the culture of the business.
- It may help them to work more safely.
- They may learn skills relevant to the job (as in the Christie's Care Home case study, see page 152).

The specific advantages of induction for the business are:

- It helps the worker to settle more quickly and to be happier and more confident about working for the business.
- The worker will become productive more quickly, thus increasing output.
- The worker will value the time invested in them, which can encourage them to work hard and conscientiously.
- Health and safety issues may be reduced, which will avoid bad publicity for the business and reduce any costs connected with compensation claims

It should be noted that there is a cost to induction. Wages need to be paid but the worker is not producing goods or services during the period of induction. It also involves the cost of someone providing the training and perhaps, as in the case of B&Q below, of using a training centre.

Case study: B&Q and induction training

B&Q.

At B&Q, the DIY retailer, new employees are sent to the B&Q University (its training centre). Here they follow a course about the history and aims of the business, the rules of the company and health and safety considerations. New employees also find out about how they are paid, opportunities for promotion, and so on. Smaller businesses also cover these things but are more likely to do them in the factory or offices that the employee will work in. They may give the new employee a tour of the business and introduce them to the other workers so that employees are made to feel welcome.

Case study: induction training and beyond at Christies Care

Christies Care runs care homes that look after people with problems such as dementia, learning disabilities and physical disabilities. All new employees have to go on a residential, two-week training course at the company's training centre in Saxmundham. The safety of the residents in the homes is very important, as is the safety of the workers themselves. The course teaches the employees skills such as how to move and handle patients properly, continence care, emergency first aid, infection control and how to safeguard adults. New employees take tests during the course and, if successful, will gain a care certificate. Once achieved, the new employee is ready to work in one of Christies Care homes.

Adapted from christiecare.com

Activity 5 – Explanation activity

a) What is induction training?

b) Explain one advantage to the worker of induction training.

c) Explain two advantages to the business of providing induction training for its employees.

Staff development

Staff development is about developing the person over a period of time while training is more short term. Staff development can lead to both vocational and academic qualifications. Vocational qualifications are specific to a job. They are usually gained through a mix of practical, hands-on learning, alongside some classroom study. Academic qualifications are more general. The learning is more theoretical and predominantly class-based, though there may be some practical activities to reinforce the theoretical learning. It can be that staff development involves some training as part of the development process. This section looks at two common forms of staff development – **apprenticeships** and professional development programmes. (Remember that the term professional development refers to vocational and academic development.)

Evaluation point

The type of training relevant for a worker will depend on the needs of the worker and the business. On-the-job training helps to develop a person's job skills while they are still in work and producing goods or services. It would not be suitable in dangerous work or situations, or in service provision where the customer demands a high standard of care. On-the-job training can cause problems, particularly if it leads to mistakes in production. Off-the-job training can be very high-quality and focused on the needs of the worker. However, it tends to be more expensive than on-the-job training. Induction training is useful for new staff – helping them to settle in their new place of work as well as helping them to learn the job.

Apprenticeships

Case study: apprenticeships at Bentley Motors Ltd

Bentley.

Bentley Motors Ltd makes very grand, very luxurious and very expensive cars at its factory in Crewe. What follows is the story of one its apprentices, Charlotte, taken from the company's website.

'I currently work in the Quality Metrology department, learning how to use machines to measure Bentley components. We are constantly busy, and the job is challenging but rewarding. I have the opportunity to go on placements that will allow me to explore various roles within my department.

At the very start of my apprenticeship it was necessary that I completed my NVQ2 in engineering. This gave me the opportunity to develop an understanding of the basics of engineering, which helped me ease into my department. Each week, I attend South Cheshire College to complete my HNC/HND mechanical engineering qualification, and in a further two years I will be studying at university to gain a degree.'

From bentleycareers.com

Charlotte's experience at Bentley Motors Ltd is typical of many apprenticeships. They are long-term, structured programmes, often completed over two or three years and leading to a formal qualification. They involve a mixture of college-based work and training in the workplace. The apprentices will do some work for the businesses at its factory or office. The learning will be part on-the-job and part off-the-job, as well as being part practical and part theoretical.

Advantages and disadvantages of apprenticeships to the business

For the business, there are many advantages of taking on apprentices:

- Apprenticeships are a good way of recruiting workers, often people who are enthusiastic and ambitious.
- It can work out cheaper to train an apprentice than to hire workers who are already skilled.
- There may be a subsidy from the government to help to pay for the cost of apprenticeships.
- Learning can take place in the workplace so that it is tailored to the specific needs of the business.
- Apprenticeships may help to avoid **skills shortages**.
- Having apprentices may improve retention as they may lead to satisfied, loyal workers.
- The apprentice can do work for the business while training.

There are also disadvantages of apprenticeships to the business:

- If the apprentice is not motivated and does not finish their training, the business has wasted money on them
- It costs the business to develop an apprentice, for the cost of courses they go on and the time of experienced workers who may give them on-site support.
- There is always the risk that apprentices who are not fully trained in their job role may make mistakes, leading to quality issues and a waste of resources that could cost money and lead to a loss of customers.

Advantages and disadvantages of apprenticeships to the worker

The main advantages of apprenticeships for the worker:

- The apprentice can gain qualifications that can help them to progress with their careers.
- Apprentices earn an income while learning.
- The learning involved is often both practical and theoretical and many people like the variety of activities that this will involve.

The main disadvantages of apprenticeships for the worker:

- The pay is usually quite low while the apprentice is learning.
- The qualifications are quite specific, usually to one job. Some people prefer to follow academic qualifications such as degrees because these can open up more varied job opportunities.
- In the long term, the evidence shows that those with a degree earn more on average than workers who followed apprenticeships.

Professional development programmes

Professional development programmes (vocational and academic) are a type of staff development. Like apprenticeships, professional development programmes are long term and are about developing the knowledge and skills of the worker. They are often about developing the long-term potential of the employee. Businesses are willing to support professional development of the employee in the hope that it will benefit the firm at some time in the future. They often lead to qualifications that can be vocational or academic. The learning may involve academic study at a college or university or online, and there may also be elements of practical, hands-on training.

Table 3.26 summarises the potential advantages and disadvantages to businesses of the professional development of their staff.

Advantages of professional development	Disadvantages of professional development
■ It develops the long-term potential of workers. This can improve the efficiency of the business ■ It can help to meet future staffing needs, for example, producing future managers. ■ Workers may be motivated to work harder as they appreciate the investment that the firm is making in them.	■ These programmes can be expensive. ■ The worker may have to be away from work as part of their development and this may mean that they are not producing output. ■ It may be necessary to pay for staff to cover the worker who is away from work on a development programme. ■ The worker may leave the firm once they have been developed meaning that the business does not get a reward for developing the worker.

Table 3.26 Advantages and disadvantages of professional development

Case study: Capgemini degree sponsorships

Capgemini is a technology consultancy company that operates in 40 countries. It helps businesses to become more efficient by advising about how to use technology and will also manage their IT systems for them. Capgemini offers 'advanced apprenticeships' supporting employees to work part-time for a BSc Software Engineering, BSc Business Information Systems or a professional qualification.

Case study: CIMA and online learning

CIMA offers online training in business accounting. Employees can follow studies to gain qualifications such as the CIMA Certificate in Business Accounting. This is a widely-recognised qualification for workers involved in financial management of businesses.

Activity 6 – Zone activity

The statements below are either advantages or disadvantages of professional development (vocational and academic) for businesses or for workers. Put them under the correct heading in the table below.

- It can improve the motivation, performance and the productivity of the worker.
- The worker can gain qualifications and experience that can lead to career opportunities in the future.
- It can help to retain workers if they see opportunities for career progression in the business.
- It can help to meet the future staffing needs of the business – as a worker leaves, there may be another ready for promotion.
- It can cost a lot of money.
- It can be very hard work.
- There is no guarantee that it will lead to career progression.
- It can be satisfying to be supported at work and is good for self-esteem.
- Once the worker is better qualified and skilled, they may find it easier to get jobs in other businesses leading to problems of retention.
- It can increase the earnings of the worker.
- It can help to recruit high-quality ambitious workers.

Advantages of professional development for businesses	Disadvantages of professional development for businesses
Advantages of professional development for workers	**Disadvantages of professional development for workers**

Table 3.27 Advantages and disadvantages of professional development.

Evaluation point

The benefits to employees and businesses of staff training and development

Training and development can be very expensive for businesses. They are not always successful and can even make it easier for workers to find jobs in other businesses. However, they can bring many benefits.

Training and development can help to make or keep a business competitive by improving their performance and productivity.

Training and development are good for motivating and retaining workers.

Training and development help to recruit good workers.

Training and development help to increase the quality of the goods and services a business produces, increase sales and reduce costs and prices. This is equally important for businesses that compete with other businesses in the UK as it is for those that compete with businesses abroad.

Businesses that are going through difficult times may decide to save money by cutting back on spending on training and development. Sometimes, however, it may make sense to increase training and development to improve the performance of the business.

Staff development is particularly important for helping a business to meet its future staffing needs.

On the whole, the productivity of workers in the UK is not as good as that of workers in other countries with which UK businesses compete. Training and development are ways in which this 'productivity gap' can be closed.

Evaluation point

Training and development does not come without costs for workers. It may mean additional work, and some workers find it stressful because it can challenge them to do things they are not used to. However, it can bring benefits. Training and development can:

- lead to a great deal of satisfaction for the worker
- raise their self-esteem – workers feel valued because the business has invested time and money in their training and development
- lead to better skills and qualifications that can help the worker to earn more and gain promotion.

Activity 7 – Research activity

Investigate an occupation that you are interested in. Find out the qualifications that you will need to do the job. Your careers library and the internet will be good sources of information. Develop a plan to describe how you will gain those qualifications. Write up your findings and your plan as a personal action plan. Note that you may need to gain both academic and vocational qualifications as part of the plan.

Key facts

Training costs money.

Training and development are different. Training is more short term and is specific to the job; development takes longer and is about the person.

Training and development can improve the performance of workers and of the business.

Training and development can improve the business' ability to retain workers.

Training can be on- or off-the-job. There are different types of each.

Professional development can also be on- or off-the-job. It often leads to a vocational or academic qualification.

Both training and development are essential for the long-term ability of businesses to be competitive both in the UK and globally.

Useful words

Training is short term and is focused on helping a worker to do his or her job well.

Development is long term and is focused on the worker to help to realise their longer-term potential.

On-the-job training occurs at the place of work and while the worker is doing their job.

Off-the-job training occurs away from the job. It may still be at the place of work, or the employee may be sent somewhere else for the training.

Induction training is training to introduce a new worker to the business, place of work and their fellow workers as well as their job.

Professional development includes both vocational and academic development. It involves learning over a long period of time. Workers may learn through external courses with this learning being reinforced by practical activity in the workplace. Professional development often leads to qualifications. It is about developing the long-term potential of the employee.

Apprenticeship is a long-term development programme for workers to learn job skills while they work through a mixture of on- and off-the-job training and study. Apprenticeships lead to some kind of vocational qualification.

Productivity is measured by output per person.

Skills shortage refers to a situation in which businesses cannot recruit workers with the skills they need.

Customer service is the service given to customers, including service at the time of sale and after the sale.

Motivation is when workers are incentivised to work and to work efficiently. Workers are motivated by pay and non-pay rewards.

Retention is when workers can be kept employed by businesses rather than them leaving to work elsewhere.

Practice questions

Multiple choice questions

1 Which of the following is a feature of off-the-job training?
   a) The worker continues to produce goods or services while training.
   b) It is a cheaper way of training workers than paying for them to go on courses.
   c) This is when workers are trained in a college or training centre away from where they do the work.
   d) It never leads to a qualification for the worker.

2 Which of the following is a feature of professional development?
   a) It is a kind of short-term training.
   b) It is designed to realise the potential of a worker in the long-term interests of the business and the worker.
   c) It is designed to improve the skills of the worker to do a specific task.
   d) It usually involves on-the-job training only.

3 Which of the following statements is true?
   a) A vocational qualification is specific to a particular type of job.
   b) An academic qualification prepares a worker for work in a specific business.
   c) An apprenticeship is offered to senior managers who want to develop their skills further.
   d) An apprenticeship involves only studying at university.

Data response 22

Dream Days Ltd is a travel firm that sells special event trips and holidays. It employs a range of staff including cabin crew who serve clients on flights on Dream Days Airlines. The company is rigorous in the training it gives to its cabin crew so that it meets the industry requirements and so that they can provide a high level of service.

1 Dream Days Ltd must train new cabin crew staff about what to do in an emergency. Recommend whether Dream Days Ltd should use on-the-job or off-the-job training for this. Give reasons for your answer. (7 marks)

2 Dream Days Ltd is concerned that some of its cabin crew do not deal with complaining passengers very well. Recommend a method of training that would improve the personal skills of the cabin crew. Give reasons for your answer. (7 marks)

3 Dream Days Ltd provides induction for all new workers. Analyse how i) the workers and ii) Dream Days Ltd will benefit as a result of the induction course. (6 marks)

How to answer data response 22

1 Think about the type of training that is needed. Would it be safer to give on-the-job training or off-the-job training? Analyse the advantages and disadvantages of the different methods and then provide an evaluation – recommend the method and justify your answer.

2 Think about the type of skills that the cabin crew need. How could they learn these skills? Would they need to see someone demonstrating the skills? Would they need to practise the skills? Would it be useful to give them feedback on how they deal with customers? There is no one correct answer here – make a decision and justify it.

3 Think about the things that the new employee will learn. How will they feel if they are given good induction training? How might this affect the way they work and why? How will Dream Days Ltd benefit – think about how quickly the worker settles in, what kind of work the worker does and analyse why fully-trained workers are essential.

UNIT 3.7 Employment law

Learning outcomes

By studying this unit, you will be able to:

- explain the purposes of employment laws
- explain the main laws that exist to protect workers in the UK
- apply the main laws that exist to protect workers in the UK to case studies
- analyse the benefits and costs of employment laws for workers and for businesses
- evaluate the impact of current legislation on recruitment and employment.

Introduction

Read the following extracts. They highlight some of the different ways that people in the UK may experience **discrimination** at work.

Extract One – Disability (House of Lords Report on the Equality Act 2010)

'There are over 11 million disabled people in the United Kingdom, and the number grows year by year. Disability affects us all – as disabled people ourselves, as the carers, family, friends, employers, colleagues, and educators of disabled people – and it is the task of all of us to remove the barriers that prevent some from participating fully, and equally, in society.'

Extract Two – Ethnicity (*Guardian* newspaper, November 2015)

'Ethnic minorities are under-represented in almost all professions – in the City, the media and FTSE 100 companies, and across the board at every management level. That is compared, like for like, to white counterparts with the same level of education and attainment.'

Extract Three – sex discrimination (unison.org.uk)

'Men and women have the right not to be discriminated against at work because of their gender. Some employers have outdated ideas about what work is appropriate for women, what work is appropriate for men, and how that work should be rewarded. Some employers allow or ignore sexual harassment in the workplace or apply rules that put either women or men at an unfair disadvantage. Although there has been an Equal Pay Act in force in the UK since 1975, women still earn an average of 19.8 per cent less than men, according to the Office for National Statistics.

As well as earning less than men, women are more likely to face sex discrimination and harassment at work.'

'What were you saying about equality?'

Extract Four – Religion or belief (personneltoday.com)

'Employees may require time off to observe a religious festival not covered by current statutory holidays, or for prayers. There is no express right to take time off in these circumstances and employers are not required to grant all requests for leave for religious observance.

However, employers risk liability for direct discrimination by refusing to grant leave if leave is refused because of an employee's religion. Employers also risk indirect discrimination by having rules that are particularly disadvantageous to members of a particular religion, and which are not objectively justifiable.'

Extract Five – Sexual orientation (bp.co.uk)

'BP's LGBT employee network has been instrumental in driving forward the organisation's work on recruiting people of all sexual orientations and creating a culture where LGBT people can flourish.'

Extract Six – Hours worked – The impact of the working time directive on the UK labour market (Department for Business, Innovation and Skills 2014, gov.uk)

'Since 1998, there has been a decline in the incidence of long-hours working in the UK and a general trend towards shorter working hours. It is possible that this is, at least in part, due to the introduction of the 48-hour maximum working week despite the existence of the opt-out.

Long-hours working is generally more prevalent in high-income and highly-skilled occupations compared to lower-income and medium- and low-skilled occupations. It is more prevalent among males, people with management positions, and in certain sectors. Evidence suggests that many people working long hours do so for short periods of time, perhaps indicating that employees do exercise a choice over whether they work long hours.'

Extract Seven – Holiday entitlement for UK workers (workingmums.co.uk)

'Your employer cannot suddenly reduce your holiday leave entitlement without your consent and without consultation. If he does so, then you potentially have a breach of contract claim which could entitle you to resign and make that claim. Also you might have an unlawful deduction of wages claim if the likely result of this is a change or reduction in pay.'

The impact of current legislation on recruitment and employment

The extracts give examples of some ways in which a person can be discriminated against in employment. In summary, the law states that there should be no discrimination against a worker because of gender, sexual orientation, age, their marital status, disability, race or colour or ethnicity and religion. If a firm breaks the law it can be fined and forced to pay compensation.

The case studies on pages 162–3 illustrate that not all employers treat their employees fairly. Employment law exists to control the behaviour of employers. Usually employers have more power than their employees, and so employment laws give rights to workers. If a worker feels that their rights have been breached, they can take the employer to an **employment tribunal**. A tribunal is a panel of people – a legally qualified chairman as well as other people with expertise relevant to the case to be heard. A tribunal will hear evidence from the employee and the employer and then come to a decision. It can impose fines or award compensation and costs. Often, when a case goes to a tribunal for a hearing, the worker will be supported by a **trade union**, if they are a member of one. The trade union will give them legal advice and may pay for legal representation.

An employment tribunal offices.

The law also guides the recruitment of workers. The recruitment process, including the advertising of the job, cannot normally discriminate against potential employees on any of the grounds mentioned above. There are some exemptions. For example, a school can advertise for a female PE teacher as she would have to have a presence in the changing rooms where girls change. Also, a business has the responsibility of making its premises and operations suitable for disabled people, for example, by facilitating access for people in wheelchairs or providing documents in Braille for blind people. Legal action can also be taken against businesses that flout the laws when recruiting workers.

Activity 1 – Research activity

Choose one of the ways in which workers may be unfairly treated from the seven extracts. Research an example of a real-world case where a worker has been treated unfairly for the area that you have chosen. Use a search engine such as Google. Write a brief summary of what happened.

Discrimination laws

The Equality Act 2010 brought together 116 pieces of legislation into one single Act. The Act is designed to provide a legal framework to protect the rights of individuals and advance equality of opportunity for all. The Act relates to protection in the workplace and outside.

Discrimination at work can affect the following:

- recruitment
- pay
- terms and conditions of employment
- promotion opportunities
- training opportunities
- when an employee is dismissed.

Table 3.28 shows some types of discrimination.

Type of discrimination	Main points of the 2010 Equality Act
Equal pay discrimination	The Act was introduced to make sure that women are paid the same as men when they do work of equal value.
Racial discrimination	The Act aims to prevent people of one race, colour, nationality or ethnic origin being treated differently from others. An example would be if one worker is given a promotion when another employee is actually better qualified. There are some exceptions to the law – for example, if, for some reason, the job must be carried out by someone of a particular ethnicity, such as a waiter in a Chinese restaurant.
Sex discrimination	The Act was introduced to prevent men or women being treated differently. A job advertisement that says the job is for a woman would be breaking the law. There are some exceptions – for example, if, for some reason, the job must be carried out by someone of a particular sex (such as a female PE teacher who would need to deal with female pupils in the changing room).
Disability discrimination	The Act is designed to give equal opportunities to disabled people. For example, employers cannot discriminate against disabled people when recruiting staff. They are expected to make reasonable changes to premises to permit access and mobility around them. They have to provide appropriate equipment so that disabled people can work.
Sexual orientation discrimination	The Act applies to the employment of lesbian and gay people, heterosexual and bisexual people and those who have had gender reassignment. An employer should not give preference of any kind to a person of one sexual orientation over another because of their sexual orientation.
Religion or belief discrimination	The Act protects workers from being discriminated against either because of their religious beliefs or because they do not have any. An example is that an employer should allow people to have a holiday on a day that is an important festival for their faith.

Table 3.28 Features of the Equality Act 2010.

Activity 2 – Matching terms activity

The left-hand column of the table below gives cases that have been before an employment tribunal. Match each one against the provision of the Equality Act 2010 that covers that case.

- Equality pay
- Race relations
- Sex discrimination
- Disability discrimination
- Religion and beliefs discrimination

Case	Provision in the Equality Act 2010
Erik Pietzka was a manager at the Cardiff offices of PricewaterhouseCoopers (PwC). His marriage broke down and his wife moved to Bury St Edmunds with his daughter, then two years old. Mr Pietzka asked bosses at the firm if he was able to work flexibly, to take two days off work a week to spend with his daughter, as seeing her involved a four-hour drive. This was initially refused but he was later allowed to take one day off. Bosses later blocked his chances of promotion. Mr Pietzka resigned and then took the business to a tribunal on the grounds that this was unfair as women at the company were much more likely to be approved for flexible working. *Adapted from telegraph.co.uk, 4 November 2014*	
Meseret Kumulchew worked at a Starbucks café in Clapham Junction in London. Ms Kumulchew was responsible for taking the temperature of fridges and water at specific times and recording the results. She made mistakes entering this information on forms. This was due to her dyslexia, which she had informed Starbucks about and which caused her difficulties with reading, writing and telling the time. Starbucks gave her lesser duties and told her to retrain. This left her feeling suicidal. *Adapted from bbc.co.uk, 9 Feb 2016*	
Two Muslim workers at Tesco, Abdirisak Aden and Mahamed Hasan, took Tesco to a tribunal after supermarket bosses kept their prayer room locked. They were among a number of devout Muslim employees who had lobbied for a prayer room since 2006. In 2008, managers agreed to set aside a security office at the distribution depot in Crick, Northamptonshire, as a prayer room for Muslims. But in 2012, bosses set new restrictions on the use of the room, which included keeping it locked when it was not in use. Muslim workers were forced to tell managers when they were going to pray and had to ask for the key and fill in their names in a book every time they entered the room. They also claimed they were forbidden to worship in groups and were only allowed to pray one at a time. *Adapted from dailymail.co.uk 12 June 2016*	
Female shop workers at Asda say that they have been unfairly treated because they consider their jobs to be of equal value to those of men in distribution centres who are receiving higher pay. One Asda store worker said that the work was the same whether you were in the shop or in the warehouse – packing and unpacking pallets of clothes and food and putting stock on shelves, often through the night. The outcome of the case had not been decided at the time of writing this book. *Adapted from bbc.co.uk, 24 October, 2014*	

Carol Howard was a black, female firearms police officer in the Diplomatic Protection Group (DPG) in London. She claimed she had been discriminated against in two ways. She said that her boss had undermined, discredited and belittled her. Her 'every absence' was assumed not to be genuine, her commitment was challenged in front of colleagues and her application for an armoured response vehicle role was not supported. *Adapted from independent.co.uk, 1 July 2014*	

Table 3.29 Cases involving the Equality Act 2010.

Evaluation point

The case studies in Activity 2 illustrate a number of ways in which workers can be discriminated against. The best business practice is to avoid discrimination taking place. Businesses need to take care when recruiting workers, for example, they need to avoid breaking the rules about advertising for a man or a woman when the job could be done by either men or women. Also businesses must take care to avoid discrimination once workers have been appointed. This will require policies about how workers should behave, and staff will need training to educate them about discrimination and then to monitor their behaviour. This will cost the business money.

There are other costs involved in obeying rules about discrimination. For example, a business may have to install ramps and lifts for disabled people. Also, if found guilty of discrimination, firms often have to pay compensation to the person they have treated unfairly. Another cost that cannot be measured easily is that to the reputation of the business. If found to be guilty of discrimination, it may lead to a loss of sales or difficulties in recruiting workers. There is a moral or social point about discrimination. In the UK, we believe that all people should be treated equally, fairly and with dignity.

Activity 3 – Research activity

Research each of the cases described in Table 3.29. Find out whether the claims were accepted and what reasons were given for the judgement by the tribunals in each case. You will find it useful to use a search engine such as Google and the website addresses given at the end of each case.

Holidays

In the UK, the law says that all workers are legally entitled to have 5.6 weeks holiday each year. Bank holidays are included in this total – there are eight bank holidays in the UK at present. While on holiday, the worker must be paid by the employer. The amount of pay has to reflect what the worker would normally earn.

'I have earned this.'

The purpose of the law is so that all workers get a break from work for part of the year when they can do other things. Some employers will not allow workers to have time off to attend interviews or go for medical appointments, and the worker has to use their holiday entitlement for this.

The actual number of days' holiday that a worker has depends on how many days per week they work. For example, if a worker works for five days per week, their holiday entitlement would be calculated as follows:

Days worked per week x 5.6 = holiday entitlement

```
5 x 5.6 = 28 days
```

Remember that eight of these days will be bank holidays.

Another example shows the holiday entitlement of someone who works two days per week.

Days worked per week x 5.6 = holiday entitlement

```
2 x 5.6 = 11.2 days
```

When planning human resource needs businesses will have to take in to consideration these rules. It may mean they need to employ more workers so that they always have the workforce they need. It may mean

Case study: pay while on holiday – an employment tribunal ruling

Mr Lock was employed by British Gas as a salesman. He was paid a basic salary each month and, on top of this, he was paid commission for the number and type of contracts he persuaded customers to enter into. However, when he took periods of annual leave, he would be paid just his basic pay with no payment for commission. This was significantly less than his normal pay and was a disincentive to take annual leave. Mr Lock challenged this. It was eventually decided by a tribunal that Mr Lock should be paid a sum equivalent to his average monthly earnings – his salary plus the typical commission he earned.

Adapted from oldsquare.co.uk

Activity 4 – Explanation activity

The following case went to an employment tribunal. It was settled in 2014.

16 workers – a mix of electricians, scaffolders and semi-skilled operatives – worked on a project at the West Burton power station site in Nottinghamshire until it came to an end in 2012. During that time, they were consistently required to work overtime and received payments for travel time. Payments for that work were not included in holiday pay, meaning that the workers received considerably less pay when on holiday, compared to when they were working.

Should the workers have been paid more in holiday pay? Give reasons for your answer.

they need to control when people take holidays so that too many workers are not on holiday at the same time.

Hours worked

How many hours a worker can work per week in the UK is controlled by the 'working time directive'. The limit on the number of hours an employer can ask an adult worker to work is 48, but this is an average over a 17-week period. (The limit is 40 hours or 8 hours a day for someone under 18.) This means that an employer could ask a worker to work more than 48 hours in some weeks in a 17-week period, so long as in other weeks that worker works less than 48 hours.

The average number of hours worked by a worker would be calculated by the following formula:

$$\frac{\text{Number of hours worked}}{17} = \text{Average number of hours}$$

For example, suppose an employee worked 799 hours in a 17-week period and that in four of those weeks she worked for 52 hours. The average hours per week in this period would be:

$$\frac{\text{799 hours worked}}{17} = \text{47 hours on average}$$

The employer would not be breaking the law in this case.

Workers do have the right to 'opt out' of this law. Opt out means that they can choose, voluntarily, to work more than 48 hours per week. However, sometimes workers may feel obliged to work more than the 48-hour average if they fear their employer might look for some kind of reason to sack them if they refused (the employer cannot sack them for refusing to work more hours than the law allows).

There are some exceptions to the law. For example, people in the armed forces, the police or emergency services, seamen, security workers and servants in private households can be directed to work more than 48 hours. Also, if a person's working time is not measured in hours, and they are in control of a business, that person may have to work more than 48 hours. This would include managing directors of businesses. The law applies to employees but not to self-employed people.

Activity 5 – Calculation activity

A worker has worked 914 hours in a 17-week period.

a) Calculate the average number of hours that they worked during that period.

b) The worker was a plumber who was a full-time employee. Has the firm asked them to work longer than allowed by the working time directive? Explain your answer.

c) Another plumber also worked 914 hours for the firm in the same 17-hour period. they were self-employed. Was the firm guilty of breaking the working time regulation in this case? Explain your answer.

There are other rules. Workers must be given a 20-minute rest break every six hours, under 18 year olds can only work up to 40 hours in a week. These rules will again impact on the human resource needs of a business – how many people it will employ, the ages of the people it will employ and so on.

Contract of employment – the statement of employment particulars

A contract is a legal agreement between two people. When a business offers a person work and the person accepts, a contract has been made, in this case, between the employer and employee. The Employment Rights Act 1996 states that a business does not need to give a worker a written **contract of employment** but it must give a **statement of employment particulars** within eight weeks of starting work. Usually referred to as a statement of particulars, it is a written statement of the agreement that exists between the employer and the worker.

The purpose of a statement of particulars is to make it clear for the employer and the employee what both agree to. It helps to avoid disputes over, for example, the hours that should be worked, pay or holidays.

The statement covers information about the job title, when employment began, hours of work, pay, holiday entitlement and how much notice must be given for terminating employment.

Once agreed, the statement restricts the amount of work that the employee can be asked to do. This will affect the human resource needs of the business.

Complying with Employment Laws – the impact on recruitment and employment

Businesses often benefit from complying with employment laws.

- Workers will see the business as a good employer and will be motivated if firms treat them according to the laws. This may make the business more efficient.
- If workers are treated respectfully in terms of the legal requirement, it can also help with the retention of workers and so reduce recruitment costs as workers may be happy to stay.
- Firms with a good reputation for their recruitment and employment practices will find it easier to attract new workers.

There can be costs to firms of complying with recruitment and employment laws. Table 3.30 summarises the costs that employment laws can have on businesses.

Cost	Explanation	Example
Wage costs	Firms may need to employ more workers than they want to.	There is a limit on the hours that they can ask workers to work. OR They have to let workers have the holidays they are entitled to.
Wage costs	Firms will need to employ workers (managers) or pay consultants to make sure they are complying with the laws.	The firm will need to put in place policies, such as recruitment policies, to make sure their advertisements are legal. OR The firm will need make sure that staff are provided with a contract of employment.
Court costs	If an employee takes legal action against the business, the firm will have to pay for lawyers to represent it in court or an employment tribunal.	If a worker takes the firm to court for discrimination it will need to employ a barrister to present its case.
Fines	If the firm is found guilty of breaking the law it may have to pay a fine or compensation to the worker.	If a firm is found guilty of discrimination it will have to pay compensation for the upset to the worker.
Publicity costs	If a firm is taken to court it may lead to bad publicity.	If a firm is criticised for discriminating against workers, bad publicity could lead to a fall in sales or it could make it difficult for the firm to recruit workers in the future.

Table 3.30 Costs to businesses resulting from employment laws

Activity 6 – Zone activity

The following statements have been taken from a real statement of particulars for a physiotherapy clinic and an employee (the names of the employer and the employee and some details have been changed to protect their privacy). The table below shows the headings typically found in a statement of employment particulars. Write each statement in the place where it should go in the table to create a case study of a statement of particulars. The first statement has been written into the table for you.

- £36,000 per year.
- Clinical manager and lead physiotherapist
- 1 June 2016
- The employer will be entitled to two months' notice from you and you will be entitled to two months' notice from the employer.
- Payment in arrears on the last day of each month.
- The employer will comply with pension duties in accordance with Part 1 of the Pensions Act 2008.
- Narendra Kumar, 15 Woodlands Road, Aigburth, Liverpool L17 5HR
- 25 days per year.
- No payment will be made for absences due to illness.
- Managing the physiotherapy team and treating patients.
- 37.5 hours per week, normally between 8.30 a.m. and 5.00 p.m.
- Three months, during which time your employment may be terminated at any time.

Statement of particulars	
Name and address of employer	Aigburth Physiotherapy Clinic, 22 Aigburth Road, Liverpool L17 2UG
Name and address of employee	
Start date of employment	
Title of job	
Description of job	
Hours of work	
Pay	
When paid	
Probationary period	
Pension rights	
Holiday entitlement	
Sick pay	
Termination of employment	

Table 3.31 Statement of employment particulars.

Activity 7 – Explanation activity

Suppose that you own a local newsagent's shop. Draw up a statement of particulars for a shop assistant that you have appointed to a full-time post. Use the example of a statement of employment particulars in Activity 6 to help you.

Key facts

A contract of employment is a legal agreement between an employer and an employee.

Workers must be given a written statement of employment particulars within eight weeks of starting work. It is a part of the employment contract.

Employment laws are designed to protect workers from employers who may treat them unfairly.

The Equality Act 2010 protects workers from different types of discrimination including gender, race, disability, sexual orientation, religion or belief and unequal pay for men and women.

All employees are entitled to paid holidays each year.

The number of hours that employers can ask workers to work is limited by law, although there are some exceptions and employees can voluntarily opt out from accepting the limits if they wish to do so.

Employment tribunals will hear cases where a worker's rights may have been breached by a business.

Trade unions will support members when there is evidence that their rights may have been breached.

Useful words

Employment law is designed to protect workers from employers who may treat them unfairly.

Discrimination is when one worker is treated differently from another for no acceptable reason. There are several unacceptable reasons for different treatment.

Working time directive is a statement of the maximum number of hours that a person can be asked to work.

Holiday entitlement is the amount of paid holiday that a worker can have in a year.

Employment tribunal is a panel that hears cases where employment laws may have been broken and which comes to a decision either in favour of the employer or employee.

Trade union is an employee organisation that exists to represent the interests of its members.

Contract of employment is a legal agreement between an employer and an employee.

Statement of employment particulars is part of the employment contract. It gives details of the terms of employment.

Practice questions

Multiple choice questions

1 Which of the following is true?

a) An employer must give a worker a written contract of employment.

b) An employer must give a worker a written contract.

c) An employer does not have a contract with an employee until the worker has been given a written contract.

d) An employer can cancel a contract of employment without notice at any time.

2 Which of the following would break discrimination laws?

a) An employer pays a woman sales manager more than a male salesperson.

b) An employer promotes a white person who has more experience than a similarly qualified black person.

c) An employer does not send a gay man on a training course attended by all heterosexual workers doing the same job as him.

d) An employer spends money providing wheelchair access for workers.

3 The working time directive states that employers cannot normally ask workers to work more than an average of 48 hours per week in a 17-week period. Calculate in which of the following cases the employer has broken the working time directive.

a) An employer asks a worker to work 54 hours for 10 weeks and then 36 hours for the next 7 weeks.

b) An employer asks a worker to work 714 hours in a 17-week period.

c) An employer asks a worker to work 850 hours in a 17-week period.

d) An employer asks a worker to work 60 hours for 9 weeks and 34 hours for 8 weeks in a 17-week period.

Data response 23

Svetlana Lokhova has been awarded over £3 million from an employment tribunal. Ms Lokhova was highly regarded by Sberbank's senior management. The bank had agreed to pay her over £300,000 a year plus bonuses. However, some workers at Sberbank CIB's London office did not want her there because she had been appointed from head office. Her new job was in a small, quiet office and she immediately felt hostility from her new colleagues. 'The atmosphere was sort of strange and I started getting reports from people when I'm not in the office. People, especially my direct boss, calling me derogatory names. Names like "Miss Bonkers"' – but there was much worse being said by her direct boss, David Longmuir, in emails and messages to her colleagues and clients in major investment banks.

Adapted from bbc.co.uk 15 April 2015

1 Analyse two ways in which Sberbank may be affected as a result of failing to comply with discrimination legislation in relation to Ms Lokhova. (6 marks)

How to answer data response 23

The impact on the business may be financial – on fines, on training and the costs involved on sales and on future recruitment of staff. Analyse these points.

Business 2: Operations, finance and influences on business

4 Operations

UNIT 4.1 Production processes

Learning outcomes

By studying this unit, you will be able to:

- explain the **job**, **batch** and **flow production** processes
- analyse the benefits and costs of the different production processes
- evaluate when different production processes are appropriate
- explain how the use of technology within production processes has developed
- analyse the benefits and costs of the use of technology in production processes
- evaluate the impact on businesses of the use of technology in production processes.

Introduction

This unit is about how goods are made and services provided. It focuses on **production processes** and methods of production.

Different production processes and their impact on businesses

There are three types or methods or processes of production: job, batch and flow production.

Introductory case study: job production at the Coppice Co-op Ltd

Louis Le Glas – using job production to make hand-crafted furniture.

The Coppice Co-op Ltd is a small business run by a group of friends and like-minded people. Based in Carnforth in Lancashire, the company is fiercely concerned about sustainable production. The main work of the group is coppicing. When some trees are cut back to their stumps or roots, strong new growth will result. Coppicing is managing woodlands in this way. The Coppice Co-op are paid by the owners of woodlands to manage their woodlands, and the wood that is cut will be sold by the woodland owners, some of the wood is also used by the members of the Coppice Co-op to make charcoal and other products. One of the owners of the Coppice Co-op is Louis Le Glas. He is a skilled woodworker. Louis designs and carves out his own furniture and each piece is unique. Customers can have furniture made exactly as they want it so the products are bespoke.

Job production

This process involves producing each product individually. The furniture that Louis le Glas makes is produced using job production. The coppicing of the woods by the Coppice Co-op is also job production as each job is done exactly as the owner wants it. Other examples of job production include: building a bridge, factory or shopping centre, craft production of works of art – paintings, pottery, sculptures etc., building ships, creating an advertising campaign, taking wedding photographs, making a film or TV or radio programme, tailoring hand-made dresses and suits, and cutting hair.

The table below shows the advantages and disadvantages of job production.

Advantages of job production	Disadvantages of job production
■ Products are usually high-quality. ■ Products can be made to meet the needs of individual customers. ■ Workers often get more satisfaction from working on something until it is finished.	■ Costs of production will be high. ■ Labour costs may be high because job production often requires skilled labour.

Table 4.1 Advantages and disadvantages of job production.

Batch production

Case study: batch production of paint at Crown Paints

Crown Paints is based in Darwen in Lancashire. It makes a range of paints used for decorating. It makes different types of paints – silk and matte emulsions, gloss paints, primers – and, of course, different colours and shades of paints. The paints are made using batch production. The 'ingredients' are mixed to make a type and colour of paint. Once this is done, the paint then goes to the canning room. The tins of paint will be labelled and filled with paint and then the lid will be pressed in to position. Once that batch of paint has been manufactured, the factory switches to make a different type and colour of paint.

The batch process of production involves producing one type of a product for a while, then changing production to another type of product as described in the case study. The firm will switch back to the first product made when more is needed.

Bakers use batch production. They may bake a batch of one kind of bread and then switch production to make a batch of a different kind of bread.

Some clothing manufacturers use batch production, switching production between different types of garments.

Other goods made using batch production are furniture, newspapers, books (this book will have its own print run at the printers), and electrical goods.

The table below shows the advantages and disadvantages of batch production.

Advantages of batch production	Disadvantages of batch production
■ The needs of different customers can be met by making batches of different goods. ■ Batches are made to meet specific orders from customers and this may reduce costs because the goods do not need storing. ■ It may be possible to use specialist machines and to automate product on so that costs are saved.	■ It takes time to switch production from a batch of one product to a different batch. Machinery may need to be re-set. This adds to the costs of production and reduces output. ■ It may be necessary to keep stocks of materials and components to be able to switch production when required. Holding stock is a cash flow problem – the materials have been paid for but revenue is not being earned. There are also storage costs. ■ There will usually be less choice of products for customers compared with job production. ■ The tasks may be repetitive and boring for the workers.

Table 4.2 Advantages and disadvantages of batch production.

Working in batch production is as boring as watching paint dry.

Flow production

Case study: flow production at Heinz

Heinz makes its baked beans at its factory just outside Wigan. Over 1 billion tins of beans are made each year in the factory. The beans are made using a continuous flow method of production. The beans are mixed with the sauce and then put into tins that are sealed. The beans are then cooked. From the ovens, the tins go to be labelled. This process takes place every day throughout the year.

Adapted from BBC TV. 'Inside the Factory', 9 August 2016

The flow process of production involves an assembly line. One type of product is made continuously. The goods are mass-produced. Other examples of flow production include:

- Ford (and most other car manufacturers) uses flow production to make cars. The cars are assembled on a production line. The cars move along a conveyor belt. Different workers and machines complete different tasks as the car moves along.
- Plate glass is made using flow production. The raw materials are heated and mixed. The glass is moved on flowing water to be cooled and polished.

The table below shows the advantages and disadvantages of flow production.

Advantages of flow production	Disadvantages of flow production
■ Large amounts can be made. ■ The costs of production for each unit made are low because the firm benefits from economies of large-scale production. (Economies of scale are reductions in costs that large businesses can benefit from.) ■ Machinery can be used, helping to keep costs low. ■ Improvements in technology mean that not all of the products need to be the same; some variations in design can be programmed into the computer-controlled machines.	■ Goods are mass-produced and may not be of good quality, although this is not always true. ■ It is very expensive to set up a production line. ■ Large stocks of materials may have to be kept to keep the production line supplied and this may be expensive. ■ If the production stops at any point on the assembly line (because of a mechanical breakdown or industrial action) there may be a complete shutdown of production. ■ Jobs on an assembly line can be repetitive and boring.

Table 4.3 Advantages and disadvantages of flow production.

Evaluation point

In deciding which production methods to use, people in businesses must consider the amount that their business will sell, the importance of low costs and prices, and what customers want to buy and at what price. Businesses often want to keep production costs down to a minimum so that they can charge low prices or just so they make more profits. Batch production and flow production are ways of producing goods at low cost. However, these methods of production require a sufficient level of demand to justify the investment in machinery that is often necessary. For some products – where customers want bespoke products and are willing to pay high prices – job production is appropriate.

Activity 1 – True or false activity

The table below gives statements about the different production processes. Tick one box next to each statement to indicate if the statement is true or false.

Statement	True	False
Modern businesses do not use job production.		
Goods produced by flow production are usually made to suit the needs of individual customers.		
Flow production is suited to the manufacture of upmarket sports cars.		
It is cheap to set up a flow manufacturing process.		
Flow production is suited to large-scale production.		
Job production does not require skilled labour.		
Working in a batch production process can be repetitive and boring.		
Flow production does not require a workforce.		
Flow production workers are usually highly skilled.		
Job production workers are often highly skilled.		
Goods produced by job production are usually high quality.		
Many dangerous processes are best carried out by automated machinery.		
Supermarket in-store bakeries use the batch production method.		
All businesses will try to introduce flow production.		
Job production enables products to be made to suit the needs of individual customers.		

Table 4.4 Different production processes.

Activity 2 – Missing words activity

Use the words below to help you fill in the gaps in the following paragraph.

- advantages and disadvantages
- volume of production
- disadvantages
- process of production
- another type
- batch
- product
- technology

There are several different types of production process – job, ___ and flow. Each ___ will usually be appropriate for a particular ___ There are ___ for each type of production but it does not necessarily follow that the ___ of one type of production can be overcome by changing to ___ of production. Much will depend on the ___ being produced, the ___ and the ease with which ___ can be introduced in to the production process.

Activity 3 – Explanation activity

a) For each of the production activities in the table below, recommend one appropriate method of production from the following list:

- job
- batch
- flow

b) Give reasons for your recommendations.

c) Explain the problems that the business may face as a result of using the method or methods of production you have recommended.

Production activity	Method of production	Reason for recommendation	Possible problems
A specialist tailor makes made-to-measure suits.			
A specialist sports car manufacturer produces cars to order.			
A multinational car company produces large numbers of cars in the UK for export to the rest of Europe.			
A local bakery produces a range of bread and cakes for distribution to shops within a 20-mile radius of the bakery.			
An office furniture manufacturer produces solid wood office furniture to order.			
A sugar refinery produces hundreds of tons of sugar each day.			
A business produces thousands of bottles of beer each day. The bottles need to be washed, filled, capped and labelled.			
A small company produces three different models of caravan. Each model requires a different steel frame. Some of the components the company makes are used in each of the three types of caravan.			

Table 4.5 Methods and reasons for production activity.

The influence of technology on production and the impact on businesses

Technological development is nothing new. It has been happening for hundreds of years, but what is different is the increasing speed and level of sophistication of developments. The section below deals separately with three aspects of technology which, in practice, are difficult to separate.

Automation

Case study: automation at Crown Paints

As we saw in the earlier case study on Crown Paints, the production process can be divided into two parts – mixing the paints and then canning them. The whole process is highly automated. When it comes to canning the paint, the process goes as follows:

> Empty tins are put onto a line and rolled along automatically. The tin is first rolled past a machine that drops glue onto it. It is then rolled further along a line where a machine presses a label on to the part of the tin that has been glued. After this, the tin is turned upright and will pass beneath a hopper. (A hopper is a big vat which tapers at the bottom so that, in this case, paint can be poured into the tin as it passes below it.) The weight of the tin is measured during this process and when there is the correct weight of paint in the tin, the pouring stops and the tin moves on down the line. It will come to a machine that will put a lid on the top as it passes it before moving along to another machine that will press the lid tight shut.

Production in many industries can be controlled automatically by programming a computer to control machinery. Machinery here includes a wide range of things such as mechanical, electronic and hydraulic equipment. **Automation** can refer to the process of production used in a factory but it also covers processes by which aeroplanes and ships are now guided and stabilised automatically. In each case, the role of workers is to oversee the use of the computers and that production is taking place correctly. Workers in a factory will check that the production is taking place as it should do. The pilot in an aircraft will check that the computer controlling the take-off, flight and landing is working safely.

'Time to wake up sir, we have arrived.'

Computers

Computers are helping to automate production, particularly in service industries. Many people now bank online. Payments into and out of bank accounts are handled automatically by the computer system the bank uses. It has been suggested that cash will disappear and we will make payments using our mobile phones that will transfer money between bank accounts – something that is already happening, as with Android Pay and Apple Pay.

'Do you want me to pay by cash, cheque, card or phone?'

Computer systems are being used increasingly in schools. Data about attendance, punctuality and performance is all stored on computers; the same computers can alert teachers to problems such as pupils being regularly absent on particular days or from particular lessons, and automated texts and emails can be sent to parents to let them know their child has not registered for school. Much of the information that goes on to school reports can be generated automatically, ready for the teacher to add their comments. Teachers can post homework tasks and supporting resources on the website: showmyhomework.co.uk, and an email is sent to notify parents and guardians of this. There are a number of systems that can be used by parents and guardians to pay for school meals, trips, uniforms and so on without having to send in cash.

Other service industries use computerised systems in similar ways – insurance, financial and health services, energy companies, businesses selling tickets for concerts, football matches and flights.

Robotics

Case study: robotics – China's robot evolution

We usually think of China as a low wage economy. The wages of workers are generally lower than in the UK, but wages have been rising as the Chinese economy grows and this has added to the costs of production. As in the UK, businesses in China are looking to reduce costs by introducing technology into the production process. The managers of the Ying Ao sink foundry in the Guangdong province have invested in nine robots which will replace 140 workers. This will save on wages but the machines will make fewer mistakes than human workers and will be able to work 24/7 which will also help to reduce costs.

Adapted from ft.com, 6 June 2016

Robotics is really an extension of automation. With robotics, a computer is programmed to control a machine to do specific tasks. Robots are used very widely in car manufacturing and in the manufacturing of components used in cars. This accounts for about 65 per cent of the use of robots in manufacturing. Other industries that use robots are metals, food, semi-conductors and electronics, life sciences, plastics and rubber. Robots are being introduced into service industries as well. Some hotels have started to use them on their reception desks and they have been trialled (not very successfully so far) as waiters in restaurants. Hospitals can use them for collecting laundry to be washed. Some trains are already operated without human drivers. Until recently, robots did predominantly unskilled and repetitive tasks such as lifting a car door in to place before it is fixed (by a human worker or by another robot), welding and painting. More recently, through the development of artificial intelligence, robotics is developing and robots are being programmed to do skilled and complicated work. This may require complex tasks where the robot needs to adjust what it is doing according to the situation it is in. Robots can write reports and make decisions about the best place to position an advertisement in a magazine. They are used by surgeons to help them perform operations with great accuracy. It is even possible for robots to do operations without a surgeon. Robots went in to the remains of the nuclear power station in Fukushima in Japan after it exploded in 2014 to start the clearing process early despite the dangerous conditions – it would not have been safe for humans. The driverless car is already possible. How long will it be before all lorries, trains and planes travel without drivers and pilots?

The two tables below summarise the impact of technology on businesses in the production process.

Advantages of technology in the production process	Disadvantages of technology in the production process
■ Costs are reduced as the number of workers required is reduced. Goods and services can be produced faster, increasing the productivity of workers. Fewer workers may be needed, the average costs of production will fall and this will help the business to keep prices down and to compete. ■ Machines can be more accurate than human workers, improving quality and reducing waste – again helping to cut costs. ■ Production can be more flexible because the computers can be programmed to produce a variety of products. ■ The machinery is never absent from work. ■ Machines can work 24 hours per day, 7 days per week. ■ Machines can do dangerous and boring jobs that human workers may be reluctant or unable to do. ■ New technology can lead to new products creating demand – think tablet computers and mobile phones.	■ Workers may be redundant when the new technology is introduced and this may result in redundancy payments, adding to the short-term costs of the business. ■ New, skilled workers may need to be recruited. Often, the types of workers needed are in high demand and the business may have to pay them big salaries. ■ Workers may need training to work with the new technology, which adds to the business costs. ■ Machines can break down and this will disrupt production. ■ It can be expensive to buy and finance the purchase of technology. ■ Customers sometimes do not like technology as with automated telephone systems. ■ Where systems store data about people, there are security issues.

Table 4.6 Advantages and disadvantages of using technology in the production process.

Activity 4 – Zone activity

The statements below are either advantages or disadvantages to businesses of introducing technology. Put each statement under the correct heading in the table.

a) Machines never have days off sick.
b) Output can be lost because of machine break-downs.
c) Making workers redundant costs money.
d) Workers have to be trained and this raises costs.
e) Machines do not mind doing dangerous or boring jobs.
f) New products lead to new demand.
g) Lower production costs mean fewer mistakes, less waste.
h) Technology can be expensive to buy and install.
i) Lower production costs mean fewer workers are needed.
j) Customers do not always like technology.
k) Recruitment of new, skilled workers can be expensive.
l) Machines work 24/7.
m) Data needs protecting.
n) It allows for flexible production.

Advantages of using technology	Disadvantages of using technology

Table 4.7 Advantages and disadvantages of using technology.

Evaluation point

The application of technology in the production process is becoming increasingly important as technology is becoming more and more sophisticated. In the past, it was often used for simple tasks, replacing unskilled workers, but it will increasingly replace skilled workers as well. The key advantage of using technology in production is that it can reduce the costs of production by reducing the number of workers and waste caused by human error. It can also help with marketing, for example, by improving the speed and quality of services. As global competitiveness grows, the importance of technology also grows. Much is written about the effects of technology on levels of employment. One report has suggested that 11 million jobs could disappear in the UK as a result of technological progress. However, new technology can create jobs – skilled jobs for people to design and programme technology and jobs that result from the expansion in production and demand that technology can bring.

Key facts

There are three main methods of production – job, batch and flow production.

Each method of production has its own advantages and disadvantages.

Technology is being used increasingly in the production of goods and services.

Technology includes automation, computers and robotics. Technology development has focused on replacing unskilled jobs in the past.

Progress in developing artificial intelligence is making it possible for technology to perform more and more skilled work, even work requiring judgements and decision-making.

Technological progress can lead to some jobs disappearing but it can also create new jobs.

Useful words

Job production is the process of production where products are made individually.

Batch production is the process of production where one type of product is made and then production is switched to make a different product.

Flow production is production of one product that takes place continuously using a production or assembly line. This is sometimes called mass production.

Automation is a production process involving machinery that is not controlled by a person but usually controlled by a computer.

Robotics is the use of robots in the process of production.

Product processes are the three methods or processes of production – job, batch and flow.

Practice questions

Multiple choice questions

1 Jenny Carson makes and ices wedding cakes. Which method of production is she likely to use?

- a) job production
- b) batch production
- c) flow production
- d) robotic production.

2 Warburton's bakery uses batch production to make its bread. Which of the following is a disadvantage to Warburton's of using batch production to make its bread?

- a) The costs of production are lower than using other methods.
- b) It can meet the demand for different types of bread from different customers.
- c) It may have to reduce the range of bread it can offer.
- d) It can make bread to order so the bread does not need to be stored.

3 Which of the following is not an example of automation?

- a) Beer bottles are labelled by a machine when they pass it on the production line.
- b) The hand-making of a wedding dress.
- c) A business has sensors on its doors to make them open when someone approaches.
- d) Customers of Vauxhall Motors can configure and order their own car online which is added to production without any further input.

Data response 24

Kiva computing moving a shelf in an Amazon warehouse.

Amazon has 12 warehouses in the UK. Kiva robots are being used in its Doncaster warehouse. When a customer orders a product, the request is passed automatically to one of the robots. The robot follows digital patterns on the floor of the warehouse to find the shelf where the product is stored and brings it to a human worker, who will box the product and then ship it off. Previously, the products would have been collected by workers called 'pickers' whose job was physical and demanding, as they had to walk many miles at speed each day. No workers have lost their jobs at the warehouse since the robots were introduced. However, the warehouse is now handling many more deliveries than before. More importantly, according to Amazon, the speed at which the orders can be delivered has increased. Amazon has introduced a 'Prime' delivery service that promises delivery within one day. Amazon was planning to introduce 2,500 new jobs in the UK by the end of 2016.

1 Evaluate the impact of the new technology on production processes at Amazon. (9 marks)

How to answer data response 24

1 Analyse the benefits of introducing the technology and the problems or disadvantages. When evaluating you may want to state what will determine whether the benefits are negative or positive. Consider, for example, the impact of using robots on the work conditions of workers at the warehouse, the overall level of employment at Amazon, and whether or not they are introduced into other warehouses in the UK.

UNIT 4.2 Quality of goods and services

Learning outcomes

By studying this unit, you will be able to:

- explain the concept of **quality**
- explain the different methods of ensuring quality – quality control and quality assurance
- evaluate methods of ensuring quality
- evaluate the importance of quality in both the production of goods and the provision of services.

The concept of quality

Introductory case study: Alpha Guest House Trip Advisor review

Customers of hotels, restaurants and tourist attractions can post reviews on the Trip Advisor website. It is widely used by customers who are looking for places to stay, eat or to visit. A good review can encourage customers to visit, a bad review can have a disastrous effect on the business. The review below is one bad review about the Alpha Guest House in Bristol. Would it encourage you to stay there?

'As a well experienced traveller [sic] who has come across some appalling hotels & B&Bs, this place takes the crown as the worst B&B absolutely disgraceful how is this place open to the public it's disgusting and dangerous, your met by the proprietor who is desperate to get her hands on your money, there is a five-minute money back refund. If you do not want to stay they keep your money, the rooms are absolutely shocking and appalling with a disgusting stench and the place is full of junkies who just doss about the place all day I am absolutely flabbergasted that Bristol council & the authorities have allowed this place to stay open to the public it's an absolute disgrace!

Stayed April 2016, travelled solo'

From tripadvisor.co.uk

The term 'quality of production' means that a product or service is fit for purpose (it does what it is supposed to do), meets the legislative rules (about design and safety, for example) and meets customer expectations. On the latter, sometimes when a person buys a cheap product, they will not expect it to be top quality but will have some idea in mind of what is satisfactory quality.

'It costs five times more to gain a customer than to keep a customer.' This saying indicates the importance of quality. It is easy to lose a customer by supplying goods or services that are of poor quality. To attract new customers requires all manner of marketing activities and costs a lot of money. Once gained, businesses will find it worthwhile spending on quality procedures in order to avoid losing customers.

Case study: Samsung Galaxy Note 7

Samsung Galaxy Note 7 had to be withdrawn from sales on the day – 1 September 2016 – it was to be available in the UK. 2.5 million phones had been sold already around the world. There were reports, around 35 in all, of phones catching fire during or after they had been charged. This was bad publicity for the company that is the market leader. Its main rival, Apple, was due to start sales of its new iPhone 7 days later. Samsung decided to recall all of the phones already sold in order to check that they were safe – a move that would also reassure the public. However, Samsung share price fell with the news.

The importance of providing quality goods and services

There are many benefits to providing quality goods:

- It avoids waste – if goods are not of a good quality, they may not be able to be sold and so the producer has wasted money. Goods sold may be returned by dissatisfied customers and may need to be replaced. Goods that cannot be sold as good quality can sometimes be sold as seconds. The producer will have to reduce the price for these and so will lose revenue.
- It avoids recalls – this is when an unsatisfactory product is offered for sale and problems arise after the sales have been made, as was the case with the Samsung phone.
- Reputation and sales – the customer will not be happy if they receive poor-quality goods or services. They may decide to buy from another seller in the future. They may tell friends and family. Once a seller develops a poor reputation, the business will lose sales and it may be difficult to change that reputation. The consequence for the business here is that it does not retain its customers, nor is it likely to gain new ones.
- Disrupted production – production may be disrupted if the quality of materials produced at an early stage in the process of production is not good enough for them to be used at a later stage.

Methods of ensuring quality

Quality control and **quality assurance** are methods or approaches to ensure that a business provides high quality goods or services. There is a difference between quality control and quality assurance, and the section below looks at this in more detail.

Quality control

Case study: Heinz Beanz

Cans of Heinz baked beans.

Heinz Beanz are made in Wigan. Some three million cans per day are manufactured in the factory using a highly-automated process. The machinery is programmed to detect faults in the cans or in the labels. If, for example, a can is not the correct weight or has not been sealed properly, it will be ejected from the production line so that it is not sold to customers.

Adapted from BBC TV. 'Inside the Factory', 9 August 2016

Quality control is about checking that the product or service produced meets the required standards. For goods, this can be a physical inspection. Inspectors may sample the raw materials or the goods during the process of manufacture and/or once the production is complete. Some products may be tested in a laboratory to see if they have been made properly. The inspection might be done by the machinery, as in the case of Heinz Beanz. For services, it can be through a customer satisfaction survey.

An alternative method is to use a mystery shopper. With this method, a person pretends to be a normal customer but will check that the service provided is up to the right standard. A lot of retailers use mystery shoppers to check that shop assistants are providing service to customers according to the policy of the business. The retailer will hope that the shop assistants will always give good service. The form below is used by mystery shoppers who are paid to eat a meal at a restaurant. The restaurant manager and waiter will not know that the person is testing their service until the buyer introduces him or herself after the meal. The test result would be sent to the owner of the restaurant or manager of the chain who can then act on its findings, if necessary, in order to improve the service provided.

(RESTAURANT NAME)

Mystery Shopping Report

Shopper's Name ______________ Date __________ # in Party ________

Location ______________ Server's Name ______________

Manager on Duty ______________ Day of the Week ____ Meal Period ______

CATEGORY	POINTS EARNED	POSSIBLE POINTS	PERCENT
Facility/Environment		125	
Service/Personnel		175	
Food & Beverage		50	
TOTALS		350	

Comments:

The 3 top things this restaurant did very well:

1. ______________
2. ______________
3. ______________

The 3 top things that could be improved:

1. ______________
2. ______________
3. ______________

Overall comments/observations:

____

____

____

____

A typical mystery shopper form

Activity 1 – Research activity

Choose a service that you are familiar with. It could be the school canteen or a local shop or service such as the bus that you travel to school on. Use the internet to research forms that mystery shoppers can use – use Google or a similar search engine. Get some ideas together as to what you would look for in the service that you have chosen – think about who provides the service, how it should be provided, any goods that might be involved (e.g. as in canteen meals), the facilities in the place you buy the service from and so on. Once you have done this, design a form that could be completed by a mystery shopper using the service you have chosen.

Carry out a test and write short notes on the form. Write a short report about your findings. Make recommendations about how the service could be improved.

Activity 2 – Research activity

Complete the table below with:

a) the names of three businesses that have a good reputation for good-quality products or services (one product is given as a suggestion)

b) an explanation of why these businesses appear to have earned this reputation and how they use it to help sell their products.

Name of business with good reputation	Explanation of how reputation is used by the business
Chanel perfume	This has been marketed as a high-quality perfume for many years – advertised and priced as such.

Table 4.8 How a good reputation is used by businesses.

Advantages and disadvantages of quality control measures

The table below shows the advantages and disadvantages to business of using quality control measures.

Advantages of quality control	Disadvantages of quality control
■ It can help to prevent faulty goods and services being sold. ■ It is not disruptive to production – workers continue producing, inspectors do the checking. ■ As with any quality system, the business may benefit from an improved reputation for quality and this may increase sales.	■ It does not prevent waste of resources when products are faulty. ■ The process of inspecting the goods or service costs money, e.g. the wages paid to inspectors, the cost of testing goods in a laboratory. ■ It does not encourage all workers to be responsible for quality.

Table 4.9 Advantages and disadvantages of quality control measures.

Activity 3 – Presentation activity

Suppose that the company which does the cleaning in your school has to compete with other companies for the work. Prepare a presentation (use PowerPoint or similar) to explain to the company:

a) what quality control involves and how the cleaning business may ensure that quality is good

b) the advantages to the cleaning business of ensuring good quality control

c) problems the business may face in using quality control methods.

Quality assurance

Quality assurance is about preventing problems with quality. It involves designing products and services that meet consumer needs. It is relevant to service industries as well as manufacturing.

Quality assurance creates a culture of quality in the business. Every employee is involved at every stage in the process of production. Each employee is expected to treat other employees at a later stage in the process of production as customers who use what they have produced – the 'customer employee' should be happy with what has been produced.

Quality assurance is also about encouraging employees to suggest ways in which the business can be improved. There will be meetings of employees at different levels in the business where they come up with ideas about improving quality further.

Case study: Toyota Motors – quality assurance

Toyota Motors is perhaps *the* company more than any other that is associated with quality assurance. Its quality assurance process stresses continuous improvement and encourages all employees to make suggestions about how the business can do better, and all employees are responsible for their part in the process of production of the cars. Toyota tries to reduce waste as much as possible and to produce cars which meet the needs of the customer. The two basic principles on which the company is run are 'customer first' and 'respect for people'.

Advantages of quality assurance	Disadvantages of quality assurance
■ There may be less wastage and this will reduce production costs. ■ Workers may feel valued because they have been given responsibility for quality and this may motivate them to work harder and better. As a result output may increase and quality improve. ■ As with any quality system, the business may benefit from an improved reputation for quality and this may increase sales.	■ It may disrupt production because workers are stopping to check the quality of what they have produced. This may slow down production and raise costs. ■ It may cost the business a lot to train a worker to be able to assess the quality of the work that they have done. ■ Workers may worry about the extra responsibility of having to check their own quality. They may resist the introduction of quality assurance methods for this reason.

Table 4.10 Advantages and disadvantages of quality assurance.

Case study: Disney World, Florida

Disney World provides an example of quality assurance applied to a service business. All the employees at Disney World are called 'cast members', whether they are actors in the pageants, street cleaners or queue supervisors. The whole service is considered as a 'show' that all workers contribute to. Each 'cast member' is responsible for providing their own high quality of service to provide a great experience for the customers.

Activity 4 – Poster activity

Draw a poster that shows:

a) the quality assurance idea

b) the advantages and disadvantages of quality assurance.

You should use pictures and symbols or numbers in your poster. You can only use ten words in the poster.

Evaluation point

Quality is very important for businesses in competitive markets. If the goods or services of a business are not of a quality that satisfies customers, the business will have a bad reputation, lose sales and incur extra costs. How a business ensures quality will depend on the type of product or service it offers. Quality control is good for very technical products where testing is necessary – for example, with chemicals and with pharmaceutical drugs – to make sure that the final product is produced to the correct standards. Quality assurance is an alternative approach that has its advantages and is useful where workers are able to make appropriate judgements about the quality of their own work.

Key facts

Building a reputation for good quality takes time.

Losing a reputation for good quality can happen very quickly if products and services are not of good quality.

There are two main methods of ensuring quality – quality control and quality assurance.

Useful words

Quality control is a system for inspecting the quality of the goods or services produced and that they are of a good standard.

Quality assurance is an approach that involves the whole business focusing on quality, thus aiming to prevent quality problems arising.

Quality is about a product being fit for purpose.

Returns are goods which customers take back to the shop because there are problems with the quality of them.

Recalls are when a fault occurs with a product and the business asks for the product to be brought back so it can be repaired or replaced.

Practice questions

Multiple choice questions

1 Which of these statements describes quality assurance?

   a) Inspectors are used to check the quality of the goods being produced.

   b) All workers are involved in and responsible for the quality of their work.

   c) Only finished goods are checked so that no faulty products are sold to customers.

   d) Quality assurance does not disrupt production because quality is only checked once production is finished.

2 Which of the following is a disadvantage of the quality control method?

   a) Inspectors do not need to be paid because the workers check their own quality.

   b) Inspectors are better at checking the quality of goods than workers.

   c) Inspectors have to be paid for the work that they do, adding to the cost of production.

   d) Workers do not have to disrupt production to check the quality of what they have made.

3 Which of these statements is true about the importance of quality?

   a) It is easy to gain a reputation for quality.

   b) It is easy to lose a reputation for quality.

   c) Producing high quality goods always increases sales.

   d) Producing high-quality is always cheaper than producing low quality.

Data response 25

'Providing great food is Sainsbury's core purpose. Customers continue to rate us above our main supermarket peers on product quality ... We are making good progress in our programme to improve the quality of 3,000 own-brand products, investing in the products that matter most to our customers. For example, we improved the quality of our Taste the Difference burgers, our Sainsbury's cheesecake and our Sainsbury's all-in-one dishwasher tablets recently won Which? Best Buy 2015. The rate at which we launch these new products will increase at pace over the next 12 months.'

From j-sainsbury.co.uk

1 Evaluate the importance of selling good-quality products for Sainsbury's supermarket. (9 marks)

2 Explain one method that Sainsbury's could use to make sure that its shop assistants provide a good quality of service to the customers. (3 marks)

How to answer data response 25

1 You need to discuss both the advantages and the disadvantages (including, for example, the costs involved) of ensuring quality. Then you need to discuss why, in a competitive market, quality is essential to avoid goods being returned or recalled, and the potential loss of customers to competitors if Sainsbury's quality is not good enough. Make sure that you apply your answers to Sainsbury's and the grocery market in general – mention the competitors.

2 You can choose any method here but the easiest method to explain would probably be the use of mystery shoppers. Make sure you apply your explanation to explain how this approach would be used in a supermarket.

UNIT 4.3 The sales process and customer service

Learning outcomes

By studying this unit, you will be able to:

- identify and understand the different methods of selling that a business might use
- evaluate the influence of **e-commerce** on business activity
- evaluate the importance of **customer service** in business activity
- explain how product knowledge and **customer engagement** help develop successful businesses
- analyse and evaluate the different methods of selling a business might use, and make justified recommendations as appropriate
- evaluate the contribution of product knowledge and customer engagement to customer service in business activity.

Introductory case study: John Lewis

John Lewis.

'Never Knowingly Undersold' (NKU) has been our unique promise to our customers for over 75 years, on quality, service and value. You can trust that we will always stock the best quality, responsibly sourced products. We work hard with all our suppliers to ensure they pay full attention to the wellbeing of their employees, their communities and the environment in which they are based. This includes using sustainable materials and methods wherever possible, and trading ethically at all times.

Our staff (Partners) are highly trained to offer helpful, impartial advice on all products and we provide an excellent after-sales and a great choice of expert services from delivery to installation. We set highly competitive prices for all our products: if we find a national high street competitor offering a better nationwide price for the same individual product, sold with the same service conditions, we'll lower our price to match in all our shops and on our website, including when a competitor is having a sale.'

From www.johnlewis.com

Methods of selling

Businesses are able to use a range of selling methods. These are:

- e-commerce
- face to face
- telesales.

E-commerce

E-commerce is the process of bringing a buyer and seller together electronically. It is more commonly described as online sales. E-commerce is linked to digital distribution (see Unit 2.4) but where digital distribution means the product is *delivered* digitally, e-commerce will involve some form of physical delivery after an online sale.

The influence of e-commerce on business activity

The introduction of e-commerce is having a wide-ranging effect on business activity. It is also a fast-changing situation: you need to make sure that you have up-to-date information on new developments. Industries that have adapted well to this type of selling include some retail, travel and finance businesses.

There have been many changes in business activity due to changes in e-commerce. These are:

- location
- new skill development
- levels of employment
- creation of specific departments
- click and collect
- delivery options.

Location

The locations of some parts of business activity have become more adaptable than before thanks to e-commerce, and now businesses are able to locate almost anywhere. A business will only need a telephone connection to take orders, this being referred to as the 'front end' of the business. A warehouse, storing goods to be sent to the customer when ordered, need not be in the same place as the office taking the order. For the warehouse, a location near the motorway network may be more suitable. In this way, locating different functions of the business needs different considerations.

New skill development

A business launching a product or service through e-commerce will need the workforce to have different skills. Some people will be needed to maintain the website, some to reply to emails from customers and some people will be needed to pack goods in a warehouse for delivery. All of these jobs may not have been required before e-commerce started. Extra training may well be required for all levels of staff. Workers may be recruited with the skills that a business does not have in any of its current staff. Some staff may feel threatened by the introduction of the new technology connected to e-commerce, especially if they are older and less familiar with technology.

Levels of employment

The move to e-commerce may well increase or decrease the overall level of employment. An existing business switching some of its operations to e-commerce may well find that it needs fewer staff due to the technology being used. Banks and building societies now offer many accounts that are available only over the internet. This enables them to reduce the number of staff needed in traditional branches.

A business may find it has to make some staff redundant if they do not have the skills to transfer to digital technology. However, a new business starting with e-commerce operations will likely need to recruit new workers.

Creation of specific departments

Many large businesses have a separate 'online arm' that deals with online sales. Shops such as Marks & Spencer, Next and John Lewis have seen online sales increase rapidly, and a separate online department within the business will be seen as necessary to make sure that no business is lost to competitors who may be offering a better price or service.

Click and collect

This is another growing area within e-commerce. A problem of having goods delivered at home is that the customer might not be in. This can be solved by the customer ordering online and then collecting the goods from a store at a later time. Prior to this, a customer could go shopping only to find that the goods are not in stock. **Click and collect** solves the problem. Click and collect is a competitive area for many businesses, in particular the speed at which the product is ready for collection. Supermarkets are now looking at click and collect on grocery shopping that is done within the same day. Many local shops are now being developed as click and collect centres to further help this growing trend. This is a fast-changing situation – look out for further developments in the future.

The success of click and collect has meant that businesses who use this method of selling are having to dedicate more space in-store for click and collect customers. This affects the business because they have to think of the best way they can use their available space within a store.

Delivery options

The speed at which products can be delivered will be increasingly important in the future. If a business can deliver goods faster than its competitors, then it could well attract more customers. Amazon has a well-established next-day delivery service, Amazon Prime, although this is a paid-for service. The new development may be in drones, used to deliver certain goods (not perhaps washing machines) within hours. There are, however, problems of security and safety. Amazon is looking carefully at the potential for drone delivery to keep the business at the cutting edge of delivery – such a key element in a world that requires quick service. As with click and collect above, businesses are being more inventive in how they deliver their goods, always trying to stay ahead of their competitors.

Could drones be the answer to speedy delivery?

Activity 1 – Explanation activity

a) Explain why some businesses using e-commerce can be adaptable and located almost anywhere.

b) Many businesses using e-commerce may want to be located near the motorway network. Why is this?

c) Explain how the following have changed due to e-commerce:

- booking a summer holiday
- operating a bank account
- buying clothes.

Advantages to businesses using e-commerce

Sell world wide

A business using e-commerce can sell goods and services to a worldwide market. This will mean that even the smallest business could sell goods and services throughout the world, helping to increase sales and profit.

Open all the time

There is no restriction on opening times with e-commerce. A business can sell throughout the day and night, again helping to increase sales and profit.

Professional look at little cost

A website can make a small business appear very professional, helping to create a positive image with potential customers. This positive image will hopefully tempt customers to buy from the website.

Lower operating costs

A business using e-commerce will not have to pay expensive city centre rents for a shop or office to sell its goods and services. It can operate from anywhere where there is a suitable internet connection. This will lower costs for the business, helping to keep profits high.

Disadvantages to businesses using e-commerce

Worldwide competition

As all businesses using e-commerce will have a potential worldwide market, businesses will have greater competition from other e-commerce operations. Customers can easily compare prices and service levels. This may lead to greater competition on price, which could lower sales and profits.

Problems of delivering goods and accepting returns

A business operating in a town high street will sell goods direct to a customer. An e-commerce business needs to arrange delivery for all goods moved physically (some goods could be sold in digital format where there is less of a problem). In this case a business may have to rely on other businesses to deliver the goods, which adds to costs. A customer may buy many items to try and then return. The return of goods again adds to the costs of an e-commerce business.

Online security

Businesses must operate a secure website for customers and keep data safe. If there is a problem with the security of the website then the business will suffer from a loss of customers who do not trust the site. Making sure the website is secure will add further costs to operating an e-commerce business.

Advances in technology

An e-commerce business must keep up to date with any technological improvements which influence customer buying habits. The recent increase in the use of mobile phones to order goods and services means that an e-commerce business must make sure that it has developed its technology to make sure that customers can use phones, tablets (and other future devices) to order from its website. As with other advances in technology, this will add further costs to the business operations.

Customers and e-commerce

It is important that a business is aware of the needs of its customers so that those needs can be met. The reaction of customers to e-commerce developments will influence business activity.

For any product or service, customers can be other businesses as well as general customers, for example, Next will buy the clothes they sell from a business that make the clothes. The following advantages (and disadvantages) should be seen from the point of view of a business buying on e-commerce as well as an 'ordinary' customer.

Advantages to customers of using e-commerce

Price comparison

When buying using e-commerce, prices can be compared easily, enabling the buyer to get the best possible deal and save money. There are now a number of price comparison sites, which are a business in themselves. Businesses must be aware of their prices being checked against competitors. This has led to Tesco, among others using a 'brand price guarantee'. John Lewis are 'never knowingly undersold' which has helped them increase sales despite online competition.

Seven-day availability

Just as it is an advantage for a business to open digitally seven days a week, the customer can also buy at whatever time they wish. Businesses therefore must plan for seven-day working.

Wide range of products

Because the internet can provide world-wide access to goods, the customer has a much wider choice of products. The correct product, at the correct price, can be chosen more easily. Businesses must be aware of the range of products being sold by competitors – are they losing business because they are not offering the same online range?

Disadvantages to customers of using e-commerce

Buying online may be frustrating at times.

Lack of personal contact

With e-commerce, there is often no person to talk to directly. This may put some potential customers off using the internet as a means of buying goods. On the other hand, it may encourage others who prefer not to deal with people! Businesses must make sure that their website is easy to navigate and that the 'buying experience' is as good as possible, even though there is no personal contact.

Problems returning goods

If goods purchased on the internet from a business in the UK are faulty, then customers have the same rights as if the goods were bought from any other business. The goods must be of 'satisfactory' quality and match the description given. Despite this protection, some customers may feel that it is easier buying from, say, a shop and being able to sort problems out much more easily. With more online retailers offering free returns on goods, many customers are now happier to order online and return what they do not want.

Only image of goods seen

When you buy something from a shop, you can see and touch the product, inspecting the quality. When buying digitally, only the image is available, which may not be suitable for some customers. If the customer knows the product well, such as a DVD, there is less of a problem buying it with just an image given on screen. The website is important here in making the images as clear as possible, using magnification to help customers look closely at the goods on offer.

Security

Security is seen as a problem for some customers, as well as the business using e-commerce to sell goods and services. Credit card protection using encryption may be available, but this may still not be enough for some customers.

Methods of payment

Customers wishing to pay by cash will not be able to use digital distribution. Much of the payment is geared towards credit cards, which are not used by all customers. There is little a business can do for a customer who only has cash to pay for goods.

Technology

To buy using e-commerce, a customer needs access to the internet. Although the number of people having internet access is increasing all the time, large groups, particularly the elderly, do not have the necessary access. A business wanting to sell using digital distribution must think carefully whether the target markets for the product are likely to be able to buy on the internet.

One important aspect of e-commerce is the ability of the customer to order goods from a number of devices. Mobile phones are now an important tool to order goods and services. This has a clear benefit to the customer, being able to order goods anywhere, anytime, but it also means that businesses need to keep up to date and make sure their products and services are available through phones and tablets.

Evaluation point

When evaluating the advantages and disadvantages of e-commerce, remember to check whether it is from the point of view of the *customer* or the *business*.

The suitability of e-commerce will be affected by the target market, and the product or service itself. Some products and services are much more suited to e-commerce than others.

Activity 2 – Research activity

a) Complete a survey of your business group on how they use e-commerce to buy goods on the internet. You need to make up your own questionnaire to find out:

- what they bought through the internet
- what technology did they use (phone, tablet, laptop, desktop)
- why they used the internet rather than traditional shops
- if they do not use the internet to buy goods, what are the reasons?

b) Make a graph of your results.

c) Explain why certain goods may be bought on the internet, with other products still being bought in traditional shops.

d) Explain how your own views on digital distribution are similar to the group and how they differ from the group.

Activity 3 – Presentation activity

Working individually or in small groups, think of a new product or service you think would sell well, or provide a profitable service, by being sold through e-commerce. Make a short presentation to the rest of the business studies group to cover:

- a description of the product or service
- who your target market is
- why you believe the product or service will sell on the internet
- the location and general organisation of the business.

Face to face

Face to face selling for a retail organisation is normally seen as selling through a shop. Here there can be good interaction between the business and its customer. There is an opportunity for advice to be given and questions to be asked and answered. The business will have a belief and hope that a customer feels they have been well served and will return. For the customer, they feel that the shop has provided much more in the way of service than an online service could offer.

However, shops are expensive to operate. There are staff to be paid, as well as rent, local taxes on the property, cleaning and general maintenance costs. People have to visit shops and in poor weather customers may simply want to stay at home and shop online. Some people may feel that face to face selling does not provide the level of service it should. Other shoppers know exactly what they want and the service element of face to face selling and buying is simply not needed.

Face to face selling can also be seen in businesses such as banks and travel agents where the same features given above will apply. Face to face is applicable wherever a person is doing the selling, whether it is the Avon person calling at your door or buying a brand-new Ferrari from a showroom.

Where a business is concerned with service, then face to face selling becomes more important. Compare buying a book with buying a wedding dress. It may not matter that you have not seen or touched the book you want. It may not matter that you have not been served by a helpful assistant in a shop. However, a wedding dress is a much different proposition. Here the service element comes into play with selling. Seeing the dress, touching the dress and talking to staff will all help the face to face sale.

Telesales

Telesales, or telephone sales, can be a bridge between e-commerce and face to face selling. While older people may not be comfortable with online shopping, they may well be happy to talk to someone online and be helped through the buying process. Larger businesses will have a separate telesales department. Smaller businesses may not have the staff to offer such a service.

Telesales also has the advantage of allowing the customer to argue for a better deal with the business. Renewing a mobile phone by telephone enables the customer to try and bargain for a reduction in price, or more minutes and so on. A business therefore must have staff trained to deal with this situation and be able to offer a deal that pleases the customer and enables the business to make a profit.

A growing issue with telesales is customers being called at home at inconvenient times. This 'cold' calling is seen as a nuisance by many people.

The importance of customer service and after-sales service

Businesses are increasingly seeing the importance of good customer service along with **after-sales service**.

Why is customer service important?

Put quite simply, it helps maintain or increase sales. A business must at least retain its existing customers and try to gain new customers wherever possible. The last thing a business wants is an unhappy customer, who may not return to spend money at the business. Competitors are all too ready to take customers from any business that is seen to fall in the standard of its customer service.

Activity 4 – Zone activity

Complete the table below to indicate the suitability of selling different goods. For some products, it may mean a tick in all three boxes

Product or service	Suitable for e-commerce	Suitable for face to face	Suitable for telesales
An expensive sports car			
A CD			
Fresh vegetables			
Shoes			
A house			
Designer clothing			
Newspapers			
A laptop computer			

Table 4.11 Products suitable for e-commerce, face to face or telesales.

Pick three of the products in the table and explain why you think they are suitable for that method of selling.

How a business might provide good customer service

Customer service areas are a familiar sight in many stores.

After-sales service

It is one thing providing good service when someone is buying a product. But what happens if things go wrong? After-sales service is vital in a competitive business environment. This might mean offering refunds if a customer simply does not like a product and wants to return it (there is nothing in law that states that a business must do this) or it could mean organising a speedy repair if appropriate. It might also mean keeping the customer informed about a problem that is difficult to solve.

Whatever is done in after-sales service, the customer must be left happy in the knowledge that the business has done all that it can. No customer wants things to go wrong, but most customers will appreciate a business that does all it can to solve a problem, and then will be more likely to return to spend more money at a later date.

The importance of good product knowledge

This will depend on the product itself. If a customer wants a plant to go in a particular garden space, it is reasonable to expect some knowledgeable staff at a garden centre to provide different suggestions to give the customer a choice. In electricals, knowledge of the latest television technology should be available from staff to help the less well-informed customer. If a customer feels that they have been given clear help, then they are more likely to buy.

This all comes with training from the business (see Unit 3.6). Training takes time and money, but with better **product knowledge** helping to provide better customer service, this should lead to increased sales and help pay for the money invested in the training.

In other businesses, such as newsagents, product knowledge may be less important. It is not a case, however, of smaller businesses not needing to have much product knowledge. A hairdresser has to know which product is required for a particular look.

Sometimes, customer engagement simply does not work.

Customer engagement

Customer engagement is the contact between a customer and the business. Few, if any, people will appreciate being served by rude staff. If staff are well trained with good product knowledge and manners, then there is more chance of a sale being made. There is at times a fine line between being too helpful and being 'pushy'. Car salesmen have at times had a reputation of trying too hard to persuade customers to buy. They may have excellent product knowledge, but the engagement with the customer might simply not work. A customer might just have *too* much information!

Customer engagement is not just important in face to face selling. The friendly, helpful voice at a telesales company might be enough to persuade someone to buy. Some e-commerce companies have put a lot of thought into how they can engage with customers without actually seeing or speaking to them. Constant feedback and communication is vital, with the words sent as an email or text being carefully thought through to replicate the engagement that a face to face seller might have.

Activity 5 – Explanation activity

Look back at the information on John Lewis at the start of this unit.

a) Explain how John Lewis provides good customer service.

b) Explain why good customer service is important to a business such as John Lewis.

Activity 6 – Missing words activity

Complete the following paragraph using the words provided.

- sales
- interaction
- maintain
- training
- After
- telesales
- product

Customer service is important if a business wants to ___ or increase the level of ___ Customer service can be helped by staff having better ___ as this will increase their ___ knowledge and help with customer ___ Businesses that use e-commerce and ___ also have to provide good customer service, otherwise they will lose customers to competitors ___ sales service is also important to any business as it is important to provide service after a product has been sold.

Key facts

There are a number of ways of selling that are open to a business.

Not all businesses are suited to every method of selling.

E-commerce continues to grow in importance.

Speed of delivery is a key area of competition within all businesses, though especially those in e-commerce.

Click and collect is growing in importance in e-commerce businesses.

Customer service is a vital part of successful selling.

After-sales service, product knowledge and customer engagement are areas that more businesses are developing to help their selling.

Staff training is an important part of successful selling and good customer service.

Useful words

E-commerce is the bringing together of buying and selling electronically.

Customer service is the name given to an area of business that deals with customer enquiries.

Customer engagement is the contact between the business and customer.

Click and collect is ordering online and collecting goods from store at a later time.

Face to face selling is usually completed in a shop where there is direct contact between buyer and seller.

Telesales is sales completed over the telephone.

After-sales service is advice and help given to a customer after they have bought a product or service.

Product knowledge is the detailed knowledge of a product or service that staff within a business use to help persuade a customer to buy.

Practice questions

Multiple choice questions

1 E-commerce is:
- a) selling goods and services from a shop
- b) selling goods and services through a large warehouse
- c) selling goods and services through the internet
- d) selling goods and services at airports.

2 E-commerce can help business activity by:
- a) enabling customers to buy goods 24/7
- b) giving advice in a shop
- c) making sure the goods are up to standard
- d) taking time to send goods securely.

3 Face to face selling will help a business:
- a) when goods being sold are cheap
- b) when service is important
- c) when goods being bought are small
- d) when the customer has a computer.

Data response 26

Amazon Prime is a service offered by Amazon. It was introduced in 2007 as an unknown idea, never before had a retailer tried to offer a year of next-day delivery for a fixed fee. It is a subscription service, with an annual fee to take advantage of the service. A Prime customer can have unlimited next-day deliveries throughout the year. Amazon also offers, as part of the package, free access to movies and music.

Amazon offers alternative delivery options, including free delivery (subject to minimum spend) and next-day delivery for a fee without having to pay the annual charge.

New developments include same-day delivery in certain areas (usually large cities) and one- or two-hour slot deliveries through the Prime Now mobile app.

1 Explain two reasons why Amazon might offer a range of delivery options. (4 marks)

2 Explain two difficulties for a business wanting to set up a next-day delivery service. (4 marks)

3 Analyse two impacts of Amazon's same-day delivery service on its competitors. (6 marks)

How to answer data response 26

1 Here you need to think about the different customers that Amazon might have. Will everyone want to pay an annual fee for Amazon Prime, for example, when they only buy one or two items a year from the business? Does every customer want same day or next day delivery?

2 In this question, you must think a little wider. Think of a customer in one part of the country ordering a product that is kept at a warehouse hundreds of miles away.

3 This question requires you to analyse and so needs to look at the effect on *other* businesses. These may be in e-commerce or not, though they should be selling the same types of goods as Amazon. Try and cover a range of possible effects.

UNIT 4.4 Consumer law

Learning outcomes

By studying this unit, you will be able to:

- identify and understand the ways in which customers are protected by law
- identify the ways that **consumer law** affects business activity
- explain how the law can affect different businesses in different situations
- analyse and evaluate the impact consumer law has on different business situations.

Introductory case study: Which? – the consumers' champion

Which?

Which?, formerly the Consumer's Association, was started in 1957 and since then it has worked on behalf of customers. It has made customers aware of their rights in law as well as tested products to see if they comply with the law, making recommendations on 'best buys'.

Which? has the power to make businesses look at how they treat customers, having taken issue with supermarkets and banks among others in the past, in an effort to make them treat customers more fairly.

While an individual customer may feel that they cannot win a legal case against a large business, Which? exists 'to make individuals as powerful as the organisations they deal with'.

Businesses are under pressure to make sure they stay within the law when dealing with customers.

Customer rights

There are laws that help protect customers, and by giving customers protection, there is an impact on businesses.

How customers are protected by law

Customers are protected by the **Consumer Rights Act** 2015. This act of parliament gives customers protection when they buy goods *and* services, which must be:

- **of satisfactory quality** – goods must not be damaged or faulty when you buy them. The quality expected in different products should be taken into account. Cheaper 'bargains' should be expected to have a lower quality than luxury goods
- **fit for purpose** – goods must do what they are meant to do. If the seller claims that a product does a particular function, then it must be able to do that
- **as described** – goods must be as they are described. If you ordered an orange-coloured bike, then you should receive an orange bike, not a green one.

Other customer rights

Rights within 30 days

There is a 30-day time period for you to return faulty goods for a full refund, though businesses might offer more time than this as a gesture of good customer service. This part of the Consumer Rights Act does not apply to digital products such as music and apps that have been downloaded. A customer could ask for a replacement of such products, and if that is not given, the customer is entitled to a price reduction, which could be 100 per cent.

Rights within first six months

If a product develops a fault within the first six months, it is presumed that the fault was there at the time of buying. It is up to the seller to prove that the fault is with the customer. A customer may wish to argue for a reduction in price or a replacement in this time period. The only exception here is cars, where there is a reduction from any agreed compensation for the use of the car in that time.

Rights after six months

If a fault develops after six months, it is up to the customer to prove that the fault was there at the time of delivery. This would be a much more complicated procedure for most customers. Customers have six years to complete any claim against a seller.

Services

The points above relate to products. Services, such as entertainment, accountants, solicitors, estate agents and kitchen fitters are treated slightly differently by the Consumer Rights Act. If the work is not completed in the agreed time, or to a reasonable standard, then a customer can ask for the work to be completed again. If this is not possible, a price reduction should be agreed, which could be up to 100 per cent.

The impact of consumer law on business

There are a number of ways that consumer law can impact on business activity.

Production of quality goods

A business must make sure that the quality of the goods it produces is up to standard. They must not be damaged or faulty when bought (see also Unit 4.2). All goods need not be the best standard possible, but must reflect the price being charged. The production of quality goods will affect the training given to employees (see Unit 3.6) with businesses having to ensure that training is sufficient to make sure that goods are of the expected quality.

If a business does not produce goods 'of satisfactory quality' it may face customers returning goods for refund under the Consumer Rights Act. This in turn will cost the business money and may lower profits.

Maintaining or improving quality of goods can be expensive.

Safety of goods

If goods are produced that are defective in any way customers can claim compensation for damage, death or personal injury. This could result in huge costs for the business. Once again this puts pressure on a business to ensure that it has procedures in place to make sure that the goods it produces are free from defects.

Loss of reputation

If a business produces goods that are of poor quality or defective, then there will be claims from customers against the business. This can be very costly for the business in compensation payments.

In addition to the compensation payments is the loss of **reputation**. Reputations take a long time to build, and can be quickly destroyed if customers report defective products or poor service. Social media provide a way for customers to voice their anger at organisations that supply faulty goods, or provide inadequate service. Customers who see that a business has been supplying defective goods or services will likely buy from another business. This can further affect any business, possibly even leading to the business being closed down.

Evaluation point

When evaluating the impact that consumer law might have on a business, always look carefully at the situation you have been given. If a business is large and has a well-established reputation, will one complaint from a customer really put that reputation at risk?

Activity 1 – Research and presentation activity

Using the Consumer Rights Act, make a PowerPoint presentation titled 'How consumer law affects business activity'.

Activity 2 – True or false activity

Complete the following table by putting a tick in the correct column.

Statement	True	False
The Consumer Rights Act says that goods must always be of the best possible quality.		
Customers can return faulty goods for a full refund within 30 days of purchase.		
All goods must be described correctly only when they are over £100.		
Safety in goods bought by customers is covered by the Consumer Protection Act.		
Digital goods are covered in the same way as all other goods by the Consumer Rights Act.		
Good training will help in the production of quality goods.		
After 30 days, a customer cannot claim for faulty goods against a business.		

Table 4.12 Customer rights.

Key facts

The Consumer Rights Act 2015 is the key law that protects customers.

Goods and services must be as described, fit for purpose and of satisfactory quality.

The Consumer Protection Act 1987 protects customers over safety issues.

Businesses may have to pay for goods to be replaced under consumer law.

The loss of a good reputation could be very damaging to a business if it supplies faulty goods or services.

Useful words

Fit for purpose means that goods must do what they are meant to do.

As described means that goods must be as the business described them.

Consumer law is the area of law which protects the customers of a business. This is mainly through the Consumer Rights Act of 2015.

Satisfactory quality of goods means that how the goods are made will reflect the price. A high-priced product must be of high quality.

Reputation of a business is what customers say and feel about a business. Damage to a reputation can seriously affect a business.

Practice questions

Multiple choice questions

1 When buying any goods or services, customers are entitled to expect:
   - a) the goods to be of the best standard possible
   - b) the goods to be of satisfactory quality
   - c) the goods to be guaranteed for three years
   - d) the goods to be the same price as competitors.

2 A business must sell goods that:
   - a) do what they are meant to do
   - b) perform as well as competitor goods
   - c) are made to last for years
   - d) are as cheap as possible.

3 A way in which a business can be affected by consumer law is:
   - a) having compensation claims because goods are of high quality
   - b) losing reputation due to defective goods
   - c) having to sack staff who are always late for work
   - d) profits being reduced by paying higher wages.

Data response 27

QAU Ltd are a well-established business making washing machines. They have had no problems reported on their products for many years and have always advertised their products to be the best on the market for cleaning clothes. 'You cannot beat QAU clean' and 'Clean every time with QAU' have been their advertising slogans.

After recently opening a new factory to increase production, QAU have had reports from customers of clothes being left dirty and the washing drum not emptying. There have been a number of negative comments on social media to add to the problems faced by QAU.

1 Explain two ways how customers who have bought washing machines from QAU Ltd would be protected by law. (4 marks)

2 Analyse two impacts that the faulty washing machines might have on QAU Ltd. (6 marks)

3 Recommend what actions QAU Ltd might take to solve the problem of the faulty washing machines. Give reasons for your answer. (9 marks)

How to answer data response 27

1 In this question, you need to use your knowledge of the correct consumer law and explain how it would apply in this particular case.

2 Here you need to 'analyse' the effects that the faulty washing machines *might* have on the business. There is no clear right or wrong answer here. Look carefully at what you are told about QAU Ltd.

3 In question 3 you should look at what appears to be the problem – the new factory. What can be done there to make sure that the washing machines meet all the requirements of consumer law? Here you will have to think beyond this consumer law unit.

UNIT 4.5 Business location

Learning outcomes

By studying this unit, you will be able to:

- explain the main factors that influence where businesses decide to locate
- evaluate the importance of different factors that influence location decisions.

The importance of location

For many businesses, the decision of where to locate is one of the most important decisions it takes. Make the right decision and the business may flourish and become very successful. Make the wrong decision and the business may find it very difficult to succeed. As a result of globalisation, anywhere in the world can be considered a possible location for some businesses. Multinational businesses make choices about the country they should locate in, not just which region within a country. (See Unit 6.3 Globalisation.)

The wrong way to decide where to locate.

Factors influencing the location of business

There are a number of factors that can have an influence on the location of business activity. It is rarely only one factor that affects the decision to locate in a particular area but often a combination of factors.

Some of the location factors covered in this unit will have little or no influence on the location decision that a particular business makes, while others will have a significant influence. Much will depend on the type of business activity. For instance, a bakery producing bread and cakes will usually need to be located near to the market it is serving (unless it uses temperature-controlled storage).

On the other hand, a business producing clothing will probably need good access to the road network so that it can deliver to its customers who may be located in many different parts of the country.

The right way to decide where to locate.

Fresh cream cakes do not travel well in warm weather.

Costs

Case study: Burberry

Burberry, made in China.

Burberry produces expensive, upmarket clothes – it has a Royal Warrant, which means that it has sold goods to the Royal Family. The clothes used to be produced in Wales. This factory was closed and production now takes place in China. Burberry said it had decided to move production because the costs of producing in the UK were higher than almost anywhere else in the world, particularly factory costs and labour costs.

Case study: Cambridge Research Biochemicals Ltd (CRB Ltd)

CRB Ltd produces peptides and antibodies. Peptides help with building muscle and are also found in anti-ageing creams. Antibodies deal with viruses and bacteria that can make us ill. The company was founded in 1980 and was originally based in Cambridge and then, partly, in Northwich in Cheshire. In 1999, production was moved completely to Billingham in Teeside in the north-east of England. The company moved there because costs were so much lower than in Cambridge. The high demand for offices and laboratory space in Cambridge meant rents were very high. Rents in Billingham are now only 10 per cent of those in Cambridge. Labour was cheaper too and this remains the case. Much lower housing costs in Teeside meant workers were better off in Teeside than in Cambridge even when paid lower wages. In 2014, CRB Ltd spent £900,000 renovating premises to facilitate a move from Billingham to the Teeside Valley enterprise zone. It had won a 'Let's grow' grant of £65,000 from the government's regional growth fund that helped pay for the move. The fund is designed to protect jobs in the north-east.

The two case studies illustrate how the choice of location may be affected by the costs of production in different places. Costs of production will be affected by a number of factors:

- **The cost of the site** – the price of land or of premises such as offices and factories can vary significantly in different areas of the United Kingdom. The CRB Ltd case study shows the huge difference in the rental costs of premises and **labour** in prosperous towns such as Cambridge where land, premises and labour are in short supply, compared to places like Teeside that have suffered from the decline of its industries, including steel manufacture. The cost of the location will have to be paid for through the prices charged for the goods or services supplied to the customer and higher prices might make a business less competitive.

- **Transport infrastructure** – refers to the roads, railways, airports and ports that exist in an area. Infrastructure also includes ICT infrastructure covering broadband and other telecommunications networks. These are important for keeping the costs of transporting **raw materials** and finished products low as well as for communications. Some areas of the country are better served by motorways, main roads and railways than other areas. The ease with which businesses can gain access to the transport system will have a significant influence on where to locate the business. ICT communications are now so important for many businesses, that the ICT infrastructure has become a significant factor affecting location.

Government and costs

The national or local government may want to influence where businesses locate, usually to encourage them to set up in an area and so increase incomes and employment. There are 24 enterprise zones in the UK that have been set up by the national government. Four are in South Wales – Cardiff Central, Cardiff Airport and St Athan, Ebbw Vale and Port Talbot Waterfront. Businesses moving into enterprise zones are offered reduced business rates (taxes on business premises), higher capital allowances (lower corporation and income taxes when a firm invests), superfast broadband, sped-up planning application procedures and ready-built premises. These benefits can significantly reduce business costs.

Activity 1 – Research activity

Research information about production costs in your area – rents, wages etc. You will find it useful to use a search engine such as Google.

Try your local council website – often these promote the area to attract businesses.

Proximity or nearness to the market

Case study: the Posh Sardine, Arnside

The Posh Sardine sells to tourists.

Arnside is a small resort in the north-west of England. (If you are looking for exciting funfairs and night life, it is probably not the place for you!) It has a total resident population of around 2,300. It is in an Area of Outstanding Natural Beauty (Arnside and Silverdale AONB) and is popular with day-trippers and with people who own static caravans (there are 15 caravan sites in and around the AONB area). In a line of shops stretching for just 200 metres opposite the pier, the Posh Sardine (its name is an anagram of Arnside shop) is one of four cafés. It also sells craft goods and antiques. As well as the other three cafés, there are three other souvenir/craft shops, an art gallery, a clothes shop, a chemist, a restaurant and a public house that sells beer and food. Customers are predominantly the tourists who visit the town. Other retailers, more geared to serving the local residents – grocers, newsagents, hairdressers, the post office and so on – are situated away from the promenade.

Being near to its potential customers is crucial for many businesses. Clearly, as with the Posh Sardine, tourist businesses need to locate where tourists will visit. Other retailers may be looking for very large numbers of local, regular buyers. When deciding whether to locate in a particular area, retailers will need to consider the number of potential customers as well as the amount of competition already there and whether the customers will buy the kind of product it sells. There would be little point setting up an amusement arcade in Arnside. While there are no competitor businesses, it is unlikely that many of the type of people who visit the resort would want to spend time and money in an amusement arcade.

There is no retail park in Arnside. There are simply not enough potential customers for the large retailers, who tend to locate on retail parks. The nearest town to Arnside is the town of Kendal about 12 miles away, which acts as a regional centre for people who live in the Lake District and areas to the south of it. There are large supermarkets – Morrisons and Asda – and national chains such as Halfords, B&Q and Currys on the retail parks in Kendal.

Proximity to the market is important not only for retailers but also for service providers who may also need to locate close to where the customers live – care homes, hairdressers, doctors, dentists and opticians and many more. If a business creates larger products that can be costly to transport long distances then it makes sense to locate near to the buyers of the product to reduce these costs. The Midlands is a major centre for car production in the UK, particularly for Jaguar Land Rover (JLR) cars. Some businesses that supply components for the car industry have located nearby so that they can be in close communication with their buyers and also to reduce the costs of delivery. For example, Toyota Tsusho UK (TTUK) makes wheels used on JLR cars. It has sited production at Castle Donnington just 33 miles from Castle Bromwich where JLR has a major assembly plant. It is easy for TTUK to communicate with people at JLR about the type and quality of wheels needed. The cost of transporting the finished wheels is kept low because it involves only a short distance.

'We have made these fantastic, low-cost wheels but the car producers do not want them!'

Evaluation point

Proximity to the market remains a very important factor for many businesses. However, the growth of internet selling and the reduction in transport and shipping costs has made it possible for more and more sellers to compete even when they are not located near to their customers. A business like Amazon would be an example of a retailer which has competed effectively by being able to sell vast quantities at low prices. The growth in the number of delivery businesses has reduced transport costs.

Activity 2 – Research activity

Research your local area to find businesses that have located near to their market. There are three main reasons for locating near to the market. Find one example that fits each reason. In practice, one business may fit more than one reason. Write up your findings.

a) There are potential customers – think about the numbers and type of customers.

b) There is easy communication with customers – think about suppliers or service providers.

c) Costs of delivery are low – think about suppliers or service providers again.

Activity 3 – Research activity

Research how the local government near you tries to attract businesses to locate in the area. List the different incentives and benefits offered and key details about each one.
You might include benefits that will reduce business costs but also other features such as the available labour supply, the culture of the area and so on. Local government websites and local newspapers will have the type of information you are looking for.

Proximity to raw materials

Case study: Cargill Foods – being near to its raw materials

Cargill needs to be near its raw materials.

Cargill Foods is a multinational company. It has a factory in Liverpool that processes wheat imported from several countries. The factory is based on the docks in Liverpool, so that it is as near as possible to the supply of materials coming from abroad. The wheat arrives by ship and can be unloaded directly into the factory for processing. If the factory was located away from the docks it would have to be loaded on to lorries, transported and then unloaded. This would be very expensive.

Easy access to raw materials is necessary for some manufacturers, like Cargill. The costs of transporting some raw materials to a factory for processing can be very high, especially if they are bulky raw materials. Businesses that depend on a particular raw material may choose to locate near to where it is available to help reduce transportation costs.

Increasingly, the waste products of one business are becoming the raw materials for another, as businesses seek creative ways of making production more sustainable. Olleco is a business which uses waste oils and fats from restaurants to create the power needed to manufacture biofuels. Olleco is located in Liverpool so that it is near to a lot of restaurants that supply its raw materials.

There is also an environmental angle to locating near to a supply of raw materials. Buying from local suppliers means that the carbon footprint of the business is reduced (as well as the transport costs). Dewlay Cheesemakers in Garstang in Lancashire buys milk from dairy farms within six miles of its dairy and uses this claim to highlight its 'green' credentials alongside its pride about being the first cheese producer to generate its own electricity from its wind turbine.

Activity 4 – Research activity

Research businesses in your local area to find one that has located there to take advantage of a local supply of raw materials. Write up an account of the activity of the business.

Proximity to labour

Case study: proximity to labour in Newcastle

The website startups.co.uk described the following about Newcastle in 2014:

- 67,800 or just over one-third of the population of the city have a NVQ Level 4 or higher qualification – around average for a city of its size.
- £466.93 was the average weekly earnings, making it cheaper to employ workers than other cities, including Birmingham and Liverpool.
- The city has two major universities – Newcastle and Northumberland – while Durham University is nearby.
- Businesses based in the area can benefit from a range of services offered by Newcastle University, including collaboration on R&D projects, development and training and access to laboratory facilities. Overall, the student population is estimated at around 42,000.

Adapted from startups.co.uk

All businesses need labour, some more than others. Many require workers with different skills, others need lots of low-skilled or unskilled labour. Where large amounts of labour are needed or labour with specific skills is required, the availability of labour will be a significant influence on location. In some parts of the country, where traditional industries such as coal mining, shipbuilding, steel and textiles no longer exist, the supply of labour is usually plentiful. The CRB Ltd case study shows that the business had moved to Teeside partly because there was a plentiful supply of cheap labour in this area as a result of the decline in steel production. The Newcastle case study above illustrates some of the issues about labour – wage costs and skills in particular – that can influence the location decision of a business.

Activity 5 – Research activity

Research the amount and type of labour available in the area in which you live. You may find this on publicity information produced by your local council or simply use a search engine such as Google. Write a brief summary of your findings.

Evaluation point

Businesses will be affected in different ways by the factors that influence location, depending on what they produce. Businesses will need to consider the various influences on production costs – the cost of land or premises, of transporting raw materials and finished goods, and the cost of recruiting and employing labour. They will need to consider if they need to be near to their market. Often a location may present some advantages but also disadvantages. Oxford Street in London has a massive supply of possible customers that would make it a good location for a retail outlet but the rental costs of premises will be more than many businesses can afford. An IT firm may feel that it can locate where property prices are low to save money but there must be people with the relevant skills in the area. A manufacturer may wish to be based in a port for access to its raw materials but there may not be a good transport infrastructure to use to deliver the goods it makes. Businesses will need to weigh up all of these factors.

Activity 6 – Designing and drawing activity

Using the information in Activities 1 to 5, design and then draw a leaflet to attract businesses to locate in your area.

The interdependent nature of business

Unit 7 The interdependent nature of business, describes the links that exist between the different areas of business. The location of industry illustrates some of the links that exist. For example, a decision where to locate may be influenced by a number of factors – costs in the area, the supply of labour, the market size and type, and environmental considerations. Costs may be influenced by the availability of labour. How important this is, will depend on the type of business. The supply of labour may be linked to the market – a plentiful supply may mean low incomes in the area and a market where customers cannot afford expensive products.

Activity 7 – Explanation and presentation activity

This activity is based on a question that appeared in an OCR examination paper and is designed to make you think about the factors which might affect the location of a garage business in the imaginary town of Marston.

Read the information in conjunction with the map of Marston and use your knowledge of the factors which affect the location of a business to answer the questions that follow.

John Taylor is thinking of opening a new garage business in Marston. He intends to sell petrol, provide car maintenance and fit car alarms. He is considering two possible sites for the location of the garage. They are marked A and B on the map. Both sites have suitable premises for the business he is considering opening.

1 State and explain two advantages of locating the garage business at Site A.
2 State and explain two disadvantages of locating the garage business at Site B.
3 Explain what other information John might need before making a final decision on the location of his garage business.
4 Explain how John's business might benefit if the town of Marston grows in size.
5 Recommend to John location A or B for the garage business.
6 Produce a leaflet for distribution to houses in Marston advertising the new garage. Do not forget to include a location map and information on some of the services which John's garage might provide.

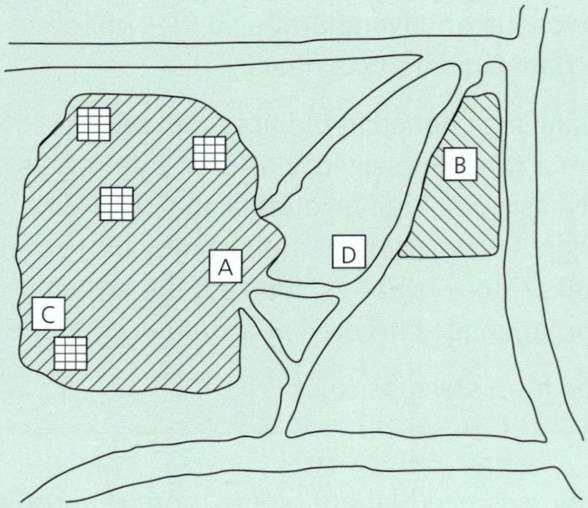

Key

A – Available site with garage premises

B – Available site with garage premises

C – Car alarm specialist fitting business

D – Existing garage – petrol retail and shop

⊞ – Existing garages – petrol retail and maintenance/repair services

▨ – Marston (population: 46,000)

▧ – Industrial estate

Figure 4.1 Map of Marston

Key facts

Location is very important for many businesses but not for all.

Costs at different sites may be taken in to consideration when deciding where to locate.

The government may help to reduce the cost of locating in a particular region in order to create jobs and raise incomes in that area.

Locating near to its customers helps a business to sell to them, to know what they need and to reduce costs if delivery is required.

Locating near to the source of the raw materials can be important for businesses that use bulky raw materials to produce a smaller finished product and for those who wish to be thought of as environmentally friendly.

Firms need to locate where there are sufficient quantities of the required type of labour.

The location of a business may be influenced by more than one of the factors affecting location.

Different sites are likely to have advantages and disadvantages for different types of businesses.

Multinational businesses may consider different locations in different countries when deciding where to locate their businesses.

Useful words

Transport infrastructure is the provision of roads, railways, ports and airports in an area for transporting goods and people.

Proximity means 'nearness to'. It can refer to proximity to the market, to raw materials and to labour supplies.

Location refers to the place where a business is sited.

Labour is a factor of production. It is the labour employed by businesses to produce goods and services.

Raw materials are materials that are processed in some way as part of the manufacture of a product.

Practice questions

Multiple choice questions

1 Which of these is not a reason for a business locating near to its market?

- **a)** It produces a large finished product.
- **b)** It uses bulky raw materials to produce a smaller, finished product.
- **c)** Its customers are not likely to travel far or shop over the internet to buy what it sells.
- **d)** It sells fresh products such as cream cakes.

2 Which one of these statements is not true?

- **a)** Firms that produce small, finished products are best locating near to their market.
- **b)** Governments often influence the location of businesses so that they can reduce unemployment and raise incomes in certain parts of the country.
- **c)** Low-cost locations are important for every single producer.
- **d)** Where a business locates is often influenced by more than one location factor.

3 A firm has identified four possible locations to set up. Based on the figures available, which offers the lowest cost per unit produced?
   a) Site W. Output per year – 10,000 units. Annual rental costs of premises – £30,000. Annual total wage costs – £80,000.
   b) Site X. Output per year – 12,000 units. Annual rental costs of premises – £42,000. Annual total wage costs – £102,000.
   c) Site Y. Output per year – 11,000 units. Annual rental costs of premises – £34,000. Annual total wage costs – £81,500.
   d) Site Z. Output per year – 9,000 units. Annual rental costs of premises – £32,000. Annual total wage costs – £71,500.

Data response 28

Heathrow is the UK's busiest airport with around 75 million passengers passing through each year. EuropCar, Sixt, Hertz and Avis Car Hire are some of the car rental companies located at Heathrow Airport. The cost of renting the service desk to deal with customers at the airport is high, as is the cost of the parking spaces needed for the cars when they are not on hire. A new car hire company, Lo-Cost rental, is considering offering car rentals from Heathrow. As its name implies, it offers cars with low rental charges. It offers low specification, cheap cars.

1 Explain one advantage to car rental companies of locating at Heathrow Airport. (3 marks)

2 Explain one disadvantage to car rental companies of locating at Heathrow Airport. (3 marks)

3 Recommend whether or not Lo-Cost should start to offer car rentals at Heathrow Airport. Give reasons for your recommendation. (7 marks)

How to answer data response 28

1 You might explain the amount of competition or costs.

2 You might explain the amount of competition or costs.

3 You need to weigh up the advantages and disadvantages of Heathrow for Lo-Cost. In coming to a decision, you might consider if there are likely to be enough customers to justify the cost or you might discuss whether the types of customers who will fly are likely to want low specification, low-cost cars. There is no right or wrong answer to questions like these – you will be credited for how well you use the data available to you and how well you explain the reasons for your decision. You may not even wish to make a decision but prefer to suggest further information that Lo-Cost would need to research.

UNIT 4.6 Working with suppliers

Learning outcomes

By studying this unit, you will be able to:

- identify and understand the role of procurement in a business context
- understand the importance of logistics
- understand the importance of logistical decisions made by businesses
- explain how procurement and logistical decisions affect particular businesses
- analyse and evaluate the impact of procurement and logistical decisions in a given business context.

Introductory case study: Eddie Stobart and the importance of logistics to a business

Eddie Stobart lorry.

Eddie Stobart lorries are a familiar sight on the roads of the UK. They are part of the supply chain for businesses, making sure that businesses, such as Tesco, have the correct number of goods on the shelves each day for us to buy. We take this for granted – imagine if we went into Tesco and there was nothing to buy!

Businesses must take care to ensure that the goods they buy are from a reliable seller. Those goods then need to be transported to their final destination. This is the role of businesses such as Eddie Stobart (now the Stobart Group), who must also be reliable in order that we have the products we need and at the time we need them. Eddie Stobart and other such businesses are said to be part of the **logistics** business, that is the transportation and storage of goods. This is a very important area for many businesses.

Procurement

Procurement is the management of the buying or purchasing area in a business. For some businesses, it will be a very large department. Think of the number of goods a supermarket such as Tesco sells; these goods are bought to be sold in their shops. This in turn means that a business has to deal with many other businesses that make the products. If something goes wrong, it will be Tesco who will take much of the blame, rather than the supplier of the product. It is therefore vital that procurement works well in choosing and managing where products are bought.

Activity 1 – Research and presentation activity

For a service business (which may be a shop, bank, insurance etc.) and a manufacturing business, investigate the number of different goods and services they require in order to operate fully. For example, a business selling clothing, such as New Look, will obviously need clothes, but the business will also have offices – what might be required there for the business to operate fully? Present your ideas in any form you feel comfortable with, which may be computer-based.

The role of procurement

Procurement has a number of roles within a business. These are:

1 identifying goods and services to buy
2 choosing suppliers
3 ordering goods and services
4 receiving deliveries from **suppliers**.

Identifying goods and services to buy

Any shop, large or small, has to constantly make decisions as to what they should offer for sale. It is a similar decision for manufacturing businesses; they have to decide where to buy their materials. Service businesses, such as banks, will have to decide where to buy their computer equipment, where to buy their paper for the printer – the list is endless!

There are a number of factors that can affect which goods and services to buy. These include:

- **the time of year** – clothes shops, for example, will have to think carefully as to what they order at what time of year. A change in the weather can catch them out and result in losses. Should a local shop stock up on ice cream at the end of September? Should a local DIY centre stock up on paint in January – will most people be decorating their houses in the middle of winter or is it more of a spring job? A business such as B&Q will change its shop layout in September, putting away, or selling at a discount, outdoor furniture and barbeques. Fresh stocks will be bought in for sale the following spring, along with spring plants for the garden.
- **changes in technology** – for some products, technology changes rapidly. A business must be careful to make sure that it does not buy too much of a product that is being replaced in the near future, unless of course it is offered a huge discount!
- **changes in fashion and lifestyle** – this obviously applies to clothing – buying the correct styles will certainly help sales. Fashion and lifestyle can also apply to food. There has been a growing movement towards vegetarian meals and gluten-free food, which has meant that many supermarkets are buying in greater ranges of these products for their customers to buy. Furniture changes in style over time along with many other household items. Cosmetics are linked closely to lifestyle, too. There are many businesses that must be 'on trend' and make sure that they have identified goods and services to buy that are in line with current fashion and lifestyle.

It is important that goods are bought at the correct time of year for a business.

Activity 2 – Explanation activity

Complete the table below, explaining how different factors can affect the buying of different goods and services by businesses. Try and think of a number of different examples of goods and services.

Factors that can affect the buying of goods and services by businesses	Examples of goods and services	Why goods are affected by this factor
Time of year		
Changes in technology		
Changes in fashion and lifestyle		

Table 4.14 Different factors that affect the buying of goods and services.

Activity 3 – Design and explanation activity

Design your own chart to explain how certain goods and services, such as the need for food, are not affected by the factors that you have covered in Activity 2.

Choosing suppliers

A business should choose its suppliers carefully. Factors that can affect that decision include:

- **the quality of the goods supplied** – as well as reliability (see page 216), quality is important to a business. It is not to say that quality must be the highest possible level, but quality must be at the expected standard all of the time. Car manufacturers use parts made by many different businesses. These parts must be at the expected standard, otherwise the reliability of the car may fall and customers will buy from another maker.
- **the reputation of suppliers** – while a supplier might provide the goods a business needs, if those goods are made in an unethical environment (see Unit 6.1) then the decision may be made to look for an alternative source. The poor reputation of a supplier can affect the reputation of the final seller of the goods.

Ordering goods and services

Procurement will deal with the actual ordering of the goods and services needed by a business. This may include paper for the printer or staff to clean the premises. Once again, the list could be a long one! In smaller businesses, however, such as a newsagent's shop, all of the ordering will no doubt be done by the owner, who is likely to do the cleaning as well.

Procurement will look at the amount of goods and services to be ordered. Is there a discount if more of a product is ordered? If a cleaning contract is signed for a year rather than six months would the price be lower?

Receiving deliveries from suppliers

The orders made by procurement have to be stored when received. This will clearly have an influence on the amount being ordered. It is no use doing a great deal on washing up liquid only to find you have no room to store the 50,000 bottles you have bought.

In some businesses, deliveries are made at night and so arrangements have to be made for staff to receive the goods. There needs to be access to the premises if bulky goods are being delivered. Once again, it is no use ordering large quantities if the delivery van cannot get near your business.

Impact of logistical and supply decisions on businesses

When a business makes decisions to buy goods and services, those decisions have an impact upon the business. The impact may be slight, such as in the case of a local chip shop that changes potato suppliers and the delivery day becomes Tuesday rather than Monday. In the case of a global industry such as cars, where parts are bought from all over the world, the effect of changes in supply can be enormous.

Decisions on logistics and supply are affected by:

- time
- reliability of supply
- length of the supply chain
- costs
- customer service.

Time

For some businesses, time can be vital for the delivery of supplies. If a plumber is in the middle of a complex job and finds that a part is needed, it is important that the particular part is supplied quickly. If not, there will be a serious impact on the job. In larger manufacturing business, parts are often delivered just at the time they are needed for production to take place. Once again timing is vital. If goods do not arrive at the correct time, then there is an impact on the business.

Reliability of supply

A business must have reliable supplies. A shop needs products to sell. In the case of fresh products such as fruit and bread, daily supplies are required. If the delivery is not made, the shop concerned will not only have no fruit to sell, but also risk compromising its own reputation. This links with the section on time above. Reliability and supplies being on time go together.

The reliability of supply also involves the delivery of goods, which may be by a specialist logistics business such as Eddie Stobart (see the case study at the start of this unit). It is vital therefore that the supplier, if required, uses a reliable delivery service. If not, the supplier and the final seller will both be seen as unreliable and may lose customers.

Length of the supply chain

The supply chain is the organisation of people and resources that brings goods and services to the consumer. For some business situations, the supply chain might be shorter than others. A potter selling handmade pottery direct to the public will still have to buy clay from a supplier, who may themselves buy clay from where it is mined.

For other goods, the supply chain may be rather longer. Looking at the car industry again, a car maker who buys brake systems from a specialist supplier is relying on the supply chain of the brake manufacturer, who themselves may be relying on other businesses to supply them with materials and parts to make the brakes.

When decisions are made about which suppliers to use, the length of the supply chain may well be a consideration. If there is a long and complex supply chain that involves large distances in addition to many businesses, any problem within that chain can affect the final product. A shorter supply chain will usually be more reliable and easier to manage.

Some supply chains are very complex.

Costs

Clearly the costs of items being bought by a business will have a direct impact on business performance. Costs, however, must be balanced against other logistic and supply considerations. Is it better to have lower costs rather than a reliable supplier? Is it better to have lower costs but wait longer for supplies to arrive?

Factors such as costs, reliability, timing and quality must be considered together when decisions are made as to which supplier to use. A saving on costs may result in lower quality, less reliability in a product and consequently a loss of a good reputation that might be difficult to get back. However, paying too much for supplies must also be avoided, provided that all other considerations have been made.

Customer service

It must be remembered that businesses are themselves customers. They buy goods and services from other businesses. Decisions on choice of supplier may take customer service into consideration. If a business fails to deliver certain items, or items have a fault, when will the problem be corrected? This problem is the same as a customer buying goods. When a business sells to another business it must have an organisation in place – customer service – to deal with any problems that might occur, otherwise the business that is buying may take their custom elsewhere.

Evaluation point

Remember that choosing a supplier is a complex matter. There are many factors to consider, along with just how many and at what time goods should be ordered. There are many ways in which decisions on suppliers can impact on businesses. Generally speaking, there is no single factor, at any one time, that is more important than others. It is usually the case that factors such as cost, reliability, quality and so on, are all seen as important.

Activity 4 – Explanation activity

The following factors impact on the decision-making of businesses in the supply of the goods and services they need in order to operate:

- time
- reliability of supply
- length of the supply chain
- costs
- customer service.

In the following business situations, which of the factors would be the most important? Give reasons for your recommendations, remembering that a number of factors may be of equal importance.

a) A discount shop selling all of its goods at £1.

b) A high-class perfume manufacturer, keen to keep its upmarket reputation.

c) A business wanting to create a good customer service image after bad publicity in newspapers.

d) An online supplier of clothing has had difficulty in meeting promised delivery dates.

Key facts

Procurement in a business has a number of roles in the ordering of supplies.

There are a number of factors to consider when choosing a supplier.

When making a decision on which supplier to choose, there are a number of considerations that will have an impact upon the business.

Useful words

Logistics is the management of the transportation and storage of goods.

Procurement is the management of purchasing within a business.

Suppliers are parties who supply goods and/or services to a business.

Practice questions

Multiple choice questions

1 Procurement is:

a) the process of making sure the best-quality product is ordered

b) how a business makes sure that deliveries are made on time

c) the process of managing the ordering of goods and services required by a business

d) the part of a business that manages the level of production to increase efficiency.

2 A longer supply chain will mean:

a) a business will have to make do with lower-quality goods

b) it may be more difficult for a business to manage supplies

c) it will take longer to find the right kind of supplier

d) the supplier could demand higher prices.

3 Logistical decisions in a business are concerned with:

a) the transportation and management of supplies

b) the management of the quality control system within a business

c) the methods a business will use to examine goods upon delivery

d) the management of costs in the production process within a business.

Data response 29

Korean phone manufacturer Samsung had 35 cases of its newly launched phone exploding while being charged. Samsung suspended sales of the phone and offered replacements for anyone who had already purchased one, but stopped short of recalling all of the phones sold.

Koh Dong-Jin, president of Samsung's mobile business, said, two weeks after the Note 7's launch: 'We have received several reports of battery explosions on the Note 7... and it has been confirmed that it was a battery cell problem. There was a tiny problem in the manufacturing process so it was very difficult to find out.'

Koh refused to name the supplier of the faulty battery, but said that Note 7s sold in China used batteries from a different supplier and were unaffected. He said that Samsung was working with two or three different battery suppliers for the smartphone, including its own Samsung SDI.

Adapted from the Guardian, *2 September 2016*

1 Identify two factors that can affect how a business might choose a supplier. (2 marks)

2 Analyse two possible impacts on Samsung of the faulty batteries that have been supplied. (6 marks)

3 Evaluate the problems of a complex supply chain to a business such as Samsung. (7 marks)

How to answer data response 29

1 This question requires identification, so no explanation is necessary

2 This question requires analysis, so you need to look at the potential effects (good or bad) on the business.

3 This question is examining analysis and evaluation. Look at the potential effects on the business of a complex supply chain, and then identify which is the greater potential effect on Samsung.

UNIT 5.1 The role of the finance function

Learning outcomes

By studying this unit, you will be able to:

- explain and evaluate the role of the **finance function** in businesses
- explain and evaluate how the finance function can influence business activity.

Introductory case study: EasyJet

EasyJet investors are expecting the low-cost airline's weakest full-year results in three years after the summer 2016 plunge in sterling wiped £90 million from its earnings to drag its full-year profits down by a third.

In its first profit warning since 2009, the airline admitted last month that it expects to make between £490 million and £495 million in this financial year, almost a third less than the £686 million it made in 2015 and the lowest full-year profit since 2013.

The post-Brexit currency crash wiped a third from the airline's market value, after dealing a heavier than expected blow to the airline that has since reduced ticket prices to encourage more people to fly on its planes.

Adapted from telegraph.co.uk, 12 November 2016

The details above on EasyJet show how events outside the control of a business can affect its finances. The finance function will have to keep a careful check on finances at EasyJet to cope with the problems it and many other businesses face in the modern business world.

Purpose of the finance function

Only larger businesses will have a separate finance function. Sole traders and partnerships would normally employ an accountant to check their finances. Larger limited companies will have their own finance function.

Provide financial information

Financial information can take many forms. These include:

- the costs and revenues of the business, for use in cash-flow forecasting (see Unit 5.5)
- information on the profit or loss of a business
- data on average rate of return and profitability (see Unit 5.3).

It is vital for any business that this data is accurate and up to date so that any decisions the business might take, are taken using the correct information.

A finance department will provide a range of information that can help the successful operation of a business.

Supporting business planning and decision-making

We have seen that finance is important for business. It influences business activity by making it possible for a business to start up, expand, replace equipment that has depreciated and pay for day-to-day expenses. The finance function in a business will have an input into the business plan (see Unit 1.2).

An inability to gain finance will restrict business activity. Many small businesses remain small because they could not raise the finance to expand.

The need for finance may affect the legal form of the business. The owner of a sole trader business who wishes to expand may invite someone who can provide finance to become a partner, changing the business into a partnership. Partnerships may become private limited companies so that they can sell shares, expanding ownership and finance. Private limited companies may become public limited companies so that they can sell their shares publicly and gain funding from a wider range of investors.

Influence of the finance function on business activity

Part of how the finance function can influence business activity is by providing the information that other departments need in order to make decisions, as well as raising the finance that is needed. In the rest of Unit 5, you will look in more detail at the financial information that the finance department will provide. It is helpful to give a basic description of this information and illustrate when it may be useful.

- Sources of finance are where businesses get money from to make payments. Sources include savings, loans, overdrafts and share issues. (See Unit 5.2.)
- Revenue is the money that businesses receive from selling goods. Costs include the cost of making and selling a good or service and expenses involved in production. Profit or loss is found by taking the total costs of production away from the total revenue made by a business. (See Unit 5.3.)
- Break-even is a calculation of the number of products a business needs to sell in order to cover all of its costs. It is based on assumptions about the price it can charge and its costs of production. (See Unit 5.4.)
- Cash flow records the inflow of money and the outflow of money. From this, a business can see if it will have enough income to pay upcoming bills or if it will need to finance this somehow. (See Unit 5.5.)

Some examples of decisions where financial information will be useful are given below.

- A business that decides to become more environmentally friendly will have possibly increased costs and may need to monitor cash flow. It may need additional finance, for example, to change the way it produces or to market itself as environmentally friendly as possible. Its break-even output may change as its costs change. The finance department will have to provide the information about these so that relevant people in the business can monitor what is happening. It may need to take action to raise the finance.
- A business may be affected by a recession when demand in the economy and sales may be reduced. The finance department would need to provide information about revenues and costs that would help the business decide how to respond.
- A business that is considering changing from job to batch or from batch to flow will need information from the finance department predicting changes in revenues and costs, what finance it would need to raise and how it might do this, how the change might affect the cash flow of the business and how its break-even output would change.
- A business may want to change the way it markets its product, perhaps by advertising on TV. The finance department would provide the information about the costs of these and may raise the finance needed.

- A business may wish to change the way it sells its products, perhaps by selling online as well as through retail outlets or perhaps by opening up retail outlets if it only sells online currently. Again, the finance department will provide the information needed about the effects on revenues and costs.

What we are seeing in these examples is the interdependent nature of business. This is covered in more detail in Unit 7.

Activity 1 – Explanation activity

A business has decided that it needs to change the way it behaves in order to be an ethical business. It has decided to raise the wages of its workers and increase the measures it takes to ensure its workplace is healthy and safe.

Explain how the following data from the finance function might influence the decision-making at the business.

a) The costs of production.

b) The profit of the business.

c) The cash flow of the business.

Evaluation point

All businesses need finance. The owner or owners in a small business will deal with finance issues in their business. Large businesses usually have finance departments that specialise in this type of work. The work is crucial to the start-up and continued success of a business. It also influences the way in which the business operates. It is important to be able to evaluate the importance of the finance function in business decision-making.

Key facts

The finance function is vital for all businesses – all businesses must manage their finance well to succeed.

Accurate financial information is vital to a business when planning and developing.

Useful words

Finance function is sometimes referred to as the finance department. Only found in larger businesses.

Financial information includes details of profit, loss, cash flow, break-even, profit margin and average rate of return. These can be used in helping business decision-making.

Practice questions

Multiple choice questions

1 Which of the following is a role of the finance function?

a) advertise for temporary Christmas staff

b) decide on the style of a new television advert

c) monitor the costs and revenues of a business

d) make sure that the quality of goods made is of the highest standard.

2 Which of the following statements is false?

a) Business growth may be limited by problems of raising finance.

b) Finance is needed to pay for the start-up costs of a business.

c) Marketing costs are always paid out of revenue the business raises so finance is not needed.

d) A business may need to change its legal form to raise finances.

3 A business that makes clothes decides to increase production. Which of the following is not likely to happen?

a) Expenditures measured on the cash flow forecast will increase.

b) The firm may need to raise finance to expand the production facilities at the business.

c) The total cost of production will increase.

d) The firm will spend less money on raw materials.

Data response 30

LP Ltd is a company that has begun to develop some new drugs. It now needs to trial the drugs, which is very expensive. If the trials demonstrate the drugs are successful, LP Ltd could either produce the drugs itself to sell or allow other manufacturers to produce them under licence. LP Ltd will need to invest in a new factory if it is to produce them and it will also have to market the drugs. Drug companies advertise their products online, by mail shots and by sending sales representatives to visit hospitals and doctors' surgeries. Using sales representatives is considered to be the most effective way of marketing drugs but is also the most expensive.

1 Explain three reasons why financial information will help the business develop and trial its new drugs. (6 marks)

2 Evaluate the importance of the finance function in supporting the planning at a business such as LP Ltd. (7 marks)

How to answer data response 30

1 This question asks you to explain, so you must look carefully at the information you are given in the case study and look to see how financial information will help the business. For example, you are told that a trial is expensive so careful planning is necessary. How will financial information help in this situation?

2 The case study gives examples of the planning necessary to develop and trial the new drugs. The question directs you to evaluate, so you must make a judgement on how useful the finance function is in this planning process. How will the finance function help it to succeed?

UNIT 5.2 Sources of finance

Learning outcomes

By studying this unit, you will be able to:

- explain and evaluate the reasons that businesses need finance
- explain and evaluate the main ways of raising finance, and the costs and uses of these
- evaluate how and why different sources of finance are suitable for new and for established businesses.

The reasons businesses need finance

The purpose of the finance function is to manage the money that businesses need to operate.

Case study: Chineasy – long-term business start-up through crowdfunding

Crowdfunding makes Chineasy.

Chineasy was founded by ShaoLan Hsueh. She appreciated that learning to read Chinese was very difficult for many Western people because of the different writing used – it is made up of thousands of symbols. ShaoLan also realised that there was a business opportunity as a lot of people want to learn Chinese because of the increasing importance of trading with China. Her intention was to develop a course for beginners to help them to learn basic Chinese characters and then build on this to learn further characters. To support learning, ShaoLan designed materials including a book, flash cards and online films (you can find some on YouTube, if you are interested). Funding was needed to develop and produce the materials and set up the website. She also needed finance to pay for advertising. ShaoLan did this through crowdfunding. She used the website Kickstarter.com to let people know she needed money for the business and to collect the money offered by investors. In addition, she promoted her business idea through social media and other, more traditional media. Such was the interest in her business, ShaoLan was able to raise nearly £200,000 within a month, well above her target of £75,000.

Case study: Makerfield Services Ltd – short-term financing

Makerfield Services Ltd is a small, electrical contractor. The business contracts to do the electrical wiring needed as part of construction or refurbishment projects. Money is needed for day-to-day purchases, such as electric wiring and sockets, and for paying the wages of the workers. These are financed partly out of the revenues that the business makes. However, the cash flow into the business is not always enough to pay for these materials. Makerfield Services Ltd has a current account at the bank into which it pays revenues and out of which it makes payments for the materials and other business expenses. Makerfield Services Ltd has also arranged an overdraft facility, which means that it can overspend on the account up to an agreed amount. Makerfield Services Ltd pays a monthly fee for the facility and **interest** on the amount that is overdrawn. When Makerfield Services Ltd receives enough revenue, it will reduce the overdraft. The overdraft is an example of external finance. It is short term because it can be repaid to the bank quickly. It is used in this example for the day-to-day running of the business.

The two case studies illustrate different reasons why businesses need finance. All businesses will need finance at some stage in order for them to:

- establish a new business start-up, which means spending money on capital equipment, recruiting workers and marketing activities
- fund expansion when a business grows in size, either by internal or external growth
- run business recruitment, paying for the recruitment costs
- develop marketing activities such as to fund marketing campaigns to maintain or increase sales and market share.

Sometimes finance is needed for just a short period of time to help overcome a temporary shortage of funds, for example when waiting for a customer to pay a large bill – a cash-flow problem. On other occasions, finance may be needed for a much longer period of time, for example when buying a new building.

Ways of raising finance

Businesses can raise finance either internally or externally. They can raise it to meet their short-, medium- and long-term needs.

Activity 1 – Matching terms activity

In the table below match the reason for needing finance in the left-hand column with the example of that reason in the right-hand column.

Reason for needing finance	Example
1 Starting up a new business	a) A pharmaceutical company seeking to develop a new drug to treat cancer.
2 Replacing old machinery, equipment and premises	b) A person setting up a new business installing and maintaining burglar alarms.
3 Internal growth	c) A theme park that is only open from Easter to October needs money during the closed season for maintenance and promotional activities.
4 External growth – the takeover or acquisition of another company	d) Buying new computer equipment to replace old computers that have been in use for several years.
5 Day-to-day expenses – dealing with cash flow problems	e) Buying new manufacturing equipment as a result of increased demand for products.
6 Development purposes – research and development	f) Walmart, the USA retailer, has taken over Jet.com, an online retailer, which is the main challenger to Amazon.

Table 5.1 Reasons for needing finance.

Case study: Peter Hobson, Gardener – own savings start up and expand

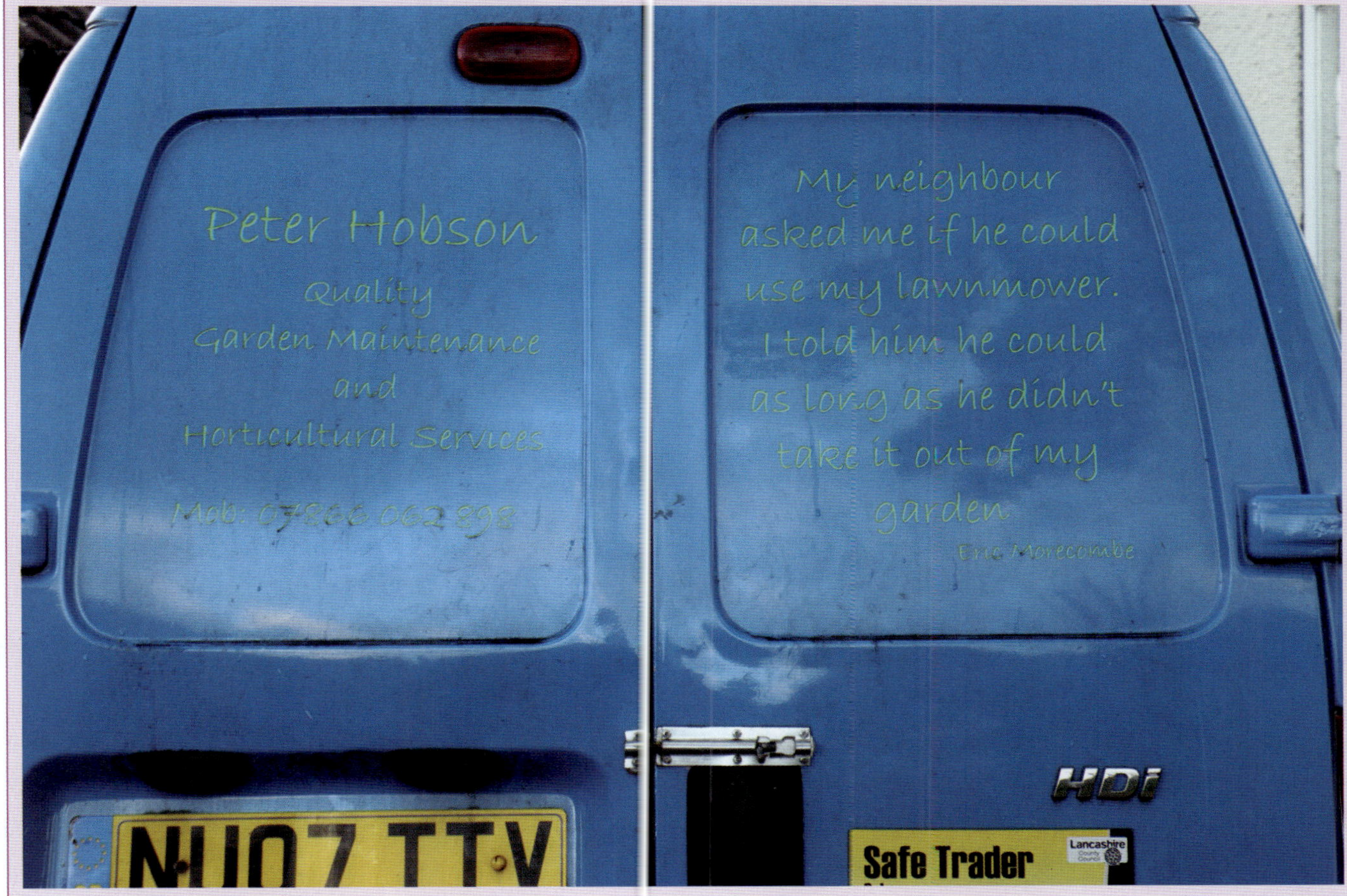

An example of a business owner using savings to finance the business

Peter Hobson is a self-employed gardener. He had worked for a number of years as a qualified horticultural instructor at a special school in Ormskirk. He saved £12,000 from his wages to have enough to buy a van (and have it painted) and the gardening tools he needed to start up his gardening business. It was a risk he was prepared to take because he had always wanted to start his own business. At first, he got work on the recommendations of friends and ex-work colleagues. The number of customers increased rapidly based on recommendations from satisfied customers. In 2016, he took on a partner, his son Matthew. To increase the number of customers further, Peter paid for 5,000 leaflets to be printed that were then distributed to homes and businesses in the area. He used more savings from the business to buy new tools to be able to offer a greater range of services such as patio and path laying, garden design and the construction of pagodas. Peter may have been able to get a loan from a bank to start up the business but he might have had to provide some kind of security – perhaps his house – against the loan. As the amount required was fairly small in business terms and he had the savings needed, it made sense not to put his family home at risk. The finance Peter needed was medium-term because the capital equipment he bought would be used over the next three to five years.

Case study: Leon – loan

Leon is a fast-food chain selling 'healthy' foods. On its menu are foods such as salads, wraps and chicken in pots. In 2016, it borrowed £19 million from OakNorth to finance the opening of 50 more new restaurants. OakNorth is a specialist bank that lends to businesses it identifies as fast-growing. There are already over 40 Leon restaurants in the UK, mainly in London, and it has expanded abroad having opened a restaurant at Schipol Airport, in Amsterdam. It is planning further expansion abroad, in Holland and in the USA. The loan is a long-term loan. Leon has financed its expansion from an external source because it did not have sufficient reserves to finance it. It has had to provide security against the loan – an asset that OakNorth could sell to get its money back should Leon not be able to repay it. OakNorth will accept fixtures and fittings, stock and property, including intellectual property as security. It is long-term finance because Leon will not need to repay the loan before five years have passed.

Not all sources of finance are available to every business. Some reasons why are given below:

- Sole traders and partnerships (unincorporated businesses) are not able to raise finance by selling shares.
- Limited companies (incorporated businesses) cannot take extra partners in the hope of raising more finance.
- Businesses with a poor financial record are unlikely to find many banks willing to lend money to them.

Business activities that are considered to be very risky or have a poor future will also find it difficult to raise finance.

Evaluation point

Obtaining finance for business development is a serious matter. The business will need to consider carefully the advantages and disadvantages of each source of finance before making a decision as to the most suitable source. In some circumstances, a combination of different sources of finance may be appropriate. Not all sources of finance will be available for every business.

Most sources of finance represent a commitment to repay a debt at some time in the future.

Identifying how economic and business conditions may change in the future is very difficult but an important part of the decision-making process when considering obtaining additional finance. Getting it wrong may spell the end for the business but being too cautious may mean that the business is not able to grow and develop in order to compete with its rivals.

How and why different sources of finance are suitable for new and established businesses

Advantages and disadvantages of different types of finance

Table 5.2 lists different types of finance that businesses can use. The types of finance have been divided into internal and external. The first column describes the different types of finance, what they are typically used for and whether they are suitable for new and established businesses. The second column indicates the time period for the finance and which types of businesses, in terms of ownership, it is available to. The third and fourth columns give advantages and disadvantages respectively.

Most businesses will find the choice of finance difficult to make.

Description and uses	Type and availability of finance	Advantages	Disadvantages
Owner's capital ■ The owners use their own savings. ■ Typically used for buying start-up, expansion or replacement capital equipment or for paying for start-up or development activities. It can also be used for day-to-day running expenses. ■ New and established businesses.	Short, medium or long term, sole traders and partnerships.	■ No need to repay the money. ■ No interest has to be paid. ■ No cost to raise the finance.	■ If the owner or owners do not have enough savings, they will need to use another source of finance as well.
Retained profit ■ Profit that is made by the business but which is not distributed (paid out) to the owners is invested back in to the business. ■ Typically used for buying, expansion or replacement of capital equipment and paying for start-up or development activities. ■ Established businesses only.	Medium or long term, all businesses.	■ No **interest** has to be paid. ■ No need to repay the money. ■ No cost to raise the finance.	■ Only available to businesses that have made profits.

Description and uses	Type and availability of finance	Advantages	Disadvantages
Sale of assets ■ A fixed asset, such as machinery or premises that the business owns, is sold. ■ Typically used for buying expansion or replacement capital equipment and for development purposes. The money can also be used for day-to-day expenses. ■ Established businesses only.	Short, medium or long term, all businesses.	■ Good if the asset is no longer of use to the business.	■ Can take time to sell the asset. ■ May not be possible to find a buyer.
Overdraft ■ An arrangement with a bank that the business can spend more money than it has in its bank account. ■ The amount of the overdraft may vary on a daily basis as money is paid into and taken out of the account by the business. ■ Used for day-to-day expenses such as wages, stock, bills. ■ New and established businesses.	Short term, all businesses.	■ An overdraft can meet short-term cash flow problems. ■ The business can continue trading in the short term. ■ The size of the overdraft varies monthly and interest is paid only on the amount borrowed.	■ Interest is charged on the daily amount of money that the business owes to the bank. It can be expensive.
Trade credit ■ The business does not need to pay the supplier for goods for a period of time – often 30 days. Sometimes a longer period of time may be agreed. ■ Used for buying stock or raw materials. ■ New and established businesses.	Short term, all businesses.	■ This source of finance allows the business buying the goods to sell them on to a customer before payment is made to the supplier. ■ It helps businesses that may have a temporary shortage of funds – a cash flow problem. ■ The period of credit is usually interest free.	■ The goods must be paid for even if they do not sell. ■ Interest is charged if the credit is not repaid within the time limit.
Taking on a new partner ■ A new partner contributes finance to the business. ■ Typically used for buying expansion or replacement capital equipment and for development purposes. ■ Established businesses.	Long term, partnerships only or sole traders who become partnerships.	■ A new partner may bring new skills to the business. ■ No cost to raise the finance.	■ The new partner will have a say in the running of the business. ■ The new partner will be entitled to a share of any profits.

Description and uses	Type and availability of finance	Advantages	Disadvantages
Loan ■ An amount of money borrowed from a bank or other lender usually for a stated purpose. In some cases, the bank may want to take a **security** – an asset that it can sell to recover its money – in case the loan is not repaid. The loan is usually for a fixed period of time. ■ Typically used for buying start-up, expansion or replacement capital equipment and for paying for start-up or development activities. ■ New and established businesses.	Medium or long term (depends on period of loan).	■ Repayment is spread over time. ■ Business knows the amount to be paid in instalments which helps budgeting.	■ Interest has to be paid. ■ Business may need to risk an asset as security.
Share issue ■ New shares are sold, raising money for the business. The buyers become shareholders. They are part-owners of the business. ■ The investor can earn a 'dividend' – a share of the profit (if profits are made and paid out) or a capital gain – if the value of the shares rises. ■ Typically used for buying start-up, expansion or replacement capital equipment and for paying for start-up or development activities. ■ New and established businesses.	Long term, limited companies only.	■ A lot of finance can be raised from many investors. ■ Money does not have to be paid back. ■ No interest is payable.	■ Dividends may have to be paid on the shares to shareholders. ■ Shareholders are entitled to have a say in the running of the company. ■ The business may be taken over and existing shareholders no longer own the business (less likely with private limited companies who can control who can become shareholders).
Crowdfunding ■ Money is raised from 'sponsors' usually by advertising a business idea on a crowdfund-raising website such as seedrs.com or kickstart.com. ■ Sponsors can either: a) donate money – usually for community projects b) lend money c) become a part-owner of the business (get equity in the business). ■ Typically used for buying start-up, expansion or replacement capital equipment and for paying for start-up or development activities. ■ New and established businesses.	Medium or long term, all businesses.	■ A lot of money can be raised from a lot of contributors. ■ Used for start-up or expansion. ■ No security is needed for loans.	■ Interest will need to be paid on loans. ■ Profits may need to be shared if equities are sold.

Table 5.2 Different types of finance available.

Activity 2 – Definitions activity

Match the sources of finance listed with the definitions in the table below.

a) crowdfunding

b) share issue

c) trade credit

d) overdraft

e) loan

f) retained profit

g) sale of assets

h) owners' capital

i) taking a new partner

Type of finance definition	Name of finance
1 A business borrows a sum of money from a bank or other lender.	
2 A bank allows a business to spend more money than there is in its current account.	
3 Money is raised by a business by inviting sponsors to contribute money, provide a loan or buy equity in the business.	
4 Money is raised by selling a share of the business.	
5 Money is raised by inviting someone to become a new partner in a business.	
6 Goods are obtained from another business without immediate payment being made.	
7 Money is earned by the business but not paid to the owners.	
8 Money is received following the sale of capital items owned by the business.	
9 The owner or owners use their own savings to provide capital for the business.	

Table 5.3 Business definitions.

Activity 3 – Zone activity

The statements below are possible advantages or disadvantages connected with different sources of finance. Match each one to the relevant source of finance. Note that some statements should be used more than once.

a) The money does not need to be paid back.
b) No interest has to be paid.
c) There is no cost for raising the finance.
d) Owner may not have enough savings.
e) Goods can be sold before they are paid for.
f) Can raise money from the public.
g) Interest is paid on loans.
h) Profits are distributed to owners of equity.
i) Useful when there is a cash flow problem.
j) The new owner may bring new skills as well as more finance.
k) Interest is charged daily on the amount borrowed.
l) Interest is paid.
m) Can raise money from non-shareholder investors.
n) Interest will be paid if the money is not paid back by the due date.
o) Interest is only paid on the amount borrowed.
p) Existing owners may be bought out in a takeover.
q) Security may be required by the lender.
r) The business must have made and saved some profits.
s) The existing owner(s) may have to share control with the new ones.
t) Unwanted equipment can be sold to raise finance.
u) No one may want to buy the assets.
v) The existing owner(s) may have to share control with the new ones.
w) Payment is made in instalments over time.
x) The money does not need to be paid back.
y) It can take time to find a buyer.

Type of finance	Advantages	Disadvantages
1 Crowdfunding		
2 Owners' capital		
3 Trade credit		
4 Taking on a new partner		
5 Overdraft		
6 Sale of assets		
7 Retained profit		
8 Loan		
9 Share issue		

Table 5.4 Advantages and disadvantages of different types of finance available.

Activity 4 – Explanation activity

Using the table below:

a) identify the most suitable source of finance from the list below for each of the business situations.

- share issue
- owners' capital
- trade credit
- retained profit
- loan
- taking a new partner
- overdraft
- crowdfunding.

b) give a reason for your choice of finance.

Business situation	Most suitable source of finance	Reason for choice
1 A small, sole trader building business wishing to buy a second-hand lorry		
2 A family textile business, trading as a private limited company, wishing to invest in some new manufacturing equipment		
3 A veterinary partnership needing to raise finance to help it buy some new premises		
4 A new business wishing to sell tapes and CDs via the internet		
5 An established hairdresser wishing to open a tanning and nail studio		
6 An established family-owned fish and chip shop business wishing to take over a rival business		
7 A nationwide 'coffee shop' business seeking to expand in the north of England		
8 A large public limited company wishing to takeover another public limited company		

Table 5.5 Most suitable finance for different business situations.

Activity 5 – True or false activity

Tick one box next to each of the statements in the table below to indicate if it is true or false.

Statement	True	False
A loan has to be repaid with interest.		
Shareholders are part-owners of a business.		
Banks will always lend a business money.		
New partners are usually easy to find.		
An overdraft is a cheap way of borrowing money for long-term projects.		
Selling assets is a quick way of raising finance.		
All businesses will have some retained profit.		

Table 5.6 Finance statements – true or false.

Activity 6 – Calculation activity

a) Bowton Manufacturing plc is attempting to raise additional finance by offering shares for sale at £1 per share. It has 50,000 shares available for sale. Calculate how much money it would raise if it sold:

Number of shares sold	Answer
Only 10,000 shares	
All of the shares	
50% of the shares it has available for sale	

Table 5.7 Finance calculation.

Short-, medium- and long-term finance

You will not be tested directly on short, medium and long term finance but it is useful to think about this when recommending the type of finance a business should use for a particular need. The section that follows helps you to think about the time periods connected with types of finance. Business may require finance for different lengths of time. These **time periods** are usually classified as short, medium and long term.

Short-term finance is usually money required for up to a year, but often in the immediate future, to pay for day-to-day expenses such as wages, stock and bills.

Medium-term finance is money usually needed for one to five years and is spent on, for example, new machinery and building or extending premises.

Long-term finance is money that is needed for over five years. This could also be for spending on new machinery and buildings or extending premises. This is usually for major business investments such as building a nuclear power station which may take ten years or more.

Table 5.8 summarises the different sources of internal and external finance and the different terms of finance. Different sources of finance may be used for different time periods. In some cases, the same source of finance may be used to finance an activity over different time periods. Understanding these sources of finance is useful when you come to the section dealing with 'Ways of raising finance - how and why different sources of finance are suitable for new and established businesses.

Time period	Short term (up to 12 months)	Medium term (1 to 5 years)	Long term (5 years or more)
Internal source of finance	Owners' capital Sale of fixed assets	Retained profit Sale of fixed assets Owners' capital	Retained profit Sale of fixed assets Owners' capital
External source of finance	Overdraft Trade credit	Bank loan Crowdfunding	Bank loan Taking on a new partner Share issue Crowdfunding

Table 5.8 Types of internal and external, short-, medium- and long-term finance.

Activity 7 – Tick the box activity

The first column of the table below lists all of the different types of finance that you need to know about. Tick the boxes next to each type of finance to state whether the type of finance is short, medium or long term. Note that some may be short and medium or even all three terms.

Type of finance	Short term	Medium term	Long term
Crowdfunding			
Owners' capital			
Trade credit			
Taking on a new partner			
Overdraft			
Sale of fixed assets			
Retained profit			
Loan			
Share issue			

Table 5.9 Types of finance.

Key facts

Finance is vital for all businesses – all businesses will require finance at some stage.

Finance may be used for different lengths of time.

Not all sources of finance are available to all forms of business.

For most types of finance, there is usually a cost involved.

Some sources of finance are best suited for particular uses.

Useful words

Interest is the amount of money that has to be paid on borrowed money.

Security is something of value that is offered to a lender as a form of guarantee of payment.

Time period is the length of time for which the finance is required.

Loans are sums borrowed for a certain period at an agreed rate of interest.

Overdraft is an arrangement with a bank that a business can spend more money than it has in its account.

Trade credit is when the business has the goods to sell and agrees to pay at some time later.

Retained profit is profit that not distributed to shareholders as dividend.

Sale of assets are items sold by the business.

Owners' capital is money from savings put in to the business by the owner.

Taking on a partner is adding a new partner who contributes some new capital.

Share issue is money raised from investors by selling new shares.

Crowdfunding is money raised through an appeal to the public.

Practice questions

Multiple choice questions

1 Which of the following is not a feature of trade credit?
   - **a)** The supplier does not need to be paid for 90 days.
   - **b)** Interest has to be paid if the money is not paid within the time limit.
   - **c)** It is useful for dealing with a short-term cash flow problem.
   - **d)** It can be used to finance the purchase of new machinery.

2 Which of the following is not a good source of new capital?
   - **a)** taking a new partner
   - **b)** overdraft
   - **c)** share issue
   - **d)** crowdfunding.

Data response 31

Pleasurewear plc produces a range of casual clothing for men and women. It has been very successful since its start-up six years ago. Sales have increased significantly and the business has made good profits over the period. It cannot increase production any further at its existing factory. Pleasurewear plc now intends to build a new and larger factory. The board of directors has to decide whether to finance the new factory using retained profit or to take out a bank loan.

1 Discuss one source of finance that Pleasurewear plc should use to finance its new factory. (9 marks)

How to answer data response 31

1 Discuss one source of finance that you think will be suitable. Analyse an advantage and a disadvantage, and then justify why the business should use this.

UNIT 5.3 Revenue, costs, profit and loss

Learning outcomes

By studying this unit, you will be able to:

- explain the meaning of **revenue**, costs, profit and loss in a business context
- identify examples of different costs
- calculate costs and revenue for a given business situation
- calculate profit/loss
- calculate profitability ratios
- evaluate the importance of revenue, costs, profit and loss in business decision-making
- calculate the average rate of return from data provided
- use quantitative skills to analyse and evaluate profitability ratios and average rate of return, interpreting the importance of such data.

Introductory case study: revenue, costs, profit and loss at Xpipe

Plastic pipes used in the building trade.

Xpipe makes plastic piping for use in building houses and other buildings. With the reduction in the number of housing projects, its revenue from the sale of piping has gone down, while the costs of operating its factory have stayed much the same. This has affected profits and the general profitability of the business as a whole has been questioned. Managers at Xpipe are looking at investing in a new, more efficient pipe-making machine. It will cost £750,000, which at a time of falling profits is a big decision to make. The management at Xpipe is investigating just how much they will gain from having such a machine in the factory. To help with this they are looking at the average rate of return, which will give a percentage figure to show the value of the investment in the machine, over a period of years.

Revenue

Revenue is income coming into a business from the sale of products and services. It is calculated in the following way:

Revenue = quantity sold x selling price

So, if a bookshop sold 300 books at £20 each, revenue would be:

300 x £20 = £6000

Costs

Costs are the payments that a business makes in order to make goods and provide services.

Wages, cost of materials, rent, telephone bills, interest on loans and transport costs are just some of the costs that businesses must pay. These costs can be classified under two headings:

- **fixed costs**
- **variable costs**.

Fixed costs

These are costs that do not change when the business changes the amount it produces. Rent and business rates (a local tax on business property) are examples of fixed costs. For example, Arshia is a professional photographer. She pays £1,000 per month rent for her shop and photographic studio. This cost will not change in the immediate future even if she sells nothing.

Variable costs

These are costs that do change when the business changes the amount it produces. Arshia's variable costs will include buying photographic paper, ink and chemicals. The more she sells, the more she will spend on these items. Variable costs may be calculated as follows:

`Total variable costs = quantity sold x variable cost per unit (the unit here is a photograph)`

Arshia pays £3 in variable costs for each photograph that she produces. The total variable cost of producing 100 pictures would be:

`Total variable cost = 100 x £3 = £300`

Total costs

The **total costs** of a business are found by adding together the total for *all* of its fixed and variable costs. If Arshia pays £1,000 in rent and £800 in business rates, the total cost of producing 100 pictures would be:

`Total costs = all fixed costs plus all variable costs`

`Total cost = £1,800 (£1,000 plus £800) + £300 = £2,100`

It is important for any business to keep a careful eye on costs.

Activity 1 – True or false activity

Tick the correct column to show whether the cost is fixed or variable.

Cost	Fixed	Variable
Insurance		
Wages		
Rent		
Heating		
Business rates		

Table 5.10 Variable or fixed costs.

Profit and loss

A business makes a **loss** when its costs (money going out of the business) are greater than revenue (money coming into the business). Profit is the money that is left over from revenue once the costs of operating the business have been paid. Profit is calculated over a period of time; in many businesses, this is a year.

There are two types of profit:

- **gross profit**
- **net profit**.

Gross profit

Gross profit is the amount of profit made by a business as a result of buying and selling goods or services, but without paying for any of the day-to-day or other expenses of running the business.

Calculation of gross profit

Gross profit is calculated by using the following formula:

`Gross profit = Revenue` *`minus`* `the cost of sales`

Example:

If you bought a box of chocolate bars for £30 (the cost of sales) and sold the chocolate bars for £50, your gross profit would be:

`£50 – £30 = £20`

Activity 2 – Calculation activity

Calculate the gross profit in each of the following examples:

a) Weekly sales revenue from DVD sales is £15,000. The cost of buying the DVDs is £8,000.

b) Daily sales of one type of chocolate bar in a local shop are worth £75. The cost of the chocolate is £44.50.

c) The school canteen sells 200 cartons of fruit juice for 50 pence each. The cost of buying each carton is 30 pence.

d) Last term, a school sold 20 electronic calculators for £4.50 each. The cost of buying each calculator is £3.85.

Net profit

Net profit takes into account the profit made as a result of buying and selling goods or services but also makes an allowance for the costs involved in running the business – for example, wages and telephone calls. It is seen as a more accurate reflection of the performance of a business and is calculated using the following formula:

Net profit = gross profit *minus* the costs of running the business

Example:

	£	£
Gross profit		500,000
Wages and salaries	300,000	
Rent	50,000	
Heating and lighting	10,000	
Insurance	5,000	365,000
Net profit		135,000

Table 5.11 Net profit.

In this example, the gross profit is £500,000. The expenses of running the business (wages and salaries, rent, heating and lighting and insurance) are added together and then taken from the gross profit figure. This gives the net profit figure of £135,000.

Activity 3 – Calculation activity

Calculate the net profit in the following examples by adding up the expenses and subtracting them from the gross profit:

a)

Gross profit	£20,000
Electricity	£2,000
Wages	£10,000
Telephone	£500
Rent	£3,000
Net profit	

b)

Gross profit	£30,000
Advertising	£1,000
Salaries	£20,000
Heating and lighting	£3,500
Insurance	£1,000
Net profit	

c)

Gross profit	£3,500,000
Wages and salaries	£2,200,000
Transport	£50,000
Heating and lighting	£150,000
Rent	£250,000
Net profit	

d)

Gross profit	£580,000
Labour	£275,000
Energy	£120,000
Maintenance	£50,000
Heating	£25,000
Net profit	

Note that when the costs of operating a business are more than the gross profit, then the business is making a loss.

Profitability ratios

Profitability ratios are calculations using financial data to measure the performance of a business. It is always important to be able to judge performance accurately. Simply saying 'sales have increased so we must be doing well' is not good enough. Sales could increase, but with analysis it could be shown that really the business is not doing as well as first thought.

Two profitability ratios are:

- **gross profit margin**
- **net profit margin**.

Gross profit margin

The gross profit margin is usually calculated as a percentage. Using the figures from gross profit calculations above, where the gross profit from selling chocolate was £20 and the sales were £50, the gross profit margin can be calculated by the following formula:

$$\text{Gross profit margin} = \frac{\text{gross profit}}{\text{revenue}} \times 100$$

or

$$\frac{£20 \times 100}{£50} = 40\%$$

Net profit margin

The net profit margin is the amount of net profit a business makes as a percentage of sales revenue. Like the gross profit margin, it is expressed as a percentage. It is calculated as follows:

$$\text{Net profit margin} = \frac{\text{net profit}}{\text{revenue}} \times 100$$

Example:

If a business selling chocolate made a net profit of £1,500 and has sales of £30,000, its net profit margin is:

$$\frac{1,500 \times 100}{30,000} = 5\%$$

Activity 4 – Calculation activity

Use the figures from Activity 2 to calculate the gross profit margin in each example.

Activity 5 – Calculation activity

Calculate the net profit margin in the following examples:

a) Net profit £25,000, revenue £260,000.

b) Net profit £10,000, revenue £45,000.

c) Net profit £22 500, revenue £65,500.

Interpreting gross and net profit margins

It is all very well being able to calculate the gross and net profit margins, but what do the figures actually mean for a business?

Look at the following example of figures from Jacquelyn Williams booksellers:

	Year 1 (£)	Year 2 (£)
Revenue	150,000	225,000
Cost of sales	80,000	140,000
Gross profit	70,000	85,000
Business expenses	40,000	55,000
Net profit	30.000	30,000

Table 5.12 Bookseller sales.

Points to note from the figures:

- Revenue has increased by £75,000 or 50 per cent from year 1 to year 2.
- Gross profit has increased by £15,000.
- Cost of sales has increased by 75 per cent.
- Business expenses (wages, rent, heating, insurance etc.) have increased by 37.5 per cent.
- Net profit has stayed the same.

So how has Jacquelyn Williams booksellers performed? Which is the better year – year 1 or year 2? Or, as the net profit is the same for both years, is there no difference in performance?

If the gross profit margin is calculated:

Year 1

$$\frac{\text{Gross profit} \times 100}{\text{Revenue}} = \frac{70{,}000 \times 100}{150{,}000} = 46.66\%$$

Year 2

$$\frac{\text{Gross profit} \times 100}{\text{Revenue}} = \frac{85{,}000 \times 100}{225{,}000} = 37.77\%$$

If the net profit margin is calculated:

Year 1

$$\frac{\text{Net profit} \times 100}{\text{Revenue}} = \frac{30{,}000 \times 100}{150{,}000} = 20\%$$

Year 2

$$\frac{\text{Net profit} \times 100}{\text{Revenue}} = \frac{30{,}000 \times 100}{225{,}000} = 13.33\%$$

What do the figures tell us about Jacquelyn Williams booksellers?

1 The gross profit margin figures

The fall in gross profit margin from 46.66 per cent to 37.77 per cent would indicate that while sales have increased (good news), the business is paying more than it did in year 1 for the books it is selling. Could the business buy books from a different supplier, or ask its present supplier for more of a discount, after all it is selling more books! If the business continues in this way, it will not be performing as well as it could and should be. Action should be taken.

2 The net profit margin figures

The net profit margin has also fallen from 20 per cent to 13.33 per cent. Why is this?

Although the gross profit has increased, the net profit has stayed the same. The reduction in the net profit margin is because expenses (the costs of running the business) have increased by 37.5 per cent. Jacquelyn should therefore look carefully at why the expenses have risen so much. Can she really cut down on any expenses such as wages, heating, lighting and insurance? There could be any number of examples as to why the expenses have increased – look back at all of the different headings in the costs of running a business. The point is that an increase in itself is not a problem if there is the same or greater percentage increase in the net profit. However, it is always important for any business to keep a close eye on its costs and reduce them wherever possible when it does not harm the business itself.

Activity 6 – Calculation activity

Using the following data, use the gross and net profit ratios to interpret the performance of the business over the three years.

	Year 1 (£)	Year 2 (£)	Year 3 (£)
Revenue	30,000	50,000	60,000
Cost of sales	15,000	22,000	30,000
Gross profit	15,000	28,000	30,000
Business expenses	10,000	14,000	15,000
Net profit	5,000	14,000	15,000

Table 5.13 Gross and net profit.

Importance of revenue, costs, profit and loss in business decision-making

It is important for a business to analyse data to help decision-making.

As you can see from the data covered in this unit, it is important for a business to analyse carefully all of the data on performance that it can. So how does this fit into decision-making?

Revenue and decision-making

Remember that revenue is the income from sales. This is important but must not be looked at on its own. It is very easy for a business to sell more – simply cut the price. This might mean an increase in revenue, but the business might be losing income on every item it sells. It is important therefore that a business looks carefully at its pricing strategy (see Unit 2.4 The marketing mix) and makes sure that any price reductions are carefully thought through. It may also be the case that increasing prices, while putting off some consumers, might lead to an increase in revenue. Once again, a business has to be careful as to just how much it increases the price of its product or services. If all consumers stop buying because of a price increase, the business will be in trouble. Decisions have to be made carefully.

Examples of how decisions on price might affect revenue:

An electrical manufacturer can sell 2,000 toasters a year at £25:

```
Revenue = 2,000 x £25 = £50,000
```

If the price is raised to £30, it can only sell 1,800:

```
Revenue = 1,800 x £30 = £54,000
```

If the price is reduced to £20, 2,100 toasters can be sold:

```
Revenue = 2,100 x £20 = £42,000
```

In this example, it is better for the business to sell the toasters at £30. Although the amount sold will be less, the revenue is higher.

Activity 7 – Calculation activity

Look at the following figures and explain which price the business should charge for a product to maximise sales revenue.

Price	Number expected to be sold
£22	300
£25	280
£28	270
£30	250

Table 5.14 Which price should the business charge?

Factors that can affect revenue due to price changes

The number of competitors	If there are no competitors, a business could raise prices without seeing a fall in revenue as there is nowhere else for consumers to buy the product or service. If there are a lot of competitors, sales (and so revenue) might fall as consumers switch to buying from another business.
The action of competitors	If competitors raise their prices, there is an opportunity to raise prices without the fear of losing customers to other business. This will increase revenue, unless customers feel they can manage without the product or service you are selling.
The starting price of the product	If the product or service is already very cheap, a large percentage rise in price will not really affect consumers too much and revenues might still rise.

Table 5.15 Factors that can affect revenue.

Increasing revenue through increasing sales

A business might expand in the hope of increasing revenue. This could work very well, but it is not a guaranteed way to increase revenue. Asda increased revenue by opening supermarkets throughout the UK. However, this can also create problems with competitors taking business from you and so reducing revenue.

A business might advertise more to increase revenue. Again, this could work well, but the effects of advertising must be clearly analysed to make sure that the advertising is providing value for money. Once again, decisions have to be carefully made.

Examples of the effect of advertising on revenue:

- A business spends £10,000 on advertising, revenue rises by £12,000.
- If £20,000 is spent on advertising, revenue rises by £24,000.
- If the business spends £30,000 on advertising, revenue rises by £30,500.

In this example, revenue rises with each stage, but the best value from advertising is at £20,000.

Increasing revenue through increasing product range

Another way of increasing revenue is to increase the number of products sold. Dyson started with vacuum cleaners. It has now developed products in hair care, lighting, air treatment and hand dryers. Tesco started by simply selling groceries, but now it sells electrical goods, telephone services, clothing and insurance. For other businesses, this might not be easily done. It is often expensive to develop new products and there is no guarantee that there will be an increase in revenue after all the costs have been met.

Tesco now sells a wide range of different products.

Activity 8 – Explanation activity

Suggest what would happen to sales revenue in each of the following situations. Give reasons for your answers.

a) A shopkeeper decided to raise the price of a box of matches from 15 pence to 20 pence.

b) The world price of oil rose. The Local Service Station, like all other petrol stations, decided to raise the price of its petrol price to cover the costs.

c) A supermarket decided to reduce the price of its bread by 50 per cent. Competitors left the price of their bread unchanged.

d) The pizza delivery service in a village five miles away from Ryan's Pizza Place reduces its prices by 20 per cent. Ryan decides to leave his prices unchanged.

Costs and decision-making

Decisions on revenue have to be taken carefully as shown above. In the same way, decisions on costs need careful analysis. If a business has high fixed costs, then it must sell a high number of products or services to cover those fixed costs (see also Unit 5.4). If a decision is made to move to a larger factory with higher fixed costs, such as rent, then the business must make sure that it can sell an increased number of products to cover those higher fixed costs. If not, then revenue and profit will fall.

The variable costs of a business also need to be carefully analysed. The materials that a manufacturing business needs might go up in price, thus increasing variable costs that will affect net profit. If this happens, a business could decide to:

- accept the price increase and look for savings elsewhere in variable costs
- look to buy from a different supplier, though they would need to check on quality and reliability of the new supplier
- negotiate with the present supplier on a reduction in price.

There is no right or wrong decision here. All three options have their merits. You simply need to understand that there are a number of decisions that can be made regarding the costs of a business. With other variable costs, the decision-making process is much the same – if the insurance or electricity bill goes up, a business could look for another quotation from another supplier or ask for a reduction, or simply do nothing.

Profit, loss and decision-making

The profits or losses a business makes will have a significant effect on decision-making.

If a business makes large, increasing profits it could:

- buy new equipment and buildings
- look to take over other businesses
- pay increasing dividends to shareholders if a limited company, or allow the sole trader or partners to withdraw an increasing amount of money from the business
- develop new products and services.

Clearly all of the above is good news. But if profits are falling and losses start to occur, a business might be faced with the following:

- Decisions on buying new equipment and buildings will have to be postponed.
- A decision may have to be made as to whether to agree to be taken over by another business.
- Dividends will be reduced or scrapped. This will not please shareholders who may sell their shares causing the business further problems. For sole traders and partnerships there will be less money to draw from the business.
- Can the business afford to invest in new products or services? If the decision is not to invest in new ideas and competitors bring out new products, then the business faces further problems as consumers switch to the rival businesses.

Activity 9 – Presentation activity

Make a PowerPoint presentation to show how important profits are in decision-making for a business. Be creative in your designs to show how different decisions may have to be made when a business goes from profit to loss.

Average rate of return (ARR)

The phrase 'rate of return' is the amount you receive from making an investment. So, if you put £100 in a bank account and received two per cent interest, your rate of return will be two per cent.

Sometimes the rate of return for investment is not very high.

It is the same for a business when they make investments in new equipment. They will want to know what the 'return' is likely to be on that investment in order to judge whether it is going to be worthwhile. If the expected return is very low, the business may well look at other possible investments to see if they produce a better return.

The 'average' in **average rate of return** is the amount of return, on average, over the life of the investment. So, if a business is buying new equipment that it expects to last for five years, the average rate of return will give a percentage return *on average* for each of the five years.

Calculating average rate of return

A gardening business spends £5,000 on a new ride-on grass mower, which it expects to last for five years. The following table shows the expected income from cutting grass for each of the five years when the mower is used.

Cost of equipment	£5,000
Income year 1	£2,000
Income year 2	£2,500
Income year 3	£3,000
Income year 4	£3,000
Income year 5	£2,500
Total income	£13,000

Table 5.16 Expected income.

Calculation part 1

The first part of calculating average rate of return (ARR) is to calculate the profit from using the mower. The total income is £13,000 and the cost of the mower was £5,000.

$$\text{Profit} = \text{total income} - \text{cost of machine}$$
$$= £13,000 - £5,000$$
$$= £8,000$$

Calculation part 2

The next stage is to calculate the average profit for the five years. The total profit for five years was £8,000 so average profit is:

$$\frac{8,000}{5} = 1600$$

Calculation part 3

The formula for average rate of return is:

$$\frac{\text{Annual average profit}}{\text{cost of investment}} \times 100$$
$$= \frac{1,600}{5000} \times 100$$
$$= 32\%$$

Interpretation of average rate of return

As with the calculations for gross and net profit margins, calculation of the average rate of return is the first step in the process of understanding its value to a business. It is important to be able to interpret the results and understand how they may be used.

Average rate of return (ARR) is useful when comparing different investments. In the above example, the gardening business could also look at different mowers costing different amounts and consider what profit they would bring in over their lifetime. Figures could then be compared and the mower that gave the best ARR would be the one to buy.

A business might also look at what else it might do with its money. If it can get, say, two per cent return without any risk from putting money in a bank, why should a business take a risk if the ARR is only four per cent? In the example above, the ARR is 32 per cent which is very high compared with returns from investing money in bank accounts. This looks to be a very good investment if the future income is achieved.

Remember that average rate of return is a calculation based on what is expected in the future, so any interpretation of results must take this into account. As with any predictions in business, many things can change and events may not turn out as you had planned.

Evaluation point

When evaluating data, you need to understand that there are a number of options open to a business. Always consider the situation a business is in – is it in profit, is it making a loss, is its revenue increasing, could it cut its costs? The list can go on. All will have an effect on the decision a business makes. Check any calculations you complete to make sure that you are making a judgement on the correct figures!

Activity 10 – Calculation activity

Calculate the average rate of return over three years from the following figures.

Cost of investment	£20,000
Income year 1	£6,500
Income year 2	£7,000
Income year 3	£8,000

Table 5.17 Average rate of return.

Key facts

Costs are split into fixed and variable.

Fixed costs stay the same when output changes.

Variable costs change as output changes.

It is important for a business to keep a check on its costs.

There are a number of ways a business might increase its revenue.

Profit is vital to the success of a business.

There are two types of profit, gross and net. They are calculated in different ways.

If a business continues to make losses, it will go out of business.

Gross and net profit margins are a way of measuring and comparing the profitability of a business. Net profit margin is considered to be the more accurate measure of profitability.

Average rate of return calculations can help a business compare the profitability of different investments.

Useful words

Revenue is the money from sales.

Fixed costs are costs that stay the same as output changes, for example, rent.

Variable costs are costs that change as output changes, for example, wages.

Total costs are the addition of fixed and variable costs.

Gross profit is sales minus the cost of sales.

Net profit is gross profit minus the expenses of operating the business.

Gross profit margin is gross profit divided by sales multiplied by 100.

Net profit margin is net profit divided by sales multiplied by 100.

Average rate of return (ARR) is a method of measuring and comparing the profitability of an investment over the life of the investment.

Loss occurs in a business when costs are greater than revenue.

Profitability ratios are calculations such as gross profit margin and net profit margin which help to interpret financial data.

Expenses are the costs of operating a business.

Practice questions

Multiple choice questions

1 Variable costs in a business:

- **a)** do not change as the business increases production
- **b)** increase as the business increases production
- **c)** stay the same until a certain level of production is reached
- **d)** reduce when a certain level of production is reached.

2 Calculating the net profit margin allows a business to:

- **a)** understand how sales influence revenue
- **b)** understand the relationship between net profit and sales
- **c)** understand how net profit is calculated
- **d)** understand the connection between net profit and loss.

3 The average rate of return can help a business to:
   a) compare the profitability over time of different investments
   b) compare the rates of return on offer from different banks
   c) judge whether or not to raise prices
   d) compare performance against that of a competitor.

Data response question 32

Alan Cropley Guitars Ltd (ACG) makes electric guitars. The business has expanded in recent years after a top band used ACG guitars at a festival.

	2015	2016
Sales revenue	£550,000	£700,000
Cost of sales	£230,000	£400,000
Costs of running the business	£250,000	£270,000

Table 5.18 ACG sales and costs

1 Idenvtify one cost that ACG would classify as a fixed cost. (1 mark)

2 Identify one variable cost that ACG is likely to have. (1 mark)

3 The net profit margin for 2015 is 12.72 per cent. Calculate the net profit margin for 2016. Show your working. (3 marks)

4 Using the figures from question 3 and your calculations, explain what the results show about the profitability of ACG. (4 marks)

5 ACG is considering buying a new delivery van and is looking at three different models. Explain how using average rate of return can help ACG decide on which model van to buy. (4 marks)

How to answer data response 32

1 Here you need to simply identify one fixed cost. Always remember what type of business ACG is.

2 Here you need to simply identify one variable cost. Always remember what type of business ACG is.

3 When completing any calculation question, always show your working, as a wrong answer with the correct working can be rewarded.

4 This question asks you to explain what the results show. You must explain, so to have a chance of full marks you must do more than say the profit has gone up or down. Always use the figures you have, even if you think they may be wrong, you can still get marks for knowing the method of calculation.

5 This question tests your knowledge of the benefits of using average rate of return. This question is not testing any knowledge of delivery vans!

UNIT 5.4 Break-even

Learning outcomes

By studying this unit, you will be able to:

- explain the concept of break-even and its uses
- calculate the break-even quantity of a business
- evaluate the usefulness of break-even analysis in business decision-making.

Case study: Lord Digby Jones and Hereford Furniture

Lord Digby Jones

Lord Digby Jones, a respected businessman, made a TV programme for the BBC. It was called *The New Trouble Shooter*. In the programme, Lord Jones visits Hereford Furniture run by Mike Muxworthy and his daughter, Kate. The family-owned business had been successful but, at the time of Lord Jones' visit, it was making a loss of £80,000 and there was a risk that the 40 workers it employed would lose their jobs. Lord Jones gave the owners a lot of advice about how to improve the business. The first piece of advice concerned **break-even forecasts**. He lambasted the owners for not doing these and told them they were essential for good business planning.

BBC Television, The New Trouble Shooter, *14 march 2014*

The concept of break-even

Businesses use information about revenues and costs to calculate the break-even level of output. A business breaks even when its total costs of production are equal to its total revenue from sales. This means that the business does not make any profit, nor does it make a loss

Calculating the break-even quantity

Tables and graphs used to calculate break-even

Break-even calculations are usually done as a forecast. The forecast predicts the revenue, fixed, variable and total costs for a business for a range of outputs.

The information about costs and revenue may be estimated, from what these have been in the past, or what the business thinks they will be in the future. A break-even forecast is usually presented in the form of a table or a graph.

A break-even calculation using a table and a graph is illustrated below. David Adams plans to open a sandwich bar.

Table 5.19 on page 248 shows the costs and revenues that David expects for a range of sales from 0 to 1,200 sandwiches per week.

Sandwiches sold	Total revenue	Fixed costs	Variable costs	Total costs	Profit (Loss)
0	0	400	0	400	(400)
200	160	400	60	460	(300)
400	320	400	120	520	(200)
600	480	400	180	580	(100)
800	640	400	240	640	0
1,000	800	400	300	700	100
1,200	960	400	360	760	200

Table 5.19 The Sandwich Bar – break-even table.

From Table 5.19 (and the graph – Figure 5.2 – below), we can see that David will make a loss if he sells either 200, 400 or 600 sandwiches per week. If he sells 600 sandwiches, his loss is £100 per week. To avoid making a loss, he must sell at least 800 sandwiches per week – this is the break-even output where he does not make a profit nor a loss because total revenue is equal to total costs of £640.

When David sells more than 800 sandwiches, he will make a profit. If he sold 1,200 sandwiches, he would make £200 profit for the week. The amount by which his actual sales are greater than the level of sales he needs to break even is known as the **margin of safety**.

If David does sell 1,200 sandwiches in a week then his margin of safety is:

Margin of safety = actual sales – break-even sales

= 1,200 – 800 = 400 sandwiches

(There will not be any direct questions asking you about margin of safety. However, it is an idea that is useful to businesses when planning and it is included in this unit for this reason.)

It is normal for businesses to present break-even figures in the form of a line graph. The graph below shows the break-even forecast for David Adams' sandwich bar.

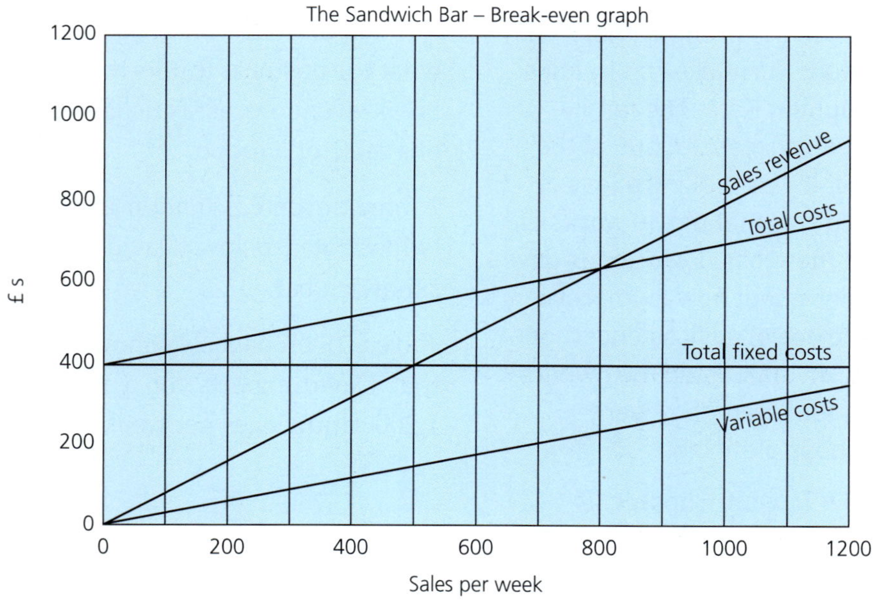

Figure 5.2 The Sandwich Bar – break-even graph.

Activity 1 – break-even calculation and presentation activity

Paul Brown runs a driving school. The fixed costs of running the school include the repayment of loans on the cars he owns and administration costs. He calculates these to be £500 per week. The variable costs are the costs of labour and petrol. He calculates these to be £20 per lesson. He charges £30 for each lesson.

1 Use the information above to complete the table below.

Lessons per week	Total revenue	Fixed costs	Variable costs	Profit/Loss
0				
10				
20				
30				
40				
50				
60				
70				
80				
90				
100				

Table 5.20 Break-even calculation.

2 Use the information in the table to draw a break-even graph for the driving school.

Remember that you will need to measure sales revenue and costs in pounds on the vertical axis and lessons sold on the horizontal axis. You will need to plot four lines – fixed costs, variable costs, total costs and total revenue. It is important to label the axes and the lines clearly. Figure 5.2 is an example of a break-even graph.

3 Draw a line on the graph to show the break-even level of output. Using the information in the break-even graph calculate:

a) how much profit or loss Paul Brown would make if he sold:

(i) 70 lessons in a week

(ii) 20 lessons in a week.

b) Paul Brown's margin of safety if he sold 90 lessons in a week.

4 Suppose he raised the price of his lessons to £35. Draw a new total revenue line on the graph to show the effect of this change. What would be the break-even level of output?

5 Suppose that, at the original price of £30 per lesson, Paul Brown was faced with variable costs rising to £25 per lesson. Draw a new graph to show the effect of this change. What would be the break-even level of output?

6 Word-process a report, including the spreadsheet and graphs, about the break-even analysis for the driving school.

Activity 2 – Constructing a break-even graph activity

Suppose you plan to raise money for a charity by selling home-made biscuits at morning break. The food technology teacher has said you can cook in his room at lunchtime if you pay £1.05. This will be your fixed cost of production. You estimate that the cost of the ingredients will be £2 in total. You plan to produce 20 biscuits and sell them at 30 pence each.

Divide the total cost of ingredients by the number of biscuits you will produce. This will be your variable cost per biscuit.

a) Using your knowledge of break-even analysis, complete an appropriate table and graph.

b) Using the information in your graph, calculate:

i) how many biscuits you will need to make in order to break-even

ii) how much profit you will make if you sell all of the biscuits.

c) Explain why you may not make as much profit as you predict. You may find it useful to read 'limitations of break-even analysis in business decision-making' below to help you to answer this.

Calculating break-even using a formula

It is possible to calculate the break-even output without constructing a table or graph. This can be done by using the following formula:

$$\text{Break-even output} = \frac{\text{total fixed costs}}{\text{price} - \text{variable costs per unit}}$$

Using the following information, the break-even output would be calculated as follows:

- Fixed costs of £10,000 per year
- Selling price per unit = £50
- Variable cost of each unit = £30

$$\text{Break-even output} = \frac{£10{,}000 \text{ (total fixed cost)}}{£20 \text{ (price} - \text{variable costs per unit)}}$$

$$= 500 \text{ units}$$

Activity 3 – Calculation activity

The figures below show costs and revenues for a toy manufacturer:

- total fixed costs of producing the toys are £50,000 per year
- variable costs per product sold are £2
- the selling price of the toys is £6 each.

Using the calculation method, work out how many toys the manufacturer must sell to break even.

The usefulness of break-even analysis in business decision-making

Uses of break-even analysis in business decision-making

In the case study, we read that Lord Digby Jones was critical of Hereford Furniture for not completing break-even forecasts. The uses of break-even forecasts are discussed below:

- The figures in the forecast will help the business to plan how much to sell in order to make a profit.
- If a person needs a loan from a bank, the bank manager will often ask to see a break-even graph as part of the business plan. It will show that the owner has thought about how many products the business must sell to break even and the bank manager will be able to question the owner about the plan. It will give the manager some idea about the quality of the applicant for the loan as a business owner.
- The forecast can be used to make judgements about prices and costs. The figures may show a need either to increase the price of the product, to raise revenue, or to reduce the costs. For example, David Adams may decide that a break-even figure of 800 is too high. He might be able to raise prices

to increase the sales revenue. Alternatively, he may feel that this is not possible, perhaps because of the competition that he faces. If this were the case, he would have to see if he could cut the costs. Perhaps he could use cheaper ingredients in the sandwiches to achieve this? This illustrates how cash flow analysis can be used to inform marketing and production decisions.

- The forecast can be used to find the expected profit at an output.
- It can show the margin of safety. The business can assess the impact of any external changes on the margin of safety and on the profit or loss the business may make. For example, it can estimate the effect that a new competitor might have on prices and revenues or the effect of a rise or fall in the cost of raw materials.

Limitations of break-even analysis in business decision-making

Break-even forecasts need to be treated with care. Businesses should remember that forecast figures may turn out to be different from those predicted. Figure 5.2 shows that the break-even forecast for the sandwich bar is based on estimates of what price David *thinks* he will be able to charge in the future and what he *thinks* his costs may be. Prices, revenues and cost may not be as forecasted for the following reasons:

- The number of competitors in the market may change. If another sandwich bar opened in the same area, David may sell less or, to maintain sales, he may need to reduce the price he charges. David would find that he would have to sell more than forecasted to break even.
- The business may make promotional offers particularly at the start-up of trading or when launching a new product. For these reasons, the price may therefore be less, for a time, than the predicted price on which revenue calculations were based.
- The cost of ingredients may change. If the cost falls, he will find he does not have to sell as many sandwiches to breakeven.
- A price increase may not lead to an increase in revenue. Instead, the increase may lead to a fall in sales. Revenue could either rise, fall or stay the same depending on the size of the price rise and the change in demand for the sandwiches which results.

Activity 4 – Zone activity

The following statements are either uses or limitations of break even in business decision-making. Put them under the correct heading in the table below:

- The business can plan how many products it must sell to break even.
- The price used to calculate the expected sales revenue may change, for example, if a new competitor enters the market.
- The forecast is only an estimate.
- The forecast may be needed as part of a business plan given to a bank when asking for a loan.
- The forecast can be used to estimate the margin of safety.
- Variable costs may rise, for example, if raw material prices rise.
- The business may not sell as many as it expects at the price it uses in the forecast because a competitor reduces its prices.
- The forecast can be used to assess the effect on revenue and the break-even output of a rise in price.
- Knowing the margin of safety will help the business to know if it would be worth producing if costs rise.

Uses of break-even forecasts	Limitations of break-even forecasts

Table 5.21 The uses and limitations of break-even.

Evaluation point

Break-even forecasts are useful planning tools for businesses. They can be used to plan how much to produce and sell and what the margin of safety will be. They can support applications for loans from a bank. However, it is important that businesses recognise that they are predictions based on certain assumptions, and there is no guarantee that they will be accurate as forecasts. Businesses will need to redo forecasts and alter plans as circumstances change.

Key facts

Break-even forecasts are useful tools for business planning.

Businesses use forecasts of prices and sales revenues, fixed and total costs to calculate the break-even output.

Break-even figures may be presented in a table or on a graph or calculated using a formula.

The figures in a break-even forecast may be used to calculate the break-even output and the losses or profits that are made at different levels of output.

The figures are only forecasts of revenues and costs – actual revenues and costs may differ.

Useful words

Break-even forecast is a prediction about the break-even quantity based on estimates of future sales revenues and costs.

Break-even quantity is the amount a business must sell to earn enough revenue to just cover its costs so that it does not make a profit nor a loss.

Margin of safety is the amount by which a business' actual output is greater than its break-even output.

Practice questions

Multiple choice questions

Carlton Press Ltd publishes a business revision booklet. It forecasts the following revenues and costs for the booklet.

The variable costs are £2 per booklet and the booklet sells at £5. Carlton Press Ltd has started to produce a break-even forecast but it is not yet complete. This is shown below.

Sales of books	Total fixed costs (£)	Total variable costs (£)	Total costs (£)	Total revenue (£)
0	30,000	0	30,000	0
5,000	30,000	10,000	40,000	25,000
10,000	30,000		50,000	50,000
15,000	30,000	30,000	60,000	75,000
20,000	30,000	40,000	70,000	100,000

Table 5.22 Revenues and costs.

1 The total variable cost of producing 10,000 booklets is:

- **a)** £30,000
- **b)** £20,000
- **c)** £15,000
- **d)** £10,000.

2 The break-even output is:

- **a)** 5,000
- **b)** 10,000
- **c)** 15,000
- **d)** 20,000.

Data response 33

Samantha Dixon is starting up a cake-decorating business. She has estimated that she can sell wedding cakes at £300 each. She estimates the variable costs of each cake to be £180. Samantha has calculated that her fixed costs are £3,600 per year for her premises (making use of her own kitchen) and interest payments on a bank loan. Samantha is considering producing 10, 20, 30, 40 or 50 cakes per year.

1 Calculate how many cakes Samantha must sell to break even. Use either a table, graph or the calculation method to get your answer. (3 marks)

2 Analyse one advantage to Samantha of calculating the break-even level of output. (3 marks)

3 Analyse two limitations to the break-even forecast that Samantha has calculated. (6 marks)

How to answer data response 33

1 Use the formula. Remember that you have to subtract the variable costs from the selling price before completing the division.

2 Do not be put off by the fact that this calculated forecast is not one drawn from a table or graph. The uses are the same however the break-even is forecast. Write about one of the uses of break-even forecasts. There are three marks available so state the use, the application and then give one point of analysis.

3 Write about two limitations of break-even forecasts. State the limitation and then give two points of analysis for each one.

UNIT 5.5 Cash and cash flow

Learning outcomes

By studying this unit, you will be able to:

- identify the different parts that make up a **cash flow forecast**
- explain the difference between cash and profit
- evaluate the importance of cash to a business
- complete a cash-flow forecast
- analyse and evaluate data to make a recommendation on action that a business might take to correct a cash-flow problem
- evaluate the usefulness to a business of completing a cash-flow forecast.

Introductory case study: Broder Metals Group and cash flow

Broder supplies high-quality metal alloys for use in power stations and Formula 1 cars, although their main market is oil and gas exploration and production.

When the price of oil dropped dramatically in 2014/2015, there was a sudden reduction in oil and gas exploration. This gave Broder a real problem because orders from the oil industry also fell dramatically. Broder orders their stock of metals with a time delay of 15 months before delivery. Therefore when the oil price fell, they had orders in place that had to be paid for. This meant cash was flowing *out* of the business. The problem was that the reduction in orders meant there was less cash flowing *into* the business.

This cash flow problem had to be solved. A business needs cash to pay for expenses, and the management at Broder took the following steps to minimise the problem:

- reduced stock, even selling stock at a loss if necessary
- talked to suppliers – tried to cancel/delay orders or asked for a reduction in price – not always possible
- general cutbacks wherever they could to save cash
- talked to their bank – this was a key move to help manage the problem. A bank can help with an overdraft (see Unit 5.2) to give businesses like Broder the necessary cash to help them pay for expenses until orders improve in the future. The important element here was to talk to the bank when the problem could be forecasted – not when you actually have the problem.

The above measures did work for Broder and it now has the ability to create a cash surplus, which can help with any future cash-flow problem, should one occur.

Importance of cash to a business

Meeting short-term debts and expenses

A business needs cash to pay its expenses and meet its short-term debts. These might include:

- wages and salaries
- rent
- suppliers
- heating and lighting bills.

If any of the above are not paid, then the business may well be in some difficulties.

Providing liquidity

Liquidity is the ability of a business to turn assets (things that a business owns) into cash. For example, a shop will have stock that it sells for cash. That cash is used to buy more stock to sell, and to pay other expenses. But what if the stock is slow to sell and the electricity bill has to be paid? Having cash will give a business the liquidity to pay its bills.

It is therefore vital that a business plans carefully to make sure that it has enough cash to meet its debts and to have the necessary liquidity.

Cash and profit

It is important to understand the difference between cash and profit.

Cash

Cash is the money held in bank accounts and in cash on the premises. Cash is used to pay expenses and short-term debts. The amount of cash a business expects to have at a given time is shown in the cash flow forecast (see below).

Profit

Profit is calculated by subtracting the total costs of running a business from the total revenue it receives. A business could have a lot of cash but make little profit, or be short of cash in a particular month but make a good profit.

Cash is very important to a business.

Cash flow forecast

A cash flow forecast is an attempt to predict what could happen in the future, just as the weather forecast attempts to predict what the weather might be like tomorrow, or in a few days' time. Sometimes the forecast is accurate and on other occasions the forecast is only partly accurate. Any forecast will always have a certain amount of uncertainty.

Most businesses will try to forecast future events using previous experiences or data that they have collected. This process will help the business to plan for the future.

One of the most important forecasts that a business makes concerns the amount of money that it expects to have flowing into and out of the business in the future. This is called a cash flow forecast.

Knowing when a business might have too much or too little money is important so that plans can be made for the future of the business. Look back at the case study at the start of this unit – how Broder Metals Group saw that in the near future they would have a shortage of cash.

Cash flow forecasting in a business needs carefully estimated figures.

Example of a cash flow forecast

This table below is a cash flow forecast for HMJA fashion, a business selling teenage fashions.

	October	November	December
	£	£	£
Cash inflow			
Sales	30,000	40,000	55,000
Total inflow	30,000	40,000	55,000
Cash outflow			
Wages	6,000	7,500	10,000
Loan repayments and interest	3,500	3,500	4,000
Stock	35,000	15,000	10,000
Total outflow	44,500	26,000	24,000
Net cash flow	–14,500	14,000	31,000
Opening balance	1,000	–13,500	500
Closing balance	–13,500	500	30,500

Table 5.23 Cash flow forecast.

Understanding a cash flow forecast – the left-hand column

Look at the cash forecast flow (Table 5.23).

The left-hand column starts with cash inflow. This is the money coming into the business. In this case, it is sales from selling clothing.

Going down the left-hand column, the next section focuses on cash outflow. This is the money going out of the business. In this example, these are payments for wages for the people working in the shop; overheads, which are payments for expenses such as heating and lighting; and stock, which is the business buying the clothes it will sell. These items are added together to give the total outflow.

The next item is the **net cash flow**. This is calculated by taking the cash outflow figure from the cash inflow.

The **opening balance** is the amount of cash at the start of the month and is the same as the **closing balance** from the previous month.

Understanding the figures in a cash flow forecast

Look again at Table 5.23. In October, the business sold £30,000 of clothing – the sales figure. In the same month, it paid £6,000 in wages, £3,500 for loan repayments and interest and £35,000 on stock. The high figure for October stock will be buying items in for Christmas – this business plans early! The total outflow of £44,500 is the total of wages, overheads and stock.

Notice in October the net cash flow has a – (minus) sign in front of the £14,500. This is because the net cash flow is the **total inflow** minus the **total outflow**. In this example, it is £30,000 minus £44,500 which is –£14,500.

Looking further down in October, the opening balance is £1,000, which would have been the closing balance for the previous month, September.

The final figure for October is the closing balance. This is the opening balance minus the net cash flow. In this example, it is £1,000 minus £14,500. This again gives a negative number: –£13,500. Notice that this then becomes the opening balance for November.

A positive cash flow is always good news for a business.

The process then starts again for November.

The cash flow forecast for HMJA fashion shows that they have forecasted a **negative cash flow** for October. This means that they forecast they will have more cash going out of the business than they have coming in. For November and December, they calculate they will have a **positive cash flow**, which is more cash coming in than going out.

Is a negative net cash flow a problem?

A negative net cash flow may:

- only be temporary and may not necessarily cause a problem for the business
- require the business to obtain additional finance in the form of an overdraft to help it overcome a shortage of cash
- mean that the business has to delay payment of money it owes to others, such as suppliers.

The business will be in serious financial trouble if it forecasts a negative cash flow at the end of a number of months. Unless things start to improve, the possibility exists that the business may go out of business, not because it is unprofitable, but because it has run out of cash. A business will always need money to pay for its expenses and short-term debts.

Activity 1 – Calculation activity

Design and complete your own cash flow forecast for the next six weeks.

Under cash inflows, you might have pocket money, paper round, babysitting etc. List all of the ways you will have a cash inflow – you may even have a birthday in the next six weeks!

Under cash outflow, list all of the ways in which your cash is flowing out. This list could include mobile phone, DVDs, entertainment, clothes, bus fares etc.

Once you have completed your cash flow forecast:

a) Explain any difficulties you had in forecasting up to six weeks ahead.

b) How accurate do you think your forecast is? Why is it difficult to make it accurate?

Activity 2 – Explanation activity

Look back at Table 5.23 on page 256, the cash flow forecast for HMJA fashion.

a) Explain why wages are forecast to go up in November and increase further in December.

b) Why is the sales figure forecast for December so much higher than in October and November?

c) Explain why a forecasted negative net cash flow in October was no real problem for HMJA fashion.

d) Explain how the next three months might look for the cash flow of HMJA fashion. Give reasons for your answer.

Activity 3 – Calculation activity

Complete the following cash flow forecast for Lamick Ltd, a business that produces yoghurt.

	January	February	March
	£	£	£
Cash inflow			
Sales	80,500	92,000	88,000
Rent received	500	500	500
Total inflow		92,500	88,500
Cash outflow			
Materials	55,000	60,000	59,000
Wages and salaries	20,000	20,000	20,000
Transport	8,000	9,000	8,500
Overheads	3,000	3,000	3,000
Total outflow	86,000		90,500
Net cash flow		–500	–2,000
Opening balance	4,000		500
Closing balance	1,000	500	

Table 5.24 Cash flow forecast.

Activity 4 – Missing words activity

Use the words below to help you fill in the gaps in the following paragraph.

- run out of money
- estimate
- increase
- accurate
- plans
- too much
- out of business
- profit
- expenditure.

Cash flow forecast is only an ___ of the amount of income and ___ which a business expects. The main purpose of the calculation is to estimate when the business may have ___ or too little cash. It does not calculate ___ When a shortage of cash, to pay bills, is expected, the business may need to change its ___ so that costs are reduced and attempts are made to ___ its income. Without sufficient cash, the business may go ___ not because it is unprofitable, but because it has ___ Short-term forecasts are likely to be more ___ than long-term forecasts.

Firework manufacturers do not have a steady cash flow throughout the year.

Activity 5 – Research and presentation activity

Make a PowerPoint presentation on businesses that are likely to have a steady flow of cash into and out of their businesses throughout the year. Contrast those businesses with ones that are likely to have cash flow problems – possibly where their sales are concentrated in particular times of the year.

The usefulness of cash flow forecasting to a business

1 A planning tool

Businesses need to plan in order to give themselves the greatest chance of success (see also Unit 1.2). Part of that planning is in the completion of a cash-flow forecast. A cash flow forecast can be shown to banks in order to show that the business has thought carefully about its financial future in terms of cash. This will help to obtain loans or other finance that the business might require.

2 Anticipates periods of cash shortage

After completing a cash flow forecast, a business might see that there is a cash shortage in certain months but not others. It is quite common for a business to have a cash shortage in certain months, and in normal circumstances this will not cause any issues. A problem will arise however when a business has not seen the problem coming and it may be too late to find solutions. If the problem can be seen by completing a cash flow forecast, then the potential problem can usually be solved.

3 Enables remedies to be put in place for shortages

Once a cash flow forecast has shown that there is likely to be a cash shortage for a period of time, then solutions can be found. A common remedy is an overdraft (see also Unit 5.2) arranged through a bank. This will provide finance to pay for wages, overheads and so on in the period where there is a cash shortage. Look back at the start of this unit. The case study on Broder shows how a business faced a cash shortage caused by factors outside its control. The management at Broder took a number of steps, including cutting back on spending, talking to their bank and trying to get a better deal on the orders they had placed. The point to emphasise is that completing a cash flow forecast shows what could happen in the future and this enables remedies to be put in place to control the problem before it occurs. As we saw with Broder, the remedies put in place by the management worked well and they are now building up a cash surplus.

4 Provides targets

Completing a cash flow forecast provides targets for a business. By looking ahead, a business may see that there is a possible cash shortage. The business may then target reducing certain parts of spending to a particular level in order to make sure that it has sufficient cash. A business might also set a target of having a cash surplus by a particular date if it believes there will be a cash flow shortage later. Having the surplus could mean that there is no need to ask a bank for an overdraft.

Evaluation point

When asked how a cash flow problem might be solved, look carefully at the information you are given. What situation is the business in? How long is the cash shortage likely to last for? Is the cash shortage significant?

When suggesting possible solutions, be realistic and make sure your suggestions are achievable as far as you can see. Think of the costs involved of your solutions and the effect your proposals might have on the business.

Key facts

Businesses need to forecast the flow of cash to and from the business so that any potential future problems can be identified.

Cash flow forecasts are only estimates of expected **income** and **expenditure**.

Cash left over at the end of one month is carried forward to the beginning of the next month.

A negative cash flow in one month does not mean that the business is unprofitable.

A positive cash flow in one month does not mean that the business is profitable.

Cash flow needs to be managed so that the business does not run out of cash.

Good cash flow management is vital for the future success and survival of the business.

Useful words

Cash flow forecast is a statement showing the expected flow of money into and out of a business over a period of time.

Net cash flow is total inflow minus total outflow.

Opening balance is the amount of cash available at the beginning of the month that was the closing balance at the end of the previous month.

Closing balance is the amount of cash left at the end of a month. This becomes the opening balance at the start of the next month.

Total inflow is the total amount of cash flowing into a business.

Total outflow is the total amount of cash flowing out of a business.

Negative cash flow is when during one month, more cash is flowing out of the business than is flowing into it. It is sometimes called a cash flow deficit.

Positive cash flow is when, during one month, more cash is flowing into the business than is flowing out of it. It is sometimes called a cash flow surplus.

Income is money that the business receives.

Expenditure is money that the business pays out.

Liquidity is the ability of a business to pay its short-term debts which must be paid in the near future.

Short-term debts/expenses are the bills that a business has to pay in the near future, for example electricity.

Cash is not simply notes and coins held in the business, but also money in a bank account.

Profit is the revenue received by a business minus the costs of running the business.

Practice questions

Multiple choice questions

1 A cash flow forecast is useful for:
   a) informing the business about the profit that the business should make each year
   b) helping the business to see where cash shortages might occur in the future
   c) seeing the flow of cash from the business to the bank
   d) choosing the best method of finance to use for expanding the business.

2 A cash flow shortage in a business is often solved by arranging:
   a) an overdraft
   b) a loan
   c) crowdfunding
   d) shares to be sold.

3 Net cash flow is calculated by:
   a) adding the closing balance to the opening balance
   b) adding total inflow to total outflow
   c) taking total outflow from total inflow
   d) taking the closing balance from the opening balance.

Data response 34

Tom and Olivia own a flower shop. The net cash flows for the business are forecast as follows:

Month	£
June	–2000
July	–1500
September	–2500
October	–1500
November	–1200

Table 5.25 Net cash flow forecast.

The opening balance for the business in June is £6,000.

1 Calculate the closing balance at the end of November. (2 marks)

2 Explain one possible problem shown in the net cash flows. (3 marks)

3 Analyse two measures that Tom and Olivia could take to deal with a possible cash-flow problem. (6 marks)

How to answer data response 34

1 Here you are not given a complete cash flow forecast. You need to calculate the total of money coming in or going out of the business and add it, or take it from, the opening June balance.

2 Here you need to 'explain'. First, identify a problem shown by the net cash flow, and then show why it is a problem for the business.

3 Here you need to analyse rather than identify. Look at the figures presented to you. Does it look like a mere temporary problem, or more of a long-term problem? The measures you write about in your answer should take this into account, and look to show the effect that they will have on the business.

6 Influences on business

UNIT 6.1 Ethical and environmental considerations

Learning outcomes

By studying this unit, you will be able to:

- explain and apply the term 'ethical considerations'
- analyse and evaluate the impact of ethical considerations on businesses
- explain and apply the term 'environmental considerations'
- analyse and evaluate the impact of environmental considerations on businesses.

Introduction

This unit deals with two issues – ethical and environmental considerations. Many businesses see these two issues as part of their 'corporate social responsibility'. They recognise that business success is not just about selling goods and services and making profits, but that they will be judged on their overall contribution to society. Next plc, the clothes retailer, writes about its 'social responsibilities' that include ethical and environmental considerations on its website.

Ethical considerations

The meaning of ethical behaviour

Ethics focuses on what is the right or wrong thing to do. It is not always easy to decide what is right and wrong in business and what we think is right or wrong can change over time. Two hundred years ago, many people thought it was correct to trade in slaves, taking people from Africa and selling them in America. Nowadays, people think slavery is wrong.

Introductory case study: ethical and environmental considerations at Next plc

The bullet points summarise the ethical and environmental considerations at Next plc.

- acting in an ethical manner
- developing positive relationships with our suppliers
- taking care of our employees
- being responsible for our impact on the environment
- delivering support through charitable contributions
- delivering value to our customers.

From Nextplc.co.uk.

Examples of ethical issues for business

The treatment of workers

Case study: H&M, Welcome Break under-pay workers

In January 2015, the Swedish-owned clothes retailer, H&M, was named by the Revenue and Customs in the UK for under-paying 540 workers a total of £2604.85 during the period of their employment. This works out at £4.82 on average for each worker. H&M claimed the problem was caused by the workers' hours not being logged correctly. In the same report, Welcome Break – the motorway services business – was shamed for under-paying 20 workers. Welcome Break said their under-payment issue arose because of management changes, holiday periods and a new IT system, and that there was no deliberate attempt not to pay what should have been earned. In all, 37 businesses were named in the report.

The firms in this case study may, or may not, have deliberately underpaid their workers. However, it is clear that they have not been sufficiently concerned to make sure their workers are paid correctly. Does this mean they have not been ethical or is it just human error? You might wish to discuss this as a class.

H&M are also mentioned in a report by the Centre for Research on Multinationals which states that the firm has been employing children in Myanmar younger than 14 years old and paying as little as 13p per hour. Is this ethical? This kind of practice helps firms like H&M to sell goods to us at low prices and the children are earning money, which will help them and their families.

The case study shows one way in which businesses may be unethical when it comes to the employment of labour. These practices have been made illegal in the UK but there are still unethical employers here (as well as abroad) who are willing to treat their workers badly. Other ways include:

- using **child labour**
- paying workers low wages
- expecting workers to work very long hours
- not providing workers with safe working conditions
- discriminating against workers on gender, ethnicity or disability grounds.

The treatment of suppliers

Case study: Tesco and its treatment of suppliers

The Grocery Code Adjudicator (GCA) investigated Tesco and found that it was guilty of delaying payments to some suppliers, usually smaller businesses. One supplier had to wait for 24 months for the £2 million it was owed.

Sometimes it would use the fact that it owed money to help strike a better deal, promising payment if the supplier would agree to sell further stock to it at lower prices. Tesco apologised and improved its terms.

Late payment of bills is a real problem that affects the cash flow of many businesses. It can mean that a business is unable to pay their own bills and it could be forced into liquidation. When businesses the size of Tesco are late with payments, it is very difficult for small suppliers to do anything about it because they might put their deals with the company at risk. Losing a deal could cause them to lose profits and possibly to go out of business.

The treatment of customers

Case study: Servicing Stop and its customers

Servicing Stop organises the servicing of cars on behalf of customers. It organised a car service at a garage for one customer. The garage did the service but also replaced the disc brake pads on the car and charged an extra £441 for doing this. The customer had not asked for this work, nor was the work needed. The disc brakes had been replaced only nine months before and the car had travelled just 6,000 miles since then.

The garage that had done the work claimed the disc brakes were worn and showed them to the customer who then showed them to a second garage. The mechanic at the second garage said the pads were slightly worn as would be expected but also said that there was plenty of life left in them. The customer complained to Servicing Stop who refused to respond, so the customer wrote to thisismoney.co.uk. The story about the disc brakes does have a happy ending, however. thisismoney.co.uk contacted Servicing Stop who arranged for a refund and some compensation to be paid. The customer received £600.

Adapted from www.thisismoney.co.uk

Not all garages rip off customers!

Many customers will have stories of poor treatment by sellers. Firms like Next make statements about 'delivering value to our customers' to stress their desire to be seen to treat customers fairly.

Sourcing materials

Case study: Apple at Pergatron

Apple iPhone 6.

A BBC *Panorama* programme found that workers in a Chinese factory at Pergatron, near Shanghai, were being treated unethically. The workers were manufacturing the iPhone 6. The BBC sent undercover reporters to work in the factory who reported that workers were falling asleep as they worked because they were so tired. One employee had been made to work for 18 consecutive days without a day off, another had worked one shift of 16 hours and another lived in a small, cramped dormitory room for 12 workers. Apple, however, said that it takes worker safety seriously and trains managers and workers, and inspects the factories it buys from to make sure they are behaving according to the standards that it has laid down.

Adapted from bbc.co.uk, Panorama, *18 December 2014.*

Ethical issues are faced by all businesses. There is often fierce competition between suppliers of products. These suppliers may find it necessary to keep their costs as low as possible to help them to compete, and this is where they may be tempted to 'cut corners' when it comes to ethical work practices. The problem has become increasingly complex as globalisation has increased. Businesses can find it difficult to know exactly what is going on in the factories that supply them. In developed countries, like the UK, we expect our businesses to take these responsibilities seriously, by, for example, having proper and effective inspections of the factories of suppliers.

Marketing considerations

In 2015, news broke of a big scandal connected with VW, the car manufacturer. It turned out that VW had rigged tests that it had done on its cars. VW claimed that its cars caused less pollution than they actually did and it had been claiming this for several years. Millions of cars sold in different countries in the world were affected by this and VW is having to pay out billions of pounds in compensation.

Marketing includes price, product, promotion and place. Many firms use **ethical marketing** practices. However, there are unscrupulous people, and even firms with good track records like VW can succumb to the pressures of competition. VW was unethical in its advertising because it was making false claims about its product. In the UK, the Advertising Standards Authority (ASA) applies the advertising code, which states that advertising should be legal, decent, honest and truthful. The code explains what ethical advertising means. Advertisers must obey the spirit of this as well as being technically correct. It is a common-sense approach that seeks to make sure that advertisers are behaving ethically. Advertising should not mislead, harm or offend. The code is designed to protect children and the vulnerable. It is particularly watchful of claims related to alcohol, beauty, health, the environment, gambling and direct marketing.

Another potentially unethical practice is charging a higher price than is fair. Energy and petrol companies have sometimes been accused of this. It is said that when the price of gas or oil falls on the world markets, they do not pass these lower

Activity 1 – True or false activity

Tick the true or false box next to each of the statements in the table below to indicate whether or not they are generally thought to be ethical practices.

Statement	True	False
It is ethical for a football manager to take a bribe because other managers do the same.		
It is ethical to employ very young children as long as they are paid a fair wage.		
It is not ethical for businesses to delay paying their bills to suppliers.		
It is ethical to copy films because the producers make a lot of money from them.		
It is ethical for a business to make false claims for its products because it helps to create jobs for people.		
It is ethical to buy goods from poor countries, in order to help their businesses to develop.		
It is ethical to save money by reducing health and safety measures, as long as it helps the business to survive.		
It is not ethical to sell arms to political leaders who might use them to crush peaceful, law-abiding opposition in the country.		

Table 6.1 True or false ethical practices.

costs on in the form of lower prices for consumers as quickly as they should. Instead, they may make higher profits for a while.

Another practice that may be unethical is testing beauty products on animals.

Laws such as the Trade Descriptions Act and the Sale of Goods Act can be used to punish firms who do not act ethically. These are covered in Unit 4.4.

Whilst it is possible to prosecute firms that break the laws as mentioned above, it is not possible to punish firms that test beauty products on animals. This is because this is not against the law, though some people think it is unethical and that it should be against the law.

Sourcing of materials – Fairtrade

The **Fairtrade** movement has become increasingly important as a way of encouraging ethical business activities. The Fairtrade Foundation exists to 'bring justice and sustainable development' to trade so that 'everyone, through their work, can maintain a decent and dignified livelihood and develop their full potential'. To achieve this, it tries to help those who live and work in developing countries. It uses the Fairtrade Mark. This guarantees to the consumer that the retailer has paid a fair price to the farmers who produced the goods so that they have extra money to pay for the education of their children and other social needs. Many retailers in the UK are selling more and more Fairtrade ranges. Sainsbury's supermarket will only sell Fairtrade bananas and Marks & Spencer works with 600 Fairtrade cotton farmers.

However, some people criticise the Fairtrade idea. In India and China, many people who have not been protected by Fairtrade have managed to increase their earnings by producing the right goods at the right prices. Other critics say that the prices the producers are paid are not a lot more than they would normally be and that the focus should be on developing and providing the farmers with new technology which would increase the amount they could produce. Others say that producers in Third World countries may become dependent on Fairtrade sales rather than seeking to improve their efficiency and competitiveness.

Activity 2 – Debate activity

In groups, prepare and carry out a debate about each of the following ethical issues. You will need one group for and one group against for each proposal.

a) It is ethical to employ young children in India to work in textile factories so that they can earn money to help their families.

b) It is ethical to exaggerate claims for a product if the business is struggling to survive because it will help to increase sales and stop workers becoming unemployed.

c) Businesses should always maximise the profit they make for their shareholders. This is being fair to the shareholders who have invested their money in the business.

d) It is ethical for a football manager to pay a bribe to a football agent to make sure he can sign a player for the team.

'I only do it for the fans.'

Activity 3 – Missing words activity

Complete the paragraph using the words given below:

- child
- competitive
- right
- money
- less
- more
- survive
- human rights
- Fairtrade
- safe.

Ethics is about ___ and wrong. An example of an unethical business activity is when a firm buys products made using ___ labour. Another unethical practice would be a firm that does not provide its workers with a ___ working environment. A business that sells arms to the political leaders of a country who do not give proper ___ ___ to their citizens may not be ethical. Sometimes it saves a business ___ by not being ethical. This may be important if the business is in a very ___ market. Some of the competitors may not be ethical and so they can charge ___ for their products. The result might be that the ethical business cannot ___ However, many customers are now prepared to pay ___ for products that are sold by ethical producers.

Ethical considerations and their impact on businesses

Some businesses do not want to be ethical. The problems it can bring include:

- **higher costs** – for example, having to pay higher wages to workers, providing safe working conditions or buying from ethical and **environmentally-friendly** producers abroad
- **lost sales** – unethical businesses can make sales and increase their sales revenue by not treating their customers fairly or by not marketing honestly
- **reduced profits** – the higher costs and lost sales revenue can reduce profits
- **poor financial figures** – firms may want to make their finances look better than they are, as Tesco did by delaying payments to suppliers. Good figures are good for publicity and may encourage investors to buy shares in the business.

'I have the right to make a profit.'

However, being ethical can bring benefits to businesses.

a) Workers like it when the business is ethical because they will trust their employer. Being ethical can improve motivation that can increase both the productivity and the loyalty of the workers. If this happens, the costs of production per unit may fall and the retention of labour improve so that the costs of recruiting new workers may also be reduced. If the business does need to recruit new workers, it is likely to be easier to attract them if it has a reputation as an ethical producer.

b) Customers like it. It helps the business because:

- being ethical can help a business to gain a good reputation with customers and it can lead to an increase in sales
- sometimes, being an ethical producer can be necessary to gain a contract with a business. For example, retailers may want to be confident that the businesses they buy stock from are ethical. If not, and customers find out, they may lose their good reputation and may lose sales. Some retailers have run into problems when they have bought stock from unethical sources.

c) Investors like it. Investors feel confident that the business will make them look good and, in the long term, will be successful.

d) There is evidence that firms which have good reputations as ethical producers are, in the long term, more likely to survive and to be profitable.

Evaluation point

Many customers are willing to pay more for goods and services from businesses that behave in an ethical way. This encourages businesses to behave ethically, as they use the extra revenue to pay the higher costs that may be involved. This can benefit workers, customers and suppliers. However, some customers are very poor, even in the UK, and cannot afford to pay the higher prices. Is it fair on these customers if there are only **ethical businesses** to buy from?

Activity 4 – Zone activity

The following statements are either possible advantages or disadvantages to businesses of behaving ethically. Put each one under its correct heading in the table below.

- There is a greater chance that the business will survive in the long run.
- The costs of production may rise because workers need to be paid a fair wage.
- Workers may be more motivated, which will improve productivity.
- Sales may increase because customers think the business is trustworthy.
- A business may find it easier to recruit employees.
- A business that is honest in its marketing may find that its sales fall.

Possible advantages of behaving ethically in business	Possible disadvantages of behaving ethically in business

Table 6.2 Advantages and disadvantages of ethical business.

Environmental considerations

Many businesses are now trying to be environmentally friendly.

Case study: Unilever and its greenhouse gas target

Lynx deodorant saving the environment.

Unilever makes a range of products such as toiletries, washing powders and foods. It announced that it intends to halve the amount of greenhouse gases that it creates by 2030. It will do this by designing products and using manufacturing processes that create fewer greenhouse gases, for example, it uses a 'cool blending' process to create margarines that uses less heat and therefore less energy. Unilever has created compressed deodorant sprays that use 50 per cent less gas and 25 per cent less packaging (aluminium cans). Overall the carbon footprints of these sprays will be cut by 25 per cent.

In this unit, the environment means our natural world. Households and businesses make use of the environment in three ways:

1. **It provides us with natural resources.** These include agricultural crops, fish, animals, wood, metal, oil, coal, gas and the land itself. Businesses provide goods and services using these, which results in profits and support our standard of living.
2. **It is something from which we get pleasure.** We like fresh air, enjoy a walk in the park, fishing and swimming in rivers, lakes and the sea, looking at scenery, climbing in the mountains and so on. Again, businesses may make profits by, for example, providing leisure activities, such as coach tours or outdoor pursuits, for consumers.
3. **It is somewhere to dump waste produced by households and businesses.** Land may be filled in using rubbish, businesses may dump waste in the sea or in the rivers and gases may pollute the atmosphere. Businesses earn money by dealing with waste. Also, some businesses have lowered their costs and increased profits by dumping waste in a way that may harm the environment.

Examples of environmental considerations are discussed under four separate headings below – Sustainability, Waste disposal, Pollution and Climate change. However, the issues are often connected. The first three illustrate ways in which businesses can be green or behave in an environmentally-friendly way. The fourth – **climate change** – looks at one of the major negative effects of business (and consumer) activity on the environment.

Sustainability

Renewable energy – but do these spoil the environment?

Sustainable production is making goods and providing services without depleting natural resources. In practice, businesses that claim to use sustainable methods aim to use **renewable resources** and recycled resources, reduce waste and use energy sparingly and avoid the use of **non-renewable resources** when they can. Examples of production that is sustainable are:

- **solar and wind energy** – there is no limit to the energy that can be generated from the sun or from the wind. Using these means that we do not need to use fossil fuels, such as coal and oil, which, once used, cannot be used again and will eventually run out.
- **sustainable construction** – this is about building using recycled resources such as wood and bricks that have been used before and have been recovered when the property was demolished. It is also about building renewable resources into the new building, such as putting solar panels on the roof to generate the electricity. Building good insulation into the construction can lead to energy savings in the future.
- **rotating crops** – this can avoid having to use chemicals to fertilise the soil. It involves growing a different crop each year on a piece of land so that different nutrients in the soil are being used, and giving time for those that have been used by a previous crop to replenish.
- **saving water** – water is a scarce and expensive product. Sustainable production minimises the use of water. Even simple things help such as fixing leaks and installing taps that switch off automatically.
- **switching off lights** – many businesses (and schools) now use light sensors to switch lights off when not needed and so save on the use of electricity. Not leaving computers on standby will also save electricity.
- **dispose of waste properly** – **recycling** things like paper and ink cartridges.
- **transport** – encouraging staff to cycle, use public transport or car-share to get to work. Using fuel efficient vehicles to transport goods. Using video-conferencing rather than face to face meetings that require the workers to travel. Buying raw materials and goods from local suppliers to reduce transport costs and emissions.

- **avoid printing** – only print documents when necessary. When printing is necessary, print on both sides of the paper.
- **processing waste into products** – we saw in Unit 4.5 Business location that Olleco uses waste oils from restaurants to produce biofuel.

Waste disposal

Case study: Shanks plc – waste disposal versus recycling waste

The Shanks Group is the biggest firm in Europe dealing with waste. The website for Shanks describes its business as being 'waste to product'. This means that it aims to use waste as a raw material for making products, rather than burning it in incinerators or dumping it in landfill. Incineration can pollute the atmosphere. The number of landfill sites is limited. More importantly, as the waste in landfill sites breaks down, it produces methane gas which causes **global warming**. Shanks avoids these problems and recycles the waste using it as a raw material from which products can be made and sold. The diagram below is taken from the Shanks plc website. It shows the products that Shanks makes from different kinds of waste.

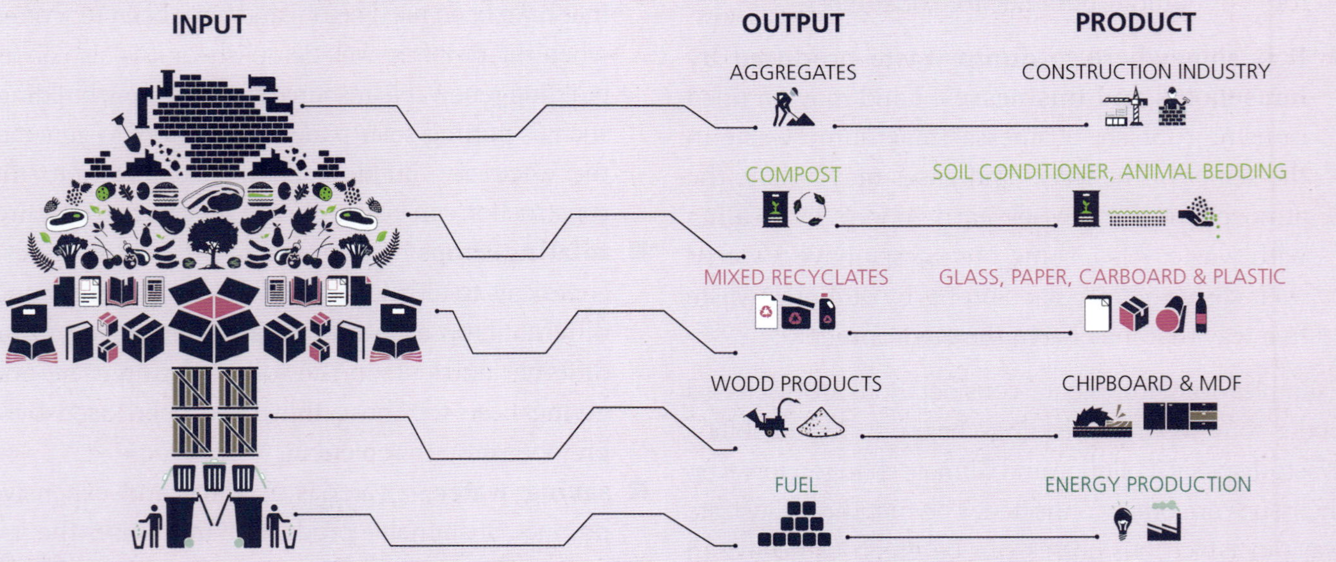

Figure 6.1 Waste to product process

Waste disposal is a huge problem. As the population and the amount that we each consume grows, waste increases. Traditionally we have used incineration and landfill but, as we have seen, these are not without their problems. More and more businesses like Shanks are seeing opportunities in using waste as a raw material.

Pollution

The main kinds of **pollution** are:

- Air pollution. This is when gases such as carbon dioxide are put into the atmosphere from, for example, cars, planes, factories and power stations. 4.6 million people are thought to die each year from illnesses caused by air pollution. 310,000 of these are people who live in Europe. The types of illness that air pollution causes include asthma, bronchitis, emphysema, lung and heart diseases and respiratory allergies.
- Noise pollution. This is when people's peace is disturbed by noise from, for example, cars, factories and planes.
- Pollution of the sea and rivers. This is when, for example, businesses pump waste produce such as chemicals into the sea and rivers.

Case study: the fashion industry – world's second biggest polluter

Eileen Fisher, a clothing industry entrepreneur, claims that the fashion industry is second only to the oil industry in the amount of pollution it causes. T-shirts can illustrate some of the problems. Many T-shirts use cotton, which is a natural product. However, fertilisers and insecticides are used on cotton plantations. Man-made fibres can also be used to make T-shirts but the production of these involves the use of chemical processes that cause pollution. Once made, T-shirts will need to be dyed using more chemicals. Then they need to be transported, often long distances from the developing countries, perhaps in Africa or in the Far East, to the developed countries, like the UK, usually in container ships fuelled by oil.

Adapted from ecowatch.com

Climate change

Climate change is the long-term change in weather conditions. There are some different views about climate change. Some scientists say it is not happening but most say that temperatures are rising, sea-levels are rising and rainfall is increasing but snowfall is decreasing. The overall effect is called global warming. It is caused by natural events such as volcanic eruptions and changes in the amount of heat generated by the sun. It is also caused by human activity – both domestic and business activity. We humans cause global warming mainly by burning fossil fuels such as coal, oil and wood used to generate energy. This creates more carbon dioxide. We also cause it by cutting down forests. Deforestation means there are fewer trees to absorb the carbon dioxide.

A report by MPs in July 2016 said that climate was having a negative effect on business activity. The report predicted problems:

- Some businesses would lose their supply of energy and their ICT connections, and have problems making and receiving deliveries. This happened in 2015 because heavy rains had caused bridges to be destroyed. This harmed the electricity, gas and IT connections carried by the bridges.
- Farming would continue to be affected by soil degradation and this would lead to higher food prices.
- The number of old people who would die from heat related causes was likely to rise.

Case study: UK winter of 2015–16 – the great Custard Cream shortage

Where are the Custard Creams?

The 2015–16 winter in the UK saw some of the worst floods in memory. The Lake District was particularly badly hit. Bridges were destroyed, roads collapsed and transport was very badly affected. It is estimated that businesses in the small village of Grasmere lost millions of pounds in business. A biscuit factory in Carlisle was so badly damaged in the floods that it was closed between December 2015 and April 2016, leading to a national shortage of McVitie's Ginger Nuts and Crawford's Custard Creams. Global warming may be causing heavy winter rains.

Climate change does create some business opportunities. The demand for insurance against the risks of climate will increase, care homes will need to install more air conditioning and flood defences will need to be built or improved.

Activity 5 – Missing words activity

Read the section above. Complete the paragraph below using the words that are given.

- compost
- fossil
- sustainable
- waste
- transported
- fertilisers
- global
- recycled
- environmentally
- landfill
- wood
- chemicals
- burning.

Shanks uses ___ as an input. From it, Shanks produces all kinds of outputs including ___ and ___ products. This is good because it saves using ___ sites or ___ waste in incinerators. For the fashion industry, there are many difficulties in being ___ friendly. Chemical ___ are often used to help to grow cotton. ___ are used to dye clothing. Clothing often needs to be ___ long distances from where it is made to where it is sold. Transport uses up ___ fuels and causes CO_2 emissions contributing to ___ warming. ___ production involves making goods and services using ___ resources.

Activity 6 – Poster activity

Think about the local area around your school. Individually or in groups, draw a poster that shows the costs to the environment in this area that result from consumers and producers. Also, show the benefits that consumers and producers gain from their local environment.

The rules for drawing this poster are that you can use lots of pictures and symbols and numbers but you cannot use more than ten words. Once you have drawn it, you need to explain it – either to the whole class or to some of the other students in your class.

Activity 7 – Research activity

Imagine that you are buying Christmas or birthday presents for your friends and family – toys, toiletries, bags, clothes etc. Research gift catalogues to find presents that are environmentally friendly. You will be able to find these on the internet – use Google or a similar search engine. Write down your list of presents and explain how each one is environmentally friendly.

Alternatively, find out about environmentally-friendly cars – use the internet. Fuel-efficiency (miles per gallon) is one measure that can be used, another is the CO_2 emissions of the car. Compare electric and hybrid cars, such as the Toyota Prius, with petrol and diesel cars. Write down a list of about ten cars, from the best to the worst in terms of being 'green'. Explain why you have put the cars in the order that you have.

Activity 8 – Explanation activity

Individually or in groups, think about your school. Decide to what extent it is environmentally friendly. Use ideas under the heading 'Sustainable production' on page 269 to help you to make a start, and add any other ideas that you have. Write down two lists. In the first, write all of the things you can think of that happen in school which can be called environmentally friendly. In the second, write down all the ways in which your school could become greener. Briefly explain the things that you have listed.

Benefits to businesses of being environmentally friendly

The Shanks and Unilever case studies illustrate ways in which businesses may be environmentally friendly. The benefits to businesses of being environmentally friendly are given in the table below.

Benefit	Explanation
Increased sales	Consumers are becoming increasingly aware of the negative effects that businesses can have on the environment. Businesses, such as Unilever, know that they can increase their sales and their market share by reducing the environmental impact of their brands. It is likely that Unilever would have lost sales if it had not redesigned its products to be more environmentally friendly.
Reduced costs	Some of the changes to business activities to reduce the negative effect on the environment can reduce production costs. For example, the cool blending process mentioned in the Unilever case study saves money because it requires less energy to heat the ingredients ready for mixing. Other ways in which businesses can reduce costs are by using energy-saving light bulbs, generating their own electricity through solar panels, reducing the amount of packaging used for their products, making products using fewer resources, buying produce locally to reduce transport distances and CO_2 emissions.
Reduced tax bills	Many governments around the world now seek to reduce the environmental impacts of businesses. To do this they can regulate activity to make sure businesses cause less pollution and emit fewer greenhouse gases. Also, they can impose taxes on businesses so that they have to pay for environmental problems they cause. Businesses can cut the amount of tax they must pay by reducing the problems they cause.
Getting subsidies	Governments may offer subsidies to businesses to help them introduce environmentally-friendly products and production processes.
Reducing resource scarcity	Resources are becoming increasingly expensive for businesses to buy as the supply of them falls and the demand for them increases. Eventually, there is the risk that we will run out of non-renewable resources. In the long term, it is in the interest of businesses to reduce the amount of resources they use.

Table 6.3 Benefits to businesses of being environmentally friendly.

Renewable energy sources save money.

Problems of being environmentally friendly

The main problem with environmentally-friendly production is that it can increase costs. The disadvantages are shown in the table below.

Disadvantage	Explanation
Raw materials costs	Raw materials that have been produced in an environmentally friendly way often cost more.
Capital costs	Another cost is that of investing in the capital equipment needed to introduce environmentally friendly production processes. For example, the costs of buying and installing solar panels may exceed the savings from using them.
Production methods may be more expensive	The cheapest way to catch fish is to put a net in the sea and just catch as much as possible. However, many of the fish caught will not be needed and will be destroyed or thrown back dead. Growing food organically is more expensive than using fertilisers and pesticides.

Table 6.4 Disadvantages to businesses being environmentally friendly.

Evaluation point

Many businesses claim to be environmentally friendly because they know that it will help them to sell their products. However, they may exaggerate just how green they are. This is misleading the public and, as such, it is unethical behaviour. It may result in customers paying higher prices, thinking that they are helping the environment when they may not be.

Activity 9 – Matching activity

Match the statement in the left-hand column of the table with the explanation in the right-hand column.

Statement	Explanation
a) Costs of production may be higher.	**1** The firm causes less pollution.
b) The business may not have to pay as much tax.	**2** Producing food organically is more expensive than using fertilisers and pesticides.
c) The business may have to spend money on equipment.	**3** The government has its own targets to meet to improve the environment in its country.
d) Production methods may cost more.	**4** It can be more economic to use green production methods sometimes.
e) The firm may receive a subsidy from the government.	**5** Items such as solar panels need to be bought.
f) Costs of production may fall.	**6** Raw materials bought from green suppliers are often more expensive.

Table 6.5 Environmentally-friendly statements and explanations.

Key facts

Ethical behaviour is about doing what is morally right.

Ethical behaviour concerns how workers, suppliers and customers are treated.

There is now a much greater awareness of ethical issues in business.

More and more consumers are concerned with ethical issues.

Being an **ethical business** can bring advantages in terms of sales.

Being an ethical business may bring costs. There may be lost sales opportunities, higher costs and prices, or lower profits. It may even threaten the existence of the business.

Some resources are renewable, others are non-renewable.

As we produce and consume more and more we are using up the Earth's non-renewable resources.

Consumers and businesses are becoming more and more aware of environmental problems.

Many businesses are aiming to develop more sustainable production.

Many businesses realise that being a sustainable business can increase their sales.

Many businesses have realised that they can cut their costs by acting in an environmentally-friendly manner.

Sustainable production can cost more than non-sustainable production.

Sustainable production can cost less than non-sustainable production.

Being ethical and sustainable are part of being a socially responsible business.

Useful words

Ethics is about what is right and wrong.

Child labour is the use of young children, below the legal age for employment, in order to achieve low-cost production.

Ethical marketing is marketing activities that seek to give customers information to make good choices for themselves.

Fairtrade is a movement that encourages businesses to pay a fair price to suppliers in developing countries and consumers to buy Fairtrade goods.

Environmentally friendly is an adjective that describes consumers and businesses that act to make production sustainable.

Sustainable production is when production does not lead to the depletion (using up) of natural resources.

Renewable resources are resources that can be used more than once, such as wind or water power, or that can be recreated such as crops.

Non-renewable resources are resources that can only be used once, such as oil.

Recycling is when resources are reused to produce something.

Global warming is the rise in average temperatures that scientists say is taking place.

Ethical businesses are business that behave in a morally correct way.

Waste disposal is the process of getting rid of unwanted materials.

Pollution is causing harm to the environment including air, land and water.

Climate change is the process is when average temperatures rise or fall and patterns of weather change.

Practice questions

Multiple choice questions

1 Which of the following statements is false?

- a) An ethical business will only employ young children when it needs to save money to survive.
- b) An ethical business will always pay suppliers on time.
- c) An ethical business will not exaggerate the benefits to customers of what it sells.
- d) An ethical business will not buy from a supplier that cuts costs by cutting back on health and safety procedures in its factory.

2 A possible disadvantage of ethical production to a producer is that:

- a) workers may need to be paid a higher wage than offered by competitors, leading to higher production costs
- b) the sales and profits will be increased by charging customers more than a fair price for the product
- c) being ethical can motivate workers and improve productivity, reducing the cost per unit produced
- d) supplies cannot be bought at lower costs from firms that employ children.

3 Sustainability:

- a) does not use up scarce resources
- b) only uses scarce resources
- c) does not produce any waste products
- d) covers the cost of the scarce resources used.

4 A possible disadvantage of sustainable production is:

- a) it can reduce production costs by using cheaper methods
- b) it can lead to a higher demand for the business' products
- c) production costs may be higher than using non-sustainable methods
- d) it can mean that the business can claim subsidies from the government.

Data response 35

Pukka Teas is based in Bristol. The business was started in 2002, when the two owners both invested £2,000. By 2012, Pukka Teas was enjoying a turnover of £9 million. Ten of the 37 herbal teas it makes are produced using herbs bought from Fairtrade suppliers and so the teas can be certificated as Fairtrade. On its website, Pukka Teas points out the benefits of doing this:

'In everyday terms, fair trade can completely transform the life of a farmer in a poor country: it can be the difference between warm clothes for their family or going cold; education for their children or staying at home; vital medical services in their village or travelling for miles for simple health care.'

From pukkaherbs.com

1 Explain why buying ethically produced goods, such as Fairtrade goods can help farmers in poor countries in the way the extract describes. (2 marks)

2a) Analyse one benefit to Pukka Teas of buying from ethical suppliers, such as Fairtrade suppliers. (3 marks)

2b) Analyse one disadvantage to Pukka Teas of buying from ethical suppliers, such as Fairtrade suppliers. (3 marks)

2c) Recommend whether Pukka Teas should continue to buy from Fairtrade suppliers. (3 marks)

How to answer data response 35

1 You need to explain Fairtrade buying and link it to the benefits described in the extract.

2a) There will one mark for stating the benefit, one mark for applying it and one mark for analysing it.

2b) There will one mark for stating the disadvantage, one mark for applying it and one mark for analysing it.

2c) Weigh up the pros and cons. There is some evidence you can use in the case study that might indicate it has done well through being a Fairtrade dealer. However, its success might not be because it is a Fairtrade dealer – there are some teas that it sells that are not Fairtrade, have these been successful and if so why? Speculate.

Data response 36

Olleco started in Liverpool. In the nine years since it began, employment has risen from zero to 550 in plants across the UK. Olleco collects food waste, cooking oils and fats from catering and hospitality businesses and recycles them. It had to design its own vehicles to collect the waste materials. The food is then converted into energy and heat in an anaerobic digestion plant that was purchased in 2013. The energy and heat are then used to power a bio-diesel plant. Here, the used oils are turned into bio-diesel. The firms that use the bio-diesel bought from Olleco produce much less CO_2. Their vehicles produce 95 per cent less CO_2 emissions than they would if they used diesel produced from fossil fuels.

1 Evaluate whether or not Olleco has benefited from producing bio-diesel in the way that it does. (9 marks)

How to answer data response 36

1 Marks will be given for stating and explaining an advantage to Olleco of producing bio-diesel in the way that it does. Marks will also be given for stating and explaining a disadvantage. An overall conclusion is then required. Use the evidence to suggest whether or not Olleco's business practice has been successful and/or state what additional information your decision would depend on.

UNIT 6.2 The economic climate

Learning outcomes

By studying this unit, you will be able to:

- define the term **economic climate**
- explain the possible impact of changes in the economic climate on businesses
- evaluate the impact of changes in the economic climate of business
- analyse how businesses may respond to changes in the economic climate
- recommend strategies that businesses can use to respond to changes in the economic climate.

Introductory case study: Comet and Carpet Right

Two businesses affected by the recession.

In the 2000s, Comet was a giant of the high street and the retail parks. It sold a range of electrical goods from washing machines and refrigerators to computers and printers. Carpet Right, another chain, retailed cheap, lower-quality carpets. It had shops on out-of-town retail parks. Both businesses had been very successful.

In 2008, the UK economy went into recession. Many people lost their jobs and their incomes fell. Others kept their jobs but had to take pay cuts. As a result, consumer spending fell, particularly on 'big ticket' items – exactly the kind of goods that both Comet and Carpet Right sold. Both companies experienced a fall in sales.

By December 2012, Comet had closed. Carpet Right, however, survived some big losses and began to do better. It started to sell better-quality and more expensive carpets and improved the quality of customer service. It also closed some stores to reduce costs and started to provide interest-free credit.

Carpet Right has continued to thrive since 2012. In the year to 30 April 2016, profits increased by 33.1 per cent and like for like sales grew by 4.8 per cent. Just to show it is not standing still, it launched a rebrand in July 2016 along with some new products. It is refurbishing 100 stores across the UK.

The economic climate

The economic climate refers to the state of the economy a business operates in. The economic climate may be favourable when it is good for business, or unfavourable when it is bad for business. However, a favourable climate for one business is not always favourable for another.

In this unit, we focus on two main aspects of the economic climate: income and employment.

Income and employment levels

Income is the amount of money that people receive from work and from assets they own such as shares and property. It influences the amount that people can spend as **customers**. Generally, when **consumer income** goes up, people have more money and so spending rises and businesses sell more goods. Businesses might also be able to raise prices to increase their profits knowing that customers can afford to pay more. When incomes fall, the opposite happens – spending falls and businesses sell less. A useful measure of income is income per head – the average income of people in the UK.

The **level of employment** is the number of people in work, while the **level of unemployment** is the number of people out of work. There is a link between employment and income. When employment rises, normally there will be a rise in income and when employment falls and unemployment rises, there will be a fall in income.

Three other terms are useful. **Gross domestic product**, usually referred to as GDP, is a measure of the amount of goods and services that a country produces in a year. The level of GDP strongly influences the **level of income** in a country. **Economic growth** refers to a period of time when GDP in a country is rising and the speed at which economic growth occurs is usually expressed as a percentage. For example, economic growth of 0.5 per cent in a year would not be very fast, whilst growth of over three per cent would be considered very good. Sometimes the GDP of a country falls and when this happens it is called a **recession**.

Changes in income and employment figures can impact on sales.

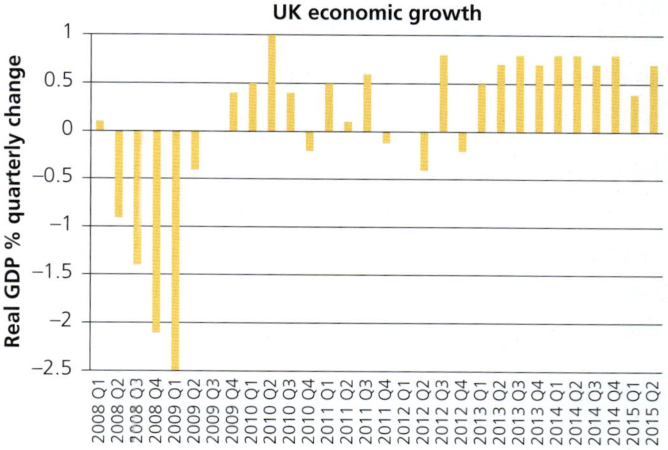

Figure 6.2 GDP changes in the UK, 2008–2015.

In a recession, incomes will fall. Businesses cannot sell as much and so cut production, while some businesses will have to lay workers off and other businesses may reduce the hours that they ask employees to work. This causes employment to fall and unemployment to rise. For both of these reasons, income will fall and this will reduce customers' spending.

The UK had a recession which started in 2008. Some economists suggest that during the period of recession which lasted into 2009, GDP in the UK fell by six per cent – a huge drop. Unemployment rose and incomes fell and this is what caused problems for businesses like Comet and Carpet Right. Many people could not afford to buy expensive items such as electronic goods and carpets, and so sales and profits fell. Economic growth was very slow in the years after the recession ended and it was not until 2013 that the UK economy began to produce more goods and services each year than it had produced before the recession. Employment did begin to rise but only slowly at first, and many of the new jobs that came into existence were only part-time jobs or jobs with zero-hours contracts. Many new jobs were not very well paid and so income and spending rose only slowly at first. In the middle of the 2010 to 2020 decade, employment reached record levels, boosted by the number of immigrants coming to work in the UK.

The impact of changes in income

Rising income often leads to increased sales for a business, increasing revenue and the profits. Customers have more money to spend and so want to buy more goods. Businesses will want to increase the amount they sell. They may need to employ more workers, buy more stock and even build or extend a factory or add more retail outlets to a chain so that output can be increased.

However, rising income can sometimes lead to falling sales, revenues and profits. This can happen with firms that produce 'cheaper' and 'lower-quality' products as customers may feel that they can now afford more expensive and better products.

Falling incomes can have the opposite effect. Sales, revenues and profits may fall as customers have less money to spend. However, some businesses may see sales, revenues and profits rise. Aldi, as shown on page 282, is an example of a business that, initially, benefited from a fall in income.

How much a business will be affected by a change in income will be influenced by:

a) How much income changes – the bigger the change in income, the bigger the effect on the business.

b) The type of product the business sells. A business that sells a more expensive kind of product may experience a large fall in sales if incomes fall, as people switch to a cheaper alternative. The producer of the cheaper alternative benefits from the fall in income.

c) How other business respond to the change in income. We will see how Aldi was able to gain market share when incomes fell. The other supermarkets were affected by this and experienced falling sales and profits (particularly Tesco at the time).

d) How the business itself responds to the change in income. Good businesses will adapt to the changes that affect them and will be able to survive and even thrive. Jaguar Land Rover (page 282) and Carpet Right (page 278) are examples of businesses that successfully changed, whilst Comet (page 278) failed to respond appropriately and so went out of business.

The impact of changes in employment

As has been noted, there is an overlap between changes in employment and changes in income. If employment in the economy is rising, it is likely to mean that incomes are also rising, while if employment is falling, incomes are likely to fall. A change in employment, by changing income, will therefore affect businesses in the ways that have been described above.

However, changes in employment can also affect production and costs. If employment rises in the UK, unemployment may fall. Firms wanting to hire more workers may struggle to employ enough workers or to find workers with the right skills as there may be a shortage. This causes competition for workers and businesses may have to offer higher pay to get the workers they need. This may increase the costs of production and reduce the profits of the business. It may also mean that businesses simply cannot get the labour they need to expand production.

How much a business is affected by a change in employment is influenced by:

a) How much employment changes – the larger the increase in employment, the larger the likely rise in wages and business costs.

b) The change in the type of employment. If there is a rise in the demand for skilled workers, this may be more difficult to deal with than a rise in the demand for unskilled workers.

Activity 1 – Zone activity

Leisure plc is considering expanding its chain of leisure centres. The statements below describe different economic conditions. Put each statement under the correct 'advantage' or 'disadvantage' heading in the table to state whether or not it would help Leisure plc to expand.

- Employment is rising.
- Consumers are not confident as they fear a recession is coming.
- Spending in the economy is high.
- Many businesses are saying that their sales are falling.
- Earnings are rising steadily as businesses increase production.
- Most new jobs are part-time.
- The international economy is growing quickly.

Advantage – it will help Leisure plc to expand	Disadvantage – it will not help Leisure plc to expand

Table 6.6 Advantages and disadvantages of different economic conditions to the expansion of Leisure plc.

Distribution of income

So far we have looked at changes in the levels of income and employment. However, it is possible for the **distribution of income** to change. This refers to the gap between the rich and the poor, which has widened in the UK since the 1980s. Lower-income people have been getting better off but so too have the rich, and their incomes have been rising more quickly. As mentioned before, in the period of economic growth after the recession of 2008 to 2009, many of the new jobs that came in to existence were only part-time or with zero-hours contracts and many were not very well paid, so income and spending rose slowly at first. The spending of the rich, however, continued to rise.

International economic climate

The **international economic climate** can also change, and this can affect business in the UK. There may be a world recession or a recession in a country or area with which UK businesses trade a lot. The European Union and the US were affected by the 2008 to 2009 recession as well as the UK, which reduced demand for UK goods and services. The US economy grew well after the recession but the European economy grew only very slowly. This restricted the growth in exports for UK firms that sold to the other businesses in European countries.

In the 2016 referendum, the UK voted to leave the European Union. It remains to be seen how this will affect UK businesses (see Unit 6.3).

Responding to changes in the economic climate

As mentioned before, Comet closed as a result of the fall in employment and income but Carpet Right was able to continue trading. Jaguar Land Rover responded to changes in the international economic climate. Other businesses actually did really well during the recession and the period of slowly rising incomes after it. How a recession affects a business will depend on what type of business it is and how it responds to the change in the economic climate.

The Carpet Right case study shows that businesses can overcome problems caused by a poor economic climate while the Aldi case study on page 282 shows that a poor economic climate can provide a business opportunity. Both businesses employed strategies which led to success.

Case study: Jaguar Land Rover

JLR is a prestigious brand in the international market.

2015 was an interesting year for Jaguar Land Rover (JLR). JLR has been one of the great British success stories since being taken over by the Indian company, Tata, in 2008. It had enjoyed huge increases in sales and profits and had increased production and employment significantly in its UK factories. A large part of its success had been its exports to China where the economic climate had been very favourable. China had enjoyed rapid economic growth for many years, often as high as 10 per cent per year. Due to a growing middle class in China with high incomes, who wanted to buy prestige goods such as expensive cars, JLR cars enjoyed strong sales.

However, economic growth in China began to slow down and the popularity of JLR cars began to wane. In the first six months of 2015, JLR sales in China fell by 28 per cent. JLR made a loss of £157 million. However, JLR responded by increasing its marketing in other parts of the world. In the UK and US, where the economic climate was more favourable, sales grew by 23 per cent and 28 per cent respectively. Sales grew by 35 per cent in the rest of Europe despite a less favourable economic climate. In addition to changes to its marketing strategy, JLR set out to reduce its production costs by £4.5 billion by 2020.

Case study: Aldi

Aldi grew out of the economic downturn in 2008.

In 2007, Aldi was just a small supermarket chain with a 2.5 per cent share of the UK market. By 2015, it had become the sixth-largest chain in the UK with a 5.3 per cent market share. Its rapid growth was helped by the poor economic climate after 2008.

Aldi focuses on selling cheaper groceries, with some of its products selling for 50 per cent less than similar products in other supermarkets. It also sells a lot of own label products which lowers the cost to the supermarket of buying stock. Aldi offers a 'no frills' shopping experience, as the stores are basic. In addition, Aldi keeps its prices low by having a very efficient distribution system – warehousing and transport costs are kept to a minimum.

Cheap prices were exactly what consumers wanted in the late 2000s and early 2010s. Customers switched from the more expensive 'big' supermarkets such as Tesco, Sainsbury's and Morrisons and many have remained loyal Aldi customers, encouraged by the continuing low prices.

When looking at possible strategies in response to changes in the economic climate, it is useful to think about the different areas of businesses – production, human resources, finance and marketing – and to see what can be done to achieve success. This is because of the interdependent nature of business which you will look at in Unit 7. Business decisions often affect more than one area of business and a decision in one area can affect another's activity. In larger businesses divided into departments, specialists will look at possible strategies in each department, but senior leaders will consider how actions in one area will impact on another area. In smaller businesses, the owner or owners will have to consider all of this. Some of the possible strategies that could be used in a recession to keep businesses going are outlined below.

Production

One strategy is to reduce production costs per unit in order to sell the product at a lower price and undercut competitors, as Aldi has done and JLR has started to do. The production department may be able to reduce costs in a number of ways:

- One way to reduce costs would be to improve control which would reduce wastage. Production could be outsourced or moved to another country where labour is cheaper (see Units 4.1 Production processes and 4.2 Quality of goods and services).
- Worker productivity could be increased so that output per worker rises. This can be improved by introducing new technology which can replace labour and speed up production.

Human resources

The human resources department might seek to improve productivity:

- It could do this by motivating workers through schemes such as bonus systems and awards for workers, or by improving their skills (see Unit 3.5 Motivation and retention).

Finance

The finance department might also look to reduce costs:

- It could do this perhaps by improving cash flow and reducing the interest payments on an overdraft to finance any negative cash flow.
- If the business has loans, it could look to change these to get a lower interest rate (see Unit 5.2 Sources of finance).

Marketing

Another strategy would be to change the marketing of the product, as Carpet Right did. This would be the job of the marketing department. Usually market research would be done first to identify developing market needs. Changing the marketing of a business would involve changes to the **4Ps** of marketing (see Section 2 Marketing):

- The **product** could be changed, perhaps making it more upmarket to appeal to wealthier customers or making it cheaper to appeal to a mass market.

Activity 2 – Group (or individual) activity

Beetham Perfumes makes a range of perfumes, selling to consumers in the UK. These are lower-cost perfumes aimed at people on low incomes. Sales and profits have been falling due to a fall in the incomes of its customers. The owners of Beetham Perfumes have drawn up a list of strategies to deal with the fall in sales and profits:

a) Reduce production costs by using cheaper raw materials.

b) Improve the motivation of workers.

c) Improve the cash flow of the business so that a lower overdraft is needed.

d) Produce a higher-quality product.

e) Sell perfumes abroad.

In groups, come up with a list of advantages and disadvantages or problems for each strategy. You might need to consider what other information is needed before a decision can be made. Discuss these as a class and come to an agreement as to what Beetham Perfumes should do.

- **Promotion** could be increased and improved, perhaps targeted at new markets including potential buyers abroad as well as customers in the UK.
- Different **pricing** strategies could be used. Penetration pricing could help to gain customers in new markets or price cuts to increase demand.
- The business might change the '**place**' part of its marketing strategy, opening retail outlets in new locations or increasing online sales.

While the above focuses on business responses in a recession, it is no less important to think about what businesses should do in a favourable economic climate when income and employment are rising. There will still be a case for looking at reducing costs and for changing the marketing strategy as the economy grows. Production may need to be increased to meet the growing demand. Customers' preferences may change as they become richer as the economy grows.

Evaluation point

When the economic climate is not favourable to a business it may cause the business to lose sales and profits, and even to close. However, some businesses will respond to an unfavourable economic climate and avoid problems, as Carpet Right did. Some businesses will see the poor economic climate as an opportunity, as Aldi did.

Activity 3 – Explanation activity

Suppose there was a recession in the UK in the next 12 months. Explain what would happen to each of the following:

a) The level of unemployment in the country.

b) The amount of competition between businesses for the workers they want to employ.

c) The level of wages that businesses would need to pay workers.

d) The likely effect of the above factors on the costs of the businesses.

Key facts

The economic climate is about what is happening to incomes and employment.

Rising levels of income and employment will lead to increases in sales and profits for many businesses. This is usually thought to be a favourable economic climate.

Falling levels of incomes and employment will lead to falls in sales and profits for many businesses. This is usually thought to be an unfavourable economic climate.

Some businesses will see opportunities when the economic climate is generally favourable, others when it is generally unfavourable.

The distribution of income can change in a country and this can affect the demand for a product. Some people in the country may be getting richer even though the general level of income is falling.

Changes in the international economic climate can affect businesses in the UK.

Businesses need to respond to changes in the economic climate either to thrive or to survive.

Useful words

Economic climate refers to how well the country is doing in terms of the levels of income and employment.

Income is the amount of money that people receive from work and from assets they own, such as shares and property.

Customers are buyers who buy goods and services for the satisfaction or benefit they will get from them. Customers largely buy from retailers.

Consumer income is the total amount of income that all the customers in the country recieve and which they have available to spend.

Level of employment is the numbers of people in work in a country.

Level of unemployment is the number of people out of work in a country.

Gross domestic product (GDP) is a measure of how much a country produces in a year. It influences the level of income and employment.

Level of income is the average income of people in a country.

Economic growth is a period when GDP is rising, causing income and employment to rise.

Recession is a period when GDP is falling, causing income and employment to fall.

Distribution of income refers to how the income is shared out amongst different people in the community. The distribution of income can become more unequal if the incomes of the rich are rising faster than the incomes of lower earners.

International economic climate refers to what is happening to income and employment in different parts of the world.

Practice questions

Multiple choice

1 Consumer spending is likely to fall when:
   - **a)** average incomes rise
   - **b)** unemployment falls
   - **c)** the country produces less than it did as measured by GDP
   - **d)** immigration rises.

2 In a period of rising income and employment most businesses can expect:
   - **a)** sales to rise
   - **b)** prices to fall
   - **c)** profits to fall
   - **d)** immigration to fall.

3 When a business loses sales and profits due to a fall in the income of consumers it should:
   - **a)** increase the amount it produces
   - **b)** reduce production costs
   - **c)** stop selling the product abroad
   - **d)** recruit more workers.

Data response 37

The UK economy has continued to grow in recent years, though the growth in the incomes of lower-paid people has not increased as much as that of higher earners. Fitspace is a gym chain which has a number of branches in the UK. It operates as follows:

- Monthly membership is less than in many other gyms.
- Customers do not have to sign up for an annual contract.
- It offers little in the way of frills such as luxury changing rooms, saunas and cafés.

1 Analyse one advantage of the way Fitspace operates. (3 marks)

2 Analyse one disadvantage of the way Fitspace operates. (3 marks)

3 Recommend whether or not Fitspace should change the way it operates. Give reasons for your answer. (3 marks)

How to answer data response 37

1 You need to analyse one benefit of the way Fitspace operates. One advantage is that customers do not have to sign up for an annual contract, so if they decide they do not want to keep going they can stop without having spent a lot of money. Another advantage is that Fitspace will attract some customers because they are cheaper than their competitors, as long as the customers are happy with the 'no frills' service.

2 One disadvantage is that the 'no frills' approach might put customers off becoming members if they prefer a more extensive provision of services and better facilities. Some customers will prefer a greater range of services such as classes, and other facilities such as a swimming pool, a sauna and a café in addition to the gym. For some, the fitness club is a social place as well as a place to keep fit so they want these different services. Another disadvantage is that the low membership fee might limit revenue and profits. As customers can choose to leave after a month or so, revenue would be lower than if they had to sign up for an annual contract.

3 You need to state and justify your recommendation – the key being to link your recommendation to the economic climate. You might say Fitspace should leave the way it operates unchanged as there will be a large potential market of lower-paid workers who will like the way it operates. This will depend on the number of customers of Fitspace gyms and their profitability. Alternatively, you might suggest that it goes more upmarket to benefit from the higher earners though this will depend on the number of other gyms in the area that sell to high earners. Consider different strategies and decide on one or state further information that you require to come to a decision.

Data response 38

Heron Holidays runs walking holidays for older people in the UK. It offers coach pick-ups in major towns on the way to holiday destinations, high-quality accommodation in its centres including full board and afternoon tea, and qualified mountain leaders to lead all walks. Customers are able to book their holidays by telephoning the booking centre. Customer incomes have been falling and Heron Holidays fears that its sales and profits will fall.

1 Analyse how the fall in customer income could impact Heron Holidays' costs. (3 marks)

2 Analyse how the fall in customer income could impact Heron Holidays' marketing. (3 marks)

3 Evaluate the overall impact on Heron Holidays of a fall in income. (3 marks)

How to answer data response 38

1 You need to analyse ways in which Heron Holidays could reduce its costs. It could look for coach companies that charge less, switch to online booking to reduce wage costs, choose cheaper accommodation or cut back on the quality of the accommodation and service offered, for example by cutting out afternoon teas.

2 You need to analyse different marketing strategies, for example, selling holidays to a different target market such as younger, better-off customers, advertising overseas or reducing the price of its holidays.

3 You need to make and justify a recommendation. You might suggest reducing the price of the holidays but also reducing costs so that the profit level is maintained. Alternatively, you might recommend marketing to a different target market that can afford the holidays, such as richer people in the UK or abroad, as it would be difficult to reduce costs without lowering the quality of the holidays. There is no correct answer to these kinds of questions – you will get marks for how well you justify your recommendation.

UNIT 6.3 Globalisation

Learning outcomes

By studying this unit, you will be able to:

- explain the concept of **globalisation**
- evaluate the impact of the growth of multinationals
- discuss how globalisation has influenced business location
- explain **international branding** and evaluate the branding strategies that can be used
- identify ways in which businesses compete internationally
- evaluate, using a synoptic approach, the different strategies that businesses use to compete internationally.

The concept of globalisation

Introductory case study: Coca-Cola – a global business

Coca-Cola is an American-owned business. It sells a range of 'fizzy' drinks. The drinks are made from a 'concentrate' manufactured by Coca-Cola in the USA. Coca-Cola factories exist all over the world including in the UK, India, Australia, Peru and Eastern Europe. The producers in each country buy the concentrate from the USA, and add water and sweeteners. Producing locally saves transport costs. Coca-Cola products are sold in over 200 countries. The products are sold in all kinds of shops, sports arenas and vending machines. Coca-Cola has invested to build factories in other countries. To do this, Coca-Cola has had to move capital (money) from the USA. American employees of Coca-Cola also move to other countries to help to set up and run these factories.

Globalisation refers to how businesses in different countries have become increasingly connected in their activities. It involves:

- buying and selling goods and services made in different countries
- the movement of workers from country to country
- the movement of capital or finance from country to country.

Coca-Cola's business activity is a good example of globalisation. As you read the case study, you should match the activities that take place against the three bullet points that define globalisation.

Globalisation has increased and continues to do so at a very rapid rate. It has been encouraged by improvements in:

- **transport** – transport costs have reduced as ships and planes have become bigger, and rail and road networks have improved. The development of containers has significantly reduced costs as the goods are basically transported in boxes that can easily be lifted by crane from a ship onto a lorry or train for onward transport.
- **telecommunications and the internet** – communication has become much faster and cheaper. A firm can use the internet to look at the products and prices of a range of possible suppliers from all over the world. Email, telephone and video-conferencing can be used to order the goods. Websites and social media can be used to promote products across the world.
- **free trade arrangements** – free **trade** exists when there are no barriers to trade. Barriers include **tariffs** (taxes on imports), **quotas** (limits on the amount that can be imported) and **regulations**

(which control, for example, the design and safety features of goods that can be sold in a country). There have been moves to reduce these barriers to trade. The World Trade Organization (WTO) exists to encourage countries to remove these barriers and, once removed, countries that are members of the WTO should not reintroduce them. Some countries have come together to introduce economic agreements. Some of these focus mainly on trade. The North America Free Trade Area (NAFTA) consists of the USA, Canada and Mexico. There are no barriers on the trade in goods and services between these countries. Other examples of areas that encourage no or lower barriers to trade include the South Asia Free Trade Area (SAFTA) whose members are Afghanistan, Bangladesh, Bhutan, India, Maldives, Nepal, Pakistan and Sri Lanka and ASEAN, the Australia and New Zealand free trade area. The UK joined the European Common Market in 1973. At that time, the Common Market permitted free trade in goods and services. In the years after 1973, the Common Market developed into the European Union (EU). By 2016, it consisted of 28 countries and, as well as free trade in goods and services, it permitted the free movement of capital and people. In a referendum in 2016, the people of the UK chose to leave the EU. Opinion in the country was strongly divided. As a result of the referendum, the UK will leave the EU in 2019. There are some fears that UK businesses will suffer by leaving the EU if they lose the benefits that result from free trade and the movement of capital and people. However, some people think that leaving the EU will mean the UK can trade more freely with other parts of the world as well as continuing to trade with EU countries, creating new and possibly better business opportunities. The government plans to make new arrangements with the EU countries and other countries across the world. We may or may not know what has happened by the time you read this.

Impact of globalisation on businesses

The impact of globalisation on businesses in the UK is discussed under four headings:

- the growth of **multinational companies (MNCs)**
- influences on business location
- international branding
- how businesses compete internationally.

Activity 1 – True or false activity

Tick to indicate whether each statement in the table below is true or false.

Statement	True	False
Globalisation has increased because countries have set up free trade arrangements with each other.		
The movement of people has increased because of better transport.		
The EU made it more difficult for people to move from one European country to another.		
The movement of goods has increased because of better transport.		
Improved telecommunications have made it easier for businesses to deal with businesses in other countries.		
Tariffs are taxes on imported goods designed to reduce the amount of imports into a country.		

Table 6.7 Globalisation.

Growth of multinational companies (MNCs)

The growth of multinational companies is a key feature of globalisation. Multinationals are businesses that operate in more than one country. The big names that you will be familiar with – Google, Amazon, Coca-Cola, Starbucks and McDonald's – are multinationals that sell in the UK as well as many other countries in the world. Coca-Cola, for example, is sold in over 200 countries around the world.

The advantages to a business of being a multinational company are shown in the table below.

Advantage	Explanation
Increasing sales	Selling in a number of countries increases the size of the market for that company and it may be able to raise sales and revenue by doing this.
Spreading risk	If one market loses sales, perhaps because of an economic recession in that country, the company may be able to compensate by increasing sales in another country that is experiencing economic growth.
Lower costs	Production costs may be reduced by making the product in a different country from that where it is sold. Sometimes, a multinational may produce different components of a product in different countries, wherever the costs of production are low, and assemble them in another country.
Tax avoidance	Multinational companies may be able to avoid paying large amounts of taxes by setting up their headquarters in a 'low tax' country even though they may sell and produce in high tax countries. Google, Facebook, eBay and Amazon are all said to have done that to avoid paying taxes in the UK by having 'sister' companies in low tax countries such as Luxembourg and Ireland.

Table 6.8 Advantages to a business of being a multinational company.

The benefits of multinational businesses to the 'host country' (the country where a multinational business locates) are shown in table 6.9.

Advantage	Explanation
Creating demand for host country businesses	The multinational may employ local people and so create jobs and increase incomes in the host country. This may lead to increased spending and opportunities for local businesses to set up or to increase their sales and profits. Also, the multinational may buy supplies and services from local businesses – components, cleaning and maintenance and so on.
Taxes and public services	The multinational may pay taxes and this may help the government in the country to provide public services such as education and health, and improve infrastructure. This will help businesses in the host country to prosper.
Lower prices and costs	By keeping costs low, multinationals may be able to offer materials and services at lower prices for businesses.

Table 6.9 Advantages to a country of hosting a multinational company.

However, there may be disadvantages to those countries where multinationals have located. These are shown in the table below.

Disadvantage	Explanation
Business closures	Local businesses may not be able to compete with the big multinationals in terms of quality or price and so may be forced out of business. The multinational may pay higher wages than local businesses and these may lose the workers they need.
Outflows of money	The multinationals may move profits out of the host country to where they have their headquarters. This may limit the benefits to the host country.

Table 6.10 Disadvantages to a country of hosting a multinational company.

Case study: Vodafone in the UK

Vodafone.

Vodafone had been accused of not paying sufficient corporation tax in the UK. Vodafone sells mobile phone and ICT services in many countries around the world. Although its headquarters are in the UK, Vodafone profits go to Luxembourg in a complex accounting practice. Taxation in Luxembourg is much lower than in the UK. However, Vodafone says that it is paying the taxes that it should pay – in the UK and elsewhere. It also says that it contributes to the UK economy through investments and by creating jobs as well as selling the phone services that customers want.

Some UK businesses sell to Vodafone in the UK – cleaning firms, advertising agencies and so on. In addition, the financial institutions buy shares in Vodafone and dividends are paid on these. These dividends go to UK citizens who have saved their money in financial institutions – pension funds, insurance companies and so on. Vodafone says that it is responsible to its shareholders to make profits on their behalf. This helps the savers who put money into the financial institutions. Vodafone is just one of a number of multinational companies that have been accused of avoiding tax in the UK.

Activity 2 – Debate activity

Motion of the debate: 'Amazon, Google, Apple, Coca-Cola, Vodafone and McDonald's are examples of the many multinational companies that do business in the UK. The problems caused by multinationals such as these are far greater than the benefits.'

The class should divide into teams. Decide whether your team will support this motion or will argue against it. Each team should research the two sides of the debate – you may find it useful to use search engines such as Google to find articles for and against multinationals, particularly about tax avoidance. The findings and ideas should be put into a presentation – you may support your presentation with PowerPoint slides but this is not essential. Agree who will be the spokesperson representing your side of the motion.

Once you have prepared the debate, present your arguments to the class. Once the main speakers have presented their arguments, other pupils in the class should be allowed to express their ideas. Once this has been done, the main speakers should then summarise their arguments and a vote be taken.

Influences on business location

Case study: Raleigh Cycles

Location affected by costs.

Raleigh was a very successful UK manufacturer of bicycles, based in Nottingham. The 2000s saw difficult times and the business went bankrupt. Some managers bought the company, becoming the new owners. Production in the UK stopped and was moved to Taiwan and other countries in Southeast Asia, to reduce the costs of production. However, sales, marketing and design departments stayed in the UK and are based in Eastwood just outside Nottingham. The business has become very successful once more and is even moving some production back to the UK. From 2016, Raleigh has assembled the Militis eTap bike (which uses an electronic system for changing gears) in Nottingham, although it still uses parts made in Asia.

Case study: the Electric Car Corporation (ECC)

Location affected by demand.

The ECC used to assemble Citroën C1 ev'ies – a battery-powered electric car – in its plant in Bedfordshire. It decided to move some of its production to Denmark as there was more demand for these cars in Denmark. The company complained that while business buyers of electric cars could get a subsidy of £5,000 from the government, consumers in the UK could not. This was holding back any increase in demand in the UK.

Adapted from autocar.co.uk

Case study: Nestor Pharmaceuticals Ltd

Skilled labour and free trade affect location.

Nestor Pharmaceuticals Ltd is an Indian-owned company that makes a wide range of common medicines. The company decided to set up and then expand its production in Suffolk. By doing this it would have access to skilled labour in the UK. More importantly, its strategy was to sell pharmaceuticals throughout the European Union. At the time that it decided to locate production here, the UK was a member of the EU and so it would be able to sell its goods freely anywhere in the EU. How Nestor Pharmaceuticals Ltd will be affected by the decision of the UK to leave the EU (Brexit) will depend on what trade arrangements are made between the UK and the EU for after the UK has left the EU.

Benefits to UK businesses of locating in another country

- **Lower costs (labour)** – for many years, UK businesses have been relocating production to the Far East because wages are lower in many of those countries. This was why Raleigh moved its cycle production to Taiwan.
- **Lower costs (technology)** – the UK has not always been very good at investing in new technology for manufacturing. Businesses abroad may have new technology that has the benefit of speeding up and increasing production and lowering costs.
- **Lower costs (properties and land)** – The prices of land and premises, such as factories and shops, may be lower in another country.
- **Expertise** – businesses wishing to undertake research and development may wish to locate in another country to take advantage of the expertise of workers there. The UK is regarded as a centre of expertise for motor car production, chemicals and pharmaceuticals and foreign firms in these industries may decide to locate their R&D facilities in the UK, rather than abroad, for this reason.
- **Skilled workers** – while there are many skilled workers in the UK, there has been a shortage of certain types of labour in the UK for some time. An example is the shortage of skilled engineers to work in manufacturing, such as car production. Firms may go abroad to take advantage of available supplies in other countries.
- **Demand** – businesses sometimes think it important to locate near to their market. The ECC case study is an example of a business that did that as it saw there was, and would remain, a greater demand for its electric cars in Denmark and other nearby European countries rather than in the U.K. Locating in Denmark would make the business more visible to its customers. The Indian firm, Nestor Pharmaceuticals Ltd, chose the UK so that it was located near to its EU market.

Disadvantages to UK businesses of locating in another country

- **Quality control** – it may be more difficult to control quality because production is taking place a long way from the head office. Sometimes the quality of goods and services produced in the UK is better than those produced abroad, perhaps because of skilled labour or the technology available.
- **Communications** – there may be problems because people may not speak English in the new plant. It may also be in a different time zone so the workers are not working at the same time as the people in the UK.

- **Transport** – the raw materials and the final products will have to be transported. Problems may arise causing the late delivery of orders which, in turn, may delay production or mean that customers do not get their goods on time.
- **Loss of sales** – if firms move production abroad and close down in the UK this will make workers unemployed. These workers will have less money to spend. If a lot of firms do this, as unemployment in the economy rises, incomes will fall and spending generally will fall. The firm that moved may find its UK sales fall.
- **Access to skilled labour** – while there may be a shortage of some kinds of skilled labour in the UK, the supply of the kind needed by a business may not be available elsewhere.
- **Costs** – if wages abroad rise, it may be cheaper to produce in the UK. Also, the **unit costs** of production may become cheaper in the UK if the business raises the **productivity** of its workers, perhaps by training them or by investing in technology.

Activity 3 – Explanation activity

Answer the following:

a) State and explain two reasons why a UK producer may be able to lower its costs of production by moving production to another country.

b) Explain why UK businesses may be affected by shortages of skilled labour and how moving abroad may help them to overcome this problem.

c) With the aid of examples, explain why a firm can increase sales by moving production abroad.

d) Explain why quality control may become a problem if a UK business moves production to a Far East country such as China.

e) Explain the communication problems that a UK firm may face if it moves production abroad.

f) Explain one transport problem that may affect a UK firm that moves its production abroad. How might the firm be affected by the problem?

g) Explain why producing goods in the UK may help sales in the UK.

- **The environment** – producing in the UK may make the carbon footprint of a business less than it would be if it produced abroad. This can be a point it can use in its marketing.

Moving production back to the UK

There are many advantages to producing in the UK. Some businesses have started to relocate to the UK despite having moved production abroad previously. However, there may be problems of producing in the UK.

Activity 4 – Tick box activity

Put a tick in one of the boxes next to each statement in the table below to indicate whether it is an advantage or a disadvantage of moving production back to the UK.

Statement	Advantage	Disadvantage
Wage costs in the UK are higher than many other countries in the world.		
Producing and selling in the UK can reduce transport costs and improve the image of the business as 'green.'		
The UK has a good supply of skilled labour.		
Customers like to buy 'British-made' goods.		
There are shortages of some kinds of skilled labour such as engineers.		
It is likely that all the workers speak English.		
Managers can visit the factories more easily to check on quality.		

Table 6.11 Advantages and disadvantages of moving production back to the UK.

Evaluation point

Many UK firms have moved their production to other countries in order to take advantage of cheaper production costs. However, many businesses are now moving back to the UK. Businesses must weigh up the overall advantages and disadvantages of production in the UK and production abroad. They need to make judgements about costs (particularly as wage costs have risen in some developing countries), the reliability and quality of production (which may not be as good as in the UK), the sales benefits of the 'made in the UK' tag, the reliability and the costs of transport (which have been rising). These considerations will change over time – so businesses may need to be prepared to move production out of, and possibly back in to, the UK. One more consideration will be how free it is to trade – will there, for example, be tariffs that increase the price of imports?

International branding

Branding is concerned with the 'truths' about a product – its image, reputation and values.

Businesses create their brands in several ways. It usually involves a logo. The brand values will be communicated using words, images and music. The communication takes place through media such as websites, TV, radio, newspapers and magazines, and through social media such as Facebook, YouTube and Twitter.

Businesses that engage in global branding will need to communicate their values around the world. There is a saying about global branding: 'Think global, act local.' This means that a business should promote the same values around the world but do it in different ways in different countries.

In international branding, businesses need to communicate their values or their image but in a way which suits the country or region where they are creating or promoting the brand. For Coca-Cola, the brand is still about refreshing, inspiring and creating value, but the way in which the message is put across is slightly different. The Coca-Cola advertisement that uses Father Christmas would not be well understood in the predominantly Muslim country of Pakistan. The brightly coloured advertisement used in Pakistan would make sense there because the buses are often painted with vibrant colours. In many countries, it would not be appropriate to use young, semi-dressed women in advertisements as this could offend people. These examples show that businesses must be aware of cultural and religious differences when creating their global brand.

Businesses also need to consider the following when creating or promoting their brand:

- Language. The Coca-Cola case study on page 295 explores how the local language and writing must be used to be comprehensible to the populations of Latvia, Poland and Russia, for example.
- Names. The naming of products is also very important and, often, products are known by different names in different countries. This may be because of legal reasons. For example, Burger King is known as Hungry Jack's in Australia because the Burger King name had already been used by another business. It may also be because the name would have a different, possibly unfortunate meaning, in another language. Burger King China's 'PooPoo Smoothie' might not go down very well in the UK!
- The level and distribution of income. There would be little point in promoting a very expensive product widely in a country where poverty is widespread. For example, it would not make sense to try to sell Patek Philippe watches that cost upwards of £7,000 to the mass of the population in the Democratic Republic of Congo (DRC) that was the world's poorest country in 2016 with an average income per head of under $400 (just over £300) per year. It would be worth promoting the brand in the DRC if the distribution of income was very uneven and there were enough rich people who were potential buyers.
- Legal factors. Businesses must obey the laws in the countries in which they operate. There may be laws about advertising concerning things like honesty

and decency, and about consumption. Cigarette smoking is banned completely in Bhutan so there would be no point trying to promote a cigarette brand there. The drinking of alcohol under the age of 21 is not allowed in many US states so it would not make sense to target teenagers.

- Bribery. In some countries, it is acceptable and even expected that bribes are given as part of the business deals. In the UK, while bribery does take place, it is not done openly and a business caught giving or receiving a bribe would receive bad press and face possible legal consequences.

Case study: Coca-Cola international branding

Coca-cola states its values online through its mission statement:

- to refresh the world in mind, body and spirit
- to inspire moments of optimism and happiness through our brands and actions
- to create value and make a difference.

The Coca-Cola logo is presented differently in different countries. The products may also be different, for example, lemon flavoured Coca-Cola is only sold in Latvia, Poland and Russia.

Think about how Coca-Cola might advertise their products in various foreign countries. You should consider the points raised in this chapter, such as cultural differences, level of income and religious sensitivites. You could draft a poster that illustrates your ideas.

Activity 5 – Matching activity

The table below is about international branding considerations. Draw a line to match a consideration in the left-hand column with the example of that consideration in the right-hand column.

Consideration	Example
Culture and religion	It is illegal to advertise alcohol in Sri Lanka.
Language	An American fast-food company sold its 'cheesy chips' as 'yassuppoi' chips in Japan – until it found out that yassuppoi means 'low quality' in Japanese.
Names	Some members of FIFA, the world governing body for football, have been accused of accepting money from TV companies in exchange for granting them the rights to show football games.
Level and distribution of income	The USA company Pepsodent advertised in Indonesia that its toothpaste would make teeth 'whiter'. Black teeth are thought to be attractive in Indonesia.
Legal factors	The USA electronics company, Best Buy, failed to compete with cheaper retailers in China.
Bribery	Schweppes 'tonic water' translates as 'toilet water' in Italian.

Table 6.12 International branding considerations.

How businesses compete internationally

Case study: Big Mac burgers – competing in India

Meeting the needs of the local market.

McDonald's needs to sell products that are acceptable to the local consumers. In India, a Big Mac is made out of chicken because people there do not eat beef. The Big Mac must be sold at a competitive price that consumers will pay, so it cannot be sold at the same price in all countries around the world. Using US dollars so that comparisons can be made, in the UK in 2016 the price of a Big Mac was $3.94 while in India it was $2.41. To promote the product, McDonald's calls the Big Mac a 'Maharajah Mac' in India (meaning king-size burger). As in the UK, McDonald's restaurants are often found in places where customers will be looking for a fast-food meal such as shopping centres, airports and on busy roads.

Competing in the international economy means both selling goods and services abroad and in the UK in markets where foreign firms also compete. The McDonald's case study shows that the 4 Ps of marketing are very important for businesses competing in the global economy. However, marketing is not the only area of business that is important and decisions about one business activity may affect decisions in another area. For example, decisions about which products to sell in a particular market may affect the method of production that should be used; decisions about the method of production may affect the finance that the business needs. This highlights the 'interdependent nature of business' that is discussed in Unit 7. The following section looks at each area of the specification (or each area of business) to suggest different ways in which businesses compete internationally.

Purpose of business activity – growth

Businesses may grow so that they can compete internationally. They may expand production in the UK so that they have more goods to sell abroad or produce abroad. This has implications for financing the growth. Two examples also show how international competition may affect business location.

- Marks & Spencer has set up shops in many countries, from Armenia to the United Arab Emirates, so that it can compete with retailers in those countries. This is an example of 'place' in marketing. It is also an example of organic growth.
- Jaguar Land Rover has set up a joint-venture with the Chinese business Chery so that it can produce cars in China and sell them there without import taxes having to be paid on the cars. One possible advantage of taking over a firm already operating in a country where a business wants to compete, is that it will have knowledge of the local market and the rules and regulations that govern its conduct.

Marketing

There is some overlap between marketing and international branding (see above). Here the 4 Ps of marketing are looked at separately to give some more ideas.

- **Product** – the product may need to be changed to meet the needs of the local market. Jaguar Land Rover produce long wheelbase versions of their cars to sell in China because rich car owners like to have a lot of space in the rear of the car where they can socialise or work while a chauffeur drives them. Coca-Cola produces different flavours for different markets. In countries where drinking coffee is very popular, such as Spain and France, coffee-flavoured Coca-Cola is available.

- **Promotion** – promotion needs to take into account the culture of the local market. Celebrities are used a lot in marketing campaigns. Some, like David Beckham, are global figures and can be used to promote products in many countries. Other celebrities may only be useful to use in a specific country. Sachin Tendulkar, a very popular cricket player in India, has featured in advertisements for Coca-Cola aimed at the Indian market. The business may also need to consider how the promotion is communicated. Traditional media – TV, newspaper, radio and so on – may remain important but the use of the internet is likely to be increasingly important so that buyers from around the world find out about the seller, its products and its prices.
- **Prices** – businesses will have to know the prices charged by firms they compete with. Prices, and profits, may have to be lower in countries where incomes are lower or there is more competition while in other countries, it may be possible to charge a higher price and make a greater profit. In Dubai, goods in the shopping malls are 20 per cent more expensive, on average, than in the UK. The difference is partly explained by higher shop rental costs but also simply because retailers know that customers who shop in Dubai are often willing to pay higher prices.
- **Place** – Unit 4.5 deals with the factors that influence location and these factors may also apply to location in the global economy. Some firms need to be near the market. McDonald's restaurants can be found in cities and shopping centres around the world. Some firms need to be near to their supply of raw materials. Extraction companies must locate where the resources are located. Rio Tinto extracts diamonds from sites in Australia and Canada. Some firms locate wherever they can produce at the lowest possible cost. The DIR Group makes furniture for hairdressing salons in China even though most sales are in Europe. Production of the furniture requires a lot of manual labour and this is cheap in China. The reduction in transport costs brought about by the development of larger ships and containers has made these costs less significant.

Human resources

Competing abroad may require the employment of workers in other countries. We have seen that Marks & Spencer have located shops abroad. Other businesses may set up offices or factories abroad. There are a number of human resources issues that will need to be considered.

- **Recruitment, training and motivation** – the business may recruit workers locally or bring in workers from other countries. In China, for the joint venture with Chery, Jaguar Land Rover (JLR) use a combination of local Chinese labour and workers from its UK plants who are familiar with the way in which JLR works and the standards its needs. The business will need to consider whether training is necessary and if it will be worth the cost. It must also think about the best way to motivate the workers – will workers be motivated by the same methods used in the UK?
- **Communications** – businesses competing abroad will need to communicate with consumers, their suppliers and any workers they employ overseas. This may require ICT but also may need workers to travel to meet directly with customers, suppliers and workers.
- **Employment law** – the business will have to comply with local employment laws. It will need to comply with regulations about working hours, pay, the use of child labour, employment contracts and so on. For example, in 2016 in Australia the minimum hourly wage rate was £10.62, in the UK it was £7.20 while in the Czech Republic it was £7.88 (currency conversions at November 2016 rates).

Business operations

A business may need to change its business operations to compete internationally.

- **Production processes and technology** – the business may need to think about changing the method of production used. It might switch from job to batch to reduce costs and prices – but this might mean an end to producing bespoke products that could affect demand. The use of technology is becoming increasingly important. Businesses in developed countries can compete with those in developing countries where wages are much lower by using technology. As globalisation increases, the use of technology is becoming more and more important. Unit 4.1 gives more detail about production processes, including the use of technology.
- **Quality of goods** – buyers in different markets will have different expectations about the quality of the goods and services they want. Also, if production takes place abroad, the business must put in place appropriate quality assurance methods to make sure that local production is up to the standard required.
- **Sales processes and customer services** – these may differ from country to country. In developed economies, high proportions of consumers are comfortable buying and paying online but, in some countries customers may prefer face to face dealing and paying in cash.
- **Business location** – it may be important to produce locally. This will be the case if the produce sold is 'fresh' and so needs to be sold quickly – fresh fish is an example. Another reason for locating production in the country where the product is to be sold is when customers wish to buy local produce. For example, 'made in Britain' is still, for many customers, a sign that the product will be of good quality. Also, consumers may want to buy locally-produced goods for environmental reasons. It may also be cheaper to produce locally and save on transport costs from the UK.

Finance

- **Sources of finance** – finance, like short-term finance to deal with cash flow issues, may be needed in order to compete abroad. The business may have to arrange for overdrafts or trade credit to pay for stock or promotional activities. Equally, long-term finance may be needed to pay for investments in new premises, machinery and so on. The costs involved may affect international competitiveness.
- **Costs** – as we saw above in the section on human resources, wages differ from country to country. A firm will need to take these into account if production or sales costs need to be paid in the countries the business competes in. Other costs such as rents and material costs will also be important. Businesses must work out whether they can sell at competitive prices while covering all these costs.
- **Break-even analysis** – when a business decides to compete in another country, it should conduct a break-even forecast that would help it to decide how much it needs to sell to make a profit.

The exchange rate and how businesses compete

Case study: Princess Yachts and changes in the exchange rate

Princess Yachts is based in Plymouth. It builds yachts that sell for between £300,000 and £20 million. 80 per cent of its yachts are sold abroad. The Chairman, Antony Sheriff, said that sales have increased recently and that this was due to the fall in the exchange rate of the pound against other currencies. He said, 'People have seen the pound move and taken the decision that it is a very good time to buy.' He also said that costs were 'a little higher' because the fall in the exchange rate made imported components more expensive.

From The Daily Telegraph, *8 September 2016*

The exchange rate is the price of one currency in terms of another, for example, £1 = €1.2. A change in the exchange rate can make exports cheaper or dearer.

- **Exports** – suppose a business wants to export (sell in a foreign country) a product for £100 in France, a country that uses the euro (€). If the exchange rate was £1 = €1.5, a buyer in France would have to pay €150 to get the £100 in sterling it needs to buy the product. If the exchange rate fell to £1 = €1.2, the buyer would now only pay €120 to get £100 sterling. This would increase the sales of the business in France (and other euro-using countries). A rise in the value of the exchange rate against the euro, however, would increase the price to the euro country buyer and the business would expect that sales would fall.

Evaluation point

Changes in the value of the pound will affect UK firms. A fall in the exchange rate may help exporters by reducing their prices to foreign buyers but harm importers by raising the prices they must pay. The effect is partly influenced by the size of the change in the exchange rate. Some UK firms will be both exporters and importers, like Princess Yachts. The effect of the change in the exchange rate will depend on the amount exported compared to the amount imported. (Only a small proportion of the costs of Princess Yachts is affected by the exchange rate, so overall it would benefit from a fall in the exchange rate.) Other factors may offset the effect of the change in the currency. For example, an exporter may deal with a rising value of the pound by reducing its production costs to keep the prices from rising. Alternatively, it may improve its quality or increase its marketing to offset the effect.

- Imports – imports are also affected by changes in the exchange rate. A fall in the exchange rate will make imports costlier and this may help a domestic producer to compete against foreign imports. However, as with Princess Yachts, it may make imported components more expensive and increase costs of production.

A useful way to remember the effects of changes in the exchange rate on the prices of exports and imports is the mnemonic, SPICED. This stands for 'strong pound, imports cheaper, exports dearer'. A strong pound is when the currency rises in value against other currencies. A weak pound has the opposite effects.

Influences on business

Influences on business may also affect how and where businesses compete internationally.

- **Ethical and environmental considerations** – while it may help to keep costs down, a business must consider the possible ethical and environmental implications of producing or selling abroad. Ethical and environmental standards of business differ from country to country. In general, employment laws and environmental protection regulations are stricter in developed economies, like the UK, than in developing countries, such as those in Asia and Africa. Rules on the use of child labour, for example, tend to be stricter and more rigidly enforced in the developed economies. However, businesses need to be aware of the possible negative publicity that they may gain if production involves practices that customers do not approve of. Customers in the UK like Primark's low prices, but Primark received some bad publicity when it was discovered that some of its goods were being produced using child labour. And UK customers may not be happy with UK firms selling goods in countries that, for example, are treating their citizens badly.
- **The economic climate** – the economic climate of a country is about what is happening to income and employment in that country. (See Unit 6.2.) The economic climate in a country will influence whether or not a business is willing to compete there. In Unit 6.2, you can read about how Jaguar Land Rover benefited from sales in expanding markets such as the USA at a time when sales in China were falling.

Evaluation point

Competing internationally is complicated. A business that is in competition with firms from other countries, whether in the UK or abroad, must consider a wide range of strategies and issues. These cover the whole of the GCSE Business specification content. When discussing recommendations about how to compete, it will not be necessary to discuss every single strategy or issue. However, any recommendations that are made will need to be relevant to that business and reasons must be given for the recommendation. It can also be appropriate to suggest further information that a business may need to research before making a decision about whether and how to compete internationally.

Activity 6 – Zone activity

The table below lists the main areas of business. Put each statement given below next to the area of business activity for which it is an example.

- A business issues new shares to raise the money to build a new factory in Indonesia.
- A retailer decides to buy a chain of shops in another country.
- A UK-based business offers generous relocation packages – free housing, free schooling for children, free flights home twice a year etc. – to its workers to encourage them to move to its new factory in Hungary.
- A business decides to start selling a product in a country because income and employment in that country have been increasing rapidly.
- A business redesigns its range of clothing so that it will sell in another country.
- A business introduces mass production so that it can meet the demand for its goods in other countries.

Area of business/the OCR GCSE specification	Example
Growth	
Marketing	
Human resources	
Business operations	
Finance	
Influences on business	

Table 6.13 How businesses compete internationally.

Activity 7 – Explanation activity

The exchange rate of the pound against the euro rises from £1 = €1.2 to £1 = €1.3 euros. For each statement below, explain how the British firm may be affected by the change in the value of the pound against the euro.

a) A British firm exports its goods to other countries in the Eurozone (the countries in the European Union that use the euro).

b) A British retailer sells goods in the UK that have been produced in a Eurozone country.

Key facts

Globalisation involves the international trade in goods and services, and the movement of people and capital between countries.

The process of globalisation is continuing at an increasingly fast pace caused by improvements in transport, ICT and the expansion of free trade arrangements.

Multinational companies are part of the process of globalisation.

Multinational companies have grown in terms of size, numbers and importance.

Multinationals have positive and negative effects on businesses in the countries where they have located.

Many UK businesses have moved production abroad.

A significant number of UK businesses that moved production abroad have moved production back to the UK.

Businesses have had to develop their brands as international brands.

UK producers have had to learn to compete abroad and at home with foreign businesses.

Useful words

Globalisation is the process by which business activity around the world has become increasingly interconnected.

International branding is creating an image or values for a product that are communicated in countries around the world.

Capital is money or assets such as machines, buildings, vehicles.

Free trade is the absence of restrictions on trade between countries.

Trade is the import and export of goods and services.

Tariff is a tax on a good or service that is imported.

Quota is a limit in terms of weight or value on the amount of a good or service that can be imported.

Regulations are rules about the goods and services that can be sold in a country.

Multinational companies are businesses that operate in different countries around the world.

Unit cost is the cost per unit produced. The greater the productivity of workers, the lower the unit cost of production.

Productivity is a measure of the output of each worker on average.

Practice questions

Multiple choice questions

1 Which statement about globalisation is not correct?

a) Globalisation involves the movement of people from abroad coming to live and work in the UK and people from the UK going to live and work abroad.

b) Globalisation includes the activities of multinational businesses that operate in different countries.

c) Globalisation involves trade between two UK businesses based in the UK.

d) Globalisation can involve a bank in one country lending money to a business in another country.

2 A UK manufacturer has decided to export a fruit juice that it produces to a country in Africa. Which of the following is not an important consideration when branding the fruit juice?

a) The amount of the fruit juice drunk in the UK.

b) The name it chooses for the product.

c) The income of the people in the country it decides to export to.

d) The language the people speak in the country.

3 Which of the following is not an advantage to a business of being a multinational company?

a) It can sell in different markets and therefore spread risk.

b) It can produce in different countries in the world to minimise costs of production.

c) It may be able to minimise the taxes it pays on its profits depending on where it locates its headquarters.

d) It is easier to manage businesses that operate in different countries.

Data response 39

Many companies that moved production abroad in the past are now returning production to the UK. One example is Symington's Ltd. Symington's has produced foods in the UK for over 185 years. Some years ago, it moved the production of its Golden Wonder Pot Noodle to China. However, it has now moved that production back to the UK.

1a) Explain two possible advantages Symington's Ltd may have gained by moving production of its Golden Wonder Pot Noodle to China. (4 marks)

1b) Explain two possible benefits to Symington's of moving production of its Golden Wonder Pot Noodle back to the UK. (4 marks)

1c) Discuss the factors that will influence whether Symington's will produce in the UK or abroad. (7 marks)

How to answer data response 39

1a) State two possible advantages of moving production abroad and explain each one. Remember to apply what you write to the production of Golden Wonder Pot Noodle.

1b) State two possible disadvantages of moving production abroad and explain each one. Remember to apply what you write to the production of Golden Wonder Pot Noodle.

1c) The command word 'discuss' means that this is an evaluation question. You need to do more than state and explain the advantages of the different options. You need to weigh them up. For example, do the cost savings outweigh the loss of the 'made in the UK' marketing benefit. To do this, you will need to discuss what this depends on, for example, the importance to customers of the sales tag, the competitiveness of the market – is it necessary to keep prices low and so on.

Data response 40

Tesco launched a number of stores in China in 2004. Other retailers such as Walmart had set up shops in China much earlier. By the time Tesco was looking to set up shops in China, rents were much more expensive. Sales were not as high as Tesco had hoped despite offering customers loyalty cards and selling produce, such as toads, which are consumed locally. Chinese customers often collect loyalty cards from several retailers and shop in whichever one sells the goods most cheaply. There were other reasons why Tesco failed. Eventually, Tesco merged its stores with the 3,000 owned by China Resources Enterprise (CRE). Tesco now owns 20 per cent of the business. The joint-venture trades under the brand name Vanguard.

1 Analyse three advantages to Tesco of going into a joint venture with a Chinese company in order to compete in the retail market in China. (9 marks)

How to answer data response 40

1 This is a synoptic question. Choose three different areas of business studies and explain how a joint venture with an established Chinese producer would help Tesco be more successful. The case study gives a couple of clues. Costs (rents) were high. Sales were disappointing – this suggests marketing issues. Maybe the existing Chinese company could help with costs and with marketing somehow? Analyse your ideas fully.

7 The interdependent nature of business

Learning outcomes

By studying this unit, you will be able to:

- analyse and evaluate the links between different areas of business
- apply knowledge and understanding to analyse and evaluate the links between different areas to business decision-making
- evaluate the impact of risk and reward on business activity
- apply knowledge and understanding of financial information in measuring, understanding and evaluating business performance and decision-making
- recommend business decisions considering the impact on different areas of business
- adopt a synoptic approach to evaluate business decision-making.

The interdependent nature of business

Below are four bullet points about the **interdependent nature of business** in the specification. Each bullet point is a feature of the interdependent nature of business:

1. the interdependent nature of business operations, finance, marketing and human resources within a business context
2. how these interdependencies underpin business decision-making
3. the impact of risk and reward on business activity
4. the use of financial information in measuring and understanding business performance and decision-making.

This unit explains and illustrates these features. In the examination, you will be tested on your understanding of how these features and the areas in them are interdependent.

Table 7.1 on page 305 summarises the four areas that are interdependent.

Interdependent here means 'linked'. Linked means that what happens in one **business area** will affect something in another. For this reason, when businesses make decisions in one area, they must consider the effect on other areas.

Three examples show how different areas of businesses are linked when a business makes a decision.

The different areas of business are all connected to, and dependent on, each other.

Section of the specification or 'area of business'	Content of the section or main 'aspects' of each area of business
Marketing	Market research, how markets can be broken down into segments, marketing decisions and activities (the marketing mix), consumer laws to consider.
Human resources	How businesses can be organised, communications in business, recruiting and selecting workers, motivating and retaining workers, training and developing workers, laws affecting employment.
Business operations	Production processes or how to make goods and services, sales processes and customer service, where to locate businesses, the supply chain and business operations.
Finance	Why businesses need finance and the sources they can get finance from, revenues, costs and profits, break-even analysis and cash flow in business.

Table 7.1 Interdependent areas of the specification.

Example 1 – Introducing new technology

This first example shows how the four features of interdependence may be a part of one single business decision.

Suppose a business has the following information:

Year	Sales	Profits
Year 1	200,000 units	£5 million
Year 2	100,000 units	£3 million

The information in the table measures business performance which is an example of feature 4 of interdependence – the use of financial information in measuring and understanding business performance.

The business must now make some decisions. First it will need to work out why sales and profits are falling. It might find that a competitor is able to sell similar products at a lower price and then it will have to decide what to do about this. The business may decide it should introduce new technology to lower its costs and so be able to reduce the price it charges.

Introducing new technology would be a decision in the business operations area as it is in the *production processes* topic. The decision would affect the human resources area as fewer workers might be needed or workers with the skills to use the technology might need to be *recruited*. The introduction of the new technology is intended to affect the finance area – it is hoping to reduce *costs*. The business would need to finance the purchase of the new technology and would have to look at *sources of finance*, another topic within the finance area. Finally, the decision should, as it is intended, affect the marketing area. Decisions need to be made about the price to be charged and also how to promote awareness of the price change. *Price* and *promotion* are both in the marketing mix topic. All the areas mentioned in the paragraph connect with feature 1. We can see that the decisions are linked with feature – the financial information which highlighted the problem.

The example can also be used to show how risk and reward – feature 3 – impact on business activity. The data showed that profits are falling. Profits are a reward for business activity – for enterprise. The fall in profits stimulates the change – the decision to introduce new technology. This decision has a risk. We saw that it needs financing. Perhaps the business takes out a loan. The risk is that the decision is not successful – the decline in sales and profits is not halted and the business will still have to pay back the loan. However, if the decision is successful, the business will gain its reward.

Example 2 – Reducing costs

Suppose that a firm is considering reducing costs by using cheaper raw materials. The firm will hope that this will increase profits, and reducing costs should help that increase. Costs and profits are part of the finance area of business. The decision to reduce costs may affect two other areas of business. Using cheaper raw materials may affect the quality of the products made by the business. Quality is a topic within the business operations area of the subject. Reducing quality may also affect sales – they may fall. Sales are connected to the marketing area of business. Any fall in sales would cause revenue to fall that could reduce profits – this, again, is the finance area of business. Any decision by the business will involve these different considerations.

Example 3 – A multiple choice question

The following question on the Specimen Assessment Materials for Component 02 (J204/02) is a question that tests the candidate's understanding of the interdependent nature of business.

1 A manufacturer has decided to run a marketing campaign on national television in a month's time. As a result of this decision, which one of the following actions might also be necessary?

A Finance should stop monitoring cash flow.

B Human resources should employ some temporary production workers.

C Operations management should reduce output.

D Purchasing should buy smaller quantities of raw materials.

Your answer ☐ [1 mark]

The answer is that the marketing campaign should mean, if it is successful, that more production workers will need to be employed. The business will need to increase production to meet the increase in demand. A decision made in marketing affects human resources.

Case study: cheese and energy production at Wyke Farm

Wyke Farm is a dairy business in Devon that made £2 million profit in 2015. It produces cheddar cheese that it exports to more than 160 countries. Wyke Farm has invested in technology to generate energy. First, it has installed some solar panels to generate electricity and it has used this to power and heat its factory, therefore reducing its electricity bills. This electricity is 7.5 pence cheaper than that supplied by the big utility companies. Wyke Farm is now looking at buying more solar panels. It also wants to invest in batteries that it can use to store the electricity it generates. This would mean it can use more of the electricity it generates itself rather than having to sell it to the national grid. Second, Wyke Farm has started to generate energy from cow dung. When cow dung decomposes, it produces the gas methane. The technology that Wyke Farm has bought converts this gas in to biomethane that can be burnt, like natural gas, to produce electricity and heat. Wyke Farm sells the biomethane to local businesses, including Sainsbury's supermarket.

The business borrowed £11 million from Barclays Bank and used £2 million of its retained profit to fund these investments. There are marketing benefits and Wyke Farm estimates that it is saving £100,000 per month on energy bills. The business hopes that the cost of the investment will be paid back in five or six years. There are risks – the firms, like Sainsbury's, that buy the biomethane must pay more for this gas than the natural gas supplied by the big utility companies. Will they want to keep paying the higher price?

Adapted from the Guardian, *27 May 2016*

The case study starting on page 306 illustrates the interdependent nature of business.

First, different areas of business are linked and underpin the decisions by Wyke Farm.

There is a decision about the production process topic in business operations – the investment in technology to produce energy. This links with the product and promotion topics within marketing. Wyke Farm has decided that it can sell energy (as well as cheese). It can also promote itself as an environmentally-friendly business. It also links with decisions about finance – Wyke Farm has used two sources of finance, a loan and retained profit, to pay for the investment. It must pay interest on the loan that adds to the business costs, a topic of finance. Wyke Farm has also calculated that investing in the technology will reduce its energy costs – finance area again.

Second, risk and reward impact the business activity. The risk for Wyke Farm is that it cannot be sure that its customers will continue to buy the energy it produces. It is a risk also because it has taken a loan and used its own retained profit. The loan will have to be repaid. Profit is the reward it hopes to gain. The business is making £2 million profit – it is gaining the reward at present. There is no guarantee that Wyke Farm will continue to make profits in the future.

Third, financial information has been used to help Wyke Farm decide what to do. It has calculated that it will save £100,000 in energy costs. It is making £2 million profit. It can conclude from these that the decision is a good one.

In an examination, there could be a question requiring an extended answer which tests your understanding of the interdependent nature of business. Below is an example of a possible question and the type of answer which would score well.

Evaluate the benefits to Wyke Farm of its investment in technology to generate energy. You should refer to the interdependent nature of business in your answer. (9 marks)

A possible answer might contain the following.

Wykes Farm's investment in technology would bring about marketing benefits. It would be able to promote itself as an environmentally friendly business which may increase its sales.

Another marketing benefit is that it will be able to spread its risks by producing energy as well as cheese. There is also a finance benefit in the form of costs being reduced by £100,000.

However, there are costs to the investment. Interest will need to be paid on the loan and Wyke Farm will lose interest on the retained profit that would have been kept in the bank. The business is making a profit of £2 million at present, which suggests that the extra costs are being covered. However, the profit could be higher if the costs had not increased as much. Also, the profit may not continue in the future. If unemployment rises and incomes fall, customers may want cheaper products. The firms that buy biomethane from Wyke Farm may want to cut costs to reduce prices. They may decide they cannot afford to buy this more expensive gas and switch to cheaper natural gas. Wyke Farm would earn less money from its investment.'

Activity 1 – Case study and questions about the interdependent nature of business

Case study: AF Furniture

AF Ltd sells bedroom furniture through retailers in the UK. Currently, it uses job production in its UK factory to produce bespoke furniture designed for individual customers. It is planning to increase its sales by exporting furniture to France and Germany. AF Ltd cannot increase production in its factory if it continues to use job production. One possibility is to switch to batch production to produce standardised furniture using new technology. Another is to take over another existing furniture manufacturer. If it did this, it would be able to continue to use job production. Increasing production would mean that finance was needed to purchase the additional wood and to pay for the take-over. AF Ltd imports wood from Finland to make the furniture. Finland uses the euro (€). AF Ltd has decided to try to increase its sales by exporting furniture to France and Germany, both of which use the euro. The exchange rate of the pound (£) is expected to rise against the euro. There is a lot competition in the French and German furniture markets, and prices tend to be lower than in the UK.

Adapted from the pre-release case study, OCR GCSE Business Studies, 2016 (A293)

Read the case study. The questions that follow are examples of questions that could be asked about the interdependent nature of business, connected to the case study.

Methods of production (business operations) and marketing

Question 1

a) Explain how using job production can help AF Ltd to market its furniture. (2 marks)

b) Analyse how using job production may make it difficult for AF Ltd to market its furniture. (3 marks)

Human resources and methods of production

Question 2

a) Analyse how the type and number of workers that AF Ltd needs to employ would change if it was to use batch production rather than producing bespoke furniture using job production. (3 marks)

b) Analyse how introducing batch production might affect the costs of production of furniture. (6 marks)

Business operations, marketing and finance

Question 3

Evaluate the possible effects on marketing and profitability if AF Ltd switches from job to batch production. (9 marks)

Activity 2 – Case study: risks, rewards and financial information

JMW Ltd is a business that makes telescopes and binoculars, targeted mainly at bird-watching enthusiasts. The business has grown in recent years as bird watching and a general interest in nature has become more popular. The present factory used by the business will become too small in the next year if sales continue to rise. A decision has to be made as to whether it is worth the risk to move to a much larger purpose-built factory.

The performance of JMW Ltd over the last five years is summarised in the following table.

Year	Total revenue (£)	Total costs (£)	Profit (£)
2012	2,300.000	2,100,000	200,000
2013	2,400,000	2,150,000	250,000
2014	2,600,000	2,300,000	300,000
2015	2,620,000	2,320 000	300,000
2016	2,625,000	2,330,000	295,000

Table 7.2 Performance over five years

Dreaming of expansion into new premises brings risk as well as reward.

Question 1

Explain one way in which JMW Ltd may benefit from if it moved to a new larger purpose-built factory. (2 marks)

Question 2

Using figures from the table above and any other relevant information, analyse the possible risks to JMW Ltd of moving to larger premises. (6 marks)

Question 3

Analyse the impact of a move to a new larger factory on business operations at JMW Ltd. (3 marks)

Question 4

JMW are planning to introduce a new range of quality binoculars that will need to be marketed through advertising and point-of-sale promotions. Analyse the effect of this marketing on the finance function at JMW Ltd. (6 marks)

A word about synopticity

In the context of the OCR GCSE (9–1) Business specification, synopticity means that knowledge and understanding about topics in Component 01 are brought together with knowledge and understanding about topics in Component 02.

There will be questions on Paper 2 (J204/02) that require candidates to give a synoptic answer. The questions below based on the Next plc case study have been adapted from the SAMs. The numbering has been changed as only the synoptic questions have been taken from the SAMs.

Questions 1 a) and b) are synoptic. 1 a) requires candidates to write about environmental issues, which is an area in Component 01, and marketing, which is an area in Component 02. 1 b) requires candidates to write about environmental issues, which is an area in Component 01, and human resources, which is an area in Component 02.

The answer to Question 2 might also be synoptic if it refers to the marketing or human resources function.

Question 3 is also a synoptic question. Knowledge and understanding about customer income levels is a part of Component 02. It has to be used in connection with knowledge and understanding about marketing, which is an area of Component 01.

Case study: Next plc

Next plc is a clothing retailer selling clothing, footwear, accessories and home products through its high street shops and online across the UK. Next plc understands the importance of creating good relationships with its customers and constantly tries to improve its levels of customer service. Customer service is important for Next plc.

For Next plc, responsible business behaviour includes addressing key business-related social, ethical and environmental impacts in a way that aims to bring value to all its stakeholders, including its shareholders. Next plc sources products from many suppliers across the world. The company takes its environmental and ethical responsibilities very seriously.

1. Analyse one way in which being environmentally friendly could impact on each of the following:
   - **a)** Next plc's marketing function (3 marks)
   - **b)** Next plc's human resources function (3 marks)
   - **c)** Next plc's finance function. (3 marks)
2. Recommend which function would be most affected by Next plc being environmentally friendly. Give reasons for your answer. (3 marks)
3. Evaluate how a fall in customer income levels might impact on the marketing activities of Next plc. (3 marks)

The interdependent nature of business and synopticity

Questions that test Section 7 of the specification – the 'interdependent nature of business' – may also be synoptic. Most of the examples given in this unit are synoptic. The Wyke Farm case study on page 306 involves Component 01 topics – marketing and human resources, and Component 02 – finance (as well as the business influence of the environment).

Answers to questions on case studies like this may require a synoptic approach, though not always.

Most questions on the examinations will be designed to assess the candidate's knowledge and understanding of one discrete area, such as marketing or human resources. Candidates will be rewarded for giving 'discrete' answers. Candidates will also be rewarded if they choose to take a synoptic approach in their answers.

Key facts

Different areas of business – business operations, finance, human resources and marketing are linked.

When making decisions, business people must consider the effects of a decision in one area of business activity on other areas of business activity.

Business decisions involve taking risks.

The reward for taking a risk is profit.

Businesses use financial information to measure business performance.

Financial information is used to make judgements and to inform decisions.

Useful words

Interdependent nature of business refers to the links between the areas of business that must be considered when business people make decisions, risks and rewards and the use of financial information to aid business decision-making.

Business areas are the main activities involved in running a business and influences outside the business that will affect the business activities. These are listed as sections on the OCR Examination Board specification.

Practice questions

Multiple choice questions

1 A shop selling expensive televisions decides to market itself as offering the best customer service on the market. This will mean:

- **a)** finance must be involved in providing funds for a new shop
- **b)** business operations must buy cheaper products
- **c)** human resources should provide additional advanced training for all sales staff
- **d)** marketing needs to advertise in national newspapers rather than television.

2 A business making ice cream wants to double its production. Which of the following will not normally be required?

- **a)** human resources to look at the need for extra staff
- **b)** finance to look at the amount of money required for the extra production
- **c)** marketing to research into why people do not like ice cream
- **d)** business operations function to check on where the products are sold.

3 A business wants to increase market share by reducing prices of its products. This would possibly involve:

- **a)** business operations function decreasing the level of production
- **b)** advertising the price reductions
- **c)** human resources looking at whether to move from a tall to a flat organisation structure
- **d)** finance providing money for a pay rise for all staff

Data response 41

Sports Direct is a large retailer of sportswear in the UK. Questions had been raised about how ethical it was when dealing with employees. The company had been severely criticised by a committee of MPs for what it called 'appalling' workplace conditions.

Sports Direct reviewed its workplace practices and decided to make changes. First, it would end its 'six strikes' firing policy. Workers got a 'strike' every time they breached company rules, for example, by being late for work, for spending too long in the toilet or if they wanted time off work to look after sick children. This policy had been intended to make sure workers would do the work they were being paid to do, but the approach was thought to be too strict. Second, Sports Direct announced that it would stop using zero-hours contracts for its shop workers and guarantee them a minimum of 12 hours of work each week. There had been criticism of workers not knowing when or if they would be given work. Third, it promised to pay workers above the minimum wage. It had been found that some workers at its warehouse at Shirebrook had, in effect, received less than the national minimum wage when they were made to stand in line after work for security checks to stop thefts.

Sports Direct also reported that its profits for the 2017 financial year were expected to fall by 21 per cent from £361 million in 2016 to £300 million.

1 Evaluate whether the proposed changes at Sports Direct will help to increase the company's profits in the future. (9 marks)

How to answer data response 41

1 Explain fully the link between the ethical image of the company and its ability to promote itself as a business that customers would want to buy from. Consider the impact of the changes on the ethical image of the company and, consequently, on the marketing mix, sales and revenues of Sports Direct. Consider also how costs and motivation of workers at Sports Direct might be affected. Compare the changes to discuss whether or not profits would be likely to fall. You might want to include some 'it depends' statements about, for example, the extent to which revenues and costs change.

Index

Photo credits

Pgs. 1 & 171, © Jacek Kadaj - Fotolia; **pg. 4**, © Francis Specker/Alamy Stock Photo; **pg. 12**, © Michael Spring/Alamy Stock Photo; **pg. 22**, © David Willis/Alamy Stock Photo; **pg. 13**, © Justin Kase zsixz / Alamy Stock Photo; **pg. 27** (*left*), © Antony Nettle/Alamy Stock Photo; **pg. 27** (*right*), © Annie Eagle/Alamy Stock Photo; **pg. 30**, © Greg Balfour Evans/Alamy Stock Photo; **pg. 31**, © VIEW Pictures Ltd/Alamy Stock Photo; **pg. 36**, © Greg Balfour Evans/Alamy Stock Photo; **pg. 53**, © vario images GmbH & Co.KG/Alamy Stock Photo; **pg. 54**, ©Ruslan Ivantsov/Shutterstock.com; **pg. 55** (*far left*), © Justin Kase z12z/Alamy Stock Photo; **pg. 55** (*second from left*), © D. Callcut/Alamy Stock Photo; **pg. 55** (*second from right*), © Justin Kase z12z/Alamy Stock Photo; **pg. 55** (*far right*), © Robert Convery/Alamy Stock Photo; **pg. 64** (*left*), © SzymonApanowicz/Shutterstock.com; **pg. 64** (*right*), © Alexey Boldin/Shutterstock.com; **pg. 69**, © Yanice Idir/Alamy Stock Photo; **pg. 70** *(top)*, © Alan King / Alamy Stock Photo; **pg. 70** (*middle*), © Skylines/Shutterstock.com; **pg. 70** (*bottom*), © Telekhovskyi/Shutterstock.com; **pg. 72**, © Robert Melen/Alamy Stock Photo; **pg. 76**, © ESB Professional/shutterstock.com; **pg. 79**, © rvlsoft/Shutterstock; **pg. 84**, © Benis arapovic/Alamy Stock Photo; **pg. 87** (*left*), © Mark Fairhurst/UPPA/Photoshot; **pg. 87** (*right*), © picturesbyrob/Alamy Stock Photo; **pg. 88**, © THOMAS COEX/AFP/Getty Images; **pg. 98**, © Greg Balfour Evans/Alamy Stock Photo; **pg. 101**, © Ekaphon maneechot/Shutterstock.com; **pg. 107**, © Chris Dorney/Alamy Stock Photo; **pg. 116**, © eye35.pix/Alamy Stock Photo; **pg. 122**, © Andy Rain / Epa/REX/Shutterstock; **pg. 126** (*top*), © Tashatuvango/Shutterstock.com; **pg. 126** (*middle*), © Zerbor/123 RF; **pg. 127** (*top*), © webpics/Alamy Stock Photo; **pg. 127** (*bottom*), © M4OS Photos/Alamy Stock Photo; **pg. 135**, © Robert Convery/Alamy Stock Photo; **pg. 138**, © Charles Polidano/Touch The Skies/Alamy Stock Photo; **pg. 139** (*top*), © REUTERS/Alamy Stock Photo; **pg. 139** (*bottom*), © Colin Underhill/Alamy Stock Photo; **pg. 141** © dpa picture alliance archive/Alamy Stock Photo **pg. 146**, © Ramin Talaie/Corbis/Getty Images; **pg. 151**, © Kevin Britland/Alamy Stock Photo; **pg. 153**, © Man Li/123RF images; **pg. 160**, © Jonathan Goldberg/Alamy Stock Photo; **pg. 181**, © REUTERS/Alamy Stock Photo; **pg. 184** (*bottom*), © Edible images/Alamy Stock Photo; **pg. 187**, © RSBPhoto1/Alamy Stock Photo; **pg. 190**, © Justin Kase z12z/Alamy Stock Photo; **pg. 192**, © Mark Agnor/shutterstock.com; **pg. 197**, © Jim O Donnell/Alamy Stock Photo; **pg. 200**, © Marc Tielemans/Alamy Stock Photo; **pg. 205**, © Rick Piper Photography/Alamy Stock Photo; **pg. 208**, © Dave Ellison/Alamy Stock Photo; **pg. 213**, © David Bagnall/Alamy Stock Photo; **pg. 223**, © ukartpics/Alamy Stock Photo **pg. 226**, © Af8images/Alamy Stock Photo; **pg. 236**, © paiboon muenchin/shutterstock.com; **pg. 242**, © marc macdonald/Alamy Stock Photo; **pg. 247**, © Dean Mouhtaropoulos/Getty Images; **pg. 258**, © rattanapatphoto/shutterstock.com; **pg. 264** (*top*), © shutterstock.com; **pg. 264** (*bottom*), © Minerva Studio/shutterstock.com; **pg. 268**, © David J. Green/Alamy Stock Photo; **pg. 269**, © Tishomir/Shutterstock.com; **pg. 271**, © STUART WALKER/Alamy Stock Photo; **pg. 278** (*left*), © Robert Convery / Alamy Stock Photo; **pg. 278** (*right*), © Convery flowers / Alamy Stock Photo; **pg. 282** (*top*), © Alexandr Blinov - 123RF; **pg. 282** (*bottom*), © Trevor Benbrook - 123RF; **pg. 290**, © Kumar Sriskandan/Alamy Stock Photo; **pg. 291** (*top*), © lovethephoto/Alamy Stock Photo; **pg. 291** (*bottom*), © MARK THOMAS/SCIENCE PHOTO LIBRARY; **pg. 292**, © gstockstudio - 123RF; **pg. 296**, © Frank Bienewald/Alamy Stock Photo.